PRODUCING WOMEN

Producing Women examines the ways femininity is produced through new media. Michele White considers how women are constructed, produce themselves as subjects, form vital production cultures on sites such as Etsy, and deploy technological processes to reshape their identities and digital characteristics. She studies the means through which women market traditional female roles, are viewed, and produce and restructure their gendered, raced, eroticized, and sexual identities. Incorporating a range of examples across numerous forms of media—including trash the dress wedding photography, Internet how-to instructions about zombie walk brides, nail polish blogging, DIY crafting, and reborn doll production—*Producing Women* elucidates women's production cultures online, and the ways that individuals can critically study and engage with these practices.

Michele White is an Associate Professor in the Department of Communication at Tulane University. She teaches Internet and new media studies, film and television studies, visual culture studies, science fiction and technology literature, gender and queer theory, and critical race and postcolonial studies. She is the author of *Buy It Now: Lessons from eBay* (Duke University Press, 2012) and *The Body and the Screen: Theories of Internet Spectatorship* (MIT Press, 2006).

PRODUCING WOMEN

The Internet, Traditional Femininity, Queerness, and Creativity

Michele White

NEW YORK AND LONDON

First published 2015
by Routledge
711 Third Avenue, New York, NY 10017

and by Routledge
2 Park Square, Milton Park, Abingdon, Oxon OX14 4RN

Routledge is an imprint of the Taylor & Francis Group, an informa business

© 2015 Taylor & Francis

The right of Michele White to be identified as author of this work has been asserted by her in accordance with sections 77 and 78 of the Copyright, Designs and Patents Act 1988.

All rights reserved. No part of this book may be reprinted or reproduced or utilized in any form or by any electronic, mechanical, or other means, now known or hereafter invented, including photocopying and recording, or in any information storage or retrieval system, without permission in writing from the publishers.

Trademark notice: Product or corporate names may be trademarks or registered trademarks, and are used only for identification and explanation without intent to infringe.

Library of Congress Cataloging-in-Publication Data
White, Michele.
  Producing women : the Internet, traditional femininity, queerness, and creativity / Michele White.
    pages cm
  Includes bibliographical references and index.
  1. Femininity. 2. Women—Identity. 3. Handicraft. 4. Home economics. 5. Feminism. 6. Internet and women. 7. Mass media and women. 8. Feminist theory. I. Title.
  HQ1154.W466 2015
  305.4—dc23
  2014032493

ISBN: 978-1-138-77678-4 (hbk)
ISBN: 978-1-138-77679-1 (pbk)
ISBN: 978-1-315-77304-9 (ebk)

Typeset in Bembo
by Apex CoVantage, LLC

Printed and bound in the United States of America by Publishers Graphics, LLC on sustainably sourced paper.

CONTENTS

List of Figures   *vi*
Acknowledgments   *vii*

    Introduction: The Technologies of Producing Women: Femininity, Queerness, and the Crafted Monster   1

1 Working eBay and Etsy: Selling Stay-at-Home Mothers   33

2 Touching Feeling Women: Reborn Artists, Babies, and Mothers   65

3 It's about "Creation, Not Destruction": Brides, Photographers, and Post-wedding Trash the Dress Sessions   96

4 Dead White Weddings: Zombie Walk Brides, Marriages, and How-to Guides   130

5 Never Cleaning Up: Cosmetic Femininity and the Remains of Glitter   157

    Afterword: A Show of Hands: Franken Polishes, Mannequin Hands, and #ManicureMonday   190

Selected Bibliography   *211*
Index   *227*

FIGURES

I.1	Pie Near Woman, photographic tableau	17
I.2	Etsy, 404 error message	21
2.1	eBay, reborn baby listing	66
2.2	Auctiva, reborn baby listing	77
2.3	eBay, reborn baby listing	80
2.4	eBay, reborn baby listing	81
3.1	Lynette Seelmeyer, Picture This Photography, LLC, trash the dress session	97
3.2	Miller + Miller Photography, engagement session	120
4.1	coreymarie, The all-new adventures of coreymarie.com, zombie hand makeup	145
4.2	Kitties26, more nail polish, zombie nails manicure	150
5.1	flinty, Polish or Perish, glitter nails manicure	158
5.2	Nail Noir, glitter nails manicure	177
A.1	Shelley and Pamela Jackson, The Doll Games, photo essay	192
A.2	The Polish Monster, monster nails manicure	197
A.3	Jayne Lim, Cosmetic Proof, manicure inspired by women scientists	205

ACKNOWLEDGMENTS

A wedding photograph depicts women in delicate pink bridesmaids' dresses standing with their backs to the camera.[1] A bride in a veil and white wedding gown stands between them but twists around to look knowingly at the photographer and presumed viewers. She opens her mouth in an expression of shared amusement and uses her hand to direct individuals to view the hiked-up skirt and underwear-clad backside of one of the bridesmaids. The other bridesmaids also have their dresses pulled up so that some of their underwear is revealed. The bride and photographer, and by analogy viewers, are positioned to see and enjoy this purposely produced accident. It is a voyeuristic view because the bridesmaids do not acknowledge their revealed buttocks or look at viewers. Yet this view of partially unclothed women is also legitimized. The repetitive aspects of their pulled-up dresses indicate that the bride and bridesmaids orchestrated this image. In similar images, bridesmaids show their partially revealed buttocks and matching underwear while twisting towards and looking at photographers.[2]

The popular media has described these images and representational strategies as a "New Wedding Trend" even though they echo many of the ongoing conventions through which women and weddings are portrayed.[3] Internet sites and computer technologies are also advertised as new and unrelated to previous developments even though they are often based in ongoing conventions. All of the articles about this "trend" are based in a similar visual archive, include a small number of images, and repeat depictions from other reports. Searches for related content suggest that these images are not massively circulated and reproduced by wedding participants. Wedding photographers produced and posted some of these images to their blogs years ago and others were obtained from porn media and sites.[4] Despite these discrepancies, the numerous articles about this wedding trend produce the visual and erotic functions of women and encourage women to produce themselves by staging photographs, sexually subjectifying themselves, maintaining fit and toned bodies, and reading about and following current conventions.

These images are part of the contemporary production of wedding culture and feminine interests. Carrie Denny identifies this "New" trend and then includes a "No, No, No, No, No, No" in her title.[5] Denny "borrowed the string of No's" from the "subject line of one of the many people" emailing to make sure that she was aware of this practice. Internet sites also direct me to such images and texts because my research has been algorithmically read as someone who is interested in wedding culture, which is correct in some ways. The resistant repetition of "No" encapsulates Denny's sentiments. Ivy Jacobson and The Knot, which is one of the largest Internet sites about wedding culture, takes a more dictatorial stance than Denny and insists on women's propriety when offering "21 Reasons Why Getting 'Cheeky' in a Bridesmaid Photo Is a Bad Idea."[6] In a similar manner to Denny, Jacobson informs women that "children and grandchildren" shouldn't "see photos" of their naked behinds. They are advised that it will be embarrassing, unappealing, and dangerous to reveal their bodies and shapewear to families, coworkers, and lecherous strangers. However, Jacobson's and some other authors' articles are illustrated with below the waist images of fully dressed women. The slight breeze blowing the bride and bridesmaids' skirts threatens to reveal their underwear and works to caution women against any accidents or misbehaviors. Readers of *The San Francisco Globe* identify brides and bridesmaids who reveal their underwear as "Classless whores" and "slutty and tacky."[7] Through such comments, women are warned against class and sexual transgressions. Women are thereby schooled by a "trend" that is constructed from varied materials and women's practices.

Women are producing women when they engage with, contribute to, and contest these images and narratives. Many of the media images of brides showing their underwear are pinned on Pinterest and combined with other images that women find notable. A Pinterest member includes the image of the bridesmaids in delicate pink dresses under the category "cool pics."[8] Another woman more fully incorporates an image of bridesmaids showing their underwear at the beach by listing it under "Wedding Ideas."[9] These posters, like the other women I study in this book, admire other women and imagine situating themselves in the pictures. Yet reporters construct this wedding practice in order to dismiss these women's interests. For instance, Tracy Moore categorizes this behavior as "insane" in her Jezebel article.[10] She demands, "Bridesmaids, explain yourselves." Critical interrogations of such constructs, practices, and images are needed but these examinations do not appear in the popular coverage. Everyday practitioners and their interests should be treated thoughtfully rather than shaming women and demanding that they explain themselves.

I greatly appreciate the friends and colleagues who have worked with me in thoughtfully engaging with and critically thinking about such practices and cultures. Some academics still believe that such studies are apolitical and feel legitimized in castigating researchers, especially younger women and queers, about the frivolity of women's cultures. These refusals of women's work and interests renew my commitment to studying women's practices, supporting scholars' work in this area, and thinking about the important ways this research complements other kinds of cultural studies and new media research. Colleagues have invited me to present early work on producing women and provided invaluable commentary. Caren Kaplan graciously included me in the Cultural Studies Colloquium Series at the University of California–Davis where I outlined some of my research on wedding dresses. Ann Cvetkovich, Ann Reynolds, and Janet Staiger encouraged my research on eBay reborn doll producers. I spoke at their rigorous Political Emotions Conference and Staiger's thoughtful observations improved the article on affect and reborn dolls that appeared in their anthology.[11] Ellis Hanson invited me to present work on trash the dress (TTD) at the Digital Desires Conference at Cornell University. In addition, he provided important critical remarks on my analysis, which appeared in *South Atlantic Quarterly*, on the ways women's erotic engagements with TTD and women are incorporated into heterosexual wedding culture.[12] Some early research on the marketing of TTD as a form of resistance was included in *Critical Studies in Media Communication* and was, at the request of Katherine Hawkins and the National Communication Association's *Communication Currents*, translated by me for the popular audience that reads their publication.[13]

Panelists and attendees at the conferences of The Association of Internet Researchers (AoIR), Console-ing Passions (CP), Society for Cinema and Media Studies (SCMS), and the Society for the Social Studies of Science (4S) also commented on the material in this book. Susanna Paasonen and other feminist and queer Internet studies scholars organized a series of panels on affect at the AoIR conference where I continued to develop my thinking on reborn babies and mothers. Mary K. Bryson and Mary Gray invited me to contribute to a roundtable, which was held at an earlier AoIR meeting, where they created one of the most rigorous conversations about Internet research and theory. A panel on loving monsters for CP at Suffolk University was conceptualized by Marina Levina, Theresa L. Geller, and myself and has been key in my thinking on monsters and monstrosity. In addition, Levina and Diem-My T. Bui included some of my research on zombie brides in *Monster Culture in the 21st Century*.[14]

My ongoing critical and intellectual engagements have also been supported by grants from the Newcomb College Institute and Tulane University. I owe a debt of gratitude to George Bernstein, Carol Haber, Tara Hamburg, Sally Kenney, Rebecca Mark, Molly Travis, Laura Wolford, and members of the grant review committees for acknowledging my work. The Seminar on Historical Change and Social Theory, which Justin Wolfe has long shepherded and I have more recently co-organized with him, has been a vital place to discuss intellectual projects and the writing process. The Feminist and Queer Theory Reading

Group and the intellectual contributions of Jean Dangler, Felicia McCarren, Supriya Nair, Mimi Schippers, and Allison Truitt have been essential to my ongoing work. They have kindly discussed many of the concerns that appear in this text. Equally important have been the scholars who visited Tulane and collaboratively discussed feminist and queer theory issues with reading group participants. Conversations with Beth Freeman, Bernadette Wegenstein, and Kathryn Bond Stockton, whose important thinking and book on the *Queer Child* resonates through this book, inform my understanding of contemporary culture and theory.[15]

A number of intellectual experiences continue to resonate in my work. These include my graduate school engagements and grounding in critical understandings of feminism, theory, and visual studies that were provided by Carol Armstrong, Rosemarie Haag Bletter, William Boddy, Patricia Clough, Setha Low, Linda Nochlin, Jane Roos, Eve Kosofsky Sedgwick, Ella Shohat, Chris Straayer, Michelle Wallace, and Sharon Zukin. My conceptualizations of the Internet are informed by the NEH-funded summer seminar on literature and information technologies, which Kate Hayles led at the University of California-Los Angeles. Hayles is a perceptive scholar with an impressive ability to outline key concepts and new media practices. Other seminar participants, including Kathleen Fitzpatrick, Will Gardner, and Tara McPherson, continue to contribute to my intellectual inquiries. My departmental colleagues, Vicki Mayer, Mauro Porto, Ana Lopez, Mohan Ambikaipaker, Connie Balides, Kai-man Chang, Kukhee Choo, Carole Daruna, Marie Davis, Emmanuel Raymundo, Beretta Smith-Shomade, Frank Ukadike, and Ferruh Yilmaz, have supported my work with departmental resources and their research knowledge.

People in my local and international community have continued to discuss producing women and femininity. Mike Syrimis has been a careful listener and provided key commentary on the manuscript. Michele Adams, Yeesheen Yang, Schippers, and Truitt have contributed literature suggestions and their critical knowledge. I have had the great pleasure of sharing vibrant conversations about contemporary culture and theory with Christopher Schaberg. Mark Anderson has kindly searched for popular sources related to my interests. His pointers and supportive observations vastly improved my knowledge of contemporary Internet and computer cultures. The anonymous reviewers and Sharon Marie Ross provided careful readings of this project at varied stages. I owe a great deal to Erica Wetter at Routledge for her early and continual enthusiasm for and critical inquiries about this project. Simon Jacobs stewarded me through some of the thornier reference questions that arise with Internet research. I also want to extend my heartfelt appreciation to Courtney Berger, Megan Boler, Emily Clark, Ken Gonzales Day, Mary Desjardins, Greg Elmer, Anna Everett, Joan Fujimura, Joy Fuqua, Radhika Gajjala, Barbara Hayley, Ken Hillis, Steve Jones, Maggie Morse, Nancy Maveety, Esra Özcan, Marline Otte, Chip Petit, Erica Rand, Alan Rosenberg, Ellen Fernandez Sacco, Leslie Regan Shade, Carol Stabile,

Jenny Sundén, Karen Taylor, Fred Turner, Ken Wissoker, and John Willinsky. Ultimately, I want to thank my family. Without the feminist support and investment in scholarship that have been expressed by Stephanie White and Pauline Farbman, this book would never have been completed.

Notes

1. Lizzie Roberts, "Bum-baring bridesmaids spark new trend for FLASHING in wedding photos," *Mirror Online*, 1 July 2014, http://www.mirror.co.uk/news/weird-news/bum-baring-bridesmaids-spark-new-trend-3792583#ixzz371P9WMyP
2. Tracy Moore, "Bridesmaids Flashing Ass Is the Hot New Wedding Photo Trend," Jezebel, 25 June 2014, http://jezebel.com/bridesmaids-flashing-ass-is-the-hot-new-wedding-photo-t-1596600362
3. San Francisco Globe, "Bridesmaids Baring Their Butts?! The Wild New Wedding Trend (Photos)," 26 June 2014, http://sfglobe.com/?id=1188&src=fbfan_1188
4. Morgan Matters, "mexico...," Morgan Matters Photography, 12 March 2009, 10 July 2014, http://morganmattersphotography.blogspot.com/2009/03/mexico.html
5. Carrie Denny, "On This New Wedding 'Trend' of Brides and Their Bridesmaids Showing Their Bare Butts for a Photo: No, No, No, No, No, No," *Philadelphia Magazine*, 27 June 2014, http://www.phillymag.com/philadelphia-wedding/2014/06/27/new-wedding-trend-brides-bridesmaids-showing-bare-butts-photo/
6. Ivy Jacobson, "21 Reasons Why Getting 'Cheeky' in a Bridesmaid Photo Is a Bad Idea," The Knot, 27 June 2014, http://blog.theknot.com/2014/06/27/21-reasons-why-getting-cheeky-in-a-bridesmaid-photo-is-a-bad-idea/
7. Don Clark, "Bridesmaids Baring Their Butts?! The Wild New Wedding Trend (Photos)," *San Francisco Globe*, 26 June 2014, http://sfglobe.com/?id=1188&src=fbfan_1188; Pam Kriesse, "Bridesmaids Baring Their Butts?! The Wild New Wedding Trend (Photos)," *San Francisco Globe*, 26 June 2014, http://sfglobe.com/?id=1188&src=fbfan_1188
8. Chelis Gomez, "cool pictures," Pinterest, 11 July 2014, http://www.pinterest.com/chelisgomez/cool-pictures/
9. Heather Church, "Wedding Ideas," Pinterest, 11 July 2014, http://www.pinterest.com/hrchurch/wedding-ideas/
10. Tracy Moore, "Bridesmaids Flashing Ass Is the Hot New Wedding Photo Trend," Jezebel, 26 June 2014, http://jezebel.com/bridesmaids-flashing-ass-is-the-hot-new-wedding-photo-t-1596600362
11. White, "Babies Who Touch You."
12. White, "Dirty Brides."
13. White, "Trash the Dress"; Michele White, "'Trash the Dress': Wedding Conventions and Resistance," *Communication Currents* 7, no. 5 (October 2012), 23 July 2014, http://www.natcom.org/CommCurrentsArticle.aspx?id=2811
14. White, "Killing Whiteness."
15. Stockton, *Queer Child*.

INTRODUCTION

The Technologies of Producing Women: Femininity, Queerness, and the Crafted Monster

A woman wanders through everyday surrounds in her strapless and full-skirted white wedding gown. The photographs of this bride, which are produced by Alley Kat Photography and posted to Rock n Roll Bride and Flickr, depict her shopping for groceries, pumping gas, browsing in a video store, and cleaning clothing at a Laundromat.[1] She is also the "Bride of Frankenstein" with white streaks in her upswept hair and a white face "stitched" onto her neck.[2] These photos depict "just a day in the life of Frankenstein's misses!"[3] Kat from the Rock n Roll Bride blog wryly suggests that these pictures and the filmic narratives associated with the bride of Frankenstein reference and distort normative ideas about women.[4] The images rely on cultural features of brides while conceptually undoing the heterosexual and reproductive futures that are ordinarily related to weddings because the Frankensteinian bride does not really have a "life." According to varied stories, she has just been electrically animated, is deathly or dead white, is stitched together from human parts rather than having been born a woman, and is about to die.

The bride of Frankenstein photos and filmic narratives highlight failed forms of normative femininity and whiteness. Weddings are the specialty of Rock n Roll Bride and Alley Kat Photography and are usually imagined to initiate women into monogamous heterosexuality. However, the "Bride of Frankenstein" designation positions her as Doctor Frankenstein's as well as the monster's wife. A photo in which she rests her head on "Frank's" gravestone suggests there is no animate groom.[5] She is expected to be the abject bride of this dead and possibly reanimated creature even though the fluid aspects of monstrosity, which include childishness, atypical bodies, uncontrollable and improper desires, and ambiguous genitals, disrupt binary gender and racial positions and normative heterosexuality.[6] Brides are usually associated with a white racial position because of the color of dresses and because whiteness is linked to such attributes as purity.[7] However, the delineated place where the white base ends on her face is a reminder of how some women produce their Caucasian whiteness and femininity through the application of makeup.[8] Her technological and prosthetic body, which is produced through medical, photographic, beauty, and new media practices, disrupts the association of femininity with naturalness.

The images of the bride of Frankenstein produce and extend ideas about women. However, they also highlight this production, convey producing women, and link weddings to women's monstrous, and thereby resistant, reproduction. For instance, Alley Kat Photography's bride of Frankenstein pleasurably acknowledges her role in a form of non-maternal reproduction by holding up a *Frankenstein* DVD at the video store.[9] She is a copy, as opposed to a "unique" individual, but does not repeat the conventional representations of passive and languid brides. Her hands are emphasized as she performs "domestic arts," including preparing to cook and washing clothing, and thereby does things. In a similar manner, the female photographer and blogger associated with these depictions are producing women who create ideas and texts. I use the term "producing" because it points to the ways women are constructed, produce themselves as subjects, form vital production cultures, work, and deploy technological processes.

Feminist and queer researchers often look to resistant and unconventional practices as ways of subverting normative identities, rigid cultural and corporate structures, and inequitable societies and governments. There are also projects such as the Bride of Frankenstein images that deploy conventional and resistant ideas about women. In *Producing Women*, I examine the ways women use traditional femininity and Internet sites as means of supporting and revising cultural conceptions of women and femininity. I focus on the social construction of mothers, brides, and cosmetic cultures because these are some of the key practices through which women and femininity are produced. For example, the role of mother is used to associate women with such feminine behaviors as caretaking and nurturing.[10] Women are further gendered and controlled by distinctions between motherhood and other forms of childcare and Western cultural assumptions that women will give up their careers and remain in the domestic home for a period of time to care for children. Brides are a somewhat transitional feminine position that is used to demarcate women's relationship to domesticity. Cultural conceptions of brides in white wedding dresses associate women with white monogamous heterosexual unions and future familial and reproductive roles. Thus, the bride and wedding form part of a script about women's traditional positions. Cosmetics play an important part in these formations of women and femininity. Women are expected to use makeup to maintain their feminine appearance and to "properly" mark their life stages and roles.[11] A group of women pleasurably communicate about such things as cosmetics, create products, and employ normative terms such as "stay-at-home mother" and "bride" in Internet settings but their practices are often different than societal conceptions.

These women engage with the positions of mother and bride and beauty culture as methods of emphasizing their role as creative as well as reproductive producers. They sustain women-focused Internet communities, trouble the association of whiteness with beauty and aliveness, market themselves and products, and render empowering roles. As a way of studying these facets of producing women, I employ the humanities methods of close textual and theoretical analysis. These close readings include an examination of site texts, the design features of settings, women's Internet postings and multimedia products, journalistic accounts, and academic literature. I identify the terms and procedures of close textual analysis in this introduction and in the following chapters. I also outline the key concepts that inform this book, including the features and social effects of normative femininity. Some postfeminist texts indicate that there is an increasing cultural redeployment of traditional femininity and feminine positions. Traditional ideas about feminine domesticity are being extended in Internet settings. There are also women who politically use Internet sites to reclaim feminine practices and celebrate "new domesticity" and crafting. I suggest the kind of changes that are occurring through such reconfigurations and the means through which academics and the individuals who use Internet settings might theorize and engage with these shifts.

Close Textual Analysis

Close textual analysis or close reading, which examines written texts and visual representations, can provide methods for studying the everyday processes of producing women. It is an often-employed method in the humanities. I identify close textual analysis as a critical, sometimes theoretical, practice. Detailed examinations and descriptions of texts are used as methods of identifying the aspects, functions, and implications of works and the ways these features convey and produce cultural beliefs. Literary theorist Jonathan Culler identifies the academic inclination to resist defining close textual analysis and to avoid explaining the ways it can be practiced. For him, the goal of these methods of close reading is not inherently to determine the overarching meaning or resolve difficulties in texts. It is rather to "describe them, to elucidate their source and implications."[12] Texts can be opaque and stubborn and resist easy comprehension. This means that close textual analysis requires time and an attention to the parts of the text. In addition, scholars have to understand the genre and attend to the relationships and dissonances between the text and associated sites and conventions. Barbara Johnson provides examples of the different kinds of conflicts in meaning making that occur in texts, including "ambiguous words," "undecidable syntax," "incompatibilities between what a text says and what it does," "incompatibilities between the literal and the figurative," and "incompatibilities between explicitly foregrounded assertions and illustrative examples."[13] Her list indicates that diverging tendencies arise from texts and that texts do not always produce coherent and consolidated meanings.

Literary studies and related researchers, according to new media studies scholar N. Katherine Hayles, tend to avoid considering the ways close textual analysis can be connected to digital practices.[14] This is not surprising since some proponents of close reading believe that digital technologies and social practices are antithetical to textual analysis. For instance, Culler indicates that we cannot "take close reading for granted" because students have been "raised in instant messaging, where language becomes a crude, ever more abbreviated code for communicating minimal information."[15] He articulates digital culture as a kind of unskilled opposite to close reading, an opposite that he also associates with "sloppy reading."[16] Yet Hayles foregrounds the ways students constantly and intently read digital texts. She argues that "reader-directed, screen-based, computer-assisted reading" is distinct from, rather than worse than, print-based reading.[17] It consists of such practices as the use of search engines and search functions, "filtering by keywords, skimming, hyperlinking, pecking (pulling out a few items from a longer text)," juxtaposing material from different windows, and scanning. Hayles proposes that we recognize the value of and relationship between such strategies as close, hyper, and machine reading. Hyper reading, which includes reading though large amounts of information and following nonlinear hyperlinks and other structures, is associated with computer and Internet use and is present in archival researchers' deployment of skimming. Machine reading, or the automatic and unsupervised understanding of texts, is used as a means of processing survey data and rendering quantitative results.

Some scholars have revised close textual analysis and related practices so that they are suitable for Internet and computer research. Internet researcher Nina Wakeford argues that the web can be studied as part of contemporary visual culture and suggests that we examine such things as the elements of the image, how things are arranged, how they are circulated, the relationships between components of the image, and instances in which images appear in multiple ways.[18] Art historian Elizabeth K. Menon offers a useful method of overview, including an attention to "technical elements, formal elements, compositional elements, display considerations and the role of the viewer."[19] As she suggests, the ways users are addressed and audiences are conceptualized and self-identify are important. Lisa Nakamura shows how close textual analysis of Internet settings can continue feminist inquiries about agency and representation.[20] She proposes that researchers study digital images of bodies by considering how physiognomies are articulated, the kinds of bodies that individuals are offered and produce, the devices (such as sliders and click boxes) through which individuals can render or upload avatars, the ways bodies are gendered and raced, and how these representations are described by sites and individuals. These considerations inform my analysis of how producing women are gendered, associated with sexual identities, produced as sexualized bodies, and raced.

The importance of these identities and varied sorts of site information are conveyed through formal arrangements. Individuals are directed and choose to view Internet and computer sites in an F pattern, according to Jakob Nielsen and Hayles, with more emphasis placed at the top and left side.[21] When researching such texts, I reconceptualize their F zone as a left bracket in order to study the menu options and information about sites and individuals that are featured at the top and left side as well as at the bottom of pages. For instance, I analyze "About" information. These texts indicate how the setting is conceptualized and the ways people are supposed to understand its values and participants. I relate this information to other texts, including individuals' posts, in order to attend to the kinds of ambiguities Johnson foregrounds. I also consider how viewers are addressed, the kinds of experiences and empowerment that they are offered, and the ways descriptions and icons articulate settings and ideal viewers. As a means of examining Internet conventions, I compare similar images and textual passages. This results in my tendency to quote and analyze specific texts and related ideas. Yet these close readings are also derived from hyper practices because skimming and searching large numbers of texts can further explicate sites and pinpoint quotations. I understand these screen-based texts as constructed representations and address the ways people shape and are shaped by texts and technologies. For example, formal Western reading patterns and people's propensity to scan from left to right and top to bottom help to hierarchize identities in the many cases where site designers include the options for light-skinned avatars to the left of or above dark-skinned representations. Related practices are used to privilege male and masculine characters over female and feminine representations, including social news sites such as Slashdot using the gendered "Chairman" as the first "Job Title" in its sign-up form.[22] My method is to closely read such widely available texts rather than engage with sites or posters through intervention or interaction.[23]

Normative Femininity

Feminists often understand normative Western femininity as a cultural category that forms and controls women. For feminist activist and journalist Susan Brownmiller, femininity is a "tradition of imposed limitations."[24] Susan Bordo builds on this concept in her feminist analysis of embodiment. She describes the ways women and their bodies are "habituated to external regulation, subjection, transformation," and "improvement," when they pursue the "ever-changing" and "homogenizing" feminine ideal.[25] Femininity is produced through personal and cultural messages about what clothing, figure, comportment, life course, and values are expected of women. Whether embraced or resented, most women recognize that there are cultural expectations for feminine norms and are influenced by these standards. Traditional femininity includes such different roles as the bride and mother, while articulating narrow and interlocked ideas about how people in varied life stages should behave. This construction of normative and other femininities also renders conceptions of masculinity. However, not all people are affected in the same way by these gendered roles. Women's disempowered position, according to sociologist Melissa A. Milkie, is constructed through "stereotypes that provide narrower, more distorted, or more harmful images about women than about men."[26]

Bordo, Milkie, and an array of other feminists consider the controlling conceptions of female beauty and behavior that are conveyed through the media. In her feminist theorizations of film, Teresa de Lauretis refers to media texts, "institutionalized discourses," "epistemologies," "critical practices," and "practices of daily life" as "technologies of gender."[27] This is because gender is a depiction and self-representation that "is the product of varied social technologies." In a related manner, Michel Foucault describes how systems of knowledge, societal beliefs, and behaviors function as "technologies of the self" that produce individuals.[28] De Lauretis is not focusing on such material technologies as computer hardware or networks but the technologies of gender, like the Internet and other contemporary technologies and social practices, extend the body by producing its meanings.[29]

Conceptions of the body and normative femininity are ordinarily associated with young, white, middle-class, and heterosexual women. However, women who are defined according to other classifiers are still shaped by these ideas and what is "appropriate" for their role. Notions of normative and appropriate femininity change over time and are culturally and contextually specific, although still informed by understandings of Western values. These practices and beliefs about femininity produce a hierarchical system in which women are rendered less powerful and valued than men. Some women can still attain a higher status by successfully enacting normative feminine behaviors.[30] This attainment of influence within a gender hierarchy is more difficult for women who are of color, queer, older, disabled, poor, and who do not meet other ideals. For instance, Western expectations that men will be strong and active and women weak and passive further stigmatize African American women who are encouraged to be empowered and outspoken. Patricia Hill Collins's study of black sexual politics points to how this "identifies a reversed, damaged gender ideology as a sign of racial difference."[31] These claims about masculinity and femininity are part of a system that still mandates that women curtail their sexual interests, codes men's casual sexual relationships as more acceptable than women's, condemns women who gain economic and other benefits from sex, and associates black men and young black women with excessive desires and improper relationships.

Cultural conceptions of traditional femininity, including the figures of the homemaker and childbearing woman, are linked to ideas about producing women. These women are imagined as best suited for domestic work and familial care. The porting of these values into Internet settings has meant that women are correlated with such social and consumerist engagements as instant messaging and "chatting," collecting and sharing images of desirable goods, fan cultures, mommy blogging, feminine forms of crafting, shopping, and customer service and imagined to be ill suited for high-level technological labor. Of course, women also participate in producing and controlling feminine and female roles. This does not mean that their roles are stable. Figures such as the bride of Frankenstein, especially when the related texts are closely read using Johnson's strategies, show signs of slipping between active and passive, beautiful and monstrous, Caucasian and of color, living and dead, straight and queer, and married and widowed.[32]

The bride of Frankenstein's shifts indicate how normativity is always in tension with and reliant on otherness. Women are at risk of being culturally read as deviant and different. This raises questions about the behaviors and positions that operate under the label of female normativity, including being frivolous, passive, servile, nurturing, home- and child-focused, and heterosexual, and the means through which these concepts are used to code and constrain bodies. Many women struggle to maintain their claims to mainstream acceptability because of threats of violence and dismissal. Contemporary culture and the processes of normative identity construction also manage to elide conflicting identity presentations and diffuse their potential significance. Normative positions are likely to be more mutable, and in some manner queerer, than ordinarily theorized. The diverse actions that are organized under normative identity can thus be deployed and expanded to support other lived practices. It is this producing, reworking, and rethinking of normative identity positions in Internet settings that I address in this book.

Postfeminism and Internet Settings

A group of popular and academic writers indicate that individuals are readopting traditional femininity and feminine positions.[33] People's acceptance and even celebration of normative femininity is often described as "postfeminism" and contrasted with feminist critiques of traditional women's roles.[34] The term was used in the early twentieth century but postfeminism is frequently associated with Susan Bolotin's 1982 article in which she investigates women who distance themselves from feminism and accept traditional identity positions.[35] Bolotin and other individuals categorize this as disempowering. In a related manner, media studies scholars Yvonne Tasker and Diane Negra identify the contemporary "'girling' of femininity" and of professional women as a means of making them less threatening.[36] Such unchallenging constructions of women are typical with postfeminism. They persist in Internet settings where girls' and women's interests are frequently deprecated. Thus, some postfeminist representations and critical inquiries, including investigations of femininity, are related to my project.

The usefulness of the term "postfeminism" and its application to Internet settings is sometimes limited. Many academics and journalists associate postfeminism with normative femininity but there is no agreed upon definition.[37] As Negra argues, the word "exhibits a plasticity that enables it to be used in contradictory ways."[38] This has led television studies scholar Amanda D. Lotz to assert that the overarching concept is "largely useless" in research unless a definition is offered.[39] As she argues, this should be of particular concern in media studies because of the many theoretical explorations of postfeminism deployed in the field. I acknowledge the conflicting definitions of postfeminism but my intent is to use some of its features as a way of understanding Internet settings. I also demonstrate how women's Internet production cultures do not meet a number of postfeminism's aspects. An overarching deployment of postfeminism in this project would elide promising aspects of women's use of Internet settings, including their articulation of creative cultures, collaborative production of identities and products, erotic engagements with other women while self-identifying as heterosexual, and challenging of whiteness. This is different than critical examinations, which associate postfeminism with individuality, heterosexuality, and whiteness.[40]

The term "postfeminism" can be a problem for feminists. Some writing identifies it as a move "beyond" feminism because people believe women are empowered in contemporary society, no longer in need of feminist politics, and resistant to being associated with feminism.[41] Writers have also argued that feminism represents women as victims. This has caused a group of feminists to identify postfeminism and related beliefs as a backlash against feminism and women's rights.[42] Yet Elaine J. Hall and Marnie Salupo Rodriguez's study found that support for feminism and the women's movement has not decreased.[43] As a kind of remedy to the view that feminism is no longer relevant, some feminist scholars have defined postfeminism as a critical and analytical strategy that is related to postcolonialism, postmodernism, and poststructuralism and that addresses multiple and intersectional forms of inequality.[44] My concern is that the term can still suggest that we are in a period where feminism is no longer relevant. I use the term "postfeminism" with some hesitancy to identify popular beliefs about contemporary women that are articulated in this literature.

Postfeminism is also associated with other cultural beliefs and practices, including women's sexual subjectification instead of objectification, reassertions about natural sexual differences, focus on the self rather than concerns for others and commitments to collective action, self-disciplining through such practices as makeovers, assertions about agency and choice, and consumerism.[45] Foucault's conception of technologies of the self has similarly been associated with subjectification.[46] From these conceptions, the characteristics of postfeminism that most apply to my interrogation are presumptions that women are empowered and able to freely choose, including their "choice" to erotically subjectify themselves, in contemporary society. As D. Travers Scott argues, postfeminism and interactive technologies provide similar narratives about equality and choice. Individuals are assured that they are "'liberated' through interactive technologies, free to choose, surf, produce," and "remix" but such things as personalization options offer people few substantive ways to change these systems and society.[47]

Women's postfeminist choices are related to opting out and retreatism. According to Tasker and Negra, there is an expectation that the "well-educated white female professional" will demonstrate "her 'empowerment' and caring nature by withdrawing from the workforce (and symbolically from the public sphere) to devote herself to husband and family."[48] In addition, women deploy opting out and retreatism, as I suggest later in this book, to tactically satisfy gender expectations while running their own "home" businesses, creating things, and selling products and their culturally approved positions. Virginia Braun rightly points to how narratives about choice elide people's different options and the normative pressures that women experience to make certain decisions.[49] At the same time, there are problems with dismissing the potentials of choice, especially when these decisions are of interest to women. Popular women's cultures, as English scholar Eva Chen argues, are not ideal sites but criticism that overemphasizes "deception and commodification may risk positioning women as passive dupes."[50] While consumerism is often associated with women and femininity and deemed to be self-motivated and antithetical to the political, a variety of scholars have pointed to the politics of consumer choices and the consumerist aspects of politics.[51] In this project, I take ecommerce selling and consumerism to be sometimes-vital parts of daily life that are coupled to varied messages, beliefs, forms of production, and political possibilities.

The Internet and Conceptions of Women, Femininity, Domesticity, and Race

Women produce Internet texts and images and remediate media content. However, Internet settings continue to link technological skill and agency to white heterosexual men and produce narrow conceptions of identity positions. Judy Wacjman identifies the Internet's military and white male hacker origins and the ways men still control the associated networks.[52] In a related manner, my analysis of social networking and news sites provides a framework for considering how women, femininity, domesticity, race, and sexuality are coded and dismissed in Internet settings. My previous research interrogated the tendency to suggest that all individuals are empowered and acknowledged Internet and computer users.[53] These narratives are common in Internet settings and are part of the erasure of social inequities, which popular and academic writers identify as a feature of postfeminism. While there are enabling aspects of Internet settings and practices, the claims that people's engagement is always a form of co-production, creation, and personalization fail to acknowledge the ways individuals are produced and controlled in Internet settings.[54] Settings have pre-structured interfaces, code that cannot be changed, limits on the kinds of production allowed, About pages, and other features that define sites and members.

Settings such as Facebook have standard styles of pages and organizational structures and limit the length of texts and number of images people can initially view. About 60 percent of Facebook members, who should be understood as content producers, submitters of forms, and constructed participants, are women.[55] However, the majority of Facebook employees are white males.[56] Facebook articulates its ideal viewer and associates the site with white masculinity by deploying a logo with a white head and cropped hair and a "Like" icon with a white hand sporting a blue-buttoned cuff.[57] Facebook's crisp blue and white banner heading and image of people linked into a global communication network work to disavow identifications of the setting as frivolous and focused on obsessive behaviors. Nevertheless, Urban Dictionary members indicate that it is for "slut-faced high school girls to post all of their drunk and high pictures" and "where fake girls can 'write on each other's walls' saying how much they 'LOVE' each other."[58] In these comments, Facebook is used as a method of condemning and shaming women and their interests. Cultural conceptions of normative white masculinity are often used to elevate sites and new media technologies while traditional femininity and women's pleasures are employed to dismiss these settings and women.

Heterosexual masculinity is also the assumed and privileged identity on social news sites that claim to offer important information, including reddit's claim to be the "front page of the internet" and Slashdot's offering of "News for nerds, stuff that matters."[59] reddit advertises that it gives "anyone who has something interesting enough to say the ability to reach millions" and continues beliefs about Internet empowerment. However, the opportunity to "downvote" comments allows members to elide the expressions of women and people of color. Women's agency and legitimacy, as suggested by analysis of the sites and journalistic accounts, are further curtailed when reddit and Slashdot posters describe women as "bitches," "sluts," and manipulative money grabbers; produce, share, and evaluate erotic images of women without their knowledge; and suggest women are best controlled through rapes and beatings.[60] Some participants also direct women and people of color, who they deem to be uninformed about technology and other knowledge work, to do menial and domestic labor.[61] For instance, Shamson responds to a reposted early Cream of Wheat advertisement in which a black cook does not recognize words and speaks in a stereotyped manner. Shamson echoes this form of speech and asks, "IS YOU IS, OR IS YOU AIN'T FIXIN' ME SOME CREAM WHEAT?"[62] Images such as the Cream of Wheat advertisement were designed to indicate that blacks had limited aptitudes, to justify slavery and segregation, and to render whites as benevolent caretakers of African-Americans who were thought to need assistance.[63] Shamson extends these intolerant conceptions into the contemporary period. As Jessie Daniels's research on racism demonstrates, new and centuries old forms of intolerance persist with the Internet.[64]

Women also encounter directives about their cultural roles on social news sites. A Slashdot poster places "militant feminists" in traditional positions and dismisses their claims to power by telling them to "GET YOUR ASS BACK IN THE KITCHEN AND MAKE ME A SANDWICH."[65] reddit posters recommend violent methods of getting a "disobedient" female partner to be more domestic and make a male poster a sandwich.[66] CookieFetish suggests that he "Shoot her in the leg and tell her to again."[67] According to Know Your Meme, "Make Me a Sandwich" is a "catchphrase often used by male internet users to mock, discredit or annoy female internet users, playing off of the sexist trope which states that women belong in the kitchen."[68] It is one of the many Internet conventions that buttress social inequality and intolerance. GeekGirlCon refuted these oppressive practices by offering a conference panel entitled "'Go Make Me A Sandwich': Barriers to Women's Participation in Online and Fan Spaces."[69] The GeekGirlCon panel indicates that narratives about gender-appropriate work, and the larger male technologists' custom of scripting women as erotic objects and passive servants, make it difficult to communicate from a female, let alone a feminist, position. Women also deploy traditional identities as part of their engagement with Internet technologies, skew these conventional roles, and lay claim to technological proficiency. For instance, women who blog about nail polish, as I suggest in Chapter 5, make comments about their highly skilled "glitter jelly sandwich" applications that refuse cultural expectations about women's work and render sandwiches designed for their own pleasures.[70]

New Domesticity and Feminism

Mary Wollstonecraft mentions domesticity in positive terms in *A Vindication of the Rights of Woman* from 1792.[71] She argues that the subjugation of women is antithetical to domestic happiness. Not surprisingly, women's relationship to domesticity and cultural understandings of this role are of ongoing concern to feminists. Barbara Welter's research on the "Cult of True Womanhood," which she dates from 1820 to 1860 in America, was published in 1966 and continues to influence women's history and feminist research and activism. Welter asserts that the virtues of womanhood by which white middle-class northern women were judged during this period, were "piety, purity, submissiveness and domesticity."[72] Women who demonstrated these "virtues" were positioned in the private sphere and "promised happiness and power." For American women who could not attain the position of "lady" in the nineteenth century, suggests historian Gerda Lerner in her related work, there were still expectations that women accept their "'proper place' in the home."[73] Women who did not follow or could not meet these mandates risked social and state censure. While Welter addresses the experiences of a specific population, Mary Louise Roberts indicates that these experiences also apply to the same period in Europe.[74] In Latin America, as

Donna J. Guy notes, true womanhood is more applicable to twentieth-century efforts, although it was not economically possible to keep women at home.[75]

Welter offers a "powerful critique" of patriarchal behaviors, according to historian Nancy A. Hewitt.[76] Welter indicates the influence women achieved by deploying such things as female domesticity and the significant limitations that these concepts placed on their rights and abilities. This emphasis on true womanhood occurred in the West at about the same time as equal-rights feminism and domestic reform. Rather than seeing these as unrelated, Nancy F. Cott proposes that the nineteenth-century feminist movement and some of its limitations grew out of the separation of public and private spheres. She argues that these conceptions offered women "domestic influence," "social power based on their special female qualities," and a "necessary stage in the process of shattering the hierarchy of sex and, more directly, in softening the hierarchical relationship of marriage."[77] In a somewhat less celebratory manner, Linda K. Kerber indicates that the notion of a women's sphere "was not necessarily protofeminist" but "domesticity and feminism were linked by perceptions of 'womanhood'" and "sisterhood."[78]

Contemporary crafters propose similar narratives about women's spheres and practices. Jean Railla, who founded GetCrafty.com, seems to reference gendered spheres and the culture of true womanhood. She uses the term "new domesticity" to describe the "movement committed to recognizing, exalting and most of all enjoying the culture that women have built for millennia."[79] Yet for her, female practitioners of the new domesticity "are not traditional women." She designed GetCrafty.com to explore the possible connections between feminism, domesticity, crafting, and the Internet.[80] Railla distinguishes her practice from women's studies and her second-wave college professors. According to her, they believed that "housework and the domestic arts were drudgery—work done by women who don't know better." Her proposal celebrates some forms of women's work, including crafting, while dismissing the work and critical thinking of second-wave feminists. This overstatement and production of what Negra describes as an "imaginary feminist" is a common feature of postfeminist texts that does political and historical damage to feminist causes and affinities.[81]

Emily Matchar writes more critically about the empowering and limiting aspects of readopting women's work. She provides a history for contemporary interests in domesticity, which includes the "Cult of Domesticity" and the separate-spheres ideology of "woman housewife, man breadwinner."[82] She defines new domesticity as "the fascination with reviving 'lost' domestic arts like canning, bread-baking, knitting," and "chicken-raising."[83] Practitioners of the new domesticity envision personal, familial, societal, and economic value in their behaviors and market some of their products through ecommerce sites such as Etsy. As Matchar starts to suggest, they also threaten to increase work expectations as the handmade and personally produced are coded as healthier and more caring options and thus as the work of good and moral women.[84] New

Introduction 13

domesticity practitioners encourage time-intensive forms of home production and often purchase expensive items for crafting rather than buying cheaper and massified consumer products. Their ideas are likely to produce further difficulties for women who are destitute and working poor. Many of these women are already working long shifts, cannot afford to substitute new domestic practices for their jobs, and cannot invest extra time and money in these behaviors. In addition, numerous women are engaged in domestic work for pay and are expected to perform domestic work as part of their family responsibilities.[85] These women's geographic, cultural, gender, racial, and class experiences are elided by claims that revived versions of domesticity are inherently creative and liberating.

Debbie Stoller, who is the co-founder and editor of *Bust Magazine*, author of a number of crafting books, and sponsor of Stitch 'n Bitch groups, has helped to promote knitting and crocheting as pleasurable and feminist projects. Stoller and *Bust Magazine* are associated with "girlie" third-wave feminism and its celebration of such things as women's work, sexual experimentation, cosmetics, and feminine garb.[86] Stoller emphasizes these investments through her published book and chapter titles, including her use of "take back the knit" as a means of referencing Take Back the Night marches, which protest rape and other sexual violence.[87] *The Happy Hooker* book about crocheting and "I Know What Boys Like" chapter, which alludes to the Waitresses' song of the same name, play up women's active, and yet culturally stereotyped, sexualities.[88] For instance, the Waitresses band indicates that they like to tease and attract boys' attention. These and other Stoller citations tend to privilege humor over criticality and verge on repeating limiting cultural conventions.

Stoller's autobiographic book passages, like Railla's narratives and other postfeminist texts, have the unfortunate tendency to identify craft production and second-wave feminism as oppositional. She describes her early experiences watching her family craft and how her investment in the feminist movement distanced her from crafting. Stoller rousingly argues that doing "needlework inextricably binds" her to "female relatives. With each stitch," she is "carrying on centuries-old traditions and paying respect to their wide and varied crafting skills."[89] Stoller also indicates that feminists do not support such connections. She believes that they validate women who want to learn activities that are coded as male but they have more trouble with activities that are demarcated as female, including knitting.[90] She identifies this position as anti-feminist because it does not celebrate women's historical work. Other feminists are concerned with the ways new domesticity depicts women's work as a "choice" rather than acknowledging cultural expectations, does not address class and race, supplants feminist politics, and reasserts mandates for women to put the care of partners and children above their own best interests.[91]

Railla, Stoller, and a group of related producers assert that they are reprieving crafting from second-wave feminists, who dismissed it.[92] They portray third-wave feminists and feminism as fun and playful and second-wave feminists as having no sense of humor.[93] This stereotype has consistently been used to dismiss the politics and values of these women. Early feminist art projects such as the collaborative Womanhouse installation from 1972, which was part of the Feminist Art Program at Fresno State College and California Institute of the Arts, explored women's work through a variety of crafting methods.[94] Judy Chicago, one of the teachers in this program, continues to employ her art as a way of celebrating women's bodies, experiences, craft traditions, and collaborations.[95] In a different manner, the academic research and curatorial practices of Rozsika Parker's *The Subversive Stitch* show how women's embroidery and other crafting work were marginalized.[96] Like Matchar, Parker identifies crafting as a "source of pleasure" and oppressive.[97]

Ree Drummond: "The Pioneer Woman" and Producing Women

Ree Drummond is another one of the key marketers of new domesticity in Internet settings, although she does not deploy the term. Her practices point to a number of the features of producing women that I consider throughout this book. Drummond is a rancher, food and lifestyle blogger, author, television personality, and spokesperson for a variety of products. She is a producing woman, who produces the category of "woman." The journalist Amanda Fortini emphasizes some of these production roles when describing Drummond as "a canny author of her own persona."[98] Drummond makes herself into an ordinary woman, who has personal relationships with blog readers, by identifying as "The Pioneer Woman," promising that she is "Keepin' it Real," describing herself as a "ranch wife and mother of four," and thanking readers for "allowing" her "to share!"[99] Thus, Drummond is the successful producer of varied domestic, and nonetheless media and marketed products, including her own feminine image and intimate details of her life. This reconceived production of the personal and rural tradition has resulted in the blog having 25 million page views per month in 2013.[100] Drummond's successful enterprises have also made her millions of dollars.[101]

Drummond is known for her step-by-step photographic tutorials on how to cook "simple" foods.[102] In the first tutorial from 2007, she assures readers, "Don't be intimidated" about making a steak; "it's one of the easiest things in the world to cook."[103] Drummond also provides instructions on food photography and writes about her imaging practices in a manner that emphasizes her limitations. Her "photography has improved from the early days" but is nowhere near that of a food photographer and friend, who "is truly an artist."[104] Drummond distinguishes her practices from skilled and artistic identities as a means of following cultural expectations about feminine self-deprecation while highlighting her role as a producer. Stay-at-home mothers who market themselves and products on eBay also make distinctions between expertise and their roles.

Drummond downplays her expertise while using images of her hands making things to emphasize her position as a producer. This practice is deployed by many of the other producers I study. Women feature their hands crafting things as a way of asserting their creativity. They also point to things and indicate that their practices are important, depict their hands in contact with objects and people and evoke touching and emotionally connecting, and display engagement and wedding rings as a means of supporting monogamous heterosexuality. Women incorporate their hands into conceptions of production by using terms such as "handmade" and "handcrafted." Some of the literature on hands identifies these corporeal features as key parts of what makes people human.[105] Philosophers have associated hands with human abilities to manufacture and control things.[106] However, hands are often used to distinguish between people, including articulating conceptions of race. For instance, Drummond includes images of her and her daughter's white hands and lives touching and connecting through cooking. She unites with and constructs readers as mothers by advising them to have their "daughter" help with the recipe; "check her fingernails and say, 'Ew!'"; hear that she "learned it from you"; and "cry and imagine a different way of life. One that involves lovely fingernails and pantyhose."[107] Drummond links her production strategies to both empowerment and gender norms, including being "properly" feminine by maintaining clean nails and other bodily features.

Drummond connects the craft of cooking, binary distinctions, and satisfying the needs of men to feminism and women's empowerment. She writes, "I am woman. Hear me roar. But my husband's tastebuds I can not ignore. And if I make the pork chops he will melt."[108] Drummond believes in "equal opportunities for men and women" and that "women can do anything men can do" except "that lumberjack stuff. That would be pretty tough." In such statements, she articulates forms of exertion that are beyond feminist and feminine interests. Drummond further intermeshes feminism and gender norms when writing about her relationship. She "used to have to open gates" when dating her "Marlboro Man" husband and driving around the ranch.[109] The "feminist" in her "wanted to object," "remain in the passenger seat," and "demand chivalry." Through these narratives, Drummond defines feminism as the empowered right to choose gender hierarchies and gendered roles in a similar manner to postfeminist texts. This is different than the feminist belief that women are subordinated to men in Western culture and the associated calls for equality, rethinking of social structures and the ways they influence people's lives, and creation of a culture that completely addresses women's and other oppressed people's desires and interests.[110]

Drummond establishes gender and embodied differences by describing her husband and their relationship. Her husband is "rugged and virile" and has irresistible buttocks.[111] She tingles, sweats, and swoons while looking at him. This is intensified when he wears chaps and she views and photographs him from behind. A story about how her craving for donuts leads to humiliation includes the admission that her "jeans are tight" and "back fat is violent."[112] In a poem, she bemoans and to a lesser extent celebrates this uncontrollable and fleshy body. She is "So very fat" because "thirteen bastard pounds" cling to her "gut."[113] However, she resists being fully contained and asks, "Bring me cheese" and "chocolate by the load." Society also associates women with insatiable appetites that purportedly make them excessively fleshy, slothful, and repulsive.[114] However, Drummond's voracious food and sexual desires also enable her to produce and consume beyond the rules. For instance, her fixation on photographically depicting her husband from behind associates the empowered gaze and sexual activity with the female producer and readers and feminizes and queers her husband. While Laura Mulvey and some other feminist psychoanalytic film theorists have argued that cinematic looking is associated with an active male viewing position and the objectification of women, who are structured as "*to-be-looked-at-ness*," Drummond holds the camera and poses women as controlling viewers of male bodies.[115]

Drummond's family, the people who comment on her posts, the employees who work on her publications, and the personnel who assist with her television programs support her production. Women have become producers because of their admiration of Drummond.[116] However, a cohort of critical readers interrogates Drummond's expertise and role as a content creator.[117] Bloggers such as The Marlboro Woman, Pie Near Woman, and Pioneer Woman Sux parody the name of Drummond's site and her literary conventions. They believe that there is a conflict between her claims to be "Real" and her deeply mediated material and life story.[118] They provide detailed examples of how Drummond has copied other people's content without acknowledgment or permission.[119] Triggered by Drummond, they practice a form of critical production, including detailed entries that mimic Drummond's writing and photographs that humorously portray her world. In a similar manner to other women who produce Internet content and are engaged with the same topic, they collaboratively produce through their conversations and develop new media practices. Pie Near Woman notes that her "blog is frequently inspired by the mad writing skillz" of "The Pioneer Woman Sux" and "The Marlboro Woman."[120] She writes, "You complete me!" and evokes the homosocial and potentially homoerotic conversations that are part of some women's Internet production cultures and that I examine throughout this book.

The Marlboro Woman, Pie Near Woman, and Pioneer Woman Sux are concerned about how women and femininity are produced, including Drummond's marketing of and profiting from a traditional lifestyle. For example, The Marlboro Woman argues that Drummond has "set back this country's women's movement at least a hundred years with her cloying adulation for her husband and the resident 'men folk.'"[121] Unfortunately, these bloggers also criticize Drummond's body size, appearance, and sexuality. The Marlboro Woman writes about Drummond's "fat, narcissistic ass."[122] Most of Pie Near Woman's carefully rendered photographic tableaux of dolls depict Drummond covered in food as a means of condemning her appetite and defiling her.[123] These feminist and media critiques enable bloggers to produce content while rendering disturbingly retrograde ideas about other women. However, they could adopt slightly different critical strategies, including commentary that does not rely on negative stereotypes about women, as a way of forwarding their form of parody and production as criticism. For instance, Pie Near Woman transforms Drummond's husband, who is based on the rugged Marlboro stereotype, into a feminized doll and portrays his chaps-clad buttocks [Figure I.1].[124] Their focus on Marlboro Man's ass, in a manner related to Drummond's own work, proposes an empowered feminine gaze and queering of monogamous heterosexuality. Their examination of Drummond's images and ethos already produces a critical viewing position for women.

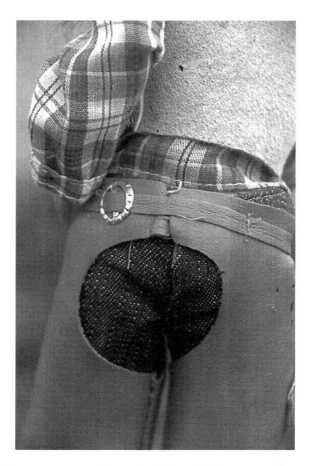

FIGURE I.1 Pie Near Woman. This remade doll parodically represents Ree Drummond's husband and his chaps-clad buttocks.

The Politics of New Domesticity and Producing Women

The Marlboro Woman, Pie Near Woman, and Pioneer Woman Sux interrogate Drummond's blog and other practices because of the ways she produces and markets motherhood and femininity. "Mommy bloggers" have also been contrarily dismissed for their purportedly insignificant subject matter and for the sometimes-substantial profits that they garner from personal and familial writing. Lori Kedo Lopez chronicles how mommy bloggers have asserted their importance and the radical act of mommy blogging.[125] She argues that mommy bloggers change cultural conceptions of motherhood. Women's expressions of personal feelings about motherhood, according to Aimée Morrison's study of mommy blogging, transmute into a communal identity and point them towards collective social action.[126] However, she argues that the political ramifications of these bloggers' practices are curtailed because they do not convey their ideas to mainstream culture. In addition, communication scholar Gina Masullo Chen finds that the empowering aspects of mommy blogging are reduced because the term reinforces normative conceptions of women and produces a kind of digital domesticity.[127] Of course, mommy bloggers' economic and literary successes and their circulation of what was once conceptualized as private information challenge some of the ways motherhood and domesticity are understood.

The academic literature on new domesticity and crafting engages with questions about women's power and gender norms. Organization scholars Stella Minahan and Julie Wolfram Cox describe contemporary knitting groups as reconceived ways of "connecting" and engaging in technological work, especially for women.[128] People's fannish commentary and critiques of Drummond have also facilitated interactive production cultures for women. Academic research on other fan communities, especially those organized around the remaking of media texts, has chronicled the ways participants collaboratively rework gender and sexuality roles.[129] In a similar manner, art historian Alla Myzelev argues that knitting can redefine "gendered roles in society" because there are a variety of subjects involved in what has been culturally understood as a feminine exercise.[130] Rather than viewing women's contemporary position as always empowered, which is the assertion made by some postfeminist texts, these considerations point to particular crafting practices where women are reworking conceptions of artistry and the associated identities.

Many researchers emphasize the in-between status of these crafts and the ways they position practitioners. Myzelev argues that knitting undoes the binary oppositions between original and copy, public and private, and gay and straight. By revising patterns, knitters produce things that are different than the directions. Contemporary crafters bring reconceptualized authorship, nostalgic ideas about crafting, reconfigured identities, and intimate and domestic practices into communal spaces through such things as Stitch 'n Bitch groups. A great deal of the literature notes that new domesticity and crafting produce hybrid structures and identities. For instance, popular culture scholars Jack Z. Bratich and Heidi M. Brush argue that new domesticity "does not transform old into new, it reweaves the old itself" so that the old meanings are changed.[131] New domesticity adjusts some aspects of normative identity positions. However, the argument that new domesticity recodes the "old" must be kept in tension with the ways it celebrates and extends the more limiting aspects of these cultures.

Behaviors that combine crafting and activism are described as "craftivism." Betsy Greer, who coined the term and implemented craftivism.com, defines craftivism as a "way of looking at life where voicing opinions through creativity makes your voice stronger, your compassion deeper & your quest for justice more infinite."[132] For her, crafting is empowering and produces political subjects. This is related to the association of the Internet and contemporary technologies with political agency, such as the marketing of Apple's iPad as "Resolutionary" and thus revolutionary.[133] Sites and practices, including blogging and tweeting, have also been linked to resistance and such social movements as Occupy and the Arab Spring.[134] People's use of these technologies to engage with community and consider the needs of others is different than postfeminism's association with the individual.[135] For American studies scholar Kristen A. Williams, craftivism practitioners are committed to "a social activism that explicitly links individual creativity and human-based mechanisms of production to broader sociopolitical cultural contexts in an attempt to influence the social world."[136] This politicization of the everyday and crafting is connected to feminist declarations that the "personal is political." However, some craftivism projects, according to Laura Portwood-Stacer's research on the topic, do not indicate the means through which the social world will be changed and equity will be facilitated.[137]

The promises of crafting-facilitated justness are compromised by the dismissal of earlier feminist projects and "older" crafters and their work. Some crafters distinguish between contemporary crafts, which they imagine to be stylish, ironic, and produced by young people, and staid and traditional work, which they relate to grandmothers. For instance, Leah Kramer founded Craftster, which is described as the "largest online community" for sharing "hip," "crafty," "do it yourself" projects, and supports the Not Your Granny's Craft Fair—Bazaar Bizarre.[138] News stories about contemporary crafting are entitled "This Is Not Your Grandmother's Knitting Shop" and "Not your Grandmother's Knitting Circle."[139] In a related manner, the Etsy seller StrungOutFiberArts lists an iPhone caddy with a cat appliqué, a headband with a rose, and a crocheted uterus under the heading "Not your grandmother's knitting."[140] Yet cats and roses have been used as craft motifs for centuries and such artists as Chicago and Tee Corinne depicted women's reproductive organs and genitals in the 1970s.[141] The contemporary claims that people are doing something more innovative than traditional women's work contrast young and old and smartly funky and ignorantly tacky and thereby render ageist and classist conceptions of crafting.

Contemporary crafters are believed to have more thoughtful and critical views of production than earlier practitioners. One of Craftster's logos depicts two women with teacups engaged in conversation and declares "No Tea Cozies without Irony."[142] In a related manner, Greer argues that contemporary craft practices include a "return to home economics tinged with a hint of irony."[143] These texts suggest that contemporary makers resist the oppressive features and unappealing goods that were part of earlier women's craft cultures. Nevertheless, blogger Gretchen Hirsch appears to be replying to Craftster when arguing, "Whether you're knitting tea cozies or a skull motif sweater, you're using the skills that have been passed down among generations of women."[144] Craftster members and other contemporary DIY producers are part of the history of tea cozy production even when they reform the rules and features of this production. After all, women have rethought craft products and the associated implications in previous decades and centuries.

Contemporary crafters are supposed to have refigured earlier conventions but these changes do not always extend to Internet settings. The people portrayed in Craftster's logos, perhaps in an ironic quotation of the 1950s that is not sensitive to racial diversity, are all fairly traditional white women in fitted and full-skirted dresses. The individuals who are responsible for the site are also depicted as white women.[145] The Etsy ecommerce setting, which focuses on handmade goods, vintage items, and crafting supplies, depicts a large cohort of light-skinned men as part of its staff but portrays members as traditionally gendered women, and to a lesser extent heterosexual couples. Etsy encourages readers to "Start Your Own Business" and "Join the movement rebuilding human-scale economies around the world."[146] It reflects the craftivism philosophy in promising that Etsy empowers "people to change the way the global economy works." Etsy underscores the idea that the site enables women by featuring stay-at-home mothers like SpinSpanSpun and her indication that "Etsy changed" her "life."[147] She thinks it "changes lives everyday, especially the lives of women."

Etsy promises women empowerment but it does not always render female authority. Its 404 error message for malfunctioning and mistyped URLs features a woman of color as a less skilled producer. This is an example of how sites code users. Individuals who submit a dysfunctional URL are informed that "Uh oh! There's something not quite right in the URL. Please check for any errors in the address bar and try again" [Figure I.2].[148] A tan-colored cartoonish woman with a "HOW TO KNIT" book and a skein of abandoned yarn illustrates this message. The crafter hunches over, frowns, and holds up a three-armed sweater for the viewer to see. The woman of color is marked as a producer but she is the "Uh oh!" and a mistake who blunders rather than a skilled crafter. Even with her instruction book, there is still something "not quite right" with her knitting. Thus, the message renders tan and other women of color as the embodiment of crafting, technological, and computer mistakes. It also suggests that it is women rather than technologies that are the cause of 404 errors and absolves the site

Introduction 21

FIGURE I.2 Etsy. Etsy's 404 error message depicts people of color as confused.

and its technologies from blame. This image and a variety of other site features promise women empowerment while posing problems for those who do not fit the most normative standards.

Chapter Summaries

Etsy describes the setting as "the marketplace we make together" and depicts traditional female sellers.[149] Etsy thereby produces a cohort of women who support the company and community and articulates what it means to be a producing woman. In Chapter 1, I study how eBay and Etsy sellers render themselves as stay-at-home mothers in order to sell products; be recognized; connect with a cohort of similarly identified women; and engage with personal and cultural investments in childcare, home, and work. I argue that these women tactically use the role of stay-at-home mother rather than following all of its constraining features. I study such portrayals because mothers are, as women's studies scholars Suzanna Danuta Walters and Laura Harrison argue, people and representations onto which we project "our most vexed understandings of womanhood and femininity."[150] I consider the kinds of labor stay-at-home mothers who sell on eBay and Etsy perform and how they mediate between cultural expectations and their diverse positions. They do traditional forms of gender and femininity, self-efface their role as business owners, connect though Internet sites, excessively work, assert the quality and importance of their crafting, and profit from their roles. For instance, sellers connect their caretaking to the kinds of products that they make and list. People purchase their products because they appear to be vetted by and a means of supporting children and generated by care. I also address the ways intensive mothering is extended by indications that individuals should perform free labor in Internet settings, including the marketplace women are directed to make together.[151] This allows me to complicate conceptions of stay-at-home mothers and suggest the methods through which women perform varied kinds of work from places that are still understood as domestic homes and feminine spaces.[152]

Women render realistic depictions of children by modifying dolls and making them into "reborn babies." Reborn artists, as I indicate in Chapter 2, use ecommerce settings and personal websites to lay claim to the feminine role of the maternal caretaker and the more professional position of creative producer. Their maternal and artistic assertions, which they suggest are interrelated, challenge cultural associations of artistry with men.[153] They further disturb stable gender and sex positions by offering to change the gender of babies and selling "anatomically correct" belly plates and umbilical cords that can be attached and removed. These babies are supposed to look as well as feel real. Reborn artists render the sensations of touching babies and their emotional calls as a means of encouraging viewers to commit to intensive childcare and conceptually shift from buying dolls to being mothers who care for babies. Eve Kosofsky Sedgwick's and other authors' considerations of affect allow me to consider the ways reborn producers use representations of hands touching and textured fabrics to make dolls emotionally matter and to have them function as viscerally felt art.[154] Buyers and viewers respond by self-presenting as "reborn pregnant" and experiencing dolls as dead and undead babies. By connecting the corporeal and emotional features of touching and feeling to the Internet, reborn artists influence viewers' conceptions of these sites and themselves.

Stay-at-home mothers who sell on ecommerce sites and women who produce reborn babies reference and torque traditional conceptions of mothers. Numerous Internet settings market traditional weddings and connect women over their shared interest in wedding rituals and white dresses. In Chapter 3, I consider how photographers work with married women and represent them wearing white wedding dresses again while posing in dilapidated surroundings and staining gowns. This is a common post-wedding practice. Photographers use Internet settings to indicate that these "trash the dress" (TTD) sessions resist photographic conventions and feminine bridal roles and, by distancing themselves from conventional wedding photography, elevate their artistic status. Brides are supposed to demonstrate their marital commitment by trashing dresses and thus promising that they will not get married in gowns again. However, women rarely wore big white wedding dresses in public more than once before the development of TTD. This ritual further challenges the centrality of marriage and traditional femininity by incorporating divorce sessions. Women indicate their distance from marital bliss by acting out the process of killing the groom just after, and even before, they have been married. These sessions associate heterosexual marriage with horror and allow the participating women to pleasurably gaze at images of women and flirt with women in Internet wedding forums. Feminist considerations of the ways women look at women allow me to theorize these brides' queer engagements.[155] While the claims that TTD is a form of resistance are overstated, women's collaborative production of TTD and engagement with other women offer them delights and erotic connections that are not so easily correlated with traditional weddings and femininity.

Women assert their active and agentive positions by arranging TTD sessions where they kill zombies. A worrying number of the women who self-present as pale zombie brides at public zombie walks and appear on image-sharing sites are light-skinned. However, women's zombie bride self-presentations and instructions, as I argue in Chapter 4, compromise some conceptions of whiteness and femininity. They wear filthy dresses and have ghastly white and blood-scabbed skin. How-to guides about zombie brides further direct people to produce whiteness by combining numerous colors and looking unhealthy or dead. They thereby pose feminine whiteness as multihued, changeable, deathly, and unappealing instead of the more usual construction of it as stable, enlivening, and beautiful. These instructions depict hands actively producing the body and delivering death to white people and whiteness as constructed rather than natural.[156] In a similar manner, representations of zombie brides and grooms legally getting wed at zombie walks pose marriages as deadening. Zombie brides dissipate into Internet sites' white backgrounds. Zombie brides' whiteness, with its monstrous and deathly features, unsettles the cultural association of feminine whiteness with beauty and health and provides some problems for the related articulation of whiteness and Caucasian people as ideals.

Zombie brides and how-to authors propose unusual qualifiers for femininity and cosmetics because they use everyday makeup to construct monstrous and deathly whiteness. Women's engagement with their appearance through such practices as applying makeup, as the feminist literature on beauty culture indicates, is one of the key ways femininity is constructed.[157] Women are reliant on metaphorical, if not physical, sparkle to maintain their beauty, appeal, and very claim to being female.[158] I analyze the connections between glitter makeup and femininity in Chapter 5. I also theorize how glitter challenges normative femininity because it is associated with childishness, frivolity, lower-class tastes, drag performances, and sex work.[159] Due to these issues, many women who blog about glitter makeup in Internet settings are attentive to the "correct" way of wearing it and try to control glitter's influences. Posters assert that there are acceptable times to wear glitter makeup, age groups who can use this material, amounts of glitter that can be worn, and parts of the face and body where it can be applied. Women also adopt glitter as a means of admiring their bodily features, rather than self-presenting for men. As commentators suggest, glitter drifts everywhere and contaminates things. I address the interlocking of the normative and unruly aspects of glitter cosmetics as a way of considering how glitter is a feature of and produces femininity, a threat to this identity category that needs to be managed, a product made by women, and a device for cultural opposition.

I focus on Shelley and Pamela Jackson's hypertexts about hands and the women who blog about nail polish in the afterword to this book because they condense and extend many of my arguments from previous chapters, including my critical considerations of femininity and hands. Nail polish bloggers use terms such as "frankening" and "franken polish," in a manner that is related to the production of the bride of Frankenstein, to reference miraculous creations, their skills, monstrosity, and problems with stable identities. They also refer to "lobster" and "zombie hands," which appear to be too pink or white, and continue the interrogations of femininity and race that are posed by some versions of Frankenstein's monster.[160] While culture and the media often render women as heterosexual and position them so that they can be looked at and objectified by men, nail bloggers photograph their hands so that they can be admired by other women and assert the part that their hands play in skillfully producing polishes and applications. Nail bloggers' practices thus support feminist interests in acknowledging and encouraging women's work and interrogating the production of bodies and categories.

Conclusion: The Technologies of Producing Women in Internet Sites

Cultural beliefs about women's identities and domestic production filter through Internet programming and design features, self-representations, site texts, and personal comments. While the functional and empowering features of computers and Internet settings are ordinarily associated with men and masculinity, arguments can be made about their relationship to women and femininity. For instance Kramer is the founder of Craftster, a craft book author, an indie crafts storeowner, and a computer programmer. Her roles continue the historical association of crafts with the technological.[161] In a related manner, the Jacquard loom automated weaving and, as feminist philosopher Sadie Plant argues, links the feminine craft of weaving to a form of computer processing.[162] People also identify knitting as a kind of computer coding.[163] Radhika Gajjala and Annapurna Mamidipuni's feminist research and weaving practices situate hand looming and its practitioners in tension with contemporary information technologies and technologists.[164] This allows them to theorize how technologies structure people and the ways they are shaped by individuals.

The Internet, as these sites and texts suggest, is the setting of multiple kinds of production. Its software technologies, design features, code, computers and screens, networks, and data centers support and render representations of bodies, spaces, and worlds. These conceptions are reliant on the work and interactions of individuals, who link functional technologies to women and other subjects rather than allowing them to only be associated with white heterosexual men. In *Producing Women*, I take these production cultures and practices seriously. Rather than choosing more conventional sorts of production, I examine cultures that have been important to cohorts of women but received little critical and scholarly consideration. Such practices as reborn doll production and trash the dress photography have been widely featured in the popular press and supported by large numbers of women but remained largely outside of academic considerations.[165] The studies in this book thus point to new research areas and complicate the ways researchers understand Internet settings as productive for participants. They also assert that women's production cultures are an important site for feminist and queer theory and politics.

Conceptions of producing women, including the ways women engage in varied sorts of material and reproductive labor and identity positions are crafted, have been key aspects of feminist theorizing and feminist searches for equity. The cultural and conceptual connections between such forms of production as new domesticity, women's work, reproduction, mothering, and Internet production cultures tend to intensify the underlying beliefs. These connections can also highlight the functions of production and thereby work as critical strategies. For instance, Internet production cultures have forms and other features that itemize the characteristics of people and allow individuals to select and construct detailed avatars and versions of themselves. They thereby provide a detailed map of the ways identities are produced and characteristics get attached to these roles. This means that individual producing women and interrogations of the structures that produce women can provide methods of engaging with and rethinking conceptions of identity and cultural production. By studying producing women in Internet sites, including practices that exceed conventions but are incorporated into traditional roles, I point to the ways women's Internet positions function and can be deployed to support a wider array of lived practices.

Notes

1. Kat, "Happy Halloween – Bride of Frankenstein," Rock n Roll Bride, 31 October 2009, 1 January 2013, http://www.rocknrollbride.com/2009/10/happy-halloween-bride-of-frankenstein/; Alley Kat Photography, "Bride of FrankinStein," Flickr, 27 October 2009, 1 January 2013, http://www.flickr.com/photos/aileycatdesigns/4050638467/in/set-72157604109132881/. Rock n Roll Bride indicates that it is dedicated to "kick ass weddingness" and people who have "picked up a bridal magazine and felt queasy." Kat, "About," Rock n Roll Bride, 1 January 2013, http://www.rocknrollbride.com/about/. In the endnotes in this book, detailed information about website references is included for each citation because there may be different authors, titles, URLs, and publication and access dates. Books and academic journals tend to have more stable features and are thus listed in the Selected Bibliography and in shortened citations in the notes. The constant reconfiguration of Internet representations and changes in Internet service providers make it difficult to find previously quoted material and important to chronicle the kinds of depictions that happen in these settings. Many Internet texts include typographical errors and unconventional forms of spelling, uppercase and lowercase typefaces, punctuation, and spacing. I have retained these formatting features in quotations

and Internet references, including those for news sites, without such qualifications as "intentionally so written" or "sic." Some of the sites listed in these citations are no longer available. Others have changed and do not offer the text or images that I describe. In the references, the date listed before the URL is the "publication" date or the last time the site was viewed in the indicated format. When two dates are included, the first date points to when the current configuration of the site was initially available and the second date is the latest access date. Some versions of referenced sites can be viewed by using the Internet Archive's Wayback Machine. Internet Archive, "Internet Archive: Wayback Machine," 6 July 2014, http://www.archive.org/web/web.php
2. Alley Kat Photography, "Bride of FrankinStein," Flickr, 27 October 2009, 22 March 2013, http://www.flickr.com/photos/aileycatdesigns/4050638467/in/set-72157604109132881/lightbox/
3. Kat, "Happy Halloween – Bride of Frankenstein," Rock n Roll Bride, 31 October 2009, 1 January 2013, http://www.rocknrollbride.com/2009/10/happy-halloween-bride-of-frankenstein/
4. James Whale, *The Bride of Frankenstein* (Universal Pictures, 1935).
5. Alley Kat Photography, "Bride of FrankinStein," Flickr, 27 October 2009, 3 January 2013, http://www.flickr.com/photos/aileycatdesigns/4050638129/in/set-72157604109132881/
6. The individual identity of the groom and the bride's marriage to one man are compromised by the continual shifts in the spelling of "Frankenstein," including "franstine" and "FrankinStein" in the previously listed photography titles. For discussions of monstrosity and heterosexuality, see Creed, *The Monstrous-Feminine*; Jackson, "Gender, Sexuality and Heterosexuality."
7. Ingraham, *White Weddings*.
8. Davis, "Remaking the She-Devil"; Poitevin, "Inventing Whiteness."
9. Alley Kat Photography, "Bride of FrankinStein," Flickr, 27 October 2009, 2 January 2013, http://www.flickr.com/photos/aileycatdesigns/4050638467/in/faves-28566859@N06/
10. Coltrane, "Household Labor"; Schaefer, "Disposable Mothers." Expectations for women to leave their careers after the birth of a child, and the later proscriptions for these women to go back to work, are examined by Sayer, "Gender, Time and Inequality."
11. Bartky, "Foucault, Femininity"; Black, *Beauty Industry*; Brand, ed. *Beauty Matters*; Davis, *Reshaping the Female Body*.
12. Culler, "Closeness of Reading," 22.
13. Johnson, "Teaching Deconstructively," 141.
14. Hayles, *How We Think*.
15. Culler, "Closeness of Reading," 21.
16. Ibid., 20.
17. Hayles, *How We Think*, 61.
18. Wakeford, "Developing Methodological Frameworks."
19. Menon, "Virtual Realities," 152.
20. Nakamura, *Digitizing Race*.
21. Jakob Nielsen, "F-Shaped Pattern for Reading Web Content," Nielsen Norman Group, 17 April 2006, 11 June 2014, http://www.nngroup.com/articles/f-shaped-pattern-reading-web-content/; Hayles, *How We Think*.
22. Slashdot, "Slashdot (15)," 11 June 2014, http://slashdot.org/
23. Many US institutional review boards, as well as the Collaborative Institutional Training Initiative (CITI) that educates researchers on human subjects issues, indicate that the methods that I use are not human subject research. They associate intervention and interaction with human subject research. While I identify my

research as the close analysis of texts, I still recognize the debates over Internet research ethics and the need to be sensitive to the investments individuals have in these kinds of renderings. For proposals about Internet research ethics, see Buchanan, ed. *Readings in Virtual Research*; Hongladarom and Ess, eds. *Information Technology Ethics*; Markham and Buchanan, "Ethical Decision-Making."
24. Brownmiller, *Femininity*, 14.
25. Bordo, "Body," 14.
26. Milkie, "Contested Images of Femininity," 839.
27. de Lauretis, *Technologies of Gender*, 2.
28. Foucault, "Technologies of the Self." For the application of this concept to Internet settings, see Siles, "Web Technologies."
29. For a related discussion of Foucault's and de Lauretis's use of technology, see Balsamo, *Technologies of the Gendered Body*.
30. Cole and Zucker, "Black and White Women's."
31. Collins, *Black Sexual Politics*, 44.
32. Johnson, "Teaching Deconstructively."
33. Press, *Women Watching Television*; Lotz, "Postfeminist Television Criticism."
34. Gill, "Empowerment/Sexism"; McRobbie, *Aftermath of Feminism*; Modleski, *Feminism without Women*.
35. Nathanson, *Television and Postfeminist Housekeeping*; Patterson, "Fracturing Tina Fey"; Susan Bolotin, "Voices from the Post-Feminist Generation," *New York Times Magazine*, 17 October 1982, 3 July 2013, http://www.nytimes.com/1982/10/17/magazine/voices-from-the-post-feminist-generation.html; Nurka, "Postfeminist Autopsies."
36. Tasker and Negra, introduction to "In Focus," 109.
37. Gerhard, "Sex and the City"; Kim, "Sex and the Single."
38. Negra, "Quality Postfeminism?"
39. Lotz, "Postfeminist Television Criticism," 106.
40. Gill, "Empowerment/Sexism"; Sarikakis and Tsaliki, "Post/feminism."
41. Brundson, "Feminism, Postfeminism."
42. Petersen, "That Teenage Feeling"; Faludi, *Backlash*.
43. Hall and Rodriguez, "Myth of Postfeminism."
44. Brooks, *Postfeminisms*; Brundson, "Feminism, Postfeminism."
45. Butler, "For White Girls Only?" Gill, "Postfeminist Media Culture."
46. Chapman, "Making Weight."
47. Scott, "Postfeminist User," 459.
48. Tasker and Negra, introduction to "In Focus," 108.
49. Braun, "Women."
50. Chen, "Neoliberalism," 441.
51. Political forms of consumerism include consumer boycotts and buycotts, buying gifts, giving away consumer items, and selling things with messages that challenge contemporary beliefs. Breen, *Marketplace of Revolution*; Schudson, "Citizens, Consumers"; Stolle, Hooghe, and Micheletti, "Politics in the Supermarket."
52. Wacjman, *TechnoFeminism*.
53. White, *Body and the Screen*; White, *Buy It Now*.
54. There is a great deal of literature on co-production and personalization, including Gauntlett, *Making Is Connecting*; Payne et al. "Co-creating Brands"; Prahalad and Ramaswamy, "Co-creation Experiences." There are also critiques of these ideas, such as Humphreys and Grayson, "Intersecting Roles"; Ritzer and Jurgenson, "Production, Consumption, Prosumption."
55. Pingdom, "Report: Social network demographics in 2012," 21 August 2012, 19 June 2014, http://royal.pingdom.com/2012/08/21/report-social-network-demographics-in-2012/. Pingdom identifies Slashdot as the "Most male-dominated site" where 87% of participants are men.

56. Sarah Gray, "Facebook releases diversity figures: They look a lot like Google's and Yahoo's," Salon, 26 June 2014, http://www.salon.com/2014/06/26/facebook_releases_diversity_figures_they_look_a_lot_like_googles_and_yahoos/
57. Facebook's "like" hand, which is garbed in Oxford cloth, also references preppy culture, the site's development at Harvard, and the setting's early function as an exclusive and Ivy League interface. Executives from the company are related to white masculinity because the like hand has appeared on the podiums that are used to make company announcements and indicated the expected identity of speakers. For an image of the podium, see Adam Schreck, "Facebook launches Mideast office in Dubai," Yahoo! News, 30 May 2012, 6 July 2014, http://news.yahoo.com/facebook-launches-mideast-office-dubai-141844339--finance.html
58. A_Really_Cool_Person, "facebook," Urban Dictionary, 25 June 2007, 19 June 2014, http://www.urbandictionary.com/define.php?term=facebook&page=6; Spazzx, "facebook," Urban Dictionary, 27 April 2010, 19 June 2014, http://www.urbandictionary.com/define.php?term=facebook&page=8
59. reddit, "reddit: the front page of the internet," 20 June 2014, http://www.reddit.com/; Slashdot, "Slashdot: News for nerds, stuff that matters," 20 June 2014, http://slashdot.org/
60. Katie J. M. Baker, "How to Shut Down Reddit's CreepShots Once and for All: Name Names," Jezebel, 10 October 2012, 2 January 2013, http://jezebel.com/5949379/; Adrien Chen, "Reddit's Child Porn Scandal," Gawker, 11 October 2012, 2 January 2013, http://gawker.com/5848653/; Adrien Chen, "Unmasking Reddit's Violentacrez, The Biggest Troll on the Web," Gawker, 12 October 2012, 2 January 2013, http://gawker.com/5950981/unmasking-reddits-violentacrez-the-biggest-troll-on-the-web/; Max Read, "Ladies: 8,000 Creeps on Reddit Are Sharing the Nude Photos You Posted to Photobucket," Gawker, 8 August 2012, 2 January 2013, http://gawker.com/5932702/ladies-8000-creeps-on-reddit-are-sharing-the-nude-photos-you-posted-to-photobucket
61. Max Read, "'Post Your Racist Opinions Here' Thread Nearly Shuts Down Reddit," Gawker, 26 September 2011, 20 June 2014, http://gawker.com/5844071/
62. Shamson, "Mmmm…. racism," reddit, 22 June 2012, 20 June 2014, http://www.reddit.com/r/WTF/comments/vfqyp/mmmmracism/; imgur, "3ERQR.jpg (JPEG Image 220 x 300 pixels)," 22 June 2014, http://i.imgur.com/3eRQR.jpg
63. Dean, "Boys and Girls"; Goings, *Mammy and Uncle Mose*.
64. Daniels, "Race and Racism."
65. Anonymous Coward, "Re: Human Sperm Produced in the Laboratory," Slashdot, 8 July 2009, 20 June 2014, http://www.science.slashdot.org/story/09/07/08/186205/Human-Sperm-Produced-In-the-Laboratory?from=rss
66. supershot666, "Help! I just asked my girlfriend to make me a sandwich, she replied, 'No, go make it yourself!' How do i stop this disobedient behavior?" reddit, 24 August 2011, 20 June 2014, http://www.reddit.com/r/shittyadvice/comments/jta6t/help_i_just_asked_my_girlfriend_to_make_me_a/
67. CookieFetish, "Help! I just asked my girlfriend to make me a sandwich, she replied, 'No, go make it yourself!' How do i stop this disobedient behavior?" reddit, 24 August 2011, 20 June 2014, http://www.reddit.com/r/shittyadvice/comments/jta6t/help_i_just_asked_my_girlfriend_to_make_me_a/
68. Variax and Brad, "Make Me a Sandwich," Know Your Meme, 20 June 2014, http://knowyourmeme.com/memes/make-me-a-sandwich. The meme's origin is credited to a 1995 *Saturday Night Live* skit. It has been included in numerous television episodes and is now circulated and remade on social networking sites.
69. GeekGirlCon, "Saturday Programming | GeekGirlCon," 2012, 20 June 2014, http://www.geekgirlcon.com/con/saturday-programming-2012/

70. Layering different kinds of glitter and "jelly" or translucent polishes makes glitter jelly sandwich applications. Women build up complicated colors and surfaces through their experimental and expert combinations.
71. Wollstonecraft, *Vindication*.
72. Welter, "Cult of True Womanhood," 152.
73. Lerner, "Lady," 12. The motto that a "woman's place is in the home" also appeared during this period.
74. Roberts, "True Womanhood Revisited," 150.
75. Guy, "True Womanhood in Latin America."
76. Hewitt, "Taking the True Woman Hostage," 158.
77. Cott, *Bonds of Womanhood*, 200.
78. Kerber, "Separate Spheres, Female Worlds," 15–16.
79. Jean Railla, "Feminism and the New Domesticity," Christy Petterson, 2 November 2004, 20 June 2014, http://christypetterson.wordpress.com/; Railla also wrote *Get Crafty*.
80. Jean Railla, as quoted in Connie Lauerman, "Feminism meets domesticity," *Chicago Tribune*, 14 December 2005, 20 June 2014, http://articles.chicagotribune.com/2005-12-14/features/0512140221_1_knitting-domesticity-crafts
81. Negra, *What A Girl Wants?* 10.
82. Matchar, *Homeward Bound*, 32.
83. Emily Matchar, "New Domesticity," 20 June 2014, http://newdomesticity.com/; Matchar, *Homeward Bound*.
84. For further reporting on new domesticity, see Peggy Orenstein, "The Femivore's Dilemma," *New York Times*, 11 March 2010, 20 June 2014, http://www.nytimes.com/2010/03/14/magazine/14fob-wwln-t.html; Michael Tortorello, "Is It Safe to Play Yet?" *New York Times*, 14 March 2012, 20 June 2014, http://www.nytimes.com/2012/03/15/garden/going-to-extreme-lengths-to-purge-household-toxins.html?pagewanted=1&hp
85. Portwood-Stacer, "Do-It-Yourself Feminism."
86. Jennifer Baumgardner and Amy Richards use the term "Girlie" in *Manifesta*. For a discussion of Baumgardner and Richards see Tamara Straus, "A Manifesto for Third Wave Feminism," AlterNet, 23 October 2000, 20 June 2014, http://www.alternet.org/story/9986/a_manifesto_for_third_wave_feminism
87. Stoller, *Stitch 'n Bitch*.
88. Stoller, *Happy Hooker*; Stoller, *Son of Stitch 'n Bitch*; The Waitresses, "I Know What Boys Like," *Wasn't Tomorrow Wonderful* (Polydor Records, 1982).
89. Stoller, *Happy Hooker*, 3.
90. Stoller, *Stitch 'n Bitch*.
91. Groeneveld, "Be a Feminist"; Emily Matchar, "The new domesticity: Fun, empowering or a step back for American women?" *Washington Post*, 18 November 2011, 20 June 2014, http://www.washingtonpost.com/opinions/the-new-domesticity-fun-empowering-or-a-step-back-for-american-women/2011/11/18/gIQAqkg1vN_story_2.html
92. For a critique of these distinctions between feminist waves, see Robertson, "Rebellious Doilies."
93. For a discussion of girlie feminism's claims about fun, see Showden, "What's Political?"
94. Meyer and Wilding, "Collaboration and Conflict."
95. These works by Judy Chicago include *Birth Project* (1980–1985) and *The Dinner Party* (1974–1979).
96. Parker, *Subversive Stitch*.
97. Parker, "Creation of Femininity," 491.

98. Amanda Fortini, "O Pioneer Woman!: The creation of a domestic idyll," *New Yorker*, 9 May 2011, 3 January 2013, http://www.newyorker.com/reporting/2011/05/09/110509fa_fact_fortini?currentPage=all
99. Ree, "About Pioneer Woman," The Pioneer Woman, 3 January 2013, http://thepioneerwoman.com/about/
100. Sarah DiGregorio, "Home on the Range: Thanksgiving with Ree Drummond," *Parade*, 16 November 2013, 15 May 2014, http://parade.condenast.com/226902/sarahdigregorio/home-on-the-range-thanksgiving/; The Pioneer Woman's traffic was ranked by Alexa at 6,702 globally and 1,477 in the United States. Alexa, "Thepioneerwoman.com Site Info," 15 May 2014, http://www.alexa.com/siteinfo/thepioneerwoman.com
101. Melanie Haupt, "A Patchwork Planet: How blogging became the (very lucrative) 21st century quilting bee," *Austin Chronicle*, 2 March 2012, 20 June 2014, http://www.austinchronicle.com/screens/2012-03-02/a-patchwork-planet/; ABDPBT, "How Much Do Bloggers Make? Case Study: Ree Drummond AKA The Pioneer Woman," 25 March 2013, http://abdpbt.com/how-much-do-bloggers-make-case-study-ree-drummond-aka-the-pioneer-woman/; Rousseau, *Food and Social Media*.
102. Ree, "Simple Sesame Noodles," The Pioneer Woman, 13 August 2010, 20 June 2014, http://thepioneerwoman.com/cooking/2010/08/simple-sesame-noodles/
103. Ree, "How to Cook a Steak," The Pioneer Woman, 30 May 2007, 20 June 2014, http://thepioneerwoman.com/cooking/2007/05/how_to_cook_a_s/
104. Ree, "Then and Now: Pots de Creme," The Pioneer Woman, 27 July 2011, 20 June 2014, http://thepioneerwoman.com/photography/2011/07/then-and-now-pots-de-creme/
105. Le Fanu, "Hand"; Slatman and Widdershoven, "Hand Transplants"; Wilson, *Hand*.
106. Rowe, *Dead Hands*.
107. Ree, "Baked Ziti," The Pioneer Woman, 26 November 2012, 20 June 2014, http://thepioneerwoman.com/cooking/2012/11/baked-ziti/
108. Ree, "Pan-Fried Pork Chops," The Pioneer Woman, 6 October 2009, 20 June 2014, http://thepioneerwoman.com/cooking/2009/10/simple-pan-fried-pork-chops. Drummond's "Cowboy Food" category provides meat and fried food "recipes that scream 'Man Food.'" Recipes that are "chick-friendly" appear in a "Cowgirl Food" section that emphasizes pastas and salads. Ree, "Cowgirl Food," The Pioneer Woman, 20 June 2014, http://thepioneerwoman.com/cooking/category/chick_food/
109. Ree, "Foggy, Foggy Morning," The Pioneer Woman, 23 August 2008, 20 June 2014, http://thepioneerwoman.com/blog/2008/08/foggy_foggy_morning/
110. I use the term "feminist" to identify people and groups who share an interest in forwarding societal equity, although the ways individuals define equity and the practices that they believe will facilitate this are quite different. Osborne, "Feminism."
111. Ree Drummond, "About Pioneer Woman," The Pioneer Woman, 9 June 2014, http://thepioneerwoman.com/about/
112. Ree, "All I Wanted Was a Doughnut," The Pioneer Woman, 23 December 2011, 20 June 2014, http://thepioneerwoman.com/blog/2011/12/all-i-wanted-was-a-doughnut/
113. Ree, "Poetry of a Madwoman, Vol. 9," The Pioneer Woman, 22 May 2006, 20 June 2014, http://thepioneerwoman.com/blog/2006/05/poetry_of_a_madwoman_vol_9/
114. Braziel and LeBesco, eds. *Bodies Out of Bounds*; LeBesco, *Revolting Bodies?*
115. Mulvey, "Visual Pleasure," 19; Kaplan, "Is the Gaze Male?"
116. Bee-Shyuan Chang, "Amanda Brooks Is Taking Her Leave," *New York Times*, 30 May 2012, 20 June 2014, http://www.nytimes.com/2012/05/31/fashion/amanda-brooks-is-taking-her-leave.html?pagewanted=all
117. PWSUX, "Ree + Photoshop = No more wrinkles," The Pioneer Woman Sux, 20 July 2011, 20 June 2014, http://www.thepioneerwomansux.com/2011/07/ree-photoshop-no-more-wrinkles/

118. Ree, "Just In Case There's Anything Left On Earth You Don't Already Know About Me," The Pioneer Woman, 19 July 2007, 20 June 2014, http://thepioneerwoman.com/blog/2007/07/just_in_case_th/. There is a provocative overlap between the pronunciation of the word "real" and Drummond's first name, which is Ree.
119. PWSUX, "Did Pioneer Woman lift your blog post too?" The Pioneer Woman Sux, 24 May 2011, 20 June 2014, http://www.thepioneerwomansux.com/2011/05/did-pioneer-woman-lift-your-blog-post-too/comment-page-1/#comment-15918; The Marlboro Woman, "The Pioneer Woman Casseroles Food Network," 6 August 2012, 20 June 2014, http://themarlborowoman.com/2012/08/the-pioneer-woman-casseroles-food-network/
120. Pie Near Woman, "Inspiration," 20 June 2014, http://www.pienearwoman.com/inspiration/
121. The Marlboro Woman, "Amanda Fortini Strips Away The Pioneer Woman's Veneer," 7 February 2012, 20 June 2014, http://themarlborowoman.com/2012/02/amanda-fortini-strips-away-the-pioneer-womans-veneer/
122. The Marlboro Woman, "The Pioneer Woman – Thanksgiving's First Responder," 16 November 2012, 20 June 2014, http://themarlborowoman.com/2012/11/the-pioneer-woman-thanksgivings-first-responder/
123. Pie Near Woman, "Aunt Edna Mae Comes Back With a Vegenance!" April 2012, 26 March 2013, http://www.pienearwoman.com/2012/04/aunt-edna-mae-comes-back-with-a-vegenance/. There is also a photo essay that is entitled "There's Dirt in my Vagina," which questions Drummond's femininity and commitment to her husband. Pie Near Woman, "There's Dirt in my Vagina – An Instagram Ode to Joe," April 2012, 20 June 2014, http://www.pienearwoman.com/2012/04/theres-dirt-in-my-vagina-an-instagram-ode-to-joe/
124. Pie Near Woman, "Cream Corned Butter – Just like Grandma Used to Make!" April 2012, 2 July 2014, http://www.pienearwoman.com/2012/04/cream-corned-butter-just-like-grandma-used-to-make/
125. Lopez, "Radical Act."
126. Morrison, "Suffused by Feeling."
127. Chen, "Don't Call Me That."
128. Minahan and Cox, "Stitch 'n Bitch," 6.
129. Cumberland, "Private Uses of Cyberspace"; Dhaenens, "Slashing the Fiction"; Hellekson and Busse, eds. *Fan Fiction*.
130. Myzelev, "Whip Your Hobby," 148.
131. Bratich and Brush, "Fabricating Activism," 238.
132. Greer, "Craftivist History"; Betsy Greer, "Craftivism Definition," Craftivism, 20 June 2014, http://craftivism.com/about/craftivism-definition/
133. Ki Mae Heussner, "Apple's 'Resolutionary' iPad Means Catch-Up for Developers: New iPad has higher resolution, faster processor," Adweek, 7 March 2012, 5 January 2013, http://www.adweek.com/news/technology/apples-resolutionary-ipad-means-catch-developers-138798
134. Khondker, "Role of the New Media"; Juris, "Reflections on #Occupy Everywhere"; Ray, "'Story' of Digital Excess."
135. For discussions of how postfeminist practices are focused on the individual, see Aronson, "Feminists Or 'Postfeminists'?" Negra, *What A Girl Wants?* Patterson, "Fracturing Tina Fey."
136. Williams, "Old Time Mem'ry."
137. Portwood-Stacer, "Do-It-Yourself Feminism."
138. Craftster, "About Craftster," 5 January 2013, http://www.craftster.org/about.html; Bazaar Bizarre, 20 June 2014, http://www.bazaarbizarre.org/
139. Barbara Burns, "This Is Not Your Grandmother's Knitting Shop," *Observer News Enterprise*, 13 October 2010, 20 June 2014, http://www.observernewsonline.com/content/not-your-grandmothers-knitting-shop; Cole Carruthers, "Not your Grandmother's

Knitting Circle," *Moose Jaw Times Herald*, 7 October 2012, http://www.mjtimes.sk.ca/Local/News/2012-10-07/article-3094592/Not-your-grandmothers-knitting-circle/1

140. StrungOutFiberArts, "Strung Out Fiber Arts by StrungOutFiberArts on Etsy," Etsy, 29 November 2012, http://www.etsy.com/shop/StrungOutFiberArts
141. Corinne, *Cunt Coloring Book*.
142. Craftster, "Craftster.org – A Community for Crafts and DIY Projects with Free Craft Ideas, Inspiration, Advice and More," 12 June 2014, http://www.craftster.org/
143. Betsy Greer, "Craftivism Definition," Craftivism, 20 June 2014, http://craftivism.com/about/craftivism-definition/
144. Gretchen Hirsch, "Gertie at STC Craft: It's Not Your Grandma's Crafting (Or Is it?)," STC Craft | Melanie Falick Books, 30 April 2012, 12 June 2014, http://www.melaniefalickbooks.com/news/2012/4/30/gertie-at-stc-craft-its-not-your-grandmas-crafting-or-is-it.html
145. Craftster, "About Craftster," 20 June 2014, http://www.craftster.org/about.html. This correlation of crafting with white femininity evokes Dawkins's study of white Detroit crafters and the unfortunate ways they distinguished their products and aesthetics from that of people of color, who were often not invited to and did not participate in their craft fairs. Dawkins, "Do-It-Yourself."
146. Etsy's representations of women and narratives about a political "movement" reference feminist waves, in a similar manner to postfeminist allusions. Etsy, "Etsy – About," 30 September 2012, http://www.etsy.com/about?ref=ft_about
147. SpinSpanSpun, as quoted in Etsy, "Etsy – About," 30 September 2012, http://www.etsy.com/about?ref=ft_about
148. Etsy, "Etsy – Your place to buy and sell all things handmade, vintage, and supplies," 26 July 2014, https://www.etsy.com/404
149. Etsy, "Etsy – About," 23 February 2013, http://www.etsy.com/about?ref=ft_about
150. Walters and Harrison, "Not Ready to Make Nice," 38.
151. Douglas and Michaels, *Mommy Myth*; Hallstein, "Conceiving Intensive Mothering"; Hays, *Cultural Contradictions of Motherhood*.
152. Dillaway and Paré, "Locating Mothers"; Hilbrecht et al., "I'm Home."
153. Nead, "Seductive Canvases."
154. Sedgwick, *Touching Feeling*.
155. Fuss, "Fashion and the Homospectatorial"; Lewis and Rolley, "Ad(dressing) the Dyke"; Vänskä, "Why Are There No Lesbian?"
156. White reaching hands are a zombie media convention that conveys mindlessness rather than agency. Research on the production of whiteness includes Peiss, *Hope in a Jar*; Poitevin, "Inventing Whiteness"; Rosenthal, "Visceral Culture."
157. Bordo, "Beauty (Re)Discovers"; Davis, "Remaking the She-Devil"; Craik, *Fashion*.
158. Leddy, "Sparkle and Shine."
159. Priest, "What's Wrong With Sparkly Vampires?"
160. In a similar manner, Drummond refers to her "alien" hands and disassociates from and fragments the body. The Pioneer Woman, "Homemade Chicken and Noodles," 25 January 2010, 20 June 2014, http://thepioneerwoman.com/cooking/2010/01/homemade-chicken-and-noodles/.
161. Buszek, introduction to *Extra/Ordinary*.
162. Plant, *Zeroes and Ones*. Susanna Paasonen provides a detailed analysis of the ways Plant and other feminist scholars associate women and femininity with the Internet. Paasonen, *Figures of Fantasy*.
163. Robertson, "How to Knit."
164. Gajjala and Mamidipuni, "Gendering Processes."
165. The small academic literature on reborn practices, includes Fitzgerald, "Let's Play Mummy."

1

WORKING eBAY AND ETSY

Selling Stay-at-Home Mothers

Mary Andrews encourages readers to "Quit Your Day Job" in a series of Etsy blog posts that provide information about sellers. For instance, she introduces readers to slippedstitchstudios who took "her career into her own hands after being laid off" during a "maternity leave."[1] Andrews associates the transformation of slippedstitchstudios into a stay-at-home mother and Etsy seller with her independence. Andrews also links this change to the productive and physical properties of slippedstitchstudios' hands and computer and Internet technologies. Etsy and members use narratives about hands as a means of referencing the experiences of being in control, touching, being touched, connecting, and making things by hand. Etsy members further highlight the affective, social, and tactile aspects of hands by choosing such member names as AtHome Hand Made, From My Hand To Yours, and The Hand Stamped Heart.[2]

These women connect through the physical and metaphorical contact of hands and Internet sites, including the ways sellers touch keyboards. Such meshing of hands and computer and Internet technologies are embodied in the term "digital." The expression, according to Jack Bratich, references fingers as well as the delivery of information. Internet technologies and sites are "extensions."[3] They intermesh corporeal digits, bodies, cultural ideas, and numerical and computational digits. In doing this, these conjunctions of bodies and technologies disrupt ecommerce and postfeminist claims about individuation.[4] Contemporary women are imagined to be distinct individuals and coherent bodies who are personally focused rather than engaged with communities. Of course, ecommerce sites and members constitute community and family because these conceptions get people to invest and engage and are thereby economically and socially productive.

Individuals' descriptions of the social features of Internet settings and hypertextual linking, which is one of the key undergirding structures of the web, present similar narratives about connecting. For instance, members indicate that Etsy and related craft events facilitate connections and community attachments. slippedstitchstudios identifies other fiber artists as a "community of mavens, connectors, and salesmen" with a "love" of "handspun" and "hand-dyed" materials.[5] These notions of animated and potentially animating hands that interweave the human, social, creative, transformational, and technological are particularly interesting when tied to crafting sites. slippedstitchstudios also contrasts her creative delight and engagement with Etsy with her previous career experiences, which include "several dead-end, soul crushing jobs." Thus, Etsy is depicted as enlivening individuals and positively intermeshing their interests. After her estranging job experiences, slippedstitchstudios "just wanted to stay home" with her child and handcraft things. She thanks readers for sustaining this way of life and makes them and Etsy into a community and an economic support system. Yet home and childcare are sites of intensive work and business for stay-at-home mothers who sell on eBay and Etsy.

Women as well as social relationships produce and are produced in Internet settings. slippedstitchstudios and other like-minded ecommerce sellers advertise that they are stay-at-home mothers in order to connect with compatible members, constitute a community, produce a marketable identity, and encourage individuals to identify and buy. These women reference traditional conceptions of motherhood and femininity while their site narratives produce much more complicated identities. For instance, slippedstitchstudios and many other stay-at-home mothers who are ecommerce sellers indicate that they work more hours than they did when juggling traditional careers and childcare. This can be a problem because stay-at-home mothers, according to sociologists Heather Dillaway and Elizabeth Paré, are expected to be "physically located within the home" and not engaging in "income earning activities that distract them from 'quality' child care."[6] Self-identified stay-at-home mothers who sell on the English language eBay and Etsy sites do not or cannot follow these economic and geographic expectations and thus help to reform cultural definitions.[7]

These stay-at-home mothers who sell things hybridize families and businesses. Their production of identities and selling positions illustrates some of the ways women negotiate conflicting social demands and work roles. By studying the ways stay-at-home mothers sell on eBay and Etsy, I demonstrate the wide scale deployment of this identity and the associated marketing strategies. Examining these sites and sellers' practices also offers opportunities to understand the different ways stay-at-home mothers are correlated with childcare, crafting, and expertise. Feminists have rightly critiqued directives for American and many Western women to perform traditional mothering roles, even as they carry out increasing amounts of career work.[8] Rather than focusing on how the role of stay-at-home mother can curtail women's opportunities, I consider women's deployment of these arrangements as methods of meeting cultural expectations, performing unconventional work, producing their identities, and garnering power. Stereotyped gender scripts leave women with limited options. This makes it important to study and understand how women negotiate their positions in relationship to cultural conventions and the ways they identify with the role of stay-at-home mother in order to develop authority and engage personal and cultural investments in childcare, home, and work.[9] It is also essential to address how the Internet has been identified as an ideal setting for these hybrid and conflicted identities.

Producing the eBay and Etsy Sites and Members

The English language eBay and Etsy sites, in a manner that is related to the complicated identifications of stay-at-home mothers and ecommerce sellers, are consumer sites that render themselves as something else. Etsy defines the setting as "the marketplace we make together" and "Your place to buy and sell all things handmade, vintage, and supplies."[10] Etsy offers individuals opportunities to present and sell their goods in personal "shops" on the site and connect with other people by using the shop messaging system. In framing the site through the terms "we" and "your," Etsy emphasizes opportunities for individualization, customization, collaboration, and ownership. It distinguishes the site from impersonal retailing and argues, "Etsy is more than a marketplace: we're a community of artists, creators, collectors, thinkers and doers."[11] Etsy thus articulates members as connected and active producers, in a manner that is related to its narratives about slippedstitchstudios, and effaces the cultural coding of Internet technologies as pacifying and isolating.

eBay emphasizes a broader array of goods and forms of production than Etsy but also asserts the agency of members. On the eBay.com domain and other country-specific sites, it offers a "Welcome" to eBay, "your community."[12] eBay indicates that the site enables connections between individuals and is produced by members. These members, as I suggest in *Buy It Now: Lessons from eBay*, both take up and interrogate eBay's promises of co-production, which asserts that the site belongs to participants.[13] eBay and Etsy market similar kinds of agency and community to members, including active forums where members can correspond. However, Chad Dickerson, who is CEO of Etsy, argues, "Ebay and Etsy are fundamentally different companies."[14] Etsy is "about people buying and selling from other people and knowing who's on both sides of the transaction." Of course, eBay encourages sellers to provide personal information so that potential buyers can feel as if they know members. Each site tries to distinguish itself with narratives concerning special ties and individualization. Through these structures, they extend postfeminist claims about empowerment but do not couple this to notions of self-focused individuals. eBay and Etsy profit from people who have detailed personal interests that can be marketed to buyers and community involvements, especially commitments to work for and promote these selling platforms.

These sites promise affective connections, especially to women, and often code participants as women. For instance, Etsy offers articles on sellers that tend to feature and address white women, and to a much lesser degree white heterosexual couples.[15] Etsy's 2008 survey determined that 96 percent of members were women.[16] According to reporter Brooke Dunbar, women are "responsible for Etsy's success."[17] She supports the company's narratives about co-production. She also identifies the interface and listed items as feminine and suggests that for women "who are trying their hand at combining full time Motherhood and homemade retail, it's a perfect platform." In a similar manner, stay-at-home mothers note that Etsy is "perfect" for their needs and allows them to "happily" create "swell and swanky things" and "be at home with the ones that" they "love."[18] eBay and Etsy sellers engage with these sites as shared feminine and maternal spheres. They get other women to care for their lifestyle by buying. At the same time, their marketing strategies and production modes skew normative understandings of who stay-at-home mothers are and what they do. Women's child rearing, as Dillaway and Paré suggest, usually functions as "invisible reproductive labor that does not receive any tangible reward or acknowledgment."[19] Through eBay and Etsy, stay-at-home mothers make their mothering visible, are acknowledged by the sites and members, and garner economic rewards.

eBay and Etsy emphasize that they provide ideal careers for mothers. eBay's newsletter chronicles how it "allows mom to focus on caretaking."[20] eBay thereby indicates that the site and selling facilitate familial connections. Readers of Etsy's Quit Your Day Job posts also learn how hobocampcrafts quit her "office job to follow her passion," "sell full time on Etsy," "work from home," "and care for her new baby."[21] Etsy claims that it makes women and families happier. Yet working at home is associated with women shifting their schedules so that they can fit in more childcare rather than working less. Jobs that facilitate familial demands are marketed to women and tend to result in increased labor for them.[22] People often imagine ecommerce sellers, especially when they are women, to be part-time workers and to have "opted-out" of careers. However, Etsy's Success Stories encourage women to work more and address them as people who are striving for bigger businesses. Etsy writes, "You've seen those big sellers" who "seem to be making sales left and right. You have to wonder how they've made it to where they are."[23] Members are encouraged to "Keep reading to find out how" sellers manage these accomplishments.

Etsy acknowledges women's labor and encourages them to generate more profit for the company. Members follow at least some of these indications. Etsy's success stories garner more than two million page views every month.[24] They are identified as inspirational and receive comments from numerous stay-at-home mothers who indicate their appreciation of the genre and interest in following these women's personal, economic, and creative trajectories. For example,

MomNMiaQuilts references these narratives in her profile. She "quit" her "'day job' to dedicate more time" to her "family" and "business."[25] mommymogul hopes to "grow" her "business to the point" that she "can quit" her "day job (like so many of the stories" she has "read about fellow etsians)."[26] These women reference cultural and postfeminist conceptions of opting-out of work in favor of motherhood. However, they claim to have replaced less valued and engaging jobs with personally fulfilling businesses. Their use of the term "day job" suggests that daytime employment is merely a means of making money while they are now focused on creative endeavors and entrepreneurial motherhood.

eBay's, Etsy's, and members' accounts about the productivity of these sites for stay-at-home mothers are mirrored and encouraged by reports concerning this phenomenon. Thus, these perceptions and formations of women and motherhood emerge from an array of cultural processes and belief systems rather than being produced by any individual site or entity. For instance, Michelle Horton, a writer for the parent-oriented site Babble, indicates that Etsy gives mothers the opportunity "to explore, develop, and share their art and craftsmanship," "work from home," and raise "kids the way they want."[27] She also describes Etsy as "the perfect environment for mothers." Individuals indicate that these ecommerce settings are economically as well as socially productive. According to designer and blogger Megan Auman, Etsy enables stay-at-home mothers to "have a creative outlet" and find "another path to financial security."[28] Karina Ioffee's news story chronicles how a seller "used to be a stressed-out single mother" but "now she works from home, selling an estimated $60,000 a year worth of jewelry online."[29] Suzanne Wells reports that people laughed at her when she started selling on eBay but she is a "Stay at home mom" who "makes $250,000."[30] These narratives downplay the kinds of career paths that many second-wave feminists strived to facilitate, including educational and professional opportunities, the ability to work in any field, prospects of career advancement, and equal pay. Instead, a form of stay-at-home motherhood where women are believed to be best suited to domestic work and thought to want to be in the home is favored. However, businesses and work remain part of these women's domestic lives. This position is depicted as a personal choice and resistant to conventional codes even though women receive intense cultural directives, as I indicate throughout this chapter, to stay at home with young children.

Stay-at-home mothers who sell on eBay and Etsy are depicted choosing their own lifestyles, being inventive, actively engaging with other women, and being empowered. For instance, eBay describes how seller "Kelli Demarco has made more than impressive profits on eBay" and "created exactly the lifestyle she wants, allowing her to raise her children at home."[31] In a related manner, eBay is believed to empower people who are otherwise "shut out of the traditional economy, such as stay-at-home mothers."[32] The Internet Based Moms website emphasizes working rather than staying at home. It contends that for "many work at home moms, online auctions provide a steady income."[33] The term "stay-at-home mother" is more common but some eBay and Etsy sellers also use the phrase "work-at-home mother" as a method of positively describing their identity and labor. However, *BusinessWeek* provides a more condemnatory account and describes the work these women perform as a "dalliance" and means of "stripping the guilt from all those" shopping trips.[34] Stay-at-home mothers who sell on eBay more positively use shopping and selling as ways of explaining their practices and connecting with other women over their consumer pleasures.

Women use their position as stay-at-home mothers to sell items on eBay and Etsy. eBay characterizes such social selling engagements as "a powerful combination of commerce, communication and community that enhances traditional buying and selling."[35] The individual is thereby productive for the site and a contributor to varied groups. eBay and Etsy train sellers in these behaviors. For instance, eBay tells how mom_in_georgia advertises that the money she earns from listings is used for her children's college education.[36] According to eBay, this gives "buyers a reason to shop with her." eBay also emphasizes the relationship between the site and stay-at-home mothers by featuring Jessica Jones, "a stay-at-home mom" who "truly enjoys selling" in its newsletter.[37] The site "gives her the flexibility to work around her family's schedule" and use "product-sourcing excursions as opportunities for one-on-one time" with her "youngest daughter." These women can be easily located by searching for "stay-at-home mother" or "SAHM" in the titles and descriptions of listings. In this and other accounts, ecommerce selling is portrayed as feminine, nurturing, and a family project, which provides opportunities to connect that would not be available with other careers. eBay's and Etsy's emphasis on the family aspects of businesses is related to corporate attempts to reframe companies, employees, and products as families.[38] These tactics keep people committed to and engaged with corporations.

Feminist Considerations of Motherhood

There is a great deal of feminist literature on how conceptions of motherhood and feminine labor have been socially deployed. Feminists have argued that being constituted as naturally maternal and solely responsible for children's needs disempowers American and many other Western women. Feminist author Betty Friedan considers the period following World War II and the ways mother blame was used to regulate American women who "were beginning to use the rights of their emancipation, to go in increasing numbers to colleges and professional schools, to rise in industry and the professions in inevitable competition with men."[39] In other words, the concept of motherhood was deployed as a controlling concept to limit women's options. Adrienne Rich, a feminist essayist and poet, was "haunted" by such regulating strategies, "the stereotype of the mother whose love is 'unconditional,'" and "by the visual and literary images of motherhood" as uniform and constant.[40] Such experiences are not surprising since narratives about women's mothering role are internalized, as philosopher

Sara Ruddick indicates, when women take on the "values of the subcultures to which they belong," which almost always include the "relative subordination of women."[41]

Cultural critics Susan J. Douglas and Meredith W. Michaels indicate that the media's insistence that women are the best "primary caretakers" and should completely devote themselves to the needs of their children, render impossible standards.[42] For Douglas and Michaels, these excessive forms of motherhood are central to the ongoing functioning of postfeminism. Sociologist Sharon Hays uses the term "intensive mothering" to describe cultural expectations that women should be the primary caregivers of their children and distinguish childcare from paid work. She shows how the mandate for intensive mothering, and the idea that "correct child rearing requires not only large quantities of money but also professional-level skills and copious amounts of physical, moral, mental, and emotional energy on the part of the individual mother," places an unreasonable burden on contemporary mothers and thereby makes it difficult for them to have careers.[43] This means that motherhood is still a controlling concept.

Being interested in profit and personal achievements does not correlate with intensive mothering. Mothers are expected to be selfless caretakers. Business people, who are still too often coded as men, are allowed to be selfish and competitive workers. Given the social, personal, and financial costs women experience because of such beliefs, some of them have sought to rework the relationship between home, work, mothering, and professionalism. For instance, Joanne Duberley and Marylyn Carrigan research women who set up businesses so that they can be "good mothers" and show how these women "construct their identities through these interlinked and potentially contradictory discourses."[44] While women may start home businesses so that they can be "good" mothers, the authors also indicate how some of these women end up having less time to care for their children.

eBay and Etsy sellers have adopted and redeployed many of the cultural directives for women to be good and self-abnegating mothers. Their depictions tend to support and extend notions of intensive mothering. However, eBay and Etsy sellers fuse and mix up conceptions of gendered work and spaces rather than fully distinguishing childcare from work and the economic sphere. Their renderings of intensive mothering and connections with other women support their careers and economic opportunities. Through such tactics, these women work within traditional gender roles; doing or performing stereotyped positions, without following all of the concomitant rules. Doing gender, as analyzed by sociologists Candace West and Don H. Zimmerman, "involves a complex of socially guided perceptual, interactional, and micropolitical activities that cast particular pursuits as expressions of masculine and feminine 'natures.'"[45] Such everyday gender performances, as feminist and queer theorist Judith Butler suggests, also "repeat and displace through hyperbole, dissonance, internal confusion, and proliferation the very constructs by which they are mobilized."[46] Thus, stay-at-home mothers who are eBay and Etsy sellers render certain pursuits as naturally associated with femininity and motherhood. Their marketing of conflicting roles also challenges these categories.

eBay and Etsy sellers use their self-articulated gender positions to perform and elide their situation as business owners. Performing entrepreneurship and doing business, according to Attila Bruni, Silvia Gherardi, and Barbara Poggio's ethnographic study, "involves a gender positioning, and depending on how gender is performed, entrepreneurial action acquires different dimensions and levels of legitimacy."[47] Their study suggests how gender and business, whether acknowledged or displaced, are inextricably intermeshed. Such events as the firing of *New York Times's* executive editor Jill Abramson and the management's identification of her as "pushy" indicate how women have difficulties being accepted in powerful business roles.[48] Women selling on eBay and Etsy enable their economic and social functioning by linking their position as businesspersons to their more feminine role as stay-at-home mothers. Yet cultural mandates for women to perform intensive mothering are also related to expectations that people should care and connect to Internet settings. They are expected to contribute to social networking sites and work more by producing profiles and texts, designing features of the system, tagging, reviewing products, and offering assistance to other members. Expectations for women to perform intensive mothering are thus extended and changed by these women's marketing of themselves through and engagement in Internet settings.

Constituting Stay-at-Home Mothers on eBay

eBay identifies stay-at-home mothers as an important part of its membership and encourages these women to participate. Individuals can ordinarily view thousands of eBay listings where sellers self-identify as stay-at-home mothers. Many of these members also employ their personal "About Me" part of the eBay site, which participants can activate, to describe themselves as stay-at-home mothers and provide more details about their personal lives. In these accounts, women establish their relationship to eBay, role as stay-at-home mothers, and goodness. They self-present as networked and community and family oriented. eBay also asserts its importance in members' lives. "With the help of eBay," claims the site, stay-at-home mothers such as Stephanie Moos and Amy White "balance work and family while boosting their families' bottom lines."[49] eBay uses these and other women as examples of how it helps others. This allows eBay to distinguish its site and processes from the majority of corporations.

Most corporations, manufacturers, and stores are culturally coded as profit-motivated and inattentive to individual and societal needs. However, companies such as The Body Shop and TOMS identify as socially conscious.[50] They address environmentally and politically concerned consumers and code their shoppers as principled. In a related manner, eBay's "Community Values" statement, which was originally established by the site developer Pierre Omidyar, indicates, "people are basically good."[51] eBay also asserts, "We care. Because we know people depend on us."[52] eBay thus portrays the site and company as caring for dependents, and as a sort of maternal figure, rather than taking fees from members. The eBay site and stay-at-home mothers who are sellers continue these articulations of care and goodness by referencing good mothers. This is aligned with contemporary cultural beliefs. Society, according to psychologist Shari L. Thurer, believes that stay-at-home mothers will save family values and the moral order.[53] They are therefore envisioned somewhat differently than postfeminist individuals and imagined to sustain cultures and communities.

eBay and Etsy feature mothers in their site texts. Individual sellers repeat these company narratives and values. For instance, eBay seller tradrmom references family and a dedication to community when indicating that she "restructured" her week so that she "can volunteer" at her children's school and "do some mommie time" with her "little one more often."[54] DeMarco echoes these commitments to community in an eBay Seller Central article. She promises that when she buys "something at a good price," she lists "it at a good price."[55] DeMarco thus codes her practice as a form of sharing with rather than profiting from members. In a related manner, jennsterb connects being a "stay at home mother" to being "an honest seller" that is willing to "work with" buyers.[56] These stay-at-home mothers perform important ideological functions because they self-present as mothers and semi-professionals who, like the company's envisioned members, privilege care. They further associate such traditionally feminine qualities as servicing and nurturing to stay-at-home mothers.[57]

Stay-at-home mothers who sell on eBay, in a similar manner to the company, credit the site with enabling them to focus on children. dianne_dp gets to "do it all" because of eBay.[58] She has her "own business" and is "a stay at home mom." tradrmom can "build whatever size business" she wants "on eBay and still be home for the kids."[59] These women explain and normalize complicated roles by self-identifying as stay-at-home mothers. For instance, tradrmom describes her formerly "very stressful job" and indicates that eBay is more "flexible."[60] Her narrative about flexibility evokes the conceptualization of telework and other flexible business models as methods of allowing women and other workers to control their schedules. Workplace flexibility, as defined by research on the subject by E. Jeffrey Hill et al., offers individuals "choices" about "when, where, and for how long they engage in work-related tasks."[61] These flexible work schedules are imagined to be particularly conducive to working mothers' varied commitments but recent research suggests that women tend to end up working more hours on the job and doing more work in the home.[62] tradrmom's list of responsibilities emphasizes the intensive aspects of her eBay work and mothering. She describes an afternoon of picking up her daughter, packing purchased items, driving to the post office, going to the market, supervising schoolwork, and getting a brownie troop prepared for their outing. eBay stay-at-home mothers and workers are positioned in a variety of places rather than only in, or focused on, the home. Such slippages between different spaces, roles, and meanings are suggested by Bruni, Gherardi, and Poggio's indication that with entrepreneurship, the "codes of a gendered identity are kept, changed and transgressed by constantly sliding between different symbolic spaces."[63]

For stay-at-home mothers who are ecommerce sellers, the household is a site where goods and services are produced and sold, a private sphere of reproductive activities, a technologically mediated space, and a place where affective engagements occur. This combination of stay-at-home mothering and ecommerce engagement is a form of immaterial labor, as articulated by the activists and theorists Michael Hardt and Antonio Negri. According to them, immaterial labor "produces immaterial products, such as information, knowledges, ideas, images, relationships, and affects."[64] It is related to affective labor that, according to cultural studies scholar Melissa Gregg, is a "meaningful and productive human activity that does not result in a direct financial profit or exchange value, but rather produces a sense of community, esteem, and/or belonging."[65] There are exploitative features of this labor. For instance, the Internet and other new communication technologies enable employers to use temporary and mobile laborers rather than committing to long-term employment and material infrastructures. Women are asked to work for eBay and Etsy by promoting the sites and providing complicated forms of customer service but have no guarantee of profits or support in return. This suggests that immaterial labor is a product of gender categories. Feminists have struggled to resolve such undercompensated and uncompensated female labor.[66] However, eBay's and Etsy's calls for women to work for family and community are easily attached to stay-at-home mothers' flexible labor because they tend to have no predetermined hours or boundaried responsibilities. Social networking sites also render immaterial labor as an aspect of participation and feminized care. For instance, Facebook's and other sites' posting "buttons" appear along with content, including eBay and Etsy listings, and use the term "share" and its association with giving and nurturance to recontextualize the work of circulating other people's materials.

Society expects women to perform affective labor, including providing sustenance and care in many settings. The women selling on eBay and Etsy respond to these expectations and emphasize their role as caring mother-producers by choosing IDs such as madebymommie. Such women's home-based activities, according to geographer Ann M. Oberhauser, "bridge private and public domains, reproductive and productive work, and the domestic arena and the workplace."[67] Many stay-at-home eBay sellers emphasize this reproductive sphere by selling handcrafted and recycled children's clothing, diapers, diaper bags, children's bedding, toys, and nursing materials. These items are directly linked to childcare and its emotional features. They clarify and consolidate what are otherwise conflicting identities. Yet IDs such as mommy$, with its use of the dollar sign rather than the letter "s," highlight cultural shifts in the meanings, values, and productivity of concepts like mother and motherhood.[68] For instance, mommy bloggers personally profit and are culturally condemned for their commodification of motherhood and securing of advertisements from mainstream companies. Motherhood has a long history of being culturally deployed as a method of articulating traditional femininity and women's positions. Homemakers have also been identified as willing buyers. Yet women's overt control and marketing of these roles have rarely been encouraged. The ID employed by mommy$ suggests how eBay uses these women's position for profit and how women find their own advantages in self-promotion.

Women's home-based ecommerce activities, in a similar manner to a range of other Internet settings and communication technologies, collapse the cultural distinctions between paid work and being at home and make individuals always available and able to labor. Stay-at-home mothers are expected to be endlessly accessible and intensively mothering children, and by extension caring for eBay buyers. This causes some sellers to provide provisos about when they are available and how they perform varied parts of the eBay selling process. shersbooksetc advertises that she tries to ship items very quickly but she may be "unable to do so due to illness or an unexpected event."[69] She curtails the otherwise never-ending customer service aspects of her ecommerce business and presumptions that worker flexibility means always being able to work. Her comments indicate how difficult it is to delimit Internet- and computer-facilitated labor. Other stay-at-home mothers who are ecommerce sellers extend conceptions of intensive mothering. For instance, elena030503 writes that people should "feel free at any moment to email" her "with questions or concerns."[70] She is there "to assist" in "every way" and "will respond within or before 24 hours." In these cases of "always on" communication, the perceived flexibility of telework is conflated with notions that women are always available and intensifies all of their responsibilities.[71]

These escalating work expectations are rarely addressed because stay-at-home mothers are imagined to have opted out and left their jobs and careers after having children. Women who describe quitting their jobs and having more flexible schedules support these conceptions. For instance, lynnber began selling on eBay while "on maternity leave and wound up never going back" to her "real job."[72] Her "kids are demanding more time" and she is "incredibly grateful" to have a "flexible enough schedule to be there for them." She self-presents as the always available and committed mother and seller by effacing the reality of her labor and that she still has a "real job." Women's schedules accommodate childcare responsibilities, which should be acknowledged as work. Etsy sellers, as suggested by my analysis of their practices in the next section, more overtly market the extraordinary hours that they commit to producing and selling items. Yet women like lynnber offer a "thank you very much" to buyers for facilitating their schedules. They encourage people to support stay-at-home lifestyles that are supposedly uncompromised by work. Expressions of appreciation address the site and members, make these people into a community, and engage everyone in the seller's life and selling. This "thank you" is a key feature of immaterial labor and customer service-based businesses, such as the "thank you" that is printed on restaurant bills. The "thank you" figures a grateful seller, server, and business rather than appreciation at being served. Personal expressions of gratitude increase tips and intensify selling.[73] Such comments also elide women's exhausting work schedules.

Stay-at-home mothers' accounts, like eBay's and Etsy's depictions, constitute the site and members as a productive community. "eBay is a great community," writes mommy2liz.[74] She has "met so many nice people through selling" and "begun several friendships as a result of initial eBay contacts." tradrmom loves the "sense of community" on the "message boards" and expects to "see you there!"[75] tradrmom's suggestion that readers will engage with her in a particular setting is designed to create ties and relationships with buyers. Sellers also employ words such as "help" to indicate how buyers provide assistance, members influence their lives, and payments are deployed. They articulate expectations about community responsibility that are related to Omidyar's indication that "community participation" is a key component of the site.[76] For instance, acornerstorecareer assures individuals that every bid they place "helps enable" the seller to "be at home" with her children.[77] mommyof2boys71 wants "to get her Internet business established so she "can stay at home" with her "kids."[78] She asks potential buyers to "help" her "get started." These requests for assistance and production of community attachments are common; they direct members to support stay-at-home mothers by buying. Like Omidyar, they indicate that consumerism is a form of social consciousness and absolve individuals from other sorts of political responsibility.

Buyers are encouraged to provide help because of expressions of gratitude, including the kinds of sellers' thanks that I have previously mentioned. Stay-at-home mothers expand the social aspects of social selling and articulate connections and purchases before they happen by offering thanks to readers. beccab312 notes, "Your purchase helps a stay at home mom stay at home! Thanks!"[79] These methods of identifying as stay-at-home mothers and highlighting the needs of children trigger the values of the sites and culture more broadly. After all, many Western government agencies and policies, educational systems, religious organizations, news reports, television sitcoms, and parenting magazines encourage women to stay home with young children. Stay-at-home mothers reply by using such mandates as methods of social selling. This happens when ysaa8773 offers a "Thank you for supporting a stay at home mom of 3 kids under the age 4."[80] Women provide personal information, including the names, ages, and genders of their children and pets. Members are therefore given a detailed portrayal of the people who they are buying from and supporting. These practices are reminiscent of charities that provide dossiers to donors about the people who they are economically assisting. They personalize the process of helping and buying.

They also shift responsibility from governmental and familial support to that of a virtual community.

Stay-at-home mothers who are eBay sellers assert that sales support families, which they distinguish from corporate interests. They self-present as mothers and business-like and manage the most culturally valued aspects of these positions. For example, shellesstore2010 is "a stay at home Mom just trying to have a small business to help pay for the groceries."[81] flowerjen started a "business as a way to share" interests and "provide income" for her family.[82] Such stay-at-home mothers portray themselves as professionalized but not too professional and business-like without having the economic identity and motivators of a large company.[83] This is distinctly different than communication researchers Caryn E. Medved and Erika L. Kirby's description of how stay-at-home mothers are employing corporate and professionalized languages and identities as a means of legitimizing their roles.[84] Their position as individuals and mothers is used to justify the community's care.

The stay-at-home mothers who sell on eBay avoid identifying as experts. This is related to cultural tendencies to link skill and professionalism with men.[85] However, stay-at-home mothers deploy these associations as business and controlling strategies. Ree Drummond self-presents as a typical woman and mother rather than an artist in order to connect with the women who read The Pioneer Woman blog. nostalgic_notions self-identifies as "not an expert but a stay at home mom that sells out of" her "home."[86] step*right*up is a "stay-at-home mom trying to make extra income" rather than "an expert in any field."[87] These women's comments are designed to control exaggerated expectations and complaints from buyers. They disavow any trained or certified knowledge of products. They also differentiate themselves from corporate behaviors. lynnber tries "to run" her "business as professionally as possible," yet it is "not a huge corporate entity and" "life sometimes happens."[88] She distinguishes between the services that she and corporations can provide. The listings are depicted as being from mother to mother and about sharing knowledge and values. These women thus disavow specialized skills while claiming maternal capability. They create a women's culture in which asserting expertise and the associated power and respect may be difficult. Of course, motherhood requires varied competencies.

Women downplay their efforts, the labor required to run eBay businesses, their position as ecommerce venues that are designed to make money, and the skills they possess by indicating that their businesses are the product of passionate shopping. In a similar manner, eBay claims to facilitate women's consumerist interests. eBay portrays women's sourcing work as "shopping" and a feminine "weakness" for clothing.[89] Women support such notions when they describe their practices as an outlet for addictive behaviors. mostly-maternity "can't resist buying adorable maternity clothes and sharing them with you!"[90] It is "an addiction!" There "IS NO MORE ROOM LEFT IN" tony3430's house but she "JUST CAN'T RESIST!"[91] Her solution is to buy things and "PASS THEM ON TO" buyers with the hope that they will "LOVE EVERYTHING AS MUCH AS" she does. These women use the phrase "can't resist" and perpetuate gendered beliefs that women cannot control their emotions or behaviors. Women are told that they are having an enjoyable time when they are working and generating detailed emotional experiences and immaterial labor for other members. However, they also validate these moments of release and use them as methods of fluidly connecting women in personal, enjoyable, and economically productive exchanges.

Stay-at-home mothers equate ecommerce selling with frivolous shopping and downplay their careers and economic gains. Unfortunately, consumerism is ordinarily not identified as a product of expertise and labor even though it requires varied skills. Women have also been encouraged to perform these negations of their labor in other settings and historical periods. As more married women began working outside the home in the 1920s and 1930s, as sociologist Viviana A. Zelizer notes, "their earnings, regardless of the sums involved" were treated as supplementary family income or "discretionary 'fun' money."[92] Liana C. Sayer's study of contemporary work and leisure indicates that the "ideology of good mothering" doesn't preclude "some engagement in paid work, but mothers are still expected to be primary caregivers, not primary earners."[93] As these studies propose, women's earnings are culturally productive when they are coded as more frivolous than their husbands' jobs and wages. Women also deploy these narratives to substantiate their own roles. However, this leaves women in other romantic and household arrangements in more precarious positions.

Stay-at-home mothers support these ideas about women's discretionary earnings by depicting their eBay selling as family motivated and their profits as a kind of supplement to men's wages. For instance, britican-empire writes that she sells on eBay "as a means to supplement" the family's "income."[94] Women assure individuals that they are focused on members and relatives when they indicate that they are "trying to make a little extra money" and "earn a little extra money" for their families.[95] They use limiting terms such as "just" to manage their roles. For instance, jamijami21 is "just a stay at home mom trying to clean out the closets and keep" her "kids in clothes that fit."[96] jordansmama17 is "SIMPLY A STAY AT HOME MOM WHO LOVES TO SHOP," "FIND GREAT DEALS," and "PASS ALONG THE SAVINGS."[97] Yet in noting that eBay allows her to "STAY HOME WITH" her "SON," jordansmama17 indicates that her eBay selling provides economic support and that she is working.

Stay-at-home mothers indicate that eBay is a hobby and that they sell in their spare time but they also describe how their ecommerce work is escalating. monkeybunsdiapers started making a small number of diapers for her son but that number "quickly turned into a LOT" for eBay buyers.[98] lynnber wonders, "how is it possible that" she has "done so many auctions while still just working" by herself out of the "spare bedroom?"[99] custombags has "made more bags and onesies than" she "ever imagined possible!"[100] These women describe reaching the boundaries of what seems possible in terms of their labor and repetitive production. There are hints that sellers are stressed to the limit. Etsy sellers more specifically detail their excessive and impossible to sustain labor. Their selling is therefore a continuation of the processes of intensive mothering. Indeed, some products are developed from stay-at-home mothers' own dedication to making things for their children.

Constituting Stay-at-Home Mothers on Etsy

The Etsy site and participants also use narratives about stay-at-home mothers to produce the setting. Individuals can read more than one hundred corporate Etsy blog posts about stay-at-home mothers, including "Featured Seller" and "Quit Your Day Job" accounts. Sellers also list thousands of tagged items that designate they are stay-at-home mothers. Etsy deploys many of the same tactics as eBay but its focus on the handmade provides somewhat different articulations of the identities of stay-at-home mothers, how they connect with buyers, their use of Internet settings, and what they make. For instance, Etsy and its members link the creative production of objects to femininity and stay-at-home mothers. This connection between creativity and motherhood is a successful addendum to conceptions of intensive mothering. It also supports ideas about new domesticity and the linking of femininity, crafting, and the Internet. As sociologist Mary Blair-Loy indicates, culture "prescribes that women find fulfillment in the creativity and intimacy of involved motherhood."[101] Contemporary conceptions of mothering mandate that children receive varied sorts of educational stimulation, including creative engagements.[102] The Etsy site and members support these ideas by relating creative production to cultural conceptions of maternal reproduction. This is significant since there have long been evaluative distinctions between the value of male artistic production and the purported insignificance, or at least the mimetic repetition, of female reproduction.[103]

eBay and Etsy indicate that they enable women to shape their own identities and work options. They evoke postfeminist narratives about women's choices. However, Etsy's "Quit Your Day Job," "Success Stories," and related narratives are solicited, selected, and posted by the company. Etsy produces members' first-person accounts by asking them a targeted set of questions. Respondents to Etsy's articles are asked such questions as, "How did you originally get into the business of making things," "What first made you want to become an artist," and "Who has been most influential in your craft?"[104] Etsy thus plays a part in manufacturing the accounts of creativity and inspiration that appear on the site. This production of members' inventiveness is counter to contemporary concepts of self-expression. The recurring aspects of posts, especially since they have been modeled and vetted by the company, indicate the kinds of creative inspiration that are most productive for the site, and purportedly for selling, and direct members to follow these models. These site-approved scripts further influence the profiles and listings members provide.

Sellers who are mothers often mention familial lineages of creativity and the relationship between their children and crafts. For instance, littlegoodall's shop "was inspired" by her child.[105] She finds "children to be very inspiring." Being a mother is an important component of mignonnehandmade's identity. Her husband is "super supportive" of her designing and selling things and she considers herself "lucky to be able to be home every day" with her children.[106] Such narratives appear to be aligned with more traditional women's roles, including that of the heterosexual wife and mother. This is extended when Horton repeats some of the more worrying conceptions of stay-at-home mothers in her review of Etsy stores. She indicates that "nostalgia for a slower-paced, pie-baking era" and "sentimentality" are why people "Love" these Etsy sellers.[107] Certainly, the eBay and Etsy sites and stay-at-home mothers who sell items appeal to members' sentiments and feelings. HolmesandWatson expresses such emotions when identifying littlegoodall's interview as "heart-warming."[108]

Etsy structures its Quit Your Day Job accounts to influence participants' emotions and engage their desires for different work schedules. Mary Andrews, who writes many of these narratives, describes how dlkdesigns worked a "9-5 desk job" and "didn't feel her full potential and creative energy were being utilized."[109] After a "maternity leave with her first child," she embraced Etsy selling and the associated artistic lifestyle. Other stay-at-home mothers write about being able to work in their pajamas, design their own schedules, focus on children and partners, and pleasurably make things.[110] In these accounts, flexible work improves not only the experience but also the kind of work women perform. Readers respond and describe their dreams of achieving similar lifestyles. In reviewing such accounts, reporter Sara Mosle critiques Etsy's claims that women can positively change their lives. Mosle provides one of the most disparaging reviews of the site and company. She argues that the site is peddling the "feminist promise that you can have a family and create hip arts and crafts from home during flexible, reasonable hours while still having a respectable, fulfilling, and remunerative career."[111] According to her, most women will not achieve this way of life, or even make an adequate living from their Etsy products, and the company is combining traditional and subcultural femininities as a lure. Other journalists express similar concerns about women leaving their careers to care for children and start home businesses.[112] For instance, Deborah Ostrovsky argues that Etsy "may, in fact, be selling an unrealistic dream" to its members and thereby making the site more profitable for the company.[113] She notes that while Etsy "isn't responsible for the sketchy financial security faced by an increasing number of highly educated North American women," it "mirrors the fact that for many women, income has become less secure."

The low number of women who make a livable income by selling on Etsy, especially when compared to the site's promises of independence and artistic expression, is deeply worrying and should not be dismissed. A number of sellers have even closed shops that were featured as successful in Etsy's Quit Your

Day Job stories.[114] Yet there are also many aspects of ecommerce sites that are meaningful to women and engage with contemporary conceptions of gender and other identity characteristics, including the ways stay-at-home mothers use eBay and Etsy to articulate their roles as crafters and businesses, constitute values and communities, reach a larger sphere of women, and render and interrogate women's roles. In these ways, women find meanings in eBay and Etsy that are distinct from their functions as selling platforms. They also unfortunately support some of the sites' marketing claims and get other women to labor for the companies and invest in the economic opportunities promised by the sites.

Stay-at-home mothers who sell on Etsy, as I have started to suggest, relate their creative practices to family members who craft and credit their children as inspiration. Horton identifies the "overwhelming similarities" in how mothers express their Etsy marketing strategies and identities.[115] These repetitive expressions are informed by and extend the ways Etsy produces its members. For these women, there are links between the familial, reproductive, feminine, maternal, artistic, and handmade. DivaBabyDesigns provides a familial lineage for her crafts that includes sewing with her grandmother and her great aunt teaching her crocheting and knitting. She took ballet classes and "loved all the beautiful tutus, but some how never got to wear one!"[116] Her daughter provided her with a reason to start "making headbands and tutus," then some of her friends wanted "them for their daughters," and she finally "set up a shop on etsy!" Thus, DivaBabyDesigns connects her own childhood desires to her contemporary fulfillment of these dreams and the nostalgic interests of other mothers and children. Debbie Stoller's narratives about knitting and other feminine work render similar links.[117]

Etsy sellers stress that there are connections between arts, crafts, the Internet, women, femininity, and motherhood. Practitioners of the new domesticity also establish these associations. However, many people continue to distinguish between female reproduction and male artistry. Feminist art historians have interrogated these gendered assumptions, especially in relationship to nineteenth- and twentieth-century visual culture.[118] Some feminist artists, especially during the 1960s and 1970s, linked the processes of giving birth, raising children, and creating things.[119] Etsy sellers indicate a similar series of correlations and do political work by associating cultural production with some female gender positions. At the same time, they often code children's items according to gender norms and extend several normative cultural presumptions. For instance, DivaBabyDesigns limits the gender of tutu wearers by identifying them as being for "Girls" and referring to the child clothed in such garb as a "pretty princess."[120] Other members also associate clothing with distinct attributes that are related to gendered expectations.

NatesMommyMadeIt uses her ID to distinguish between the male child and female mother and relate reproduction to artistry. She indicates a familial background for her crafts and that her "entire family is crafty and artsy."[121] However, she "never felt the desire to sew much." Now, "being a mommy," NatesMommyMadeIt has "so many ideas of things to create and sew." Thus, it is the mommy who is empowered and directed to make things. Her account of being inspired by motherhood and starting to create after giving birth is quite common on Etsy. Motherhood is deemed to be productive because it stimulates enthusiasm for and insights into making things as well as commitments to raising children. In a related manner, stay-at-home mothers who sell on Etsy identify the education and expertise they developed through mothering. These discourses, as Medved and Kirby argue, allow women to resist beliefs that domestic and mothering work is simplistic and mindless.[122] However, a group of eBay stay-at-home mothers take a more resistant relationship to expertise in order to control buyers' expectations and distinguish themselves from corporate selling.

Some Etsy sellers indicate that they design items to fulfill their children's needs. applenamos started to make toys because she could not find any "that were natural, educational as well as playful."[123] According to such women, items come from their direct knowledge and experiences with childcare and are designed as better functioning and healthy alternatives for children. As part of the culture of intensive mothering, women are encouraged to spend more time producing objects for their children because other goods are deemed to be unstimulating, unhealthy, or even dangerous. This means that expectations for women to work for children are extended to all the parts of their lives. Through Etsy, stay-at-home mothers continue their intensive mothering into commercial settings. They further commodify and deploy their immaterial labor for profit. In making immaterial labor more visible, Etsy sellers skew some of its features. They also reference the cultural beliefs that control their position in order to improve their sales. This is distinct from postfeminism, which individualizes and thereby minimizes the structural limitations that have shaped women's identities and life courses.[124]

bisongirl establishes her expertise and the quality of her products by referencing her knowledge as a mother, her skills as a crafter, and the adoption of these products by other parents. Her shoes are derived from the needs of her child and can thus fulfill the requirements of other children. She could not find booties that would remain on her child's feet. bisongirl put "10 years of quilting experience to work and nearly 300 pairs later," she has "a small business making and selling" these shoes from her "home studio."[125] Her use of the term "home studio" relates stay-at-home mothers to artisans. MommySaidSew further emphasizes the professional aspects of the term "home studio." She "started with custom orders from friends and family" and "is now a small business" based in her "home studio (dream come true!)."[126] Such home studios are common among artists. However, in these contexts, and possibly with critical interventions, the usual correlation of men and artistry is challenged by the female gender coding of the domestic sphere as a place of art making. Reborn doll artists, who I study in Chapter 2, extend the concept of the home studio and connect mothering, artistry, and affect in their identification of products as needy babies and elevated art objects.

Stay-at-home mothers who sell on eBay and Etsy engage buyers with their narratives about emotional feelings. For instance, they employ the term "love" with a notable frequency. Etsy supports this idea in its About page, which indicates that the site is "bringing heart to commerce."[127] People declare their love of items and sellers and further correlate the heart with shopping by using the heart-shaped "Add shop to favorites" icon. The word "love" designates Etsy members' fondness and interests, including a love of family, children, crafts and crafting, communicating, and the site. Members act as consumer fans when they express their love for the company and listings. The term "love," with its extreme affect, also evokes the feminine. MadKatDiapers loves "(sewing) and sharing the love of the insane creative potential of cloth diapers!"[128] Amy Brittingham hopes "people love the products" she makes "as much as" she "love[s] to make them!"[129] These women use the term "love" to suggest that their objects are part of passionate exchanges. For example, applenamos loves her toys and makes "sure to put that love into each and every piece."[130] She knows "you and yours will feel that come across." Thus, Etsy items have a value and emotional appeal that exceeds material objects. Like the Internet technologies through which they are viewed, these items are extensions of women's fingers and emotions. The articulations of these forms of love are social selling tactics and, as I have started to suggest, a kind of immaterial labor where women sell their passions.

Buyers of the products of stay-at-home mothers are promised that items are infused with mothers' love. The affective aspects of mothering are used as marketing strategies and a sort of connective tissue that binds members. MommyLittleTreasures' "items come straight from" her "heart to you."[131] A "lot of TLC goes into each and every item." Her listings deliver emotional content as well as material goods. Since they are "straight" from the seller's emotional feelings, the suggestion is that there is no mediation and that the computer interface does not exist or is unimportant. Sellers imagine that buyers are touched by their sentiments and by parts of their bodies, such as the way MommyLittleTreasures' heart meets the body of other members. MomNMiaQuilts also evokes touching with her items that are "Handmade with love . . . one stitch at a time."[132] Her evocation of hand-produced and textural emotions is related to Eve Kosofsky Sedgwick's indication that people interconnect tactility and affect through the dual meanings of the terms "touching" and "feeling."[133] These intertwined conceptions of tactilely sensing and emotionally connecting alter the functions of Internet settings, including the ways members can engage and material bodies and objects are conceptualized. In the next chapter on reborn dolls, I continue to consider how producers connect Internet settings, making things, femininity, and the physical and emotional experiences of touching and feeling.

MommyLittleTreasures and MomNMiaQuilts also relate emotional handiwork to the concentrated and extended periods of time that it takes to produce crafts by hand. Stay-at-home mothers describe their work in listings but they distinguish this labor from manufacturing and the kinds of business engagements that happen outside of the home. For instance, MommysLoveBugs "personally" crochets and sews all her "items with love and care."[134] As a "mother of 4," she knows "how important it is to buy high quality and unique items" and hopes buyers will "cherish" these things as much as her "love bugs do." She connects her care in producing things, her children's love of her products, and sellers' potential pleasure in these same things. Reborn doll sellers make related claims about how touch infuses objects and enlivens them. They associate artistry with the painful and time-consuming aspects of reborning and mothering. All of these artists assert emotional as well as technological networks by suggesting that their touch makes buyers feel things.

Etsy sellers also focus on hands as a kind of remedy for the features of computer- and Internet-facilitated representations. People who sell things in ecommerce settings are limited by the aspects of interfaces and the low resolution of most web-delivered images and thus have problems conveying the material and tactile features of objects. This is especially a problem for sellers who want to emphasize the one-of-a-kind and handmade details of goods. Stay-at-home mothers and reborn producers reference hands and the handmade as substitutes for physical experiences and the emotional feelings that often come with them. They deploy conceptions of corporeal digits as a way of buttressing digital technologies. Sellers also use hands and ideas about touch to further tie the different individuals who are part of their narratives together. This is because hands facilitate physical contact with objects and people as well as the associated experiences of emotionally shared touching and being touched.

Community is similarly conceptualized as a way of touching. For instance, eBay depicts its community as a series of members holding hands. eBay and Etsy use the concept of community as a means of encouraging participants to emotionally engage with each other and the setting. The stay-at-home mothers selling on Etsy, like the women employing eBay, use narratives about community in order to make the site into a support system. SkyDreams thanks the "Etsy community for sharing your knowledge so selflessly."[135] Support is a common theme in these stay-at-home mothers' descriptions and is something that they offer in forums and ask for in listings. The term is useful because it designates both emotional and economic connections. In her Etsy profile, slippedstitchstudios describes how buyers sustain her way of life: "Supporting Slipped Stitch Studios, is supporting" her "dream of staying at home" with her daughter.[136] She loves "each and everyone of you for doing that!!!" Sellers' narratives about community support involve buyers in their lives and sentiments, reference the Etsy community, and encourage members to share their ethos and worldview.

slippedstitchstudios also models the values that she thinks are important. When she needs "supplies or help," she uses "Etsy Artists, Small business owners," and work- or stay-at-home mothers because it is important to "support the community of people trying to step out and make a living doing things they love." She asks, "If you don't buy from me- please buy from someone who makes handmade items!" Kelly Herdrich conveys a similar idea in her report. According to her, Etsy is "ideal for women looking to support stay at home mothers, crafters, or those who focus on the handmade, instead of the mass produced."[137] These themes are conducive for stay-at-home mothers because they also "support" and care for children and claim to forward future generations. With these comments, the cultural belief that stay-at-home mothers sustain traditional values is further secured.[138]

Buyers are supposed to be emotionally touched by the ways children motivate and inspire the Etsy site and members. For instance, Etsy's "Handmade Kids Challenge & Sweepstakes" was designed as a "celebration of our little muses – the kids."[139] AmothersArt expresses these sentiments through her ID and narratives. She has "the most wonderful inspiration" for her craft: her children.[140] She is "sure there are a lot of moms out there who can say that." Such statements script children as the initiators of intensive art inspiration as well as requiring intensive forms of emotional and physical labor. Children shape these Etsy members' worldview. For instance, lillipopsdesigns' "children inspired not only the look of Lillipops Designs, but" her "eco-conscious philosophy."[141] These children are understandably in dialogue with their mothers and other caregivers. However, sellers' descriptions sometimes suggest that inspiration and values flow from the child to the parent rather than emphasizing women's agency and decision-making in these exchanges. Of course, it is these very connections between women and their children that vet products, connect women buyers and sellers, and provide reasons for people to buy things.

Women's Etsy shops are tied to children with store names such as NatesMommyMadeIt and MommyofTyDesigns.[142] Stay-at-home mothers who sell on Etsy are thus fused to their children and connected to motherhood and childcare through layered references.[143] This happens with littlepinkposies who uses her ID as a shop and profile name, where women often list their first names. According to her, the name was "inspired" by her daughter, who is known by a similar nickname.[144] Thus, the sellers' "name," is informed and inspired by motherhood. Yet she also states that her position as a stay-at-home mother who sells items enables her to develop an identity beyond that of mother. In "addition to providing" a "creative outlet," the shop fulfills her "desire to do a little something" for herself. To "re-capture that spirit of independence that becomes a little blurry when you devote your life to caring for your family." The seller identifies the shop and project as a method of achieving a creative and individual identity even as the references to family make her situation "blurry." This interest in having a singular and more coherent identity through Internet settings is notable. Internet engagements are often associated with fragmentation and polyvalence because of people's multiple IDs and avatars and conflation with texts and technologies.

There are sellers who describe the site, the community, and their creative production as ways of temporarily escaping their role as mothers. They reference and distance themselves from the position of stay-at-home mother, thereby potentially reaping the benefits of both positions. For example, TheHobbyRoom loves her children and is "so grateful" that she gets "to stay at home with them when they're young, but sometimes" she needs a "break from it all."[145] With Etsy she can "escape" and "create something." "Motherhood is a wonderful vocation," writes nogginsnbobbins, "but everyone needs a break."[146] She never "imagined that this escape" would become her "beloved little etsy shop." This notion of getting away may be a more palatable construction of motherhood than other career engagements because it is likely that women are still situated in the home and available to their children when they are updating listings and doing other web-based work. eBay sellers are less likely to describe the site as a method of temporarily avoiding caretaking responsibilities. However, melinda904 identifies the site as her "get away."[147] Such narratives about escapes and personal pleasures are often connected to consumerism. Yet Etsy sellers associate the role of mother-artist with production, rather than, or in addition to, consumption. They understand mother-artists as active and thus see them as more empowered. Reborn producers also use the position of mother-artist to assert their creativity and enliven dolls.

Conclusion: The Work of Stay-at-Home Mothers

Stay-at-home mothers who sell on ecommerce sites write about their escapes and pleasures. In some cases, they also emphasize the work of sourcing, producing, listing, and selling things. Descriptions of eBay- and Etsy-facilitated work are similar to conceptions of other kinds of telework that, according to Anita Greenhill and Melanie Wilson's study, are supposed to provide "a greater sense of freedom," "increased leisure time," "more contact with children," and "sustained membership in nonwork communities."[148] Despite these promises, work is a key aspect of women's experiences with eBay and Etsy. Many of them have moved from traditional careers to home-based businesses. The accompanying intensification of their labor is part of larger cultural trends. Alex Williams reports on professionals who have "cut ties with the corporate grind" to "chase second careers as chocolatiers, bed-and-breakfast proprietors and organic farmers" and "find the hours and work grueling."[149] Researchers have also investigated the "culture of overwork."[150] Women are more open to such exhaustive forms of labor because of cultural presumptions about intensive mothering, broader gender conventions, and the expectations of new media settings. Women are informed that work is part of every aspect of life. They are expected to contribute because of the association of femininity with caring and nurturing.

Women describe Etsy as an escape from corporate culture, massification, uniformity, and childcare. However, successful Etsy businesses require long work hours and repetitive production methods. Women use terms such as "assembly line" to describe their production processes.[151] They also give accounts of production schedules that provide no relief. For instance, slippedstitchstudios is "working harder" on her crafting business than she ever has.[152] There is no "off switch" for her. KreatedbyKarina indicates that there is "really no such thing as 'vacation' or 'sick days.'"[153] Sellers perpetuate these schedules by directing other stay-at-home mothers to "work hard" and "just keep on working hard."[154] Thus, women who are based in the US and many other places have lost some of the controls and promises of paid employment. Their accounts should be cause for concern, especially when correlated with the promises of freedom and care that such sites deliver. However, these narratives about intensive labor are productive for ecommerce sites and may provide validation for the women who participate. People who have established flexible work arrangements with companies, as Greenhill and Wilson indicate, are "expected to work long hours to demonstrate commitment."[155] In ecommerce settings, women underscore the time they put into making items and mothering as a means of attracting buyers and assuring them of the quality of their items and their commitment to crafting and being stay-at-home mothers. Of course, eBay and Etsy profit when people list and sell items. These companies usually charge for listings and receive a percentage of sales.

Etsy is somewhat different than eBay and mentions the work of selling quite frequently. Etsy's Quit Your Day Job form asks sellers, "Would you walk us through what a typical workday might entail?" The associated posts about sellers' labor mandate participants to work, and to thereby generate profit for the company, and may encourage escalating narratives about extreme labor. Posts also try to explain why other members have not achieved the successes of chronicled sellers. The accounts imply that other women did not work as hard as the people featured in news reports and Etsy's accounts. Caroline Colom Vasquez and her husband worked at least twenty hours a day on their Etsy store.[156] fatdaddybakeshop was a stay-at-home mother until her businesses required more space. She works "an average of 12–16 hours a day baking, plus 2–3 hours online answering convos and maintaining" her shop.[157] Women often start businesses so that they can be available for children.[158] However, this creates conflicts when most of their time is dedicated to work. The demands of crafting and ecommerce work foil the promises of personal childcare and lead some women to move their businesses from the home. For instance, Katrinakaye's business commitments conflict with conceptions of intensive and focused mothering. The "computer is on 24 hours a day" in her home and "there's always something to do on it."[159] Their large screen allows them to have "one window showing Teletubbies and one next to it with Etsy." The same screen facilitates varied engagements so that distinctions between leisure time in the home and work in other spaces, which have always been overstated, become increasingly blurred.

Mothers are assured that they can easily combine childcare with eBay and Etsy selling. Nevertheless, these amalgamations occupy even more of sellers' time. This is related to Hardt and Negri's identification of how immaterial labor practices tend "to blur the distinction between work time and nonwork time, extending the working day indefinitely to fill all of life."[160] While self-presenting as stay-at-home mothers, these women are influenced by cultural mandates for intensive mothering and career overworking and extend the workday and speed up their production schedules because there is not enough time. Women note "there's just not enough hours in the day" and they are "asking for more hours in the day."[161] lepapierstudio uses the terms "quickly" and "hurry" to describe how she goes about her day.[162] When poppychicdesigns can find the time, she works "nonstop like a crazed elf on Christmas Eve."[163] In a related manner, slippedstitchstudios uses the time that her child is napping to "sew like a crazy person."[164] Stay-at-home mothers perpetuate conceptions of insane and out-of-control women. However, it is work rather than the confining space of the home and childcare that they associate with these states. They have been marketed and adopted work models that are supposed to facilitate familial and personal time but they are still grappling with what sociologist Arlie Russell Hochschild describes as the time binds of juggling domestic and career responsibilities.[165]

Stay-at-home mothers who sell crafts and other handmade products on Etsy indicate the limits as well as the positive features of intertwining the roles of stay-at-home mother and artisan. They profit from their maternal position by triggering the interests of a group of female buyers and by providing a culturally understood category for their diverse practices. Many of these women revise the more negative cultural understandings of stay-at-home mothers by providing more detailed depictions of their lives and by demonstrating their skills and products. Given the intensity and visibility of their work schedules, they also reform the exclusive association of stay-at-home mothers with the domestic sphere and childcare. Stay-at-home mothers indicate the labor in working and staying at home. They also begin to challenge the more limiting conceptions of stay-at-home mothers and femininity. Reborn baby producers continue this marketing and interrogation of mothering roles. They use the position of mother and the experiential affects of babies as means of asserting the illusionism of their products and thus their skills as artists. Women's methods of using and revising such traditional roles, and the political potential of their challenges to norms, are practices that I continue to explore in subsequent chapters.

Notes

1. Mary Andrews, "Quit Your Day Job: slippedstitchstudios," Etsy, 1 February 2010, 21 June 2014, http://www.etsy.com/blog/en/2010/quit-your-day-job-slippedstitchstudios/
2. AtHome Hand Made, "AtHome Hand Made on Etsy," Etsy, 21 June 2014, http://www.etsy.com/people/athomehandmade; From My Hand To Yours, "From My Hand To Yours on Etsy," Etsy, 21 June 2014, http://www.etsy.com/people/FromMyHand2YoursShop; The Hand Stamped Heart, "The Hand Stamped Heart on Etsy," Etsy, 26 May 2012, http://www.etsy.com/people/stardream222

3. Bratich, "Digital Touch," 303.
4. Gill, "Postfeminist Media Culture"; Sarikakis and Tsaliki, "Post/feminism."
5. slippedstitchstudios, as quoted in Mary Andrews, "Quit Your Day Job: slippedstitchstudios," Etsy, 1 February 2010, 21 June 2014, http://www.etsy.com/blog/en/2010/quit-your-day-job-slippedstitchstudios/
6. Dillaway and Paré, "Locating Mothers," 442. See also Hilbrecht et al., "I'm Home."
7. eBay offers a number of country-specific sites but many sellers use the ebay.com domain even when they are from countries where English is not the preferred language. Etsy offers a few language and currency options. Participants can set their region and receive content from that area.
8. Friedan, *Feminine Mystique*; Douglas and Michaels, *Mommy Myth*; Snitow, "Feminism and Motherhood."
9. Deirdre D. Johnston and Debra H. Swanson identify the different ways mothers who work, work part-time, and stay at home engage with conceptions of intensive mothering and articulate the aspects of the "good mother." Johnston and Swanson, "Constructing the 'Good Mother.'"
10. Etsy, "Etsy – About," 23 February 2013, http://www.etsy.com/about?ref=ft_about; Etsy, "Etsy – Your place to buy and sell all things handmade, vintage, and supplies," 21 January 2014, http://www.etsy.com/
11. Etsy, "Etsy – Community," 21 June 2014, http://www.etsy.com/community?ref=so_com
12. eBay, "Community : Community," 18 February 2012, http://community.ebay.com/index.jspa
13. White, *Buy It Now*.
14. Chad Dickerson, as quoted in Ki Mae Heussner, "Can Etsy make the most of its 'eBay moment'?" GIGAOM, 9 May 2012, 21 June 2014, http://gigaom.com/2012/05/09/can-etsy-make-the-most-of-its-ebay-moment/
15. Etsy, "Featured Seller | The Etsy Blog," 19 February 2012, http://www.etsy.com/blog/en/tags/featured-seller/?ref=fp_featured_more
16. TechUpdates, "Survey Says: The Results Are In," Etsy, 6 March 2008, 29 March 2012, http://www.etsy.com/blog/news/category/product-announcements/page/3/; Jessica Bruder, "The Etsy Wars," CNNMoney, 15 July 2009, 21 June 2014, http://money.cnn.com/2009/07/13/smallbusiness/etsy_wars.fsb/. In an international seller survey from 2009, 97% of the respondents identified as women. muka, "Survey Says: International Seller Survey Results Are In," Etsy, 25 February 2009, 21 June 2014, http://www.etsy.com/blog/news/2009/survey-says-international-seller-survey-results-are-in/
17. Brooke Dunbar, "Etsy.com helps Moms work from home," Examiner.com, 31 August 2010, 21 June 2014, http://www.examiner.com/stay-at-home-moms-in-austin/etsy-com-creates-a-platform-for-homemade-goods
18. oneluckybaby, as quoted in Mary Andrews, "Etsy Success Stories: oneluckybaby," Etsy, 3 March 2008, 21 June 2014, http://www.etsy.com/blog/en/2008/etsy-success-stories-oneluckybaby/; eclu, "Featured Seller: eclu," Etsy, 11 March 2011, 21 June 2014, http://www.etsy.com/blog/en/2011/featured-seller-eclu/
19. Dillaway and Paré, "Locating Mothers," 451.
20. eBay, "eBay allows mom to focus on caretaking," 17 May 2014, http://pages.ebay.com/sellerinformation/tips-for-selling-online/selling-success-stories/conlan/index.html
21. hobocampcrafts, as quoted in Mary Andrews, "Quit Your Day Job: HoboCampCrafts," Etsy, 24 November 2008, 21 June 2014, http://www.etsy.com/blog/en/2008/quit-your-day-job-hobocampcrafts/
22. Wharton, "Finding Time."
23. Etsy, "Etsy Success Stories: pdxbeanies," 14 April 2008, 21 June 2014, http://www.etsy.com/blog/en/2008/etsy-success-stories-pdxbeanies/

24. Reportage Online, "Quit your day job? It's not that Etsy," 2 March 2012, 21 June 2014, http://www.reportageonline.com/2012/03/for-many-users-of-etsy-the-world%E2%80%99s-largest-online-marketplace-for-handmade-and-vintage-goods-quitting-the-day-job-is-the-dream-its-also-the-name-of-a-popular-blog-on-the-site-thats-been/
25. MomNMiaQuilts, "Maria K on Etsy," Etsy, 21 June 2014, http://www.etsy.com/people/MomNMiaQuilts?ref=owner_profile_leftnav
26. mommymogul, "mommymogul on Etsy," Etsy, 21 June 2014, http://www.etsy.com/people/mommymogul?ref=owner_profile_leftnav
27. Michelle Horton, "Top 50 Etsy Moms of 2011," Babble, 16 March 2012, http://www.babble.com/mom/work-family/best-mom-etsy-shop-handmade/
28. Megan Auman, as quoted in Karina Ioffee, "Crafty stay-at-home moms turn to online sales," Reuters, 17 March 2010, 21 June 2014, http://www.reuters.com/article/2010/03/17/us-online-crafts-idUSTRE62G40620100317
29. Karina Ioffee, "Crafty stay-at-home moms turn to online sales," Reuters, 17 March 2010, 21 June 2014, http://www.reuters.com/article/2010/03/17/us-online-crafts-idUSTRE62G40620100317
30. Suzanne Wells, "Stay at home mom makes $250,000 on eBay," examiner.com, 23 April 2010, 17 May 2014, http://www.examiner.com/article/stay-at-home-mom-makes-250-000-on-ebay
31. eBay, "eBay Seller Profile," 21 June 2014, http://pages.ebay.com/sellercentral/sellerprofiles/newbabybaby.html
32. Encyclopedia of World Biography, "Jeff Skoll Biography," 21 June 2014, http://www.notablebiographies.com/news/Sh-Z/Skoll-Jeff.html
33. Internet Based Moms, "Online Auction Resources & Education," 21 June 2014, http://www.internetbasedmoms.com/online-auctions/
34. BusinessWeek, "The Rise of the Mompreneurs," 6 June 2004, 21 June 2014, http://www.businessweek.com/magazine/content/04_23/b3886076.htm
35. eBay, "eBay Media Center: About eBay," 13 March 2008, http://news.ebay.com/about.cfm
36. eBay Seller Newsletter, "Busy mom's eBay selling takes off," eBay, February–March 2012, http://pages.ebay.com/sellerinformation/howtosell/mom_in_georgia.html
37. eBay Seller Newsletter, "Free listings bolster household budget," eBay, March 2011, 21 June 2014, http://pages.ebay.com/sellerinformation/howtosell/ca_jessica.html
38. Casey, "Come, Join Our Family."
39. Friedan, *Feminine Mystique*, 180.
40. Rich, *Of Woman Born*, 23.
41. Ruddick, "Maternal Thinking," 103.
42. Douglas and Michaels, *Mommy Myth*, 4.
43. Hays, *Cultural Contradictions of Motherhood*, 4.
44. Duberley and Carrigan, "Career Identities of 'Mumpreneurs,'" 634.
45. West and Zimmerman, "Doing Gender," 126.
46. Butler, *Gender Trouble*, 41–42.
47. Bruni, Gherardi, and Poggio, "Doing Gender, Doing Entrepreneurship," 418.
48. Martin, "Deconstructing Organizational Taboos"; Ken Auletta, "Why Jill Abramson Was Fired," *New Yorker*, 14 May 2014, http://www.newyorker.com/online/blogs/currency/2014/05/why-jill-abramson-was-fired.html
49. eBay, "Member Profiles," 21 June 2014, http://pages.ebay.com/buy/profiles/oodlecanoodle.html
50. de Chernatony, "Brand Management."
51. eBay, "Community : Community," 17 June 2012, http://community.ebay.com/index.jspa?&anticache=1333732108069
52. eBay, "What We Believe – eBay Inc." 17 May 2012, http://www.ebayinc.com/values. The company also offered the WorldofGood.com site "Where your shopping

shapes the world" until 27 August 2012. worldofgood.com, "Shop for Artisan, Handmade & Fair Trade Clothing, Clothes & Gifts on WorldofGood.com by eBay," 29 May 2012, http://worldofgood.ebay.com/; eBay, "Green Shopping, Eco Friendly Products & Sustainable Living Tips – eBay Green Team," 21 June 2014, http://green.ebay.com/#wog
53. Thurer, *Myths of Motherhood.*
54. tradrmom, "Why would Anyone go to Ebay LIVE leaving their business?????" eBay, 30 April 2003, 30 March 2012, http://forums.ebay.com/db1/topic/Ebay-Live-%20Community/Why-%20Would-%20Anyone/164474?&tstart=2640&mod=1055528568012
55. Kelli DeMarco, as quoted in eBay, "eBay Seller Profile," 21 June 2014, http://pages.ebay.com/sellercentral/sellerprofiles/newbabybaby.html
56. jennsterb, "Old Navy NWT floral tank capris jeans 18-24 2t set," eBay, 12 January 2008, http://cgi.ebay.com/Old-Navy-NWT-floral-tank-capris-jeans-18-24-2t-set_W0QQitemZ320206853784QQihZ011QQcategoryZ147184QQssPageNameZWDVWQQrdZ1QQcmdZViewItem
57. Kelan, "Emotions," 50.
58. dianne_dp, "Community Member Spotlight," eBay, 2006, 21 June 2014, http://pages.ebay.com/community/people/spotlight/archive2004.html#dianne_dp
59. tradrmom, "Tradrmom's Handbags and More eBay Store About My Store," eBay, 21 June 2014, http://cgi3.ebay.com/ws/eBayISAPI.dll?ViewUserPage&userid=tradrmom
60. tradrmom, "Why would Anyone go to Ebay LIVE leaving their business?????" eBay, 30 April 2003, 30 March 2012, http://forums.ebay.com/db1/topic/Ebay-Live-%20Community/Why-%20Would-%20Anyone/164474?&tstart=2640&mod=1055528568012
61. Hill, et al., "Defining and Conceptualizing Workplace," 152.
62. Bourne and Forman, "Living in a Culture"; Hilbrecht et al., "I'm Home."
63. Bruni, Gherardi, and Poggio, "Doing Gender, Doing Entrepreneurship," 407.
64. Hardt and Negri, *Multitude,* 65.
65. Gregg, "Learning to (Love) Labour," 209.
66. Schultz, "Dissolved Boundaries"; Weeks, "Labor, Feminist Critique."
67. Oberhauser, "Home as 'Field,'" 170.
68. mommy$, "eBay My World – mommy$," eBay, 18 August 2013, http://myworld.ebay.com/mommy$/
69. shersbooksetc, "Shers Books Etc," eBay, 25 February 2012, http://members.ebay.com/ws/eBayISAPI.dll?ViewUserPage&userid=shersbooksetc
70. elena030503, "Diane Bucki Porcelain Sleeping Baby Doll," eBay, 24 February 2012, http://www.ebay.com/itm/Diane-Bucki-Porcelain-Sleeping-Baby-Doll-/150744592175?pt=LH_DefaultDomain_0&hash=item231913ef2f
71. Greenhill and Wilson, "Haven or Hell?"
72. lynnber, "eBay View About Me for lynnber," eBay, 21 June 2014, http://members.ebay.com/ws/eBayISAPI.dll?ViewUserPage&userid=lynnber
73. Rind and Bordia, "Effect of Server's 'Thank You.'"
74. mommy2liz, as quoted in Ryan, "The Spotlight's On: mommy2liz," The Chatter Newsletter 4, no. 9, August 2005, 21 June 2014, http://pages.ebay.com/community/chatter/2005august/memberspotlight.html
75. tradrmom, "Tradrmom's Handbags and More eBay Store About My Store," eBay, 21 June 2014, http://cgi3.ebay.com/ws/eBayISAPI.dll?ViewUserPage&userid=tradrmom
76. Pierre Omidyar, "Regarding SafeHarbor 2.0," Wayback Machine, 7 October 1999, 21 June 2014, http://web.archive.org/web/*/http://pages.ebay.com/community/news/letter-011599-safeharbor.html
77. acornerstorecareer, "Old Navy mens logo fleece pullover sweatshirt~NWT~S," eBay, 31 January 2008, http://cgi.ebay.com/Old-Navy-mens-logo-fleece-pullover-

sweatshirt-NWT-S_W0QQitemZ360019339982QQihZ023QQcategory Z57988QQssPageNameZWDVWQQrdZ1QQcmdZViewItem
78. mommyof2boys71, "NWT Men's levi's jeans 34X30," eBay, 9 February 2008, http://cgi.ebay.com/NWT-Mens-levis-jeans-34X30_W0QQitemZ160207160795QQihZ006QQcategoryZ11483QQssPageNameZWDVWQQrdZ1QQcmdZViewItem
79. beccab312, "Tyco KITTY kitty Kittens 1992 Mommy large 14" white cat pink bow stuffed plush," eBay, 25 February 2012, http://www.ebay.com/itm/Tyco-KITTY-kitty-Kittens-1992-Mommy-large-14-white-cat-pink-bow-stuffed-plush-/180730880145?pt=LH_DefaultDomain_0&hash=item2a14666091
80. ysaa8773, "FREE SHIPPING IN USA New with tag baby Gap skinny corduroy pant size 4T," eBay, 24 February 2012, http://www.ebay.com/itm/FREE-SHIPPING-USA-New-tag-baby-Gap-skinny-corduroy-pant-size-4T-/180823068586?pt=US_Baby_Toddler_Girls_Clothing&hash=item2a19e50faa
81. shellesstore2010, "Crayola Crayon Maker NEW in Box," eBay, 24 February 2012, http://www.ebay.com/itm/Crayola-Crayon-Maker-NEW-Box-/290672422122?pt=LH_DefaultDomain_0&hash=item43ad6d2cea
82. flowerjen, "Aunt Martha's Standard Pillowcases Hot Iron Transfer," eBay, 24 February 2012, http://www.ebay.com/itm/Aunt-Marthas-Standard-Pillowcases-Hot-Iron-Transfer-/120478135565?pt=LH_DefaultDomain_0&hash=item1c0d0e750d
83. In Bruni, Gherardi, and Poggio's study, some women also resist being identified as businesswomen. They argue that this provides them with opportunities to manage their businesses from different positions. Bruni, Gherardi, and Poggio, "Doing Gender, Doing Entrepreneurship."
84. Medved and Kirby, "Family CEOs."
85. Thomas-Hunt and Phillips, "When What You Know."
86. nostalgic_notions, "Pureology Super Straight Shampoo 10.1 oz. $25 Value," eBay, 10 March 2008, http://cgi.ebay.com/Pureology-Super-Straight-Shampoo-10-1-oz-25-Value_W0QQitemZ160217288184QQihZ006QQcategoryZ118952QQssPageNameZWDVWQQrdZ1QQcmdZViewItem
87. step*right*up, "Huge lot KID'S COOKBOOKS children's recipes PRETEND SOUP Gingerbread House learn," eBay, 1 June 2012, http://www.ebay.com/itm/Huge-lot-KIDS-COOKBOOKS-childrens-recipes-PRETEND-SOUP-Gingerbread-House-learn-/221034378982?pt=US_Childrens_Books&hash=item3376acf6e6
88. lynnber, "eBay View About Me for lynnber," eBay, 21 June 2014, http://members.ebay.com/ws/eBayISAPI.dll?ViewUserPage&userid=lynnber
89. Member Profiles, "Staying in Style without Going over Budget," eBay, 21 June 2014, http://pages.ebay.com/buy/profiles/melrosemax.html
90. mostly-maternity, "eBay View About Me for mostly-maternity," eBay, 21 June 2014, http://members.ebay.com/ws/eBayISAPI.dll?ViewUserPage&userid=mostly-maternity
91. tony3430, "JUICY COUTURE Baby Diaper Bag +Pad+Bib+Burp Cloth $250: NWT Guaranteed AUTHENTIC or Money Back! Super Fast Ship," eBay, 10 March 2008, http://cgi.ebay.com/JUICY-COUTURE-Baby-Diaper-Bag-Pad-Bib-Burp-Cloth-250_W0QQitemZ270218707338QQihZ017QQcategoryZ146530QQssPageNameZWDVWQQrdZ1QQcmdZViewItem
92. Zelizer, "Creation of Domestic Currencies," 141.
93. Sayer, "Gender, Time and Inequality," 297.
94. britican-empire, "Britican Empire eBay Store About My Store," eBay, 21 June 2014, http://members.ebay.com/ws/eBayISAPI.dll?ViewUserPage&userid=britican-empire
95. beckyboosbargains, "Laura Ashley Mother & Child 'Isabel' Girls Crib Bedding + MANY extras – EUC," eBay, 26 February 2012, http://www.ebay.com/itm/Laura-Ashley-Mother-Child-Isabel-Girls-Crib-Bedding-MANY-extras-EUC-/

160738960753?pt=LH_DefaultDomain_0&hash=item256cc9e571; 3_little_q-ts, "Woman's Keneth too Peach Ribbed Top XL," eBay, 24 February 2012, http://www.ebay.com/itm/Womans-Keneth-too-Peach-Ribbed-Top-XL-/130483067835?pt=US_CSA_WC_Shirts_Tops&hash=item1e61659bbb
96. jamijami21, "Lot of Girls Shirts/Tops 3T Baby Gap, Old Navy, etc…(All gently worn)," eBay, 24 February 2012, http://www.ebay.com/itm/Lot-Girls-Shirts-Tops-3T-Baby-Gap-Old-Navy-etc-All-gently-worn-/280828714719?pt=US_Baby_Toddler_Girls_Clothing&hash=item4162b21edf
97. jordansmama17, "NWT VICTORIA'S SECRET PINK *PINK* BOYFRIEND SWEATS *SMALL* LOVE PINK*," eBay, 25 February 2012, http://www.ebay.com/itm/NWT-VICTORIAS-SECRET-PINK-PINK-BOYFRIEND-SWEATS-SMALL-LOVE-PINK-/160723883839?pt=US_Womens_Sweats_Hoodies&hash=item256be3d73f
98. monkeybunsdiapers, "eBay View About Me for monkeybunsdiapers," eBay, 21 June 2014, http://members.ebay.com/ws/eBayISAPI.dll?ViewUserPage&userid=monkeybunsdiapers
99. lynnber, "eBay View About Me for lynnber," eBay, 21 June 2014, http://members.ebay.com/ws/eBayISAPI.dll?ViewUserPage&userid=lynnber
100. custombags, "Custom Bags eBay Store About My Store," eBay, 19 January 2008, http://members.ebay.com/ws/eBayISAPI.dll?ViewUserPage&userid=custombags
101. Blair-Loy, "Cultural Constructions of Family," 690.
102. Vincent and Ball, "Making Up."
103. Nead, "Seductive Canvases"; Pollock, *Vision and Difference.*
104. Etsy, "Featured Seller: Mignonne Handmade," 12 February 2012, 16 March 2013, https://www.etsy.com/blog/en/2012/featured-seller-mignonne-handmade/; Etsy, "Featured Seller: rikrak," 21 April 2008, 21 June 2014, http://www.etsy.com/blog/en/2008/featured-seller-rikrak/; Mary Andrews, "Quit Your Day Job: TheShabby ChicCottage," Etsy, 18 January 2011, 21 June 2014, http://www.etsy.com/blog/en/2011/quit-your-day-job-theshabbychiccottage/
105. littlegoodall, "Featured Seller: Little Goodall," Etsy, 21 September 2011, 21 June 2014, http://www.etsy.com/blog/en/2011/featured-seller-little-goodall/
106. mignonnehandmade, "Featured Seller: Mignonne Handmade," Etsy, 12 February 2012, 16 March 2013, https://www.etsy.com/blog/en/2012/featured-seller-mignonne-handmade/
107. Michelle Horton, "Top 50 Etsy Moms: BananaSaurus Rex by Rebecca Thoms Hanley," Babble, 2010, 27 December 2011, http://www.babble.com/mom/parenting-top-50/top-50-etsy-moms/bananasaurus-rex-rebecca-thoms-hanley/#scrolltop; Michelle Horton, "Top 50 Etsy Moms: ElmStudioOnline by Erin L. Meissner," Babble, 2010, 27 December 2011, http://www.babble.com/mom/parenting-top-50/top-50-etsy-moms/elmstudioonline-erin-l-meissner/
108. HolmesandWatson, "Featured Seller: Little Goodall," Etsy, 21 September 2011, 21 June 2014, http://www.etsy.com/blog/en/2011/featured-seller-little-goodall/
109. Mary Andrews, "Quit Your Day Job: dlkdesigns," Etsy, 10 May 2010, 21 June 2014, http://www.etsy.com/blog/en/2010/quit-your-day-job-dlkdesigns/
110. loopyboopy, "Quit Your Day Job: loopyboopy," Etsy, 29 March 2010, 21 June 2014, http://www.etsy.com/blog/en/2010/quit-your-day-job-loopyboopy/
111. Sara Mosle, "Etsy.com Peddles a False: Feminist Fantasy: No, you can't quit your day job to make quilts," Double X, 10 June 2009, 27 March 2012, http://www.doublex.com/print/2422
112. Jessica Bruder, "The Etsy Wars," CNNMoney, 15 July 2009, 12 May 2012, http://money.cnn.com/2009/07/13/smallbusiness/etsy_wars.fsb/; Alex Williams, "That Hobby Looks Like a Lot of Work," *New York Times*, 16 December 2009, 20 June 2014, http://www.nytimes.com/2009/12/17/fashion/17etsy.html?adxnnl=1&pagewanted=print&adxnnlx=1329844169-cm6k02NMqlepY1D10Ta3Yw

113. Deborah Ostrovsky, "Confessions of a Reluctant Crafter," Herizon Magazine, Winter 2012, 21 June 2014, http://www.herizons.ca/node/508
114. BloomStudios' shop indicates: "***CLOSED*** I am experiencing some growing pains and have decided to close shop for a while." Bloomstudios, "bloom studios organic modern handmade jewelery by BloomStudios," Etsy, 16 May 2012, http://www.etsy.com/shop/bloomstudios#; See also fatdaddybakeshop, "Etsy :: Your place to buy and sell all things handmade," Etsy, 16 May 2012, http://www.etsy.com/shop/fatdaddybakeshop; katrinakaye, "Etsy :: Your place to buy and sell all things handmade," Etsy, 16 May 2012, http://www.etsy.com/shop/katrinakaye; SweeterThanMeDesigns, "SHOP CLOSED by SweeterThanMeDesigns," Etsy, 21 June 2014, http://www.etsy.com/shop/SweeterThanMeDesigns
115. Babble, "Top 50 Etsy Moms," 2010, 27 December 2011, http://www.babble.com/mom/parenting-top-50/top-50-etsy-moms-2010/
116. DivaBabyDesigns, "DivaBabyDesigns's Profile," Etsy, 21 July 2014, http://www.etsy.com/people/DivaBabyDesigns?ref=ls_profile
117. Stoller, *Happy Hooker*.
118. Duncan, "MoMA's Hot Mamas"; Bergstein, "Artist in His Studio."
119. Lippard, *From the Center*. One of the better-known works that focuses on these connections is Judy Chicago's Birth Project. Chicago designed a series of birth and creation images, which were produced by needleworkers and other crafters from about 1980 to 1985.
120. DivaBabyDesigns, "Birthday Tutu Outfit–Pretty Pretty Princess light pink and silver ribbon tutu set," Etsy, 12 May 2012, http://ww.etsy.com/listing/89798679/birthday-tutu-outfit-pretty-pretty?ref=pr_shop
121. NatesMommyMadeIt, "Makisha's Profile," Etsy, 7 July 2011, http://www.etsy.com/people/NatesMommyMadeIt?ref=ls_profile
122. Medved and Kirby, "Family CEOs."
123. applenamos, "applenamos's Profile," Etsy, 7 July 2011, http://www.etsy.com/people/applenamos?ref=ls_profile
124. Dobson, "Individuality Is Everything."
125. bisongirl, "Erica's Profile," Etsy, 7 July 2011, http://www.etsy.com/people/bisongirl?ref=ls_profile
126. MommySaidSew, "MommySaidSew on Etsy," Etsy, 13 May 2012, http://www.etsy.com/people/MommySaidSew?ref=owner_profile_leftnav
127. Etsy, "Etsy – About," 30 September 2012, http://www.etsy.com/about?ref=ft_about
128. MadKatDiapers, "Kathryn Cowell on Etsy," Etsy, 21 June 2014, http://www.etsy.com/people/MadKatDiapers?ref=ls_profile
129. Amy Brittingham, "Amy Brittingham on Etsy," Etsy, 21 June 2014, http://www.etsy.com/people/Abrittingham2?ref=ls_profile
130. applenamos, "applenamos's Profile," Etsy, 7 July 2011, http://www.etsy.com/people/applenamos?ref=ls_profile
131. MommyLittleTreasures, "Mommy's Little Treasures by MommyLittleTreasures on Etsy," Etsy, 14 May 2012, http://www.etsy.com/shop/MommyLittleTreasures?ref=ss_profile
132. MomNMiaQuilts, "Maria K on Etsy," Etsy, 13 May 2012, http://www.etsy.com/people/MomNMiaQuilts?ref=owner_profile_leftnav
133. Sedgwick, *Touching Feeling*, 17.
134. MommysLoveBugs, "Mommys Love Bugs by MommysLoveBugs on Etsy," Etsy, 13 May 2012, http://www.etsy.com/shop/MommysLoveBugs?ref=ss_profile
135. SkyDreams, as quoted in Mary Andrews, "Quit Your Day Job: SkyDreams," Etsy, 23 February 2009, 21 June 2014, http://www.etsy.com/blog/en/2009/quit-your-day-job-skydreams/

136. slippedstitchstudios, "Laura Lundy's Profile," Etsy, 20 February 2012, http://www.etsy.com/people/slippedstitchstudios
137. Kelly Herdrich, "Etsy allows local moms to support one another," Examiner.com, 22 June 2009, 25 August 2013, http://www.examiner.com/article/etsy-allows-local-moms-to-support-one-another
138. Thurer, *Myths of Motherhood*.
139. Vanessa Bertozzi, "Handmade Kids: Challenge Launches Tonight!" Etsy, 15 July 2008, 21 June 2014, http://www.etsy.com/blog/en/2008/handmade-kids-challenge-launches-tonight/
140. AmothersArt, "AMothersArt's Profile," Etsy, 8 July 2011, http://www.etsy.com/people/AMothersArt?ref=ls_profile
141. lillipopsdesigns, "Jayme Lillie on Etsy," Etsy, 27 December 2011, http://www.etsy.com/people/lillipopsdesigns
142. NatesMommyMadeIt, "Makisha's Profile," Etsy, 7 July 2011, http://www.etsy.com/people/NatesMommyMadeIt?ref=ls_profile; MommyofTyDesigns, "Candace on Etsy," Etsy, 13 May 2012, http://www.etsy.com/people/MommyofTy?ref=owner_profile_leftnav
143. This connection is intensified when individuals' IDs also function as their names. Some Etsy sellers use what appears to be their legal names in profiles and featured seller accounts.
144. littlepinkposies, "littlepinkposies on Etsy," Etsy, 19 May 2014, http://www.etsy.com/people/littlepinkposies
145. TheHobbyRoom, "Andrea's Profile," Etsy, 8 July 2011, http://www.etsy.com/people/TheHobbyRoom?ref=ls_profile
146. nogginsnbobbins, "Heather on Etsy," Etsy, 30 December 2011, http://www.etsy.com/people/nogginsnbobbins
147. melinda904, "Abstract Black Porcelain/Ceramic MOTHER & CHILD Statue," eBay, 25 February 2012, http://www.ebay.com/itm/Abstract-Black-Porcelain-Ceramic-MOTHER-CHILD-Statue-/130650918078?pt=LH_DefaultDomain_0&hash=item1e6b66ccbe
148. Greenhill and Wilson, "Haven or Hell?" 382.
149. Alex Williams, "Maybe It's Time for Plan C," *New York Times*, 12 August 2011, 21 June 2014, http://www.nytimes.com/2011/08/14/fashion/maybe-its-time-for-plan-c.html?_r=2&ref=style&pagewanted=print
150. Bunting, *Willing Slaves*; Hochschild, *Time Bind*.
151. oneluckybaby, "oneluckybaby on Etsy," Etsy, 19 February 2012, http://www.etsy.com/people/oneluckybaby; AliciaBock, as quoted in Mary Andrews, "Etsy Success Stories: AliciaBock," Etsy, 17 March 2009, 21 June 2014, http://www.etsy.com/blog/en/2008/etsy-success-stories-aliciabock/
152. slippedstitchstudios, as quoted in Mary Andrews, "Quit Your Day Job: slippedstitchstudios," Etsy, 1 February 2010, 19 August 2013, http://www.etsy.com/blog/en/2010/quit-your-day-job-slippedstitchstudios/
153. KreatedbyKarina, "Quit Your Day Job: KreatedbyKarina," Etsy, 8 March 2010, 21 June 2014, http://www.etsy.com/blog/en/2010/quit-your-day-job-kreatedbykarina/
154. AliciaBock, as quoted in Mary Andrews, "Etsy Success Stories: AliciaBock," Etsy, 17 March 2009, 21 June 2014, http://www.etsy.com/blog/en/2008/etsy-success-stories-aliciabock/; KreatedbyKarina, "Quit Your Day Job: KreatedbyKarina," Etsy, 8 March 2010, 21 June 2014, http://www.etsy.com/blog/en/2010/quit-your-day-job-kreatedbykarina/
155. Greenhill and Wilson, "Haven or Hell? 380.
156. Alex Williams, "That Hobby Looks Like a Lot of Work," *New York Times*, 17 December 2009, 21 June 2014, http://www.nytimes.com/2009/12/17/fashion/17etsy.html?adxnnl=1&pagewanted=print&adxnnlx=1329844169-cm6k02NMqlepY1D10Ta3Yw

157. fatdaddybakeshop, as quoted in EtsyStore, "Etsy Success Stories: FatDaddyBakeShop," Etsy, 25 February 2008, 21 June 2014, www.etsy.com/blog/en/2008/etsy-success-stories-fatdaddybakeshop/
158. Duberley and Carrigan, "Career Identities of 'Mumpreneurs.'" For a discussion of mumpreneurs, see also Ekinsmyth, "Challenging the Boundaries."
159. Katrinakaye, as quoted in Mary Andrews, "Quit Your Day Job: KatrinaKaye," Etsy, 27 October 2008, 21 June 2014, http://www.etsy.com/blog/en/2008/quit-your-day-job-katrinakaye/
160. Hardt and Negri, *Multitude*, 66.
161. KreatedbyKarina, "Quit Your Day Job: KreatedbyKarina," Etsy, 8 March 2010, 21 June 2014, http://www.etsy.com/blog/en/2010/quit-your-day-job-kreatedbykarina/; babypop, "Shery Aikens on Etsy," Etsy, 21 February 2012, http://www.etsy.com/people/babypop/?ref=storque
162. lepapierstudio, as quoted in Mary Andrews, "Quit Your Day Job: lepapierstudio," Etsy, 1 March 2010, 21 June 2014, http://www.etsy.com/blog/en/2010/quit-your-day-job-lepapierstudio/
163. poppychicdesigns, "Quit Your Day Job: poppychicdesigns," Etsy, 25 January 2010, 21 June 2014, http://www.etsy.com/blog/en/2010/quit-your-day-job-poppychicdesigns/
164. slippedstitchstudios, as quoted in Mary Andrews, "Quit Your Day Job: slippedstitchstudios," Etsy, 1 February 2010, 21 June 2014, http://www.etsy.com/blog/en/2010/quit-your-day-job-slippedstitchstudios/
165. Hochschild, *Time Bind*.

2

TOUCHING FEELING WOMEN

Reborn Artists, Babies, and Mothers

Artist Kimberly McClung, who also uses the eBay ID beachbabies2014, is one of the many women who produce reborn babies. She lists her creative work on eBay and details her practices on a personal website.[1] McClung introduces the "adult collector" and buyer of highly crafted reborns to "little Jacque/Jacqueline" in an eBay listing that includes detailed descriptions and numerous photographs [Figure 2.1].[2] Jacque/Jacqueline "is a limited edition (196/250) micro preemie reborn baby doll" made from a "sculpt by the extremely talented Tamie Yarie and there will never be another just like him/her." McClung recognizes the other producers who have contributed to this object, including Yarie who sculpted the limited edition kit, while figuring her own process as transformative and about changing a "blank vinyl kit" into a tangible presence and child. Jacque/Jacqueline triggers emotional and tactile experiences in buyers by being "kinda floppy and kinda squishy" and "very cuddly and loveable." McClung emphasizes the squishy and hybrid identity of her baby, including its open gender attribution. She includes a "non-anatomically correct tummy plate for posing" that in its painted blankness resists the usual cultural classifications. Reborn artists also complicate the association of artistry with men and masculinity by self-presenting as women artists and mother-producers, who make collectible dolls that are babies. Reborns, including McClung's listing, are thus art, visceral subjects, and Internet and material texts that make subjectivity less identifiable and stable.

The people involved in reborning describe themselves as artists and mothers and do complicated work in remaking the meaning and values of these objects. Their process includes selecting a doll kit or remaking a baby doll, cleaning the form, painting simulated skin-tone in numerous layers, inserting eyes, rooting mohair into the scalp or painting illusionistic hair, connecting the plastic doll limbs and head to a cloth body, constructing detachable umbilical cords and

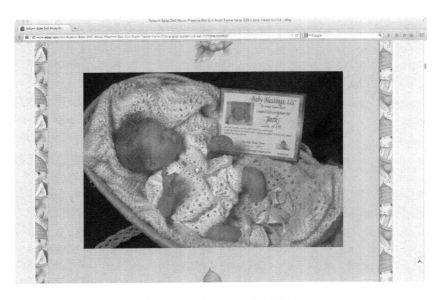

FIGURE 2.1 eBay. Reborns are portrayed as art and as babies.

belly plates, shopping for clothes and props or making these items, producing digital images of the reborn in varied tableaux, and writing about collectible babies. eBay and Etsy have active markets in reborn babies and such related items as reborn kits, clothing, and props. There are usually a few thousand reborn babies listed under "Dolls & Bears," "Dolls," "Reborn" on eBay. There are a smaller number of babies on Etsy. While there is a great deal of variance in the prices offered for these reborns, many sell for hundreds or even thousands of U.S. dollars. Yet artists downplay reborn prices by referring to sales as "adoptions" and reborns as "babies." Reborn producers further elevate their practices through biographical narratives, including their background as artists, doll makers, and mothers. For instance, reborn artists produce themselves through "About the Artist" links on their personal websites. Like the About features that are deployed by ecommerce settings, and that I discuss earlier in this book, these texts explain how readers are supposed to understand reborn producers and viewing experiences. Through these varied devices, reborn artists assert that their work is art and they are artists. Interestingly, it is through the skill and artistry of their collector objects that they also make these items into babies.

Reborn artists are producing women who use Internet settings to constitute themselves as artists and mothers and to make dolls into collectible objects and babies. I ordinarily describe reborns as "babies" in order to acknowledge the terms and values of the culture. Reborn artists also constitute the position of buyers by indicating that reborn dolls are alive because of their craft and in need of mothering. They encourage viewers to become mothers and commit to intensive childcare. For instance, McClung writes, If "this tiny sweetness tugs at your heartstrings then don't miss your chance to bring him home." McClung and other reborn artists use descriptions and images to stimulate maternal feelings in Internet settings. They also indicate the role of their own hands in producing art objects, feelings, and babies. Eve Kosofsky Sedgwick's and other authors' considerations of affect, and descriptions of the relationship between physically touching and emotionally feeling, allow me to reflect upon the ways reborn producers use representations of hands, textures, sentiments, and babies to establish their skill and enliven things.[3] I relate these analyses of the blending of tactile sensations and impassioned sentiments, and thus the ways material and affective bodies are articulated, to Louis Althusser's and Judith Butler's theories of hailing and interpellation and how individuals constitute others and themselves as subjects.[4] Reborn artists use these affective and interpellation practices to produce their creative roles and babies and thereby code production as artistic and reproductive.

Producing Artists and Mothers

McClung and other reborn artists assert the artistic qualities of reborn babies. They also highlight the feel of reborn babies in buyers' hands and the pull on viewers' "heartstrings" and emotions. The women who view reborn listings are constituted as mothers through these tactile and emotional feelings, the articulated needs of babies, and direct addresses, including listings that are directed at "you." According to dbick4, "You won't want to put her down."[5] These artists interpellate and hail viewers and make potential buyers into mothers. The voices reborn artists project and responses of buyers stage a version of Louis Althusser's model of interpellation, or subject formation. The application of Althusser's theory suggests that the ideology of intensive mothering, its dominant, comprehensive, and insistent worldview, "recruits" and "transforms" individuals into subjects through the "precise operations" of "*interpellation* or hailing."[6] In Judith Butler's reading of Althusser, a "subject is hailed, the subject turns around, and the subject then accepts the terms by which he or she is hailed."[7] Turning around, according to Butler, "is an act that is, as it were, conditioned both by the 'voice' of the law and by the responsiveness of the one hailed by the law."[8] Reborn babies ask viewers to hold and "Adopt me" and when women respond, which numerous successful auctions suggest many women do, the hailing process forms individuals into caring and laboring mother-subjects and dolls into babies.[9] Mothers and babies also constitute other subjects by calling for attention and connecting with individuals' animate and feeling hands.

Through reborn artists' and babies' addresses to and formations of these mothers, women respond to a version of the law, including gender conventions, and are conditioned by and continue mainstream conceptions of femininity and mothering. When individuals agreeably respond to social directives, they are provided with such rewards as having their purpose and desires validated and being provided with ready communities. The value, and even necessity, of such social support is not to be underestimated. Yet reborn participants also identify as adult children who mother a form of baby doll. They thereby refuse to focus on the full meaning of mainstream hails and do not follow all of the culturally identifiable maternal behaviors. This is notable since subjects are always-already interpellated and consistently hailed so that their normative roles are underscored, including their formation as gendered individuals who are directed to follow certain laws and gendered life stages. Reborn artists render structures in which they and other women are hailed and produced as traditional mothers and occupy hybrid positions as artists and mother-producers.

smallwonderskyla asserts an artistic and traditionally feminine identity by using Internet-facilitated images of herself and her reborn babies. Her eBay Store features a photograph of her working on a painted self-portrait and thus addressing and producing herself.[10] In the photographic depiction and in the realist painted image, which is included in the photograph, smallwonderskyla wears a strapless and full-skirted dress and high-heeled mules. This garb is different than the casual and paint splattered clothing that most painters wear when producing art and self-representing as working artists. Yet the tight-fitting bodice that emphasizes her breasts and the mules that enhance her legs, rather than providing stability and comfort, provide some assurance that she is properly female and feminine even when making things. smallwonderskyla uses these portrayals to depict her immobility and activity. She stands fixedly in the painting. In the photograph, she uses a stepstool to dynamically reach up and apply the brush to her canvas. Such images indicate the ways visual depictions, like written texts, contain the kinds of conflicts in meaning making that Barbara Johnson analyzes and I consider in the introduction.[11] These divergent references allow smallwonderskyla to provisionally meet cultural conceptions of passive femininity and virile artistry. smallwonderskyla gestures at her painted self with the paintbrush and hails herself as artist, woman, artwork, and representation. She also constitutes the features of her reborns, which become associated with the painting and its register of attributes. These reborn babies function as a version of the mother-artist and as live beings and collectibles.

smallwonderskyla's artistic practices are a realization of her childhood and adult investments because ever since she "was a small child," she "wanted to be an artist." smallwonderskyla uses the image of her painting the self-portrait to assert that she considers and constructs her position as artist and individual. Such creative producers are invested in a search for self and self-actualization through their work.[12] They thereby participate in larger cultural forms of self-making. For example, Internet practices, including blogging, are credited with allowing people to produce and find themselves.[13] Reality television participants often indicate the procedures of the genre and that they are supposed to discover themselves through the experiences of being filmed and commenting on their actions.

smallwonderskyla's artistic engagement is also a form of touching and making that connects bodies to their representations. As smallwonderskyla reaches her hand up to produce the self-portrait and herself, she extends her arm and the paintbrush and touches herself while being touched up. Her babies also engage in varied kinds of touching as making. Below her double self-portrait, a group of reborn babies reaches out to potential buyers and collectors with the hands that she has crafted. The realism of these hands and their lifelike qualities, with fingers flexed, reaching, pointing, and curled into fists, establish the artistry of reborn producers. These hands also expressively represent the calls of babies and make viewers into mothers who are reached for. smallwonderskyla furthers these productive and affective connections by describing them as her babies and including a picture of her gently touching a reborn baby and fixing its diaper.

Reborn artists figure the touching process of reborning as a method of finding their ultimate craft and as a form of self-realization and actualization. They are "in touch" with themselves and babies. gogirlusa "always loved dolls and babies."[14] She knew that she had found her "passion" when she "discovered Reborn Dolls." gogirlusa loops back to a previous state to establish her position as an artist. Judy Burrell "discovered the world of reborn dolls," "immediately fell in love with them," and "soon discovered" that reborning was something that she "loved to do."[15] For her, it is "a real passion." The writings of other women producers highlight similar ideas and word choices. For instance, reborn artists employ the term "discovered" to emphasize the newness and uniqueness of reborn production as well as their processes of finding their childhood and reconceived interests. Passion is also associated with artistic creation. However, in these instances, women fall in love with feminine objects as well as the processes of intensely making things. They connect their youthful pleasures of playing with dolls to girlhood and female ideas about being mothers and having babies. These women use the term "love" to link their interests in babies and dolls, which are culturally coded as feminine, to their investment in creative production. Reborn artists also employ narratives about love to articulate their relationships with collectors and the experiences that tie buyers and babies together. Love is a term that is employed enthusiastically, excessively, and parodically, and thus in conflicting ways, in Internet settings. Reborn artists and other people reference affective experiences of love in order to displace the idea that the Internet is isolating and dematerializing. They assert the intense emotions and experiences of Internet bodies. However, reborn artists' and other participants' articulations of love tend to associate their primary relationships with feminine spheres and objects rather than heterosexual and normative familial relationships.

Reborn producers' references to love render a queer set of attachments rather than being developmental and part of growing up. Kathryn Bond Stockton proposes the concept of "growing sideways" to explain queer children's resistance to, or their impossibility of, normatively growing up and fully supporting cultural categories and expectations. She argues that children's "supposed gradual growth" and "slow unfolding" have "been relentlessly figured as vertical movement upward (hence 'growing up') toward full stature, marriage, work, reproduction, and the loss of childishness."[16] Stockton associates the queer child, and related identifications and embodied experiences, with "notions of the horizontal—what spreads sideways and backwards—more than a simple thrusting toward height and forward time." The ghostly queer child, who still lingers in many people's lives, should not be seen as a testimony to their childish wrongness, but instead as an indication of the narrowness of cultural categories and values. The nonlinear and atemporal movements of growing sideways are especially appropriate in Internet and computer settings with their references to morphing and shifted times and bodies. Many of the producing women and practices studied in this book morph and spread sideways, sometimes rubbing along past experiences and delights, rather than fully following the developmental and relational stages expected of women. These women thereby play at and with the category of femininity.

There are queer resonances and forms of growing sideways even when reborn artists use the concept of love to constitute more heteronormative relationships. smallwonderskyla mentions her "husband Michael, who is also a fine artist," but after this identification and under the image of her painting are the reborns that she identifies as her babies.[17] Family is thereby part of adult life stages and creative play. After all, such creative practices are something that she has dreamed about since being a "small child" and her artistic endeavors allow her to retain this idea of herself as a child. smallwonderskyla and other women in reborn culture, like the adults Stockton considers, identify the child by thinking back, growing backwards by producing their childhood motives and interests as adults, and rendering versions of themselves as children. This alternative construction of women and mothers also happens because smallwonderskyla connects her marriage to the artistic and biological reproduction of baby dolls. Her reborn babies are depicted under but between her legs, as if they had physically emerged from her body. There are thus pleasurable and creative sideways growths in the ways reborn artists conceptualize their creations as children and their position as mothers to this handiwork. Reborn artists' associations of artistry with motherhood, like the narratives of stay-at-home mothers who are ecommerce sellers, are contrary to cultural expectations that artists will be men and that artistic genius is a feature of masculinity. Feminist art historians, including Linda Nochlin and Griselda Pollock, provide a history of how women worked within the cultural limitations of their gender and produced images of female and feminine spheres, including Mary Cassatt's images of nursing mothers in the late nineteenth and early twentieth centuries.[18] Reborn artists continue these connections by tactically using conceptions of mothering and affective nurturing to establish their positions and sell collectibles.

Reborn artists intermesh their childhood commitments to creating things with their familial and artistic training. This poses many forms of sideways growth.

smallwonderskyla keeps her youthful interests in dolls in tension with her schooling at the "Florence Academy in Italy" and at the "renowned Art Students' League." kendrasgarden references her college art education but associates reborning with her daughter's desire for a "lifelike baby doll" and thus with other versions of the child.[19] Joyce Moreno provides a "History of Reborning" that allows her to establish a familial lineage and personal claim to this form.[20] She "began creating what was to become known as a Reborn Baby" in 1989. During this period, artists' overproduction of poorly made porcelain dolls ruined the market and encouraged women to consider other kinds of doll production. Like other artistic lineages, which I consider in more detail in the next chapter, Moreno asserts her artistic genius and positions herself against previous and supposedly exhausted conventions. She poses herself as growing up and above other artists but her interests also point to sideways developments that keep her aligned with girls. Moreno's aunt, recognizing her skill in "portrait paintings of children," asked her to "paint" a very lifelike Berjusa doll so that it would "fool the eye" and look "alive." The resultant doll "painting techniques" that she "developed" were "brand new." Yet Moreno links newness and experimentation to the kinds of culturally approved production that validate and elevate artistic practices. She relies on what the "Old Master Oil Painters have used." Other Internet producers and sites also make claims about newness while relating their status to known cultural experiences and products.

Structures of Reborn Production

Reborn producers refer to themselves as "professional" artists as a way of emphasizing their skills and the value of their babies. For example, allenpia is a "Professional Reborn Artist" who has "taken many classes and studied multiple techniques."[21] 31857holly is an "award winning professional reborn artist" and is featured in newspapers and doll magazines.[22] In some cases, website designers support these identifications by including the term "professional" as part of their site designs for artists.[23] These claims about professionalism are notable. According to social geographer Alison L. Bain, it is difficult to distinguish professional artists because there are no requirements or credentials.[24] Reborn practitioners have tried to resolve these issues by establishing such things as guilds and instructional programs to validate their practices and vet practitioners. Guilds, which are "invitation only" and "comprised of 'select' reborn artists," establish their exclusivity and assert the skill of members by providing "Baby of the Month" and "Artist of the Month" awards.[25] Through these practices, reborn producers render more specific organizations and categories than contemporary artists who appear in metropolitan galleries and museums.

The women who participate in Internet-based reborn guilds continue early narratives about Internet communities and Internet-facilitated collaboration.[26] The eBay and Etsy sites and their sellers tactically market and emotionally identify ecommerce settings as communities. Individuals who engage in massive multiplayer online games also join guilds in order to collaboratively play and identify around shared interests and characteristics. Participants use the term "guild" to provide a history and context for these Internet organizations by referencing Medieval and earlier guilds that preserved and controlled knowledge about arts and technologies. Reborn artists indicate these guild structures and histories by posting membership badges and detailed affiliations on their ecommerce listings and personal sites. For instance, blondeambition3 informs readers that she is a CRIB guild artist. CRIB creators "are committed to perfection and aim only to produce Babies of Realism, distinctive Beauty & impeccable quality."[27] blondeambition3 uses her membership and these descriptions to assert her artistic commitment and expertise. CRIB further distinguishes members' skills with its hierarchically organized "outstanding artists" and regular "reborn artists" categories.[28] In a related manner, Life Like Reborn Artists & OOAK Babies Guild notes that it is "committed to exceptional quality and detail."[29] These guilds emphasize many of the attributes that culture associates with artistry, including passion and talent, as well as the reborn community's interest in realism.

Guilds also assure potential buyers that they watch over and vet the work of members. Some guilds engage with eBay's feedback system by placing members with negative reviews in a lower guild category or revoking their membership. CRIB members have to achieve "accreditation," "must meet or exceed Industry Standards," and "must strive for excellence in all areas of conduct & customer Service."[30] With these assurances, guilds render conceptions of the reborn industry that may be misleading because there are no overarching standards. At the same time, CRIB encourages members to "support one and other, and respect the work of all other artists and guilds." The purpose of Reborn Artists of Distinction is to "help and advise each other, to support and nurture each other," and "to protect and maintain reborning standards."[31] exceptional_reborn_nursery describes guild members providing assistance and critiquing and improving the art of members.[32] Guilds thereby constitute values and behaviors in Internet settings. Reborn producers' narratives about mothering echo these investments in support and care.

Reborn guilds recognize varied kinds of artistry. For instance, CRIB offers lists of reborn artists, sculptors, and crafters. Reborn babies used to be made over from mass produced baby dolls. Now, many of them are created from sculpts that are designed for reborning. In an article about reborn sculptors, Debra Jadick argues that there would be no reborn artists or collectors without sculptors because they are the "backbone of this industry" and produce wonderful "creations" that artists rely upon.[33] These sculpts are often made as limited editions in order to emphasize their originality and make them more valuable. Simply Reborn describes how a popular limited edition sculpt created "mass hysteria amongst the Reborn and Collecting communities as Artists and Collectors scrambled to get their dolls."[34] gregordonkey's reborn "originated from the brand new" and sold out "sculpt 'Saorise' by Bonnie Brown."[35] Artists are "clamoring to get a kit," so gregordonkey is "grateful" to "have a chance to reborn" it. Reborn artists mention sculptors, the number of sculpts produced in an edition, and the name of sculpts in order to emphasize the worth of sculpts and the role that this form plays in their work.

Some sculptors give their work to well-known artists to reborn and acknowledge shared forms of production, including the establishment of prestige. aleinapeterson is one of the many sculptors who features reborn artists' painted versions of her sculpts.[36] They are her customers as well as her best advertising. She is "very blessed and inspired to see" their "collaborative efforts in creating something so beautiful." She finds it "very touching" to view her sculpts from their position and sees what they have envisioned. aleinapeterson points to emotional collaborations and inter-reliant production communities that are related to new media conceptions of crowd sourcing. John Roberts and Stephen Wright's research highlights the political implications of such forms of shared authorship: "Collaboration is that space of interconnection between art and non-art, art and other disciplines, that continually tests the social boundaries of where, how, with what, and with whom art might be made."[37] These practices, according to Matthew Cornford and David Cross' discussion about collaboration, can challenge the "Modernist myth of the artist as solitary creative genius working in a studio."[38] There is a long history of artistic collaborations but male artistic genius has tended to be associated with uniqueness and individuality. As a kind of opposition to this, reborn artists emphasize the touching connections between reborn sculptors, artists, sellers, and babies.

Reborn artists do not level all hierarchical distinctions. They distinguish their work by referring to sculpts as "blanks." Other Internet producers also mention blanks, including nail bloggers who envision their nails as blanks and their bodies as uncoded until they produce and paint their nails. The term "blank" is used to contextualize body parts and artistry. Reborn artists ordinarily rename sculpts and thereby make blank forms and dolls into babies. kendrasgarden's reborns start as a "blank canvas."[39] Making "blank vinyl doll parts 'come to life' through the art of reborning is a source of tremendous pleasure and pride" for ariliv2.[40] While ariliv2 distinguishes her craft and the uniqueness of each baby, she also notes that one of her reborns is created "from the sold out limited edition 'Sharlamae' sculpt by talented sculptor Bonnie Brown." Sculpts ordinarily start as individual objects that are cast and made into multiples while reborn artists indicate that they make multiples unique. Reborn babies are identified as "one of a kind" or "OOAK" even though they share some features and an undergirding structure when the same kit is employed. ullej-13 dismisses challenges to the individuality of her artworks by explaining that reborning "is about creating the ultimate in realism through a variety of applications and particular attention to the finer details" that separate "one baby from another, making every baby a UNIQUE ONE OF A KIND CREATION!!"[41] elitecharms asserts that "No two babies can ever be the same."[42] These reborn artists undermine some of the more conceptually challenging aspects of their practices, including their creation from other artistic works and multiples, when they emphasize the uniqueness of crafted babies.[43]

Reborn artists establish the value of their work and position reborns as creative objects and babies. For instance, hannahelizabethearle conflates collectible objects and children. She tells readers that her "baby is now a collectable piece of art and should not be handled in any way you would not handle a real newborn baby."[44] shesgothelp offers a "wonderful Adult collectible baby."[45] Artists initially argued that reborning made toys into collectibles but they currently contrast these states since their process now usually starts with kits, and thus with proto-reborns, rather than with dolls that they will refurbish. For instance, ana3628's reborn "IS NOT A TOY." She is "PROUD OF INTRODUCING THIS BEAUTIFUL BABY BOY."[46] These shifts from toys to babies also allow reborn artists to articulate collectors as adults. bonniesbabies' reborn "is no longer intended as a toy for young children, but as a collectible for mature mommies."[47] littleheartsnursery offers "collectible works of art" that "should be handled only by those mature enough to handle real babies."[48] Artists try to distinguish between adult mothers who can care for reborn babies and children but their articulation of reborns are reliant on connections between children's and adults' performances and thus on sideways interests.

Constituting Women as Intensive Mothers

Artists indicate that dolls are alive and in need of mothering and thereby urge buyers to become mothers, commit to intensive childcare, and imagine touching and caring for babies. Women are encouraged to mother dolls. They are also more broadly asked to constitute themselves as mothers and hold babies in their arms. The connections that reborn artists establish between women and mothers are not surprising since, as Terry Arendell notes, "mothering has been presumed to be a primary identity for most adult women," especially since the nineteenth century.[49] Societal and media discourses encourage many Western women to be mothers and embrace intensive mothering. Women are informed that to be good mothers they have to personally spend a considerable amount of money, time, energy, and intellectual effort on raising their children. Susan J. Douglas and Meredith W. Michaels critique cultural assertions that women are the best caretakers and should completely dedicate themselves to the needs of their children.[50] However, this renders conceptions of motherhood that are impossible for women to fulfill. These expectations are especially difficult for women who have educational goals, other family responsibilities, careers, and limited incomes. Sharon Hays points to the unreasonable burdens that are placed on contemporary mothers because raising children is believed to necessitate professionalized skills and endless energy.[51] These cultural views and reborn narratives encourage women to become unconditionally subject to the will of the child or children and eschew career and personal desires that do not focus on childcare. Of course, reborn artists render ties to children and produced objects. They thereby continue and amplify certain conceptions of motherhood as marketing strategies while arguing for women's investments in other things.

Artists validate their identities and buyers by relating the processes of nurturing physical children to the experiences of owning and caring for reborn babies. Reborn artists indicate that mothers should spend a lot of time with these babies and groom their hair, clean and feed them (and many reborns come with diapers and bottles), hold and cuddle them, care for them when they are ill, shop for clothing and other items, and dress them. Reborn babies thereby provide one stand-in, at least within reborn culture, for social expectations that women should have babies and for some women's related feelings of loss and identificatory displacement when they do not have young children who recognize and need them. Artists promise to resolve individuals' personal and affective desires to be mothers. They facilitate women's forward momentum and process of growing up when asking, "Could this be the 'BABY' of your DREAMS?"[52] myforeverstory welcomes viewers to "Dream Baby Nursery" where viewers "will meet the most beautiful and lovely baby" of their "dreams!"[53] These artists indicate that women should fantasize about babies and that not engaging with these forms of motherhood and childcare is dream destroying. However, Stockton relates dreams to backward births and the reproduction of "childhood motives that cause the dream."[54] Reborn dreams are related to cultural notions about women's roles but they also bring women to a version of their childhood where dolls are babies. This occurs when kandybaby60 indicates that her reborn is "Not meant for small children, but the lil girl in all of us."[55] She genders engagements with reborns and suggests that they stimulate women's ghostly girl-child identities.

Reborn artists inform women that their mothering roles are perpetual, or could be. Women are "forever" mommies and supporters of "FOREVER ANGELS KEPT EVERLASTING"—babies who will always require care and never leave or grow.[56] Images of reborn babies crying, looking fragile, and otherwise expressing a need for love and care underscore these never-ending requirements and bonds. For instance, Kessa Lynn "calls" for viewers to "Look at my cute toes," "Look at my cute smile," "There is my cute tummy," and "Pick me up Mommy!"[57] Such renderings of cuteness, accompanied by images of babies with big eyes, oversized heads, and perpetually bent stubby legs, which prevent them from doing anything, work to trigger viewers' compassion and willingness to provide assistance.[58] Kessa Lynn continues her appeal for parental love and informs viewers, "This is my small owey! Mommy poked my forehead but didn't mean to! I'm still very cute and my beautiful hair covers it up! You still love me…right?" Through such texts, viewers are asked to choose between saving reborn babies and being bad mothers. They are directed to look so that they will feel. They are also summoned as mothers and thereby scripted into this position.

The pleas of Kessa Lynn and other reborn babies are affective and temporal binds, which are designed to connect women to intensive reborn mothering. Artists also relate intensive care giving to the large amounts of time they spend crafting babies and being mother-producers. Stay-at-home mothers who sell things on eBay and Etsy also tactically deploy these chronicles of long-term affective labor, or the persistent emotional aspects of work that are usually undervalued. tinylovenursery spends many "hours bringing" the baby to life. For her, "creating reborns is a true labor of love."[59] Producers suffer for art and for the sake of children. However, these artists claim to push the limits of bodily labor. For instance, bonniesbabies "painstakingly added just one hair at a time with the smallest possible needle."[60] Reborn artists also use the term "painstakingly" to describe the intense processes of painting dolls "by hand over many weeks" and inserting "hand rooted" eyelashes.[61] These intense commitments point to the exhausting and cyclic processes of childcare and endurance-based artworks in which individuals commit long periods of time to repetitive and painful practices as a means of foregrounding and transcending the body.

Reborn artists mention the large amounts of patience required to build up layers of paint and micro-root hair in order to represent the value of reborns, which take time rather than being manufactured or quickly made. These temporalities also stand in for feminine reproduction and crafting. Reborn layers are sedimentary processes that are supposed to be acknowledged and to meld into mothers' experiences with babies and skin. In reborning, each layer of paint ordinarily has to be heat cured before the next one is applied. dar790 uses "layer after layer of Genesis heat set paints to achieve the beautiful newborn skin tones."[62] For SonjaG, "Reborning is a time-consuming but very rewarding artform. And it is so magical to see a plain vinyl doll transform into a \'baby\' with each brush stroke and layer of paint."[63] The last layers, according to hollhollart, bring about a "HUGE transformation. Blood actually seems to start flowing through those little vessels."[64] These reborns are "carefully weighted in layers of All NEW materials" that let their bodies "shift and move" as they are handled.[65] Through these temporal commitments, reborn producers create life and render themselves as artistic mothers. The bodies of reborn participants also move against time and cultural conceptions of humanness, as they become mothers to crafted babies.

Reborn artists identify their process as painful labor that is done for love. This connects the work of reborn producers to other forms of affective labor and to women who are birthing babies. For texasbanditcat, "Creating" reborn babies "is truly a labor of love."[66] It takes her "many hours to produce a beautiful baby" and, as most participants know, they "make very little in labor." Sending them to "their new Mommy's and Daddy's and reading" their comments is the "real payment for all the hours of labor." These reborn artists, in a manner that is related to cultural mandates for intensive mothering, assert that they painfully and generously labor for mothers and babies. They also evoke the practices of stay-at-home mothers who are ecommerce sellers and disavow the economic aspects of their businesses. This encourages buyers to identify these women as mothers rather than companies and justifies reborn sales. All of this allows reborn artists to figure their babies as emotional bodies that are brought to life through love. These actions, as I suggest in more detail in the following sections, connect sellers and buyers in emotional exchanges.

Physically Hailing and Emotionally Feeling

Reborn artists present babies in need so that viewers experience emotional calls to take care of them. Reborn affect, like other embodied states, situates individuals in circuits of "feeling and response."[67] This includes sticky and drooling babies who need to be cleaned, prematurely born babies who are frail and may die, crying babies who want to be cuddled, and tiny babies who individuals can hold in their hands. magicmom2 depicts a reborn who "even has drool coming down his cheek from being so upset" [Figure 2.2].[68] In addition to the tears and saliva, the baby's eyes are screwed shut and mouth open in a call for attention. magicmom2 asks, "Look at this face, don't you just want to hold her in your arms?" magicmom2 supports these desires with images of her holding the child's hand and cradling the head. The hands of these reborn artists and babies establish an interpersonal relationship, since a "hand is not a mere neutral body part; rather, it also expresses intimacy."[69] Designers and programmers support these forms of intimacy and touching with hand-pointers and other depictions that render physical connections with and through the interface.

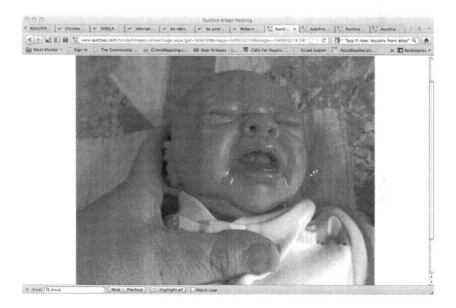

FIGURE 2.2 Auctiva. Crying reborns call for mothers to comfort them.

Reborn viewers are hailed and constituted as caring mothers by these represented hands and the gestures and textures of reborn babies. Reborn artists encourage these forms of identification and affective responses by having their babies say, "Mommy, I need a hug."[70] Buyers "turn around," reacting to and being produced by these texts, by bidding on listings, buying reborn babies, and providing supportive comments and reviews of these collectibles.[71] They respond and identify as "happy to be a new mommy."[72] Philosopher Rebecca Kukla associates such forms of hailing and interpellation with an authority figure calling out an individual's name. The person responds with a raised hand and says, "here."[73] This production of the other through self-recognition is supported by verbal addresses and hand gestures that engage, reply, point, and render. Kukla also argues, "all sorts of objects can have an interpellative voice, in virtue of being constituted and encountered as authoritative, citational representatives of the normative social order."[74] Reborn artists and babies enact these interpellative voices. By responding to these hails, buyers are implicated in the normative practices of motherhood and consent to be bound by these rules. These forms of call and response are common aspects of reborn representations. Yet, as I have suggested earlier in this chapter, producers' and buyers' interests in reborns also diverge from normative conceptions of femininity by asserting female forms of artistry and by mothering babies who are collectible dolls.

Reborn babies are depicted with their hands raised and with their hands and bodies in contact. For instance, the flexed fingers and raised limbs of silvertreenursery's baby hail the mother.[75] The directional nap of a fur rug meshes with the baby's extended limbs and emphasizes its physical call. Tousled hair and unkempt clothing function as a kind of cry for maintenance and care. In pigotts*playpen_05's listing, a chubby hand with extended finger and thumb is framed against a slightly fuzzy background. The accompanying call is intensified because pigotts*playpen_05 informs the viewer that she expects the reborn baby's "hand to reach out for" hers.[76] madelynn1 further captures this interpellative call and response. She reaches out for a tiny reborn fist and the baby holds her finger in its hand.[77] Through such gestures, a version of the mother touches and cares for babies.

Reborn artists arrange reborn bodies and image textures as a means of hailing mothers and conveying the experiences of physically touching and passionately feeling babies and other things. Sedgwick poses that a "particular intimacy seems to subsist between textures and emotions," a nexus that is conveyed by the dual meanings of the terms "touching" and "feeling."[78] "Touch and emotionally felt feelings overlap," according to Sue L. Cataldi, so that texture and tactility are affective aspects of engagements.[79] Reborn artists also use the physical hails of reborn babies to render gendered and positioned emotional feelings. This suggests that physically touching and emotionally feeling play a part in producing specific subjects. Reborn artists evoke these meshed experiences by deploying soft and fuzzy textures in order to remind hailed mothers about past instances of touching, including the feeling of fabrics, hair, and skin under fingertips and the emotional feelings that accompany them. For instance, reborn artist micheleismyname prefers "soft and sweet, babyish outfits that are nice to the touch."[80] Artists use fabrics that have a nap or hand and refer to reborns' plastic bodies as "soft vinyl" and "Extra Soft Baby Skin."[81] In doing this, they equate buyers' experiences of physically touching reborns to being mothers and feeling babies.

madelynn1 connects physically touching and hailing to emotionally feeling through the tactile surfaces of soft focus images, blurred borders, a textured bedspread, messed-up hair, and the folds of a baby's sleeper, which frame the centered vignette of the baby and mother holding hands.[82] The hail to mothers and possibility of "falling" in love are intensified because radiating folds, which are generated by the weight of the baby's body, create a cleft, direct the gaze, and enfold viewers. Through these images, reborn artists constitute mothers and situate them in the image. In bluejeanene62's images of triplets, babies and viewers are wrapped in softly colored and textured fabrics and joined together by a sinuous series of material folds.[83] The artist's depictions of babies holding each other, children reaching out with small arms, and the highly activated and folded surfaces connect babies' and mothers' bodies in physical and emotional arrangements. Such images support artists' claims about reborns because babies look more alive when they are in contact with themselves and the world. In addition, these enfoldments figure a version of the maternal body "inside" as well as in front of the screen. They create backwards births and temporal as well as material folds where individuals are drawn into images and mothers' creases. Reborn artists constitute viewers as mothers as a means of articulating babies and collectors who never fully grow up.

The hailing and production of mothers is especially visceral in instances where babies are depicted as disabled or ill. Reborn artists portray premature or preemie babies. For instance, *reborn_babies* informs prospective mothers, "Not all of the baby's circulation has developed completely, thus displaying the bluish cast to areas of his face and limbs."[84] These light-skinned preemie babies exhibit gray and blue undertones that are distinct from the peach and pink skin that are culturally coded as healthy and beautiful and that many reborn artists prefer. Preemie artists render realness and hail mothers by posing a more precarious form of liveness. They portray babies in hospital settings and wrap them in medical tubing. For instance, cherib603's reborn preemie comes "home 'on oxygen' to help" her "breathe."[85] cream-puff-nursery cradles her reborn's tiny head, which is equipped with a nasal cannula for oxygen, and torso in her glove-clad hand and underscores the baby's precarious health.[86] These reborn preemies are touched and touching because they rest in artists' large hands.

Representations of mothers' hands engaging with babies transfer materiality and embodiment between one form and the other. These experiences, like other affective engagements, place individuals in a circuit of physical and emotional feelings and responses. Through such "felt feelings," as Cataldi suggests, "we sense that our flesh is open and that our bodies are intermingled with the bodies of others and with the body of the world."[87] Hailing becomes a physical process of constituting each other through touch. Reborn artists such as cherishedangelsanddolls foreground such interconnections and argue, "BABIES ARE CREATED WITH MY HANDS TO YOUR HEART."[88] The artist's unusual phrasing suggests her hands feel, know, rest on, and make the buyer's heart. Women are thereby connected through artistry and the experience of hands touching and reworking everything. These heartfelt experiences are underscored by images of hearts that are imprinted on clothing and medical equipment. Hands transform dolls into flesh and viewers into mothers, display the highly realistic aspects of reborn art, evoke affective experiences, and stand in for mothers. This occurs when the artist ne1_4_a_baby holds her reborn preemie, which is entangled in medical tubing and wires, in her hand and thereby emphasizes its smallness and frailty [Figure 2.3].[89] However, ne1_4_a_baby also holds up its tiny feet to illustrate her painting skill. The visible veining in her hand testifies to the more detailed veins and capillaries that she has rendered on the doll's scalp and eyelids. fjords4me extends her hand so that the palm is visible and the thumb and index finger support the baby's head.[90] Yet fjords4me holds her hand in a way that signifies "look at this." In these instances, touching moves between proud artistry and impassioned mothering. Through such actions, reborn producers emphasize their creativity and women's and feminine practices.

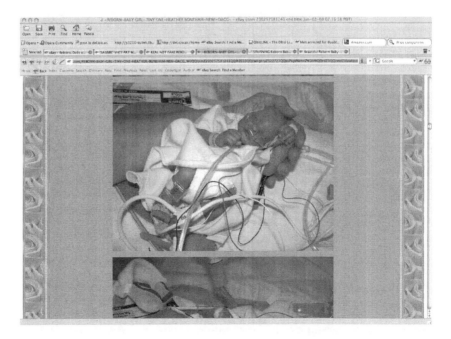

FIGURE 2.3 eBay. Reborn preemies are pictured as ill and in need of care.

Retouching Whiteness

Reborn artists tend to race their conceptions of touching. There are numerous images of light-skinned hands caressing white babies who are swaddled in soft and pale fabrics. The tufts of fuzzy white fabric, which envelope janice.fricker's reborn baby, act as fingers, foreground her hands caressing the child, and render a white affective world [Figure 2.4].[91] Reborn producers also tend to make white dolls and to associate peaches-and-cream complexions and pale skin with beauty. maggibloom argues that her reborn "has beautiful peaches and cream skin tone."[92] A "custom blend of quality paints in a peaches and cream skintone" gives nneecie's reborn a "life like baby glow" and allows her to connect pale skin to liveliness.[93] By rendering such depictions, artists continue privileging softness and whiteness, which have long been identified as ideals of Western beauty.[94] Nevertheless, the production of light and pale premature babies also associates whiteness with illness and death.

There are some reborn artists who explore conceptions of whiteness by describing the diverse colors that constitute Caucasian skin tones and the array of skin colors. sweetpeagardendolls still identifies peaches and cream complexions as beautiful but notes that the materials she uses "come in several different flesh tones."[95] She uses "more than one to make each baby" because "No real baby is all the same skin tone all over their body." tajh007 further points to the mutability of skin color and identity positions. Her reborn "started out as a peach kit but now she is a beautiful biracial baby girl."[96] tajh007 retouches reborns in a manner

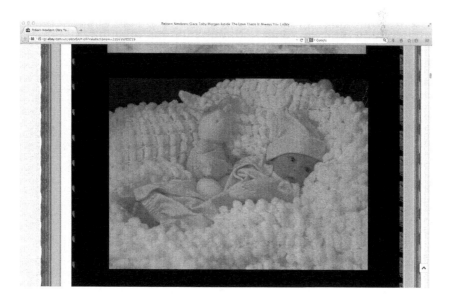

FIGURE 2.4 eBay. The textural aspects of reborn images evoke white fingers and touching.

that is related to women modifying their skin color through cosmetics, skin lighteners, and tanning. The term "retouching" suggests the ways these reborn artists render physical and emotional feelings, including the touch of brushes on skin, the corporeal sensations that are triggered by these reborns, and material changes in reborns' appearance. Reborn artists' retouching practices demonstrate that the racial positions of reborn babies are easily altered but they could further address the ways race is produced and conceptualized in these settings.

Some reborn artists pose alternative conceptions of attractiveness by describing "Beautiful light caramel skin tones" and a "stunning golden Afro /Caribbean complexion."[97] While "Caucasian Peach" and "Caucasian Pink" reborn kits are the standard and deviate from cultural categories by articulating two categories of whiteness, sculptors are increasingly offering "beautiful, biracial vinyl color."[98] Unfortunately, these offerings for "biracial" kits are related to whiteness because they include Caucasian skin color samples for "comparison purposes."[99] These biracial babies are also disassociated from the myriad of heritages and skin colors that are present in society. They are used to render light-skinned black children who are categorized as "ethnic" and distinguished as different. Reborn artists do not associate Caucasian identity with ethnic heritages or attributes. The specific heritages of Asian babies are rarely mentioned and they are stereotyped as having an "Asian Expression" and narrower eye shapes.[100] In one of the few considerations of these practices, silveroaktrading notes that she described her reborn as "biracial" but "was getting messages that she was" too "light to be biracial."[101] She tells viewers that they can identify the reborn as "biracial or not" but the baby "is more tan" than her "regular babies." silveroaktrading acknowledges different conceptions of skin color and racial identity. At the same time, she establishes pale reborns as being the "regular" form of beautiful babies. These artists foreground their fabrication of reborn babies and skin and offer some limited interventions into the privileging of whiteness in Internet settings. Without assertions about the complexity of skin color, including the foregrounding of undead and ill forms of whiteness, the aesthetic preferences of reborn producers threaten to continue the ongoing structuration of whiteness as the norm and ideal.

Producing Gender and Sex

Reborn artists, in a manner that is related to their production of race, establish babies' gender and sex positions. Reborn babies, who are produced from doll kits, have provisional genders when sculptors choose gender-coded names to represent them and use pronouns to convey the potentialities of reborn dolls and babies. Reborn artists change the names of sculpts in order to highlight their creation of new artistic objects and people. Some reborn artists also indicate that their babies could be the "opposite" gender and offer to change it for buyers. bhsgurl2013's "baby was created as a girl but can most certainly be changed into a boy!"[102]

Baby Ryan "can be a boy or a girl depending on the clothes you" choose to "dress it in."[103] These reborn artists propose that gender changes are instances of wardrobe or cosmetic alterations. Their comments point to a number of provocative questions, which reflect on cultural conceptions, about how the gender and sex of reborn babies are conceptualized and established. Reborn babies' genders can be understood as a series of cultural traits. The sex of babies is linked to specific genital features. Of course, reborns' genitals are produced by sculptors and artists and should be, but are not always, associated with gender rather than biological attributes. Feminist theorists, intersex and transgender advocates, and a range of other individuals have interrogated conceptions of natural sex and the ways scientists, doctors, lawyers, the state, and other institutions produce and regulate sex identifications and categories.[104] It would be useful to keep these vital inquiries in conversation with the ways "sex" is produced in varied objects.

Reborn artists produce sex when making "belly plates" with genital features. Even belly plates that are "NOT ANATOMICALLY CORRECT" suggest that there are reborn babies with detailed genitals.[105] "Anatomically correct" belly plates are supposed to allow artists and collectors to articulate the binary sex of reborns and distinguish between girls with labias and boys with penises. In addition, belly plates detail umbilical cords or provide detachable umbilical sections. These renderings of genitals and umbilical cords articulate the biological processes of reproduction and render reborn dolls more baby-like. Bonnie Brown indicates that these features give "dolls their individuality."[106] They also allow participants to push up and away the clothing of reborn babies. This makes it seem as if babies have wiggled out of things as part of their lively engagements. Yet reborn artists photographically portray these plates with posed and staged representations rather than action images. Thus, these features figure reborn artists and collectors as producers and facilitators of genital displays. They make the bodies of reborn babies more available to viewers. While not represented as erotic, these unveilings of reborn babies' "nude" bodies, which are not naked since there are doeskin forms under the belly plates, are unsettling. Reborn babies' genitals and plates contrarily appear to be too real because of their abrupt unveilings and perform as detachable parts that demonstrate the provisional features of gender and sex.

Reborn artists use graphical bows, butterflies, and other images to highlight and hide reborn babies' vinyl genitals. These practices of elision, which conceal something that is supposed to be but is not fleshy genitals, are represented as modesty conventions. Given the seeming humanness of depictions of reborn babies, these practices may protect artists and viewers from being identified as child pornographers and porn viewers. Partially blocked photographs are also images of reborn artists' investments in and constructions of reborn dolls as babies. The producers replace one constructed and somewhat fantastical genital creation with another body construct. In addition, their cartoon images tend to distinguish the genital area as much as they hide it. Thus, reborn artists create hybrid parts that are produced from multiple representations and objects. For instance, mummelbaerchen covers over her male reborn's genitals with an image of a powder blue but still somewhat feminine butterfly.[107] The long ovoid center of the butterfly aligns with the doll's penis and prints a seemingly concave labial and vaginal core over the folded but presumably convex genitals. It pushes in what is expected to stand out. In doing this, it reshapes the corporeal three-dimensionality of the baby.

Reborn artists use a variety of strategies to force the multiple material features of reborn babies into binary gender categories and leave their gender open to different readings. jessicasclaybabies genders her reborn as male by using pronouns, gendered narratives, blue clothing, and sports paraphernalia.[108] In one image, the reborn docilely cuddles with a teddy bear that matches and melts into his tan fleece slippers. The stuffed animal figures a contemporary moment for the reborn as a mutable and cuddly representation—a baby that is and is not a baby as the bear is a teddy but is not the animal called a bear. Yet the reborn is also associated with masculine athletic activity and has a football resting near him. The football figures a future for him, a growing up that will not happen. It references such gender performances as playing sports that the reborn is associated with but cannot enact. jessicasclaybabies further connects him to normative masculinity by indicating he is "all boy for sure" and like "'typical' boys, he already has a scrape on his leg" and "loves playing around!" She associates boyness with such masculine characteristics as activity and mischievousness. She also recontextualizes his scrape and damage as gender and sex traits.

Reborn artists' "All boy" and "all girl" indicate that reborns occupy binary gender and sex positions. They also suggest that some reborns, and perhaps other figures, cannot fit into this structure and are not all one gender or sex. snowball1994 conveys both of these positions when stating, "Dylan has a full vinyl body that is ALL BOY" and that his gender and sex are male.[109] However, her reference to Dylan's vinyl form of boyness highlights his plastic production and elasticity. While snowball1994 insists on Dylan's embodied sex, she does not indicate the specificities of his body and therefore leaves the category of boy open. mmoody7918's reborn "HAS A FULL VINYL TORSO (ALL BOY)" that she supports with images of him wearing a blue knit beanie and a genital belly plate. "TUCKED INSIDE" his belly and genitals "IS A SOFT DOE SUEDE BODY."[110] mmoody7918 locates a soft "INSIDE," or a feminized space, under the masculine body and male genitals. The belly and genitals are made into a kind of pocket that holds and gives way to another experience. Like reborn artists' images of pleated and hollowed fabrics and their conflation of concave cartoon bits and convex genitals, she creates vaginal folds that mix up boys' "all boy." Thus, reborn artists' belly plates and related constructions have a normative force and trouble gender and sex formations at the very point where these artists are trying to buttress the veracity of their babies and the sex/gender system.

Conclusion: The Generative Nana and Growing Sideways

Reborn artists produce genitals and babies, which mainstream society often associates with reproduction. Yet artists pose more mature generative women and produce babies who will never grow up or have corporeal children. These artists thus challenge some of the cultural conceptions about women's life stages and, as Rosemary Betterton indicates in her research on maternal representations, the ways the medical establishment and media have pathologized "older" pregnant women.[111] Most mature women, irrespective of how they have become pregnant, are identified as self-centered and abnormal. However, reborn producers depict more mature women as appropriate producers of children and identify as mothers and nanas with babies. For instance, connjean1958's babies come from "Nana Connie's Reborn Nursery."[112] texasbanditcat is a "grand mother" who makes babies.[113] She and other reborn artists enmesh creative and reproductive activities by using terms such as "make."

Reborn collectors also combine creative and reproductive processes by producing YouTube videos and other texts about being "Reborn Pregnant."[114] Women use this phrase to recontextualize their experiences of buying reborns and waiting for postal deliveries of babies. They grow sideways in narrating inventive pregnancies and births that echo childhood imaginings and adult interests in being mothers and doll caretakers. Some of them support these pleasurable constructions of reproductive adulthood, which a group of these women have experienced and others imagine, with depictions of their literal sideways growth in the form of fabricated pregnant bellies that they show from varied angles.[115] Women also create video montages of pregnant bellies, ultrasounds, and baby announcements in order to produce histories for their reborn children.[116] Their delay of what is deemed fully adult, including intrauterine pregnancies and births, and recrafting of pleasurable versions of childhood are underscored by donalynn's indication that reborns "ARE REALLY MADE FOR US GROWN UP CHILDREN."[117] While descriptions of women engaging with toys are ordinarily employed to dismiss and embarrass them, the individuals who are involved in reborn culture support adult interests in children's things.

Reborn participants adopt some traditional narratives concerning motherhood while refusing to follow all of the cultural indications about appropriate life stages and behaviors. Unsympathetic depictions of their practices include Victoria Silver's *My Fake Baby* documentary from 2008, which made the processes of reborning better known.[118] Silver portrays women treating their reborn dolls like children and replacing an absent grandchild with a reborn replica. There are also numerous journalistic accounts of reborn culture that over-report the number of women who engage with reborn babies because of their deceased children. These reborn dolls disturb understandings of the human. They are often misrecognized as babies when left in cars and other places, women describe them as babies, the boundary distinctions between mother and child are not maintained, and women purportedly deviate from human behaviors in mothering them.

Contemporary culture tends to ridicule women, especially older women, for caring for dolls but reborn babies emotionally touch the people who deride them. What "is intriguing," according to jcorn, "is how intensely people feel about" reborn dolls.[119] People's passionate reactions to reborns include moments of discomfort that happen across the skin and through the body. For Mara, "these human recreations" produce "the heebie jeebies" and "shivers."[120] caraMel gets "the heebie jeebies" because "they are so real looking!"[121] Klingon_Mama responds to their realism with an "Ewww."[122] In a critical assessment of the "Eew! Factor," Muriel Dimen defines it as "an excited disgust."[123] Such intense affects infuse the body with unwelcome feelings and movements. Some viewers shiver and shudder because reborn babies look dead and like tiny corpses. For Julia Kristeva, the corpse is "a border that has encroached on everything."[124] This abjection is intensified when corpses are small and cannot be explained by life courses that have been lived. For instance, haguenite learns about "Lifelike" reborns and responds with an "Eeeee! Creepy, dead-looking bubbies!"[125] Like reborns, corpses are disruptive because they are lifelike and close to people's experiential positions.

Viewers imagine reborns as similar to and physically proximate to their bodies. They envision holding reborns because these babies, and young corporeal children, call for care. However, this closeness also allows individuals to more fully conceptualize reborns as wrong. For Rich Edmondson, the reborn "simulates the sensation of carrying around a dead newborn."[126] Trend Hunter describes reborn babies as "freakishly lifelike dolls" whose "skin is cold," which causes some to compare them to "holding dead babies."[127] With these formulations, reborn artists are loosely associated with the most socially condemned kind of women—mothers who allow their children to die or kill them. Abby O'Reilly continues this construction of monstrous women when comparing a reborn artist's home to a "mortuary, bursting with tiny arms and legs waiting to be forged by Frankenstein into something resembling a human."[128] Like Kristeva, these viewers imagine death infecting the life around it. They worry that women will improperly render a form of monstrous aliveness rather than "properly" reproducing. As part of these individuals' refusals of what they identify as intimate but also improper, they express physical sensations that have been codified in horror film viewing as combinations of pleasure and discomfort. The other women's production cultures that I study deploy similar horror affects as ways of emphasizing their embodied experiences with feminine positions.

Reborn artists reference horror by producing undead reborns, including vampire and zombie babies. This also allows them to further stall childhood and render versions of growing sideways. For instance, Bean Shanine and her detailed renderings of undead reborns have been featured in numerous journalistic reports. Journalist Jill Reilly identifies Shanine as an "eccentric artist" who "is making a living out of the dead."[129] Reilly's phrasing suggests that Shanine is monstrously living off of the dead and turning the dead into the living. Shanine also emphasizes other forms of baby growth and non-biological maternal identifications by calling her shop "The Twisted Bean Stalk Nursery" and indicating that this site is where "reborn babies grow on their twisted little vines."[130] Through this phrasing, Shanine playfully codes babies as contorted and mothers as perverse. Of course, Reilly's and Shanine's representations may be misleading and encourage the kinds of close readings that Johnson itemizes.[131] All reborn artists make their living out of things that are not alive because their babies are collectible dolls. Shanine further twists society's identification of reborns as death-like and disturbing.

Shanine made the first of her "creepy monster babies" for a friend who takes part in zombie walks where people collaboratively enact undead positions in public settings.[132] This phenomenon, which I study later in this book, allows people to explore forms of embodiment where they are stalled at not quite dead. Whether they are typical reborns or Shanine's undead, these babies are understood as alive and not living affective objects that are designed to be pleasurably and eerily "soft and very easy to snuggle."[133] Shanine highlights the deathly softness and paleness of her babies with white fur and pastel clothing. At first glance, her visual effects seem to propose a world of Caucasian innocence and purity. However, small fangs punctuate the tender mouths of Shanine's vampire babies. These undead reborns, like sometimes-uncontrollable children, promise to bite because they are not innocent or ruled by reason.

Reborn artists propose intermediate states of living, including their affection for something that is seen as a baby and a collectible doll. They refuse the kinds of regimented and developmental behaviors that are expected of women. Instead, they propose other forms of growth and visions of babies. While their mandates for intensive mothering are worrying, their call to mother dolls and art objects at least partially diffuses the force of these normative feminine summonses. Reborn artists use narratives and traditional conceptions of mothers to create an unusual position for women. They deploy the role of mother-producers to establish the legitimacy of reborn artists and art practices and the possibilities for other kinds of growing in and through Internet cultures and society. These women have grown an elaborate reborn culture and women's artistic production by keeping their babies at the same age.

Notes

1. Kimberly McClung, "Beach Babies Reborn Nursery," 17 September 2013, http://www.beachbabiesreborns.com/
2. beachbabies2014, "Reborn Baby Doll Micro Preemie Boy/Girl From Tamie Yarie's Jack sculpt/Ltd. ed.! From Reborn Artist and Sculptor Kimberly McClung/ BBRON," eBay, 24 May 2013, 2 July 2014, http://www.ebay.com/itm/Reborn-Baby-Doll-Micro-Preemie-Boy-Girl-From-Tamie-Yaries-Jack-sculpt-Ltd-ed-/171044654315?pt=US_Dolls_Bears_Toys&hash=item27d30e4ceb

3. Sedgwick, *Touching Feeling*.
4. Althusser, "Ideology and Ideological State Apparatuses"; Butler, *Psychic Life of Power*.
5. dbick4, "Asian Reborn Baby Kameko by Tasha Edenholm now Lynne: Doreen's Butterfly Kisses Nursery/ MR Hair/GHSP*2 Cute," eBay, 8 September 2010, http://cgi.ebay.com/Asian-Reborn-Baby-Kameko-Tasha-Edenholm-now-Lynne-/300464402404?pt=LH_DefaultDomain_0&hash=item45f512efe4
6. Althusser, "Ideology and Ideological State Apparatuses," 105.
7. Butler, *Psychic Life of Power*, 106.
8. Ibid., 107.
9. therenewreuserecycle2014, "Adopt Me! REBORN BERENGUER GIRL BABY PERFECT FOR EASTER Blue eyes," eBay, 21 May 2014, http://www.ebay.com/itm/Adopt-Me-REBORN-BERENGUER-GIRL-BABY-PERFECT-FOR-EASTER-Blue-eyes-/271491084249?pt=LH_DefaultDomain_0&hash=item3f36212fd9
10. smallwonderskyla, "Small Wonders Kyla eBay Store About My Store," eBay, 15 September 2013, http://members.ebay.com/ws/eBayISAPI.dll?ViewUserPage&userid=smallwonderskyla
11. Johnson, "Teaching Deconstructively."
12. Taylor, "Negotiating Oppositions and Uncertainties," 356.
13. Siles, "Web Technologies."
14. gogirlusa, "eBay View About Me for gogirlusa," eBay, 21 June 2014, http://members.ebay.com/ws/eBayISAPI.dll?ViewUserPage&userid=gogirlusa
15. Judy Burrell, "About the Artist," Baby Kisses Nursery, 21 June 2014, http://www.judysrebornbabies.com/aboutme.htm
16. Stockton, *Queer Child*, 4.
17. smallwonderskyla, "Small Wonders Kyla eBay Store About My Store," eBay, 15 September 2013, http://members.ebay.com/ws/eBayISAPI.dll?ViewUserPage&userid=smallwonderskyla
18. Nochlin, *Women, Art, and Power*; Pollock, *Vision and Difference*. More recently, Tracey Emin, Mary Kelly, Alison Lapper, Cindy Sherman, Nancy Spero, and numerous other artists have depicted and interrogated women's positions as artists and mothers.
19. kendrasgarden, "Kendra's Garden Babies eBay Store About My Store," eBay, 21 June 2014, http://members.ebay.com/ws/eBayISAPI.dll?ViewUserPage&userid=kendrasgarden
20. Joyce Moreno, "History of Reborning," Sweet Dreams Baby Nursery, 7 October 2010, http://www.sweetdreamsbabynursery.com/AboutTheArtist2007.html
21. allenpia, "NB SIZE- REBORN BABY BOY FROM LAURA LEE EAGLES 'TRISTAN'- SLUMBERLAND MOHAIR," eBay, 1 March 2014, http://www.ebay.com/itm/NB-SIZE-REBORN-BABY-BOY-FROM-LAURA-LEE-EAGLES-TRISTAN-SLUMBERLAND-MOHAIR-/291086577645?pt=LH_DefaultDomain_0&hash=item43c61cafed
22. 31857holly, "Gorgeous Reborn Baby Girl SAMMIE S. Rawn **FREE SHIPPING** Canada & USA," eBay, 1 March 2014, http://www.ebay.com/itm/Gorgeous-Reborn-Baby-Girl-SAMMIE-S-Rawn-FREE-SHIPPING-Canada-USA-/291086789543?pt=LH_DefaultDomain_0&hash=item43c61feba7
23. Reborn Websets & Designs, "Reborn Websets & Designs Home," 23 May 2013, http://www.rebornwebsets.com/; Natalie Headlam, "~ Little Acre's Nursery by Professional Reborn Artist Natalie Headlam ~," Little Acre's Nursery, 23 May 2013, http://littleacresnursery.com/custom.html
24. Bain, "Constructing an Artistic Identity."
25. Terri Crisp, "Tips for buying a Quality Reborn," Sons Hobby Reborns, 7 October 2010, http://sonshobbyreborns.com/sonsReborns/index.php?option=com_content&view=article&id=6&Itemid=6

26. Rheingold, *Virtual Community*.
27. CRIB, as quoted in blondeambition3, "Sculpted Awake ERIN Fake Baby Reborn Art Doll by Eve: Truly OOAK - $300 starting bid with NO RESERVE!" eBay, 22 May 2011, 21 June 2014, http://cgi.ebay.com/Sculpted-Awake-ERIN-Fake-Baby-Reborn-Art-Doll-Eve-/160585897389?pt=LH_DefaultDomain_0&hash=item2563aa55ad
28. CRIB, "CRIB REBORN GUILD," CRIB Reborn Guild, 20 September 2013, http://cribrebornguild.webs.com/Artists.htm
29. Life Like Reborn Artists & OOAK Babies Guild, as quoted in Rosies Baby Patch, "Links Affiliations & Awards," 20 September 2013, http://www.rosiesbabypatch.com/links.html
30. CRIB, "www.cribrebornguild.co.uk," CRIB Reborn Guild, 20 September 2013, www.cribrebornguild.co.uk
31. Reborn Artists of Distinction, as quoted in Rosies Baby Patch, "Links Affiliations & Awards," 20 September 2013, http://www.rosiesbabypatch.com/links.html
32. exceptional_reborn_nursery, "Reborn Guilds," eBay, 21 September 2013, http://www.ebay.co.uk/gds/Reborn-Guilds-/10000000001623599/g.html
33. Debra Jadick, "Sculpting with Gela of Gela's Wonderful World of Babies," Examiner.com, 1 July 2012, 13 May 2013, http://www.examiner.com/article/sculpting-with-gela-of-gelas-wonderful-world-of-babies
34. Simply Reborn, "Simply reborn Ltd.," 22 September 2013, http://www.simplyreborn.ltd.uk/reborn.htm
35. gregordonkey, "Beautiful Reborn Baby Girl – NEW RELEASE 'Saorise' by Bonnie Brown," eBay, 28 July 2012, 21 June 2014, http://www.ebay.com/itm/Beautiful-Reborn-Baby-Girl-NEW-RELEASE-Saorise-by-Bonnie-Brown-/120952990043?pt=LH_DefaultDomain_0&hash=item1c295c295b
36. aleinapeterson, "Featured Reborn Artists of Aleina Peterson Original Kits," Aleina Peterson Originals, 6 July 2011, 16 May 2013, http://www.aleinapetersonoriginals.com/archives/377
37. Roberts and Wright, "Art and Collaboration," 532.
38. Cornford and Cross, "Inside Outside," 661.
39. kendrasgarden, "Kendra's Garden Babies eBay Store About My Store," eBay, 21 June 2014, http://members.ebay.com/ws/eBayISAPI.dll?ViewUserPage&userid=kendrasgarden
40. ariliv2, "Amy's Dollhouse Lifelike Reborn Baby B. Brown'Sharlamae'~MRMH~ Tummy Plate," eBay, 11 May 2013, http://www.ebay.com/itm/Amys-Dollhouse-Lifelike-Reborn-Baby-B-Brown-Sharlamae-MRMH-Tummy-Plate-/151041696063?pt=US_Dolls_Bears_Toys&hash=item232ac9613f
41. ullej-13, "Reborn Baby! New Toddler~ Leontyne~ By Danielle Zweers!: Lots Of Curls! Beautiful Lauscher German Glass Eyes!" eBay, 9 November 2010, http://cgi.ebay.com/ws/eBayISAPI.dll?ViewItem&autorefresh=true&hash=item33623d91cb&item=220691534283&nma=true&pt=LH_DefaultDomain_0&rt=nc&si=OeKXxOloyvRkJHpxP9d9rhNozdo%253D
42. elitecharms, "CUSTOM Reborn Baby Girl or Boy by Reva Schick: Choose from Ariella, Noah or Rebecca. MAKE ME AN OFFER!" eBay, 13 November 2010, http://cgi.ebay.com/CUSTOM-Reborn-Baby-Girl-Boy-Reva-Schick-/200540388823?pt=LH_DefaultDomain_0&hash=item2eb1237dd7
43. Debates about the political and aesthetic aspects of uniqueness and multiples have been a part of modern and contemporary art practices. Krauss, *Originality of the Avant-garde*.
44. hannahelizabethearle, "Reborn Gavin Bella Mia Babies," eBay, 11 May 2008, http://cgi.ebay.com/Reborn-Gavin-Bella-Mia-Babies_W0QQitemZ250247006177QQihZ015QQcategoryZ122723QQssPageNameZWDVWQQrdZ1QQcmdZViewItem
45. shesgothelp, "Reborn Madeleine, by Artist Birgit Gutzwiller-ACOF: Reborned by Debbie's Reborn Gallery. Gorgeous Rooted Ha," eBay, 30 May 2008, http://

cgi.ebay.com/Reborn-Madeleine-by-Artist-Birgit-Gutzwiller-ACOF_W0QQ itemZ170223930546QQihZ007QQcategoryZ122723QQssPageNameZWD VWQQrdZ1QQcmdZViewItem

46. ana3628, "AMAZING REBORN BABY GIRL BELLA-NE BY SYLVIA MANNING NOW IVAN: ANNABELLA'S NURSERY. REBORN ARTIST CECILIA MCDERMOTT," eBay, 2 March 2014, http://www.ebay.com/itm/AMAZING-REBORN-BABY-GIRL-BELLA-NE-BY-SYLVIA-MANNING-NOW-IVAN-/161233242233?pt=LH_DefaultDomain_0&hash=item258a400879

47. bonniesbabies, "Bonnie's Babies Reborn Biracial Ariella You Must See!: Genesis Heat Set Paint Micro Rooted Mohair," eBay, 17 May 2008, http://cgi.ebay.com/Bonnies-Babies-Reborn-Biracial-Ariella-You-Must-See_W0QQitemZ200224941979QQihZ010QQcategoryZ122723QQssPageNameZWDVWQQrdZ1QQcmdZViewItem

48. littleheartsnursery, "RARE Seldom Reborn-Like Knoops Luca Baby GORGEOUS MustC: Little Hearts Nursery Ethnic/Hispanic/Native American," eBay, 31 May 2008, http://cgi.ebay.com/RARE-Seldom-Reborn-Like-Knoops-Luca-Baby-GORGEOUS-MustC_W0QQitemZ290235255046QQihZ019QQcategoryZ122723QQssPageNameZWDVWQQrdZ1QQcmdZViewItem

49. Arendell, "Conceiving and Investigating Motherhood," 1192.

50. Douglas and Michaels, *Mommy Myth*.

51. Hays, *Cultural Contradictions of Motherhood*.

52. debbiesdaydreams, "DEBBIES DAYDREAMS REBORN, NEL de MAN MARCO BABY BOY: DOLLDREAMS NEW SOFT TOUCH VINYL, REAL FEEL BABY SKIN," eBay, 17 May 2008, http://contact.ebay.com/ws/eBayISAPI.dll?ShowAllQuestions&requested=debbiesdaydreams&iid=200224952437&frm=284&redirect=0&ShowASQAlways=1&SSPageName=PageAskSellerQuestion_VI

53. myforeverstory, "Reborn baby Jammy from Gus doll kit by Tina Kewy---SOLD OUT!" eBay 15 February 2014, http://www.ebay.com/itm/Reborn-baby-Jammy-from-Gus-doll-kit-by-Tina-Kewy-SOLD-OUT-/271329652515?pt=LH_DefaultDomain_0&hash=item3f2c81ef23

54. Stockton, *Queer Child*, 160.

55. kandybaby60, "QUEEN'S CRIB OOAK REBORN TODDLER BABY GIRL DOLL PRINCESS LOUISA by Delange," eBay, 17 February 2014, http://www.ebay.com/itm/QUEENS-CRIB-OOAK-REBORN-TODDLER-BABY-GIRL-DOLL-PRINCESS-LOUISA-by-Delange-/171240362382?pt=LH_DefaultDomain_0&hash=item27deb8918e

56. arielspretties, "Reborn Life Like Baby Doll Lanie," eBay, 21 February 2014, http://www.ebay.com/itm/Reborn-Life-Like-Baby-Doll-Lanie-/161206033587?pt=LH_DefaultDomain_0&hash=item2588a0dcb3; duchessofstonehillmanor, "SPECIAL~Reborn Girl~LE #9 Kirsten~MUST SEE~Great Price," eBay, 6 June 2008, http://cgi.ebay.com/SPECIAL-Reborn-Girl-LE-9-Kirsten-MUST-SEE-Great-Price_W0QQitemZ320260545627QQihZ011QQcategoryZ122723QQssPageNameZWDVWQQrdZ1QQcmdZViewItem

57. jnbsnursery, "*Cute Smile* Reborn Berenguer Full limb $1.00 NR L@@K!: *Jnbsnursery* Retired Face, Realistic, Take a peek!!" eBay, 8 September 2008, http://cgi.ebay.com/Cute-Smile-Reborn-Berenguer-Full-limb-1-00-NR-L-K_W0QQitemZ270274096899QQcmdZViewItem?hash=item270274096899&_trkpa rms=39%3A1%7C66%3A2%7C65%3A1%7C240%3A1318&_trksid=p3286.c0.m14

58. Allison, "Portable Monsters and Commodity Cuteness"; Morreall, "Cuteness."

59. tinylovenursery, "REBORN DOLL/BABY GIRL/E. WOSNJUK'S 'NOE'/NOT FAKE/NR!: ~No Reserve~ Adorable Layette! OOAK!" eBay, 12 September 2008, http://cgi.ebay.com/REBORN-DOLL-BABY-GIRL-E-WOSNJUKS-NOE-NOT-FAKE-NR_W0QQitemZ120304947566QQcmdZViewItem?hash=item120304947566&_trkparms=72%3A1163%7C39%3A1%7C66%3A2%7C65%3A12%7C240%3A1318&_trksid=p3286.c0.m14

60. bonniesbabies, "Bonnie's Babies Reborn Biracial Ariella You Must See!: Genesis Heat Set Paint Micro Rooted Mohair," eBay, 17 May 2008, http://cgi.ebay.com/Bonnies-Babies-Reborn-Biracial-Ariella-You-Must-See_W0QQitemZ200224941979QQ ihZ010QQcategoryZ122723QQssPageNameZWDVWQQrdZ1QQcmdZViewItem
61. scrumptiousbabiesnursery, "Reborn Baby Girl Doll ~ NICKY ~ Christa Goetzen ♥ Scrumptious Babies ♥ Ltd 500: Professional Artist Fiona Lester ~ PRA*ISE ~ ERA ~ BCG," eBay, 10 February 2014, http://www.ebay.com/itm/Reborn-Baby-Girl-Doll-NICKY-Christa-Goetzen-Scrumptious-Babies-Ltd-500-/171236039517?pt=UK_Doll_Bears_Dolls_EH&hash=item27de769b5d; popsatticritasdolls, "CrystalbyDonna Rubert Reborn Doll Little Darlins Nursery FREE SHIPPING," eBay, 13 February 2014, http://www.ebay.com/itm/Crystal-by-Donna-Rubert-Reborn-Doll-Little-Darlins-Nursery-FREE-SHIPPING-/271395111318?pt=LH_DefaultDomain_0&hash=item 3f3068c196
62. dar790, "Romie Strydom~Mommy's Angel~REBORN BY DAR'S DARLIN'S," eBay, 14 December 2008, http://cgi.ebay.com/Romie-Strydom-Mommys-Angel-REBORN-BY-DARS-DARLINS_W0QQitemZ220330060345QQcmdZViewItem QQptZDolls?hash=item220330060345&_trksid=p3286.c0.m14&_trkparms=66%3A2%7C65%3A1%7C39%3A1%7C240%3A1308
63. SonjaG, "SonjaG Artfire Shop | Bio," ArtFire, 23 May 2013, http://www.artfire.com/ext/shop/bio/SonjaG
64. hollhollart, "REBORN baby boy! - Little Chicks - Limited Edition: by Fine Artist Hollmann Hollis - Painted Hair!" eBay, 15 May 2011, 21 June 2014, http://cgi.ebay.com/REBORN-baby-boy-Little-Chicks-Limited-Edition-/280673731848?pt=LH_DefaultDomain_0&hash=item4159754508
65. kendrasgarden, "Kendra's Garden Babies eBay Store About My Store," eBay, 21 June 2014, http://members.ebay.com/ws/eBayISAPI.dll?ViewUserPage&userid=kendras garden
66. texasbanditcat, "Preemie Reborn Baby twin girl doll Tayla sculpt by Denise Pratt tummy plate," eBay, 11 February 2014, http://www.ebay.com/itm/Preemie-Reborn-Baby-twin-girl-doll-Tayla-sculpt-by-Denise-Pratt-tummy-plate-/141184672841?pt=LH_DefaultDomain_0&hash=item20df432449
67. Hemmings, "Invoking Affect," 552.
68. magicmom2, "Reborn Girl MUST SEE Taite with display bed !!!!!" eBay, 22 July 2012, http://www.ebay.com/itm/Reborn-Girl-MUST-SEE-Taite-with-display-bed-/150858265297?pt=LH_DefaultDomain_0&hash=item231fda72d1
69. Slatman and Widdershoven, "Hand Transplants," 74.
70. babymaybe, "SWEET PREEMIE/NB ReBORN OPEN MOUTH REALISM-NOT FROM KIT," eBay, 9 May 2008, http://cgi.ebay.com/SWEET-PREEMIE-NB-ReBORN-OPEN-MOUTH-REALISM-NOT-FROM-KIT_W0QQ itemZ190221274342QQihZ009QQcategoryZ122723QQssPageNameZWD VWQQrdZ1QQcmdZViewItem
71. Butler, *Psychic Life of Power*, 106.
72. Emily, as quoted in finds4unme, "REBORN Baby Boy Luna NOW Austin Stoete OOAK LR Not FAKE," eBay, 10 September 2008, http://cgi.ebay.com/REBORN-Baby-Boy-Luna-NOW-Austin-Stoete-OOAK-LR-Not-FAKE_W0QQitemZ320298023190QQcmdZViewItem?hash=item320298023190&_trkparms=72%3A1163%7C39%3A1%7C66%3A2%7C65%3A12%7C240%3A1318&_trksid=p3286.c0.m14
73. Kukla, "Talking Back," 72.
74. Ibid., 73.
75. silvertreenursery, "WOW RELISTIC ICU PREMMIE LTD ED SAM FROM HELEN CONNORS: INTESIVE CARE BABY ********NO RESERVE********," eBay, 1 November 2008, http://cgi.ebay.com/WOW-RELISTIC-ICU-PREMMIE-LTD-ED-SAM-FROM-HELEN-CONNORS_W0QQitemZ180303602892QQ cmdZViewItemQQptZUK_Doll_Bears_Dolls_EH?hash=item180303602892&

_trksid=p3286.c0.m14&_trkparms=66%3A2%7C65%3A1%7C39%3A1%7C240%3A1308
76. pigotts*playpen_05, "Pigott's Playpen Reborn VHTF Preemie Baby It's A Girl !" eBay, 16 November 2008, http://cgi.ebay.com/Pigotts-Playpen-Reborn-VHTF-Preemie-Baby-Its-A-Girl_W0QQitemZ180307140789QQihZ008QQcategoryZ122723QQssPageNameZWDVWQQrdZ1QQcmdZViewItem
77. madelynn1, "ADORABLE REBORN/PREEMIE, SO LIFE LIKE ITS AMAZING! L@@K:Details,veining,milia,mottled,genesis,sorealistic," eBay, 19November2008, http://cgi.ebay.com/ADORABLE-REBORNPREEMIE-SO-LIFE-LIKE-ITS-AMAZING-L-K_W0QQitemZ280287257588QQihZ018QQcategoryZ122723QQssPageNameZWDVWQQrdZ1QQcmdZViewItem
78. Sedgwick, *Touching Feeling*, 79.
79. Cataldi, *Emotion, Depth, and Flesh*, 128.
80. micheleismyname, "Reborn Newborn Realistic Baby Girl LLRG DADE: Sweet newborn baby girl Silver Cloud Nursery MUST SEE," eBay, 1 December 2008, http://cgi.ebay.com/Reborn-Newborn-Realistic-Baby-Girl-LLRG-DADE_W0QQitemZ330294516800QQcmdZViewItemQQptZDolls?hash=item330294516800&_trksid=p3286.c0.m14&_trkparms=66%3A2%7C65%3A1%7C39%3A1%7C240%3A1318
81. 2011-babydoll, "Hot Sale Reborn doll kits -soft vinyl DK-9," eBay, 30 July 2012, http://www.ebay.com/itm/Hot-Sale-Reborn-doll-kits-soft-vinyl-DK-9-/110925882066?pt=LH_DefaultDomain_0&hash=item19d3b2a2d2; bebepourlavie, "Holly baby doll kit by Artist Donna Rubert for reborn," eBay, 28 July 2012, http://www.ebay.com/itm/Holly-baby-doll-kit-by-Artist-Donna-Rubert-for-reborn-/110924529806?pt=LH_DefaultDomain_2&hash=item19d39e008e
82. madelynn1, "ADORABLE REBORN/PREEMIE, SO LIFE LIKE ITS AMAZING! L@@K:Details,veining,milia,mottled,genesis,sorealistic," eBay, 19November2008, http://cgi.ebay.com/ADORABLE-REBORNPREEMIE-SO-LIFE-LIKE-ITS-AMAZING-L-K_W0QQitemZ280287257588QQihZ018QQcategoryZ122723QQssPageNameZWDVWQQrdZ1QQcmdZViewItem
83. bluejeanene6, "REBORN ASHTON DRAKE TRIPLETS CHARLIE EMILY EMMA: TRULY REAL PREEMIE 10 INCH FREE SHIP WITH BUY IT NOW !" eBay, 15 November 2008, http://cgi.ebay.com/REBORN-ASHTON-DRAKE-TRIPLETS-CHARLIE-EMILY-EMMA_W0QQitemZ190267195877QQihZ009QQcategoryZ122723QQssPageNameZWDVWQQrdZ1QQcmdZViewItem
84. *reborn_babies*, "~Adoring Angels~ASHTONISHING Realism~Reborn? New born?NRMUSTC!*NOTFAKE*Awesome!U-MR,PRMA,IsHeBreathing?" eBay, 10 May 2008, http://cgi.ebay.com/Adoring-Angels-ASHTONISHING-Realism-Reborn-Newborn-NR_W0QQitemZ160239444095QQihZ006QQcategoryZ48921QQssPageNameZWDVWQQrdZ1QQcmdZViewItem
85. cherib603, "**SO REAL! MICRO PREEMIE!!!** Reborn 12.5" baby girl!!: *SOLD OUT Edition* – 3 DAYS ONLY! AMAZING Sculpt! NR!" eBay, 6 June 2008, http://cgi.ebay.com/SO-REAL-MICRO-PREEMIE-Reborn-12-5-baby-girl_W0QQitemZ140239268808QQihZ004QQcategoryZ122723QQssPageNameZWDVWQQrdZ1QQcmdZViewItem
86. cream-puff-nursery, "REBORN PREEMIE BABY BOY DOLL MUMMA'S LIL MONKEYBONNIEBROWNCREAMPUFFBABIES," eBay,13June2013,21June 2014, http://cgi.ebay.co.uk/ws/eBayISAPI.dll?ViewItem&item=360667404466
87. Cataldi, *Emotion, Depth, and Flesh*, 126.
88. cherishedangelsanddolls, "REBORN, ANGELINA, AMAZING, DETAILED, LIFE LIKE ANGEL: ROOTED HAIR, G/H/S/P/ MEMBER OF IRDA, RDAC, RHAC," eBay, 20 May 2008, http://cgi.ebay.com/REBORN-ANGELINA-AMAZING-DETAILED-LIFELIKE-ANGEL_W0QQitemZ370053749406QQihZ024QQcategoryZ122723QQssPageNameZWDVWQQrdZ1QQcmdZViewItem

89. ne1_4_a_baby, "~REBORN~BABY GIRL~TINY ONE~HEATHER BONEHAM~ NEW!~OACG~: *Many Authentic Hospital Props Included*3 DAYS ONLY!!*," eBay, 30 May 2008, http://cgi.ebay.com/REBORN-BABY-GIRL-TINY-ONE-HEATHER-BONEHAM-NEW-OACG_W0QQitemZ230257581243QQihZ013QQcategoryZ122723QQssPageNameZWDVWQQrdZ1QQcmdZViewItem

90. fjords4me, "Lifelike Reborn Baby Wendy Farmer No Reserve *A.N.F.N*: Free US Shipping/No Reserve/Genesis/MicroRooted," eBay, 29 May 2008, http://cgi.ebay.com/Lifelike-Reborn-Baby-Wendy-Farmer-No-Reserve-A-N-F-N_W0QQitemZ300228721456QQihZ020QQcategoryZ122723QQssPageNameZWDVWQQrdZ1QQcmdZViewItem

91. janice.fricker, "REBORN NEWBORN CLARA~TOBY MORGAN~WHERE BABY DREAMS ARE ALMOST REAL~: NEWBORN BABY INFANT DOLL~INNOCENCE LOVES YOU~," eBay, 10 August 2012, 21 June 2014, http://cgi.ebay.com/ws/eBayISAPI.dll?ViewItem&item=280935203219

92. maggibloom, "Reborn Baby Caleb By Heather Boneham," eBay, 23 February 2014, http://www.ebay.com/itm/Reborn-Baby-Caleb-By-Heather-Boneham-/191073674423?pt=LH_DefaultDomain_0&hash=item2c7ce0e4b7

93. nneecie, "Reborn 'Cassidy Erin' Secrist 'Teddy' sculpt," eBay, 22 February 2014, http://www.ebay.com/itm/Reborn-Cassidy-Erin-Secrist-Teddy-sculpt-/181327316326?pt=LH_DefaultDomain_0&hash=item2a37f34566

94. Palmer, "Brazen Cheek"; Peiss, *Hope in a Jar*.

95. sweetpeagardendolls, "OOAK Art Reborn Baby Doll * Painted & Rooted Hair: Cutie 10% Goes to Make A Wish," eBay, 30 July 2012, http://www.ebay.com/itm/OOAK-Art-Reborn-Baby-Doll-Painted-Rooted-Hair-Cutie-10-Goes-to-Make-A-WIsh-/190707552317?pt=LH_DefaultDomain_0&hash=item2c670e503d

96. tajh007, "Beautiful biracial baby****Cloe******," eBay, 27 July 2012, http://www.ebay.com/itm/Beautiful-biracial-baby-Cloe-/221076448441?pt=LH_DefaultDomain_0&hash=item33792ee4b9

97. ordinarymiraclesreborn, "Reborn Prototype Libby Marie Ethnic AA Baby girl sculpted by Lydia Yee Listed for charity: Ordinary Miracles Reborn Nursery Colliii Award Nominee," eBay, 30 July 2012, 21 June 2014, http://www.ebay.com/itm/Reborn-Prototype-Libby-Marie-Ethnic-AA-Baby-girl-sculpted-by-Lydia-Yee-/200798170876?pt=LH_DefaultDomain_0&hash=item2ec080eefc; katie.messou, "Big Baby Reborn Girl Ethnic African Black AA Doll Chloe by Ann Timmerman: Payment Plan Available on Request," eBay, 2 August 2012, 21 June 2014, http://www.ebay.com/itm/Big-Baby-Reborn-Girl-Ethnic-African-Black-AA-Doll-Chloe-by-Ann-Timmerman-/120957653131?pt=UK_Doll_Bears_Dolls_EH&hash=item1c29a3508b

98. dazzldayz, "BIRACIAL Reborn Vinyl doll Kit Baby KYRA by Eva Helland Realistic Lifelike 2646," eBay, 2 March 2014, http://www.ebay.com/itm/BIRACIAL-Reborn-Vinyl-doll-Kit-Baby-KYRA-by-Eva-Helland-Realistic-Lifelike-2646-/360806488787?pt=LH_DefaultDomain_0&hash=item5401be1ad3

99. *ajhunter*, "Reborn Baby Biracial Soft Belly Plate for 18-22" Doll Kit 2635," eBay, 2 March 2014, http://www.ebay.com/itm/Reborn-Baby-Biracial-Soft-Belly-Plate-for-18-22-Doll-Kit-2635-/190853153384?pt=LH_DefaultDomain_0&hash=item2c6fbc0268

100. *babies*by*bernadette*, "Asian *LI-MEI* Reborn Vinyl Doll Kit by Cathy Rowland ~20" Long & 3/4 Limbs~NEW," eBay, 2 March 2014, http://www.ebay.com/itm/Asian-LI-MEI-Reborn-Vinyl-Doll-Kit-by-Cathy-Rowland-20-Long-3-4-Limbs-NEW-/310880938776?pt=LH_DefaultDomain_0&hash=item4861f2ab18

101. silveroaktrading, "Reborn 'Cookie' Now Kylie (Lots of extras for Baby)," eBay, 24 July 2012, http://www.ebay.com/itm/Reborn-Cookie-Now-Kylie-Lots-of-extras-for-Baby-/300746054436?pt=LH_DefaultDomain_0&hash=item4605dc9b24

102. bhsgurl2013, "AA Biracial Ethnic Reborn," eBay, 25 July 2012, http://www.ebay.com/itm/AA-Biracial-Ethnic-Reborn-/261069860006?pt=LH_DefaultDomain_0&hash=item3cc8f9eca6
103. whitethunder1965, "ON SALE BEAUTIFUL REBORN BABY BOY DOLL ART TRUE LIFE BELLY PLATE MAGNETIC PACI," eBay, 12 May 2013, http://www.ebay.com/itm/ON-SALE-BEAUTIFUL-REBORN-BABY-BOY-DOLL-ART-TRUE-LIFE-BELLY-PLATE-MAGNETIC-PACI-/281103264878?pt=US_Dolls_Bears_Toys&hash=item41730f6c6e
104. For instance, individuals with intersex genitals are often operated on multiple times, starting when they are babies, to make them fit into medical and social understandings of the dyadic differences between male and female genitals. Chase, "Hermaphrodites with Attitude"; Fausto-Sterling, *Sexing the Body*; Zeiler and Wickström, "Why Do 'We' Perform Surgery?"
105. buythesewtaps, "~REBORN~Newborn Baby Boy~*Adorable*w/Tummy Plate* ONE DAY ONLY*," eBay, 21 December 2011, http://www.ebay.com/itm/REBORN-Newborn-Baby-Boy-Adorable-w-Tummy-Plate-ONE-DAY-ONLY-/250958009253?pt=LH_DefaultDomain_0&hash=item3a6e4353a5
106. Bonnie Brown, "What is Reborning?" The Bonnie Brown Collection, 2010, 14 May 2013, http://thebonniebrowncollection.webs.com/reborns.htm
107. mummelbaerchen, "Mummelbaerchens Lilian, Reborn Baby Boy, sculpt by Gudrun Legler, Ltd,bellyplate," eBay, 12 February 2014, http://www.ebay.com/itm/Mummelbaerchens-Lilian-Reborn-Baby-Boy-sculpt-by-Gudrun-Legler-Ltd-bellyplate-/301091735819?pt=UK_Doll_Bears_Dolls_EH&hash=item461a77490b
108. jessicasclaybabies, "Reborn Baby! Newborn Kyle! 1 day only! NO RES JessicasClayBabies," eBay, 21 February 2014, http://www.ebay.com/itm/Reborn-Baby-Newborn-Kyle-1-day-only-NO-RES-JessicasClayBabies-/171247285958?pt=LH_DefaultDomain_0&hash=item27df2236c6
109. snowball1994, "Reborn Berenguer Doll *Dylan* Happy Little Boy! *Full Vinyl* Curly Hair! RARE!" 23 February 2014, http://www.ebay.com/itm/Reborn-Berenguer-Doll-Dylan-Happy-Little-Boy-Full-Vinyl-Curly-Hair-RARE-/111282591237?pt=LH_DefaultDomain_0&hash=item19e8f59605
110. mmoody7918, "Baby 'Julien' 2-pc Doe Suede + Full Soft Vinyl Body So Cuddly Priced to Sell," eBay, 25 February 2014, http://www.ebay.com/itm/Baby-Julien-2-pc-Doe-Suede-Full-Soft-Vinyl-Body-So-Cuddly-Priced-to-Sell-/181328283525?pt=LH_DefaultDomain_0&hash=item2a38020785
111. Betterton, "Prima Gravida," 260.
112. connjean1958, "From Nana Connies Reborn Nursery:'Where's Mummy' a sculpt by Dee Statsny," eBay, 1 March 2014, http://www.ebay.com/itm/From-Nana-Connies-Reborn-Nursery-Wheres-Mummy-a-sculpt-by-Dee-Statsny-/301101904416?pt=LH_DefaultDomain_0&hash=item461b127220
113. texasbanditcat, "Adorable Reborn Baby doll Georgia full body w/soft body sculpt by Linda Murray," eBay, 25 February 2014, http://www.ebay.com/itm/Adorable-Reborn-Baby-doll-Georgia-full-body-w-soft-body-sculpt-by-Linda-Murray-/131120265847?pt=LH_DefaultDomain_0&hash=item1e87607a77
114. mypoeticspirit, "Oh my! I'm Reborn Pregnant! (How did this happen???)," YouTube, 25 February 2014, http://www.youtube.com/watch?v=G-vBR5sLndo; Tess Tucker, "I'm Reborn Pregnant!!! YouTube, 25 February 2014, http://www.youtube.com/watch?v=9jZq6wDomSw
115. litttleloves reborn, "Reborn pregnant for the first time!" YouTube, 25 February 2014, http://www.youtube.com/watch?v=I9du655Fc8E
116. Cuteandcuddly14, "Im reborn pregnant !!!" YouTube, 25 February 2014, http://www.youtube.com/watch?v=Ln8kIVywiko; SweetPrincessKairi, "An-Bao is coming soon! (A reborn pregnancy video)," YouTube, 25 February 2014, http://www.youtube.com/watch?v=0Fuw6JYkOMg

117. donalynn, "SWEET REBORN BABY GIRL DOLL FOR YOU!" eBay, 24 February 2014, http://www.ebay.com/itm/SWEET-REBORN-BABY-GIRL-DOLL-FOR-YOU-/151235994282?pt=LH_DefaultDomain_0&hash=item23365e22aa
118. Victoria Silver, *My Fake Baby*, 2008.
119. jcorn, "Dr. Phil Explores Reborn Dolls, Reborners and Other Obsessions," Associated Content, 10 December 2008, http://www.associatedcontent.com/article/1289266/dr_phil_explores_reborn_dolls_reborners.html?page=3&cat=2
120. Mara, "Reborn dolls," baby gaga, 30 March 2008, http://forum.baby-gaga.com/about200773.html
121. caraMel, "Dolls," Ohbaby! 18 July 2008, 21 June 2014, http://www.ohbaby.co.nz/forum/forum_posts.asp?TID=19263&goto=lastpage
122. Klingon_Mama, "Reborn dolls," baby gaga, 2 April 2008, http://forum.baby-gaga.com/about200773.html
123. Dimen, "Sexuality and Suffering."
124. Kristeva, *Powers of Horror*, 4.
125. haguenite, "Lifelike Baby Dolls: The New Trend For Childless British Women," Jezebel, 2 October 2008, http://jezebel.com/339653/lifelike-baby-dolls-the-new-trend-for-childless-british-women
126. Rich Edmondson, "The New Face of Evil," *Loudon Times-Mirror*, 27 August 2008, http://www.loudountimes.com/blogs/playstation36wii/2008-08-27/evil-has-new-face/
127. Trend Hunter, "Freakishly Real Fake Babies," 17 July 2008, http://www.trendhunter.com/trends/reborn-babies-real-fake-babies
128. Abby O'Reilly, "My Fake Baby," The F word: contemporary UK feminism, 4 January 2008, http://www.thefword.org.uk/blog/2008/01/my_fake_baby
129. Jill Reilly, "Zombie dolls are creepy new craze that just won't die!" *MailOnline*, 31 December 2012, 6 July 2014, http://www.dailymail.co.uk/news/article-2255234/Zombie-dolls-creepy-new-craze-just-won-t-die-Artist-creates-undead-babies-vampire-like-teeth-piercing-red-eyes.html#ixzz2u4vIUNAB
130. Bean Shanine, "The Twisted Bean Stalk Nursery – Where my reborn babies grow on their twisted little vines," The Twisted Bean Stalk Nursery, 13 June 2014, http://www.thetwistedbeanstalknursery.com/about/
131. Johnson, "Teaching Deconstructively."
132. Bean Shanine, as quoted in Jill Reilly, "Zombie dolls are creepy new craze that just won't die!" *MailOnline*, 31 December 2012, 6 July 2014, http://www.dailymail.co.uk/news/article-2255234/Zombie-dolls-creepy-new-craze-just-won-t-die-Artist-creates-undead-babies-vampire-like-teeth-piercing-red-eyes.html#ixzz2u4vIUNAB; Bean Shanine, "The Twisted Bean Stalk Nursery – Where my reborn babies grow on their twisted little vines," The Twisted Bean Stalk Nursery, 22 February 2014, http://www.thetwistedbeanstalknursery.com/about/
133. Bean Shanine, "For Adoption," The Twisted Bean Stalk Nursery, 22 February 2014, http://www.thetwistedbeanstalknursery.com/for-adoption/

3

IT'S ABOUT "CREATION, NOT DESTRUCTION"

Brides, Photographers, and Post-wedding Trash the Dress Sessions

Etsy's sign-up page for its wedding emails depicts a light-skinned couple and encourages readers to "Subscribe" and buy into its connection of weddings, heterosexuality, and whiteness.[1] This focus on lightness is underscored by the color of the bride's clothing and the large expanse of cream-colored sky. The woman's cream blouse and contrasting belt, which she wears over her big ivory wedding dress, mark her as a do-it-yourself bride who participates in Etsy's culture of "unique goods."[2] Rather than appearing with their family and friends in a church or groomed garden setting and following customs, the couple act as Etsy's proxy and stand alone in an overgrown field. The music for their personalized ritual seems to have come from the guitar, which now hangs over the groom's shoulder. The couple underscores their tie to each other and Etsy, rather than a proximate community, by looking at the sign-up form and each other. They hold between them a handmade string of pennant flags that is imprinted with the word "love" and two hearts. These hearts connect them to Etsy because they are handcrafted versions of Etsy's "Favorite" icon, which lets individuals express an interest in listings and the culture that the setting markets. Such wedding images are featured on web-based advertisements, photography sites, social networking pages, fashion and wedding forums, and image sharing settings. Sites such as eBay and Etsy use these heterosexual weddings to stand in for their members and ethos.

These companies reference weddings because they productively evoke distinct individuals, normative commitments, and consumer-oriented communities. The Etsy viewer is encouraged to participate in this consumer-oriented community and heterosexual union by providing an email address and learning about "Handmade and vintage picks for brides, grooms and everyone else who loves weddings." Etsy's phrasing suggests that the wedding emails offer handmade and personal selections to everyone because everyone loves weddings. Yet it also tries to control a series of incompatibilities, including its references to everyone and addresses to particular consumers. These couples and other aficionados are supposed to be linked through their love of weddings in a manner that is related to the ways they are connected through other affective experiences with Etsy. The wedding image asserts that love is unique and hand formed by individuals and couples rather than the wedding industry. It is thus related to Internet promises of personalization and choice, including the overstated opportunities to modify profiles, sites, and software. The picture poses Etsy as the best option for personal weddings and introduces a form of trash the dress (TTD) photography, which portrays couples wearing wedding clothes while exploring unusual settings.

The Rock n Roll Bride site may appear to have a different function than Etsy but its blogger Kat also focuses on varied kinds of "Crazy Love."[3] She blogs, "you're gonna absolutely love these!"[4] Kat presents photographer Lynette Seelmeyer's "True Blood" TTD session in which Hayley wears a big white wedding dress and displays her engagement and wedding rings in a cemetery. The session "had two ideas behind it," according to Kat, a "goth bride and the movie Carrie." This interest in the macabre and horrific is reflected in the location and Hayley's slightly chipped red nails and fingers that are streaked with what looks like blood [Figure 3.1].[5] Her extremely pale hand and a dead leaf—both blanched of color—are in a pool of this dark and viscous fluid. In other images, Hayley looks out at viewers and gestures violently with a knife. Blood-red fluid stains

FIGURE 3.1 Lynette Seelmeyer, Picture This Photography, LLC, Reprinted with permission. Trash the dress photographers use horror themes to reconceive traditional weddings.

the front of her gown. These visceral features are furthered by the evocative "True Blood" title of this session, which marks this blood as real and true and references the HBO television program and similarly grotesque representations.

Such portrayals of women's hands, as I have indicated in the previous chapters, are images of producing women. Women's hands displaying wedding rings usually connote heterosexual marriages and cultural expectations about nuclear families and reproducing women who will bear children. These hands work to establish women's appropriate development, compassion, connection, and normative gender. However, Hayley's hands produce a different set of affects and directions. They underscore the site's interest in diverse forms of "Crazy" love, which include passions that disrupt heterosexual unions. They make Kat want to "go watch a very scary film…maybe about sexy vampires" and evoke genre conventions and queer erotic interests that are not ordinarily aligned with heterosexual weddings. The positioning of Hayley's hands, including images where her fingers are tensed into weapons and she holds a knife, supports this association of weddings with horror. The work performed by her hands and the implications of the blood sever, and cut because of the knife, the bride from marriage and familial reproduction. The glowing burgundy blood that soaks her bodice, which is also the color traditionally associated with love, and the red-black fluid that surrounds her hand supplant the gender and racial references of her white dress and body.

Hayley's husband and the accompanying indications of heterosexual unions are banished from these images, or even murdered. Her placement in a graveyard and embrasure of a headstone forward this death of the groom. The bride's husband is also effaced in The Bride of Frankenstein images that are discussed in the introduction.[6] These representations connect weddings to women without men; female rage; blood; fluidity; gender, racial, and sexual ambiguity; horror; and death. They are part of a growing series of engagement and TTD wedding photography sessions where brides and photographers, and sometimes grooms, choose to depict brides killing their husbands. This development is based on even more troubling TTD images in which grooms kill brides and mirror the gendered conventions of domestic abuse.[7] When brides visually and conceptually kill grooms, they take up empowered but still murderous positions and stall their marriages at the point of the wedding. They refuse the growing up and through weddings, which is part of the life changes marked by these events. While married lesbians and women who are having commitment ceremonies with women rarely take part in TTD, women erotically engage with other women and discuss their queer TTD desires in wedding forums.[8] These TTD images thus forward some surprising conceptions of weddings, relationships, and women's roles.

Photographers work with married women on trash the dress post-wedding sessions and document them wearing white wedding dresses again while strolling in fields, posing in front of decrepit buildings, jumping into swamps, and smearing dirt and other fluids on their bodies and dresses. Brides extend these ideas when considering sessions in wedding forums. Photographers and journalists further feature these practices in news stories and blog accounts. On these sites, TTD sessions are identified as representing bridal rage, facilitating opposition to cultural conceptions of weddings and the visual position of women, and critiquing the limiting roles established by traditional weddings. TTD is thus associated with resistance and imagined to produce resisters. TTD is also a photographic practice that generates more representations of heterosexual women in wedding dresses.

Photographers identify TTD images as creative and better than wedding photography in their promotional blogs and other forums. They distinguish their work from wedding photography, which is culturally associated with banal images and overused conventions, and provide reasons for women to book sessions. Yet many TTD photographs depict light-skinned and traditionally gendered women passively snuggling into the bodies of male partners and seductively posing so they can be admired. These are familiar photographic conventions. The claims that TTD politically transforms weddings and women's experiences are in need of critique. After all, Etsy and other sites have incorporated TTD sessions as part of their commercial claims. However, a variety of experiences are intertwined in this cultural activity so that neither complete control nor political resistance is an apt descriptor. TTD sessions are reliant on the norm producing aspects of Western weddings, photographers need to promote and manage the oppositional functions of TTD in order to maintain their creative position, and women trouble feminine roles when staining gowns, actively fighting foes, flirting with other women, and acting out the murder of partners.

In this chapter, I analyze the similar notions of TTD that appear in photographers' blogs, Trash the Dress! sites, wedding forums, and news reports. Critical literature on resistance helps me to consider how opposition is marketed and facilitated.[9] Feminist literature provides detailed accounts of resistance, including the ways everyday acts can undermine social norms.[10] Feminist theories of the gaze, such as research on fashion magazines and horror, help me to clarify how sessions refigure women as visually available to other women and difficult to look at.[11] Examinations of dirt and abjection also suggest that women challenge normative femininity when they soil their wedding dresses during sessions.[12] Women's delighted TTD engagements with images, other women, and dirt trouble the bounded body, problematize the ways lens-based media has enabled men to look at women, and offer women forms of pleasure and desire that are not so easily correlated with white weddings and pretty brides. Photographers may associate TTD with resistance in order to elevate their practices but women's participation still produces different understandings of heterosexual brides and norms.

Resistance Studies

Photographers associate TTD with resistance as a marketing strategy, way of aligning their images with interrogations of wedding culture, and method of contesting their relationship to conventional wedding photographers. Their employment of the term suggests the fluid aspects of what resistance means and how people use it. Such conceptions of resistance are of interest to scholars because they can disrupt desired systems; challenge social, structural, and governmental control; reform identity positions and categories; provide power to more or less enfranchised groups; render affective experiences; and articulate the status of people and things. Early organizational communication researchers describe resisters negatively influencing companies and generating economic losses, organizational disruptions, and worker alienation. These academics identify resisters as deviants and their actions as something that needs to be handled and controlled.[13] Marxist informed research also examines the ways resisters challenge corporations.[14] However, Marxist investigators identify the transformative potential and politically enabling aspects of resistance.

Current work in resistance studies, as Kathleen Knight Abowitz argues in her examination of this research, recognizes resistance as more than "opposition to authority."[15] Resisters are believed to positively change environments with their attempts to eliminate oppressive societal structures and identities. These researchers also contest the binary of powerful and powerless that is established in earlier studies.[16] Scholars interrogate the identifications of domination as a "relatively fixed and institutionalized form of power" and resistance as "organized opposition to power."[17] They describe the multiple forms of domination that are present in any work or social situation, daily and micro forms of resistance, conceptions of political transformation, the critical possibilities of muteness, and the ways resisters in oppressed groups may be both powerful and resisted.[18]

Feminists also study resistance, including how ordinary behaviors can destabilize cultural conventions.[19] Instead of "focusing on revolution," note business scholars Robyn Thomas and Annette Davies, poststructuralist feminists identify "more localized and small-scale" forms of resistance, including attempts to destabilize truths, subjectivities, and normalizing discourses.[20] Such interrogations are useful for my analysis because TTD photographers claim to challenge the truths and subjectivities of wedding culture, including the emphasis on cleanliness, while working to support some wedding norms. Feminist considerations of abjection and fluidity offer critical models for interrogating traditional conceptions of the body and identity. According to Julia Kristeva, things that disrupt identities and systems and do not respect boundaries, positions, and rules cause abjection.[21] This literature identifies abjection as a possible model for resisting the clean and proper body, which feminist philosopher Elizabeth Grosz associates with an "obedient, law-abiding, social body" that is developed through directives about body fluids.[22] These forms of bodily regulation and control are supported by wedding practices. For instance, brides are told, "Don't step on the dress; don't get dirt on the dress."[23] Such directions help to articulate traditional conceptions of women and get women to act in particular ways.

Internet studies researchers are also interested in the ways technologies and social practices facilitate resistance. Some of these scholars indicate that the

Internet empowers individuals and provides ways of resisting the state, corporations, and mass media outlets.[24] The Internet, according to James Gillett, increases the "capacity for cultural resistance by creating greater opportunities for the expression of political opposition to institutional authority."[25] He offers a study of blogs as an example of these occasions for opposition. Authors have credited Twitter and other social networking applications with enabling social movements and changes in governance.[26] These texts examine conceptions of resistance but do not focus on the ways resistance is assured and promoted within particular cultures and technological applications. My research on the TTD phenomenon suggests that resistance is also commodified and eroticized in these settings. The expressive potential of technologies and sites are as likely to provide advantages to corporations and traditionally recognized producers, such as photographers, as they are to liberate women and other disempowered subjects.

There has also been critical work on how biases are continued through narratives about technologies and Internet settings.[27] Stacy Gillis describes the cyberpunk and science fiction phenomenon of the "ass-kicking techno-babe," who fights and resists inequitable systems and injustice.[28] These fictional women are technologically altered in ways that intensify their deadliness and role as objects of pleasure. For instance, Molly Millions in William Gibson's fiction is surgically transformed so that her long burgundy nails sheath knife blades and she can perform as a sex worker without limitations or memories of these encounters.[29] The power of Millions and other techno-babes is produced through their bodies and they are thereby associated with sexualized and monstrous femininities. These women fight and resist in such a manner, according to Marlo Edwards's analysis of female action heroes, that they still uphold the association of women with eroticism and commodification.[30] They are designed for men and directed to facilitate the male gaze. Thus, the techno-babe functions as a version of Teresa de Lauretis's technology of gender and encourages women to be visually available.[31]

The ass-kicking techno-babe is also part of a shift, which Elyce Rae Helford identifies in her study of female action heroes, from depicting women as passive victims to sometimes rendering them as active adventurers.[32] However, these women do not challenge cultural inequities because they have no plans for social change. There are TTD participants who render a version of the ass-kicking techno-babe's combination of powerful resistance and overt eroticism. The similarities between women TTD participants, who have performed as and identified with women who kill, and the female protagonists in action films point to the promises and limits of active and angry women.[33] The women in TTD sessions do not identify specific plans for social change but their performances propose significant reconceptualizations of bridal and familial roles. This shifts conceptions of what heterosexual monogamy looks like and how heterosexual women experience wedding culture and committed relationships. These women thereby produce a wider array of lived wedding practices, which also proposes shifts in future roles.

The Cultural Politics of Weddings

There are many reasons for people to resist and critique weddings, wedding dresses, and the industries that produce and perpetuate these rituals. Jamie Miles and The Knot, which is one of the largest sites publishing wedding content, have estimated the average cost of a wedding in the United States in 2013 at 28,427 USD.[34] Of this, the photographer costs 2,379 and the dress 1,211. A *Bride To Be* survey performed during the same time period found that the average wedding spending in Australia, including the engagement ring and honeymoon, was 54,294 AUD.[35] Couples in Australia tended to borrow 12,583 AUD for their weddings. Wedding spending in the United Kingdom was estimated between 18,244 and 24,716 GBP per event.[36] People in the UK, like individuals in other places, borrow money, request cash gifts, and sell wedding dresses and presents to pay for the event.[37] Guests report spending between 1,500 and 23,860 USD on flights, hotels, requests for event-specific clothing, and gifts.[38] Costs for bridesmaids and other women may be higher than costs for men because of expectations about feminine bodily maintenance and the ways women are supposed to appear at these events.[39] These numbers have been escalating over the last few years and suggest that weddings are expensive consumption rites with economic and social impacts.

TTD sessions allow brides to continue the heterosexual assertions of weddings while dismissing the costs by self-presenting in less opulent settings and disavowing dresses. However, this requires that women are able to afford, or at least risk, ruining gowns. Women with great affection for gowns tend to buy additional dresses for TTD sessions. Women may also have additional dresses to use because cultural mandates to find the perfect dress often result in women buying more than one. By employing different dresses, women preserve the "original" wedding gown and add to the compilation of memorable wedding items and costs. Yet this behavior means that brides are not trashing their wedding dresses. In addition to these costs and risks, there are TTD photographers' fees, which start at about 300 USD, with photographers charging additional fees for prints and other options.[40] Photographers now sell more expensive photography packages because wedding day photography has been extended to engagement, boudoir, rehearsal dinner, morning after, TTD, anniversary, and pregnancy sessions. This points to the increasing imaging and documentation of people's, and especially women's, lives. These practices are encouraged and remediated through social networking sites, which are often organized around selfies and other self-depictions.

Contemporary culture uses weddings and wedding photography as methods of structuring women's roles and life courses. Weddings mark women's expected transitions from single to coupled, young women to adults, protoheteronormative to monogamously heterosexual, and childless to reproductive. They also distinguish women who do not meet these expectations. Weddings, as

Christyana Bambacas's research on these events suggests, are "constructed as one of the defining moments of a girl's life in her progression toward womanhood."[41] Representations of weddings, according to Franka Heise's research on modern brides, "promote the idea that marriage is the only adequate framework for an intimate relationship and for the constitution of an acceptable gendered identity, meanwhile reproducing heterosexuality as norm and monogamy as societal duty."[42] Women are expected to move through wedding rituals rather than permanently being brides. Yet younger women are still directed to plan for weddings and more mature women are supposed to reflect back upon their nuptials.

Wedding images are key features of these events and have long-term functions in women's lives. They help to constitute what life looks like, including an emphasis on heterosexuality and monogamy. Images of demure brides and couples performing cake cutting and other rituals, as Charles Lewis's study of professional wedding photography suggests, almost always convey conventional ideas about heterosexual unions and gendered identities.[43] Heterosexual weddings may focus on people's choice to marry but they also, according to Ramona Faith Oswald's research on lesbians and cultural rituals, provide "profound social, legal, financial, and religious benefits."[44] These presumed and institutionalized heterosexual privileges are conveyed through wedding ceremonies, photography, invitations, dresses, and additional artifacts.

Women also confound the conventions of heterosexual unions, where they are supposed to be focused on and paired with men, when doing TTD sessions with and expressing erotic interests in depictions of other women. For instance, Alicia Robichaud Photography identifies two light-skinned women in a TTD session as "friends" but their wedding dresses and visual coupling suggest a more intimate relationship.[45] The women sit in a pond in "Mud Fight!," their buoyant skirts mesh, and their playful touching is recorded in the muck on their faces, breasts, and torsos.[46] Through these actions and images, these women choose to be erotically portrayed. Yet these women's mud play also evokes childhood states and engagements with dirty things. They thereby shift back into childish positions, which Kathryn Bond Stockton describes as queer forms of "growing sideways" and I discuss in more detail in Chapter 2, rather than asserting their movement towards the category of married and mature women.[47]

There are other wedding rituals where brides and participating women sexually subjectify themselves and are objectified. Bridal parties may now include pole-dancing classes. These events are contrarily described as empowering, body strengthening, and providing instructions on how to be sexier for male partners.[48] In a similar manner, brides are encouraged to do boudoir photography sessions, where they pose in lingerie and other revealing clothing, as gifts for future husbands and as ways of accepting and celebrating their bodies.[49] All of these practices are marketed as unconventional, encourage women to be visually available, and lead to flirtatious exchanges and same-sex erotic spheres that are contrary to the heterosexual scripts of normative weddings. Women's engagements in weddings thus tend to produce queer commitments and communities, including ongoing participation in women's wedding forums, even though these rituals are supposed to establish brides' commitments to husbands and movement into stable and heteronormative relationships.

Developing TTD

TTD photographers suggest that their practices challenge heterosexual wedding culture and photography. The wedding photographer John Michael Cooper introduced the term "trash the dress" and associated sessions with resistance in 2006. Cooper posted an article entitled "Show Off! [a.k.a. Trashing the Dress]" to the Wed Shooter blog as a means of communicating with wedding photographers and encouraging them to change their practices.[50] In the essay, he describes meetings with wedding clients as a time when photographers display their "beautiful wedding photography" and "show off" what they are "best at" and "love to do." He thus distinguishes between photographers' conventional wedding practices and their skills and creative passions. Cooper also represents his aesthetic as oppositional to traditional photographic views and the normative state of wedding dresses. He loves to depict "portraits down on the ground, in the dirt, mud, grass, trees, water, whatever," because he loves "to trash the dress." He underscores this resistance by describing these images as "anti-bridals."[51]

Cooper asked three brides to participate in the first TTD session, "told them the dress would get dirty," and had "3 flat turn downs."[52] He now shows off the resultant image and tells women "it's not a real bride 'cause the real ones turned" him "down." In doing this, Cooper suggests brides have missed being at the forefront of his photographic and artistic phenomenon and encourages new wedding clients to dismiss the sentiments of women who resist TTD. He also encourages photographers to ignore these women when he writes, "If you show" off your style or type of photography, you "might find yourself being asked" to "do just what you love to do." Cooper thus proposes that traditional wedding photography's representations of love should be replaced by the things photographers love to do.

Cooper portrays the brides who refused his TTD proposal as uninformed, unwise, and child-like. Brides purportedly misinterpret the contemporary possibilities of wedding rituals when indicating that they are "saving the dress" for a daughter, even though most women "flatly refuse to wear their mothers dresses." He suggests that brides cannot grow up through photography and weddings unless they relinquish their investments in the associated dresses. Technology manufactures and Internet sites also tend to represent women as unskilled and unwilling users and white men as employers of advanced equipment and computers. Some women who sell on eBay, as I suggest in Chapter 1, tactically perform a version of this deskilling in order to assert their position as compassionate stay-at-home mothers rather than money-oriented businesses. In contrast to these forms of feminine self-abnegation, Cooper emphasizes his creative and cultural knowledge. He asserts that his idea was innovative and important because women now ask, "pretty please style," and presumably deferentially, for sessions. These gendered narratives, which dismiss women's authority and concerns, establish Cooper as the once misunderstood artist whose talents are currently recognized.

Cooper's articulation of his aesthetic as oppositional to women's knowledge is a reminder that, as Gloria Filax argues, "resistance cannot be understood strictly to describe attempts to achieve social equality" because some people contest parity.[53] Filax considers struggles over sexual citizenship and how gays and lesbians and those who disagree with gay rights are resisters. In a related manner, Cooper uses his clients to constitute his innovative and their retrograde forms of resistance. TTD is portrayed as a form of masculine sexual seduction that requires photographers, who are rendered as male suitors, to take brides' "virginity" and thereby coerce and re-educate them.[54] Cooper asserts there "is no longer a need for the purity and innocence that the white represents" after the wedding. He never addresses the problems with these gender norms, including the privileging of whiteness and discrepant expectations about male and female sexuality. Instead, women are supposed to relinquish these conventions and their resistance to TTD after encountering the creative work of wedding photographers and, by analogy, after seeing a penis and having sex. Cooper argues, "in the real world persistent virginity sometime requires professional help." He poses TTD photographers as specialized producers who recraft wedding rituals and brides' photographic refusals. His vision of TTD is thereby based on pressuring women.

The photographer Mark Eric helped create the lineage for TTD. He read Cooper's essay; invited Shana Strawcutter to participate; posted images from their TTD session; and turned trashthedress.wordpress.com, trashthedress.com, and freetoflaunt.com into promotional venues for TTD photographers. Eric also identified Cooper as the "godfather" of TTD.[55] He thereby assigned the phenomenon a patriarchal ancestry and continued the masculinization of photography. Without such distinctions, the large number of women who are TTD practitioners, including brides who organize sessions, and feminization of this form would trouble the gender coding of wedding photography and photographers. Cooper and Eric's proposal for TTD can also be queered by emphasizing the role of women photographers. Cooper, Eric, and reporters avoid this feminization and queering by asserting a series of binary gender distinctions. They use the purportedly retrograde and frigid aspects of women's resistance and their position as objects to articulate artistic identity as masculine. This is similar to art historian Lynda Nead's description of how representations of women, and the correlation of women models with canvases and other objects, are used to associate art production and subjectivity with men.[56] Eric further distinguishes between women's representational status and men's role as artists by posting a few of Cooper's images on his TTD sites. These photographs of women in wedding dresses include *Joan* engulfed in flames, *Ophelia* drowning, and a bride's greyish feet jutting from a car trunk. A man with a shovel appears ready to bury her.

Cooper's TTD images depict dead or dying brides and aestheticize violence against women. However, Eric uses the Trash the Dress! sites to identify Cooper's photographs and processes as pioneering "a new creative, artistic, movement in the world of wedding photography," and as a form of resistance to previous conventions.[57] Cooper's images resist the clean and proper body of women and the purity of wedding dresses. However, he accomplishes this by encouraging hostility towards women. All of this is a reminder, as Filax argues, that just "as power is not owned and exerted by those in charge, resistance is not owned by those who are oppressed."[58] Even more than the usual gender hierarchy of associating male artists with activity and female models and representations with passivity, these images associate artists with life and brides with death.[59] This genre too callously mirrors images of and reports about battered women. These TTD sessions promise to move women beyond childish bridal interests but figure women's development as fatalities. TTD representations of murderous women torque these earlier conventions and narratives about appropriate development. These women figure the death of empowered subjects as a means of refusing to be controlled and harmed. They thereby offer important revisions to societal structures and TTD representations. Yet there are also problems with these representations because their reversal of the usual power structure and familial violence still means that they figure the death of other individuals. Zombie brides, as I indicate in the next chapter, further rework these conventions by associating whiteness, brides, and grooms with death.

Creativity and Resistance

A group of photographers, brides, and news reporters support Cooper and Eric's formulations and suggest TTD enables women to oppose wedding norms and being mannered. Robin Summerfield reports that TTD is an "anti-wedding" trend that sees brides getting "down and dirty with their bad selves."[60] According to journalist Izzy Grinspan, Cooper has turned "travel photography into an act of rebellion" and TTD represents "bride rage."[61] Grinspan also argues that women are performing subversion as opposed to facilitating political change. In these cases resistance, like punk and riot grrrl movements, can be political and/or a style.[62] Individuals also propose other aesthetics and interests when covering their bodies with wet and sticky materials in "fetish" magazines and in Internet representations. A few photographers combine these erotics and identify images as TTD even though they depict almost naked brides in the mud.[63] The heterosexual presumptions of TTD are disturbed when the Swimming Fully Clothed Blog highlights the times men but not women can be seen in session videos.[64]

TTD's relationship to porn practices, and what is ordinarily coded as lower class, is intriguing because proponents render wedding photography as limiting and tasteless and TTD as innovative and artistic. The wedding photographer Joel Wiebner differentiates between Cooper's images and the "cheesey guy who cracks jokes at your wedding" and "uses the same tired 5 poses every wedding that he has been using since 1972."[65] According to photographer Matt Adcock, clients identify "this stigma that is attached to their parents' wedding photos – the setting up of the shots, the perfect dress and so forth" and try to "escape" this tradition.[66] TTD photographers render wedding photography as a kind of stiff and regimented clean and proper body while TTD sessions are depicted as somewhat abject. Although such rejections of borders, systems, and rules are standard artistic moves, the in-between and ambiguous can also challenge unique artistic identities and therefore need to be carefully managed.

Eric uses the tagline "It's about creation, not destruction" to emphasize the artistic role of photographers.[67] He wants the images shown on the TTD sites to "convey the creation of beautiful art, not the destruction of a dress." Eric thereby manages concerns about trashing dresses and the damage that the position of destroyer might do to photographers' creative and commercial reputations. Photographers experience imperatives to assert their creativity because their images are understood as a trace of the real rather than artistically determined. Their practices involve other individuals, including brides, assistants, and technicians, and products are multiple rather than one of a kind. Such interrogations of the "meanings of creation and ownership," as women's studies scholar Karina Eileraas suggests, occurred with the development of photography.[68] These dilemmas have increased because digital images are easily altered and circulated. Adding to these conflicts are participants who indicate that TTD represents their choices and creativity. For instance, Cheltee T. and her partner propose to destroy their clothes by making the other person into an art "canvas."[69] They envision turning a "cheap" blank wedding dress, which would otherwise be her preserved gown, into an artistic representation of the event. Jessica chronicles her "creative idea," initiating a TTD session, and concern that the photographer will be too conventional to participate.[70] Photographers suggest that they are helping to free women from cultural constraints but Jessica proposes that women are actively reshaping culture through their TTD choices.

Some viewers further undermine TTD photographers' claims about creativity. For instance, ksl responded to Cooper's early TTD images and wrote, "Women on fire interesting, women drowning haunting (but maybe a little disturbing), women stuffed into a trunk of a car? that is just disgusting, brutal and yes perhaps misogynistic."[71] Jessica invokes the art values that Cooper and Eric reference when declaring that his message "isn't creative or artistic, it is vile."[72] Cooper quickly replied to these posts and managed his reputation. He made fun of women's inquiries by arguing that the "ladies are always try'n to confuse" him "with the long words," and their language was insufficient and unclear.[73] Eric noted that some people have commented, "without understanding the whole story."[74] The "idea for the shot was Dalisa's, John's wife" and was based on her position as a "huge CSI fan." It "was not meant to demean anyone, or promote violence." In writing this, Eric incorrectly implies that women cannot forward misogynistic ideas. He tries to persuade readers to change their opinion because "when the whole concept is explained- it sort of adds a different light, don't you think?" In these accounts, Cooper and Eric are misinterpreted photographers who work against conventions and a public who refuses to understand new art. In a similar manner to what resistance studies scholars describe, they construct oppositional roles for themselves and meanings for their art.[75]

For artists to maintain their claims to resisting conventions and being creative, they must periodically alter their strategies. Thus, in 2008, Cooper announced that he was "Retiring Joan and Ophelia," which are the images of the bride set on fire and the woman drowning, from being his initial website representations and contextualizing his practice.[76] It was "time to put up new images and start to push the boundaries once again, reinventing" his studio and "doing the unexpected." Cooper argues that *Joan* and *Ophelia* would be difficult to find and articulates a culture of rarity. However, they are still available on his site and in other settings and thereby function as reminders of his lineage. While these images are still accessible, Cooper's and Eric's initial practices are less easily determined. Cooper's "Show Off" article is only available through an archiving setting that has nothing to do with the photographers.[77] Eric has deleted a number of the Trash The Dress! sites that marketed and documented early sessions.[78] On his photography blog, sessions are listed under the term "Free to Flaunt," which indicates that post-wedding photography celebrates rather than dismisses the dress and related wedding conventions.[79]

Viewing Pleasures and Positions

Cooper and Eric tend to reject women's investments but wedding forums, where many TTD images are posted, address women. Like other sites, wedding forums use abstract representations of bodies, gender-coded colors, and About pages to indicate who their users are and how they should behave. For instance, You & Your Wedding employs such gender-coded design features as pink "buttons" and a list of "A-Z wedding dresses" to render the setting's focus on women.[80] On the opening parts of WeddingWire, an illustration of a woman in a big white wedding dress and veil codes readers as women.[81] The sexuality of readers is further articulated in a graphic that indicates couples are heterosexual and comprised of a person wearing a dress and another person wearing pants—gendered symbols that are familiar because of bathroom signs.[82]

Wedding sites articulate female, rather than male, forms of looking and evaluative gazing, including women's examination of wedding dresses and brides. There is an abundance of feminist scholarship that considers how the gaze, which is a form of power-laden staring, renders and enforces binary gendered spectatorial positions. In Laura Mulvey's study of classical Hollywood film, she indicates how the subject who gazes is structured as male and his empowered position is supported by the camera's viewpoint.[83] The object of the gaze is expected to be female and she exists in order to be viewed. Mulvey's distinctions between active male and passive female positions are related to the ways Cooper distinguishes between the aggressive role of male photographers, who not only portray but also seduce brides, and the otherwise unwilling positions of female subjects. Yet there are reasons, as Mulvey suggests, to reassess the identification of the gaze as totalizing and purely patriarchal.[84] Media studies scholar Chris Straayer reflects on E. Ann Kaplan and other feminists' psychoanalytically informed considerations of the male gaze and argues that these theories need to be combined with inquiries that determine when the gaze is heterosexual.[85] Since the gaze helps to establish what bodies mean, how they are arranged, and what they can do, research on the ways alternative gazes support and rethink these dyadic structures is critically important.

Feminists consider such forms as women's fashion magazines in order to interrogate the idea that the gaze is always organized around heterosexuality. Diana Fuss describes how women's fashion photography and the continued remediation of this material, in a similar manner to the cinema and its structures, appear to produce women who yearn to be desired by men.[86] Women's fashion photography "poses its models as sexually irresistible subjects" and invites its "female viewers to consume the product by (over)identifying with the image."[87] Yet fashion photographers also produce erotic representations of female bodies so that women will admire them. Visual culture studies scholar Annamari Vänskä adds to this analysis and argues that fashion magazines "tutor" girls and women to "consume the female body" through "gazing."[88] Reina Lewis and Katrina Rolley's research on the lesbian gaze suggests "it is difficult, if not impossible, fully to separate admiration from desiring to be and from desiring to have."[89] Women are taught to desire women and, as Fuss argues, to "look straight *at* women, it appears, straight women must look *as* lesbians."[90] These magazines, for Lewis and Rolley, "educate" the "reader into something very close to a lesbian response" and gaze.[91] While Cooper articulates a heterosexual and controlling relationship between photographers and brides, TTD images focus on brides and educate viewers, who are presumed to be women, into something similar to a lesbian gaze.

Internet wedding forums extend the lesbian looks scripted in fashion magazines and TTD photographs by providing a proliferating archive of same-sex admiration and desire. Women forum participants pleasurably view and comment on photography sessions, dresses, and women's bodies. They identify with representations and specific women when imagining wearing other women's dresses and being the subject of posted images. They therefore function as objects of the gaze. They also actively admire and express desire for the associated women, supporting their own and other people's appeal. For example, halfbaked responds to an image of a woman in a paint-splattered dress. She figures a form of what Lewis and Rolley refer to as a "lesbian response" by including an affective "Drool" in her post, signaling her process of lusting over the subject, and noting that it is her "fave."[92] Boricua_Bride renders a "woot woot, wolf call" and becomes a kind of masculinized animal in order to convey the sexual appeal of another bride.[93] These women use textual devices to convey embodied responses to other women. In such instances, the phrase "lesbian response" indicates the ways women convey their erotic sentiments, how all women admire and desire other women, and the political implications of same-sex and queer desires filtering through women's wedding culture.

Many women wedding forum participants position themselves as engaged viewers of other women and erotica collectors by searching for, gathering, storing, and posting pictures of women in TTD sessions. cld606 "found a couple of sexy pictures. Wanted to share with you girls" and asks, "Do you have any?"[94] TTD is Sarahinwonderland's "favorite type of photography" so she has "hundreds" of images that she can show to the other women who use the forum.[95] Women's wedding forums encourage women to "Find the perfect *wedding dress pictures* and *wedding gown photos*" on their sites.[96] Women participate in TTD picture exchanges and support the continuance and expansion of lesbian spectatorial positions, which all viewers must to some extent occupy, by asking other readers to post and admire compilations. This desire-expanding Internet collecting and posting is an aspect of digitally facilitated eroticism and longing. It also occurs with other kinds of image sharing, including the circulation of selfies, Pinterest boards where people "share" images of the things that they "love," sexting, and porn trading.[97] Indeed, women use the term "wedding porn" in wedding forums and blogs and reshape pornography and its emphasis on naked bodies and sexual activities into feminine pleasures in wedding and bridal images.

Women structure and ask for same-sex admiration when posting their TTD depictions and expecting other women to look at and appreciate them. Women receive such appreciative comments as "How stunning are you!!" "i can't get over how stunning you are!!" and "you are sooo gorgeous."[98] Women also persuade other women to participate in TTD sessions and fulfill their erotic fantasies. For instance, MommyLynda would "love to see" heartssetfreebylove "all rolled up in paint."[99] heartssetfreebylove responds and MommyLynda continues that her "photos would be soooooo sexy if that $25 dress got wet!!! With your ta tas???OmG!" Lallysgirl focuses on women's breasts and writes, "Nice boobs!"[100] Similar remarks concerning women's breasts and other features appear in discussions about engagement sessions, boudoir pictures, wedding dresses, and wedding photographs.[101] They extend lesbian responses and same-sex desires through the varied stages and representations of weddings and make such activities part of women's ongoing lives and cultural conceptions of heterosexuality.

The unmannered aspects of such commentary as "nice boobs" evoke sexual and queer children, who have moved away from cultural expectations of innocence without developing a "mature" voice. TTD sessions and other wedding photography also figure girl children who dream about beautiful weddings and women and thereby grow sideways rather than developing into normative married women.[102] Whether seen as positive or negative attributes, women associate TTD with childish play and self-indulgence and foil the developmental features of weddings and wedding photography. For instance, Nicolette Photography scraps professionalism and expresses her "pure childish excitement" about a TTD session.[103] Tanya Lea McConnell emphasizes the affective experiences of these sessions when contrasting the "conservative folk" who "are shaking in their Sunday's best" and the "childish charm" of people who are willing to do TTD sessions.[104] Yet Laura thinks that TTD is a form of "childish self-destruction."[105] She condemns women for not treating the ritual and valuable wedding items appropriately. Cooper also identifies women as childish for refusing his TTD ideas. Women are associated with the child and childishness when they refuse normative culture and do not focus on other people's needs.

Women may remain within a childish pre-heterosexual culture by embracing women's wedding forums rather than focusing on their married futures and husbands. Men are presumed to have a central position in the lives of women readers and, as Lewis argues, "it is for 'his' eyes that" magazine consumers "study the arts of beauty and dress."[106] Women's attention to men's desires would seem to be expanded in wedding forums. After all, heterosexual weddings legally and ideologically pair women with men. While heterosexual weddings are in some way the subject and intended outcome of the forums, there are rarely any indications in TTD narratives that this culture is produced for or directed at men. In fact, many women indicate fiancés and husbands are disinterested in dresses and TTD sessions. The roles articulated and images produced during TTD sessions figure homosocial, if not homoerotic, spheres where brides and bridesmaids are distinguished from grooms and groomsmen.[107]

Looking and Looking Away

The women who view TTD sessions grow sideways by finding visual and erotic pleasures in images of brides. These experiences may be uneasy when representations are appealing and frightening. Kat identifies Hayley and Seelmeyer's horror-inspired session as "Scary and wonderful" and a reader responds that it is "scary & beautiful!"[108] The affective expressions of brides and the features of TTD sessions can be critically considered through feminist literature on horror and the ways viewers look and look away and are fascinated with and reject things. Viewers such as JoJo Bananas characterize some TTD videos as being "like a horror movie."[109] Miss Sushi is reminded of a "scene from a horror movie" when looking at a TTD image, "but in a good way."[110] These sessions and forum posts thus facilitate bodily sensations that are related to horror viewing, including looking/looking away, pleasure/pain, and calm/shivering, when women are visually and conceptually confronted by the idea of their and other people's wedding dresses being ruined. Their interests in women's bodies may also challenge them. redbullfanatic reports that a few women "gasped in horror" because she was wearing her dress on the beach.[111] These emotional gasps and experiences of being "caught by surprise" are basic aspects of horror, according to Carol Clover's research on this topic.[112] They may echo and supplant the erotic exclamations associated with sex.

Characters in horror films, especially women, and viewers have their vision assailed by things they do not wish to observe. Viewers shut or cover their eyes as a means of protecting themselves from the things that cannot be processed and the agonizing images that convey this information. Viewers engage with, identify with, and resist the text. A version of this happens when AnneNM82 responds to the same video as JoJo Bananas and associates it with "slasher porn" and what is for her excessive, and potentially extremely erotic, violence.[113] D.Marie points out that the bride put a gun to the groom's "head in the video!!"[114] She writes, "What the heck…no way" and emotionally turns away from the associated representations. Horror spectators shift between not completely seeing, recoiling, and fully viewing/comprehending, according to media studies scholar Isabel Cristina Pinedo.[115] Viewers have mutable relationships to bodies within the text. At times, monsters are horrific versions of women's bodies. Women willingly become the monsters in the "True Blood" and "Bride of Frankenstein" sessions. Women also look at monsters and recognize, according to Linda Williams's theorization of gendered horror viewing, that women can threaten men's power.[116] For instance, AnneNM82 imagines that the bride uses the gun in the TTD video to express her feelings about "being intimate."[117] In doing this, AnneNM82 poses brides resisting and turning away from the institution of marriage and heterosexuality.

Women's conceptualization of TTD sessions, like the shivers and phantom pains that can accompany horror spectatorship and connect viewing to feeling, creates a series of corporeal sensations that affect their bodies. ginantonic indicates that trashing her dress "would just be painful!"[118] Seeing some "gorgeous" TTD pictures made ant n tilde's "belly hurt."[119] For photographer Nicola Lambert Hyde, "the thought of deliberately ripping" her dress makes her "shudder" and when she hears the "term Trash The Dress" she gets "a little squeamish."[120] She proposes changing the ways the trend is described, and to some extent enacted, to avoid these embodied responses. In these cases, literally and conceptually looking away is a powerful and controlling strategy for these women because they identify with the clean and proper body and TTD sessions pose their bodies as filthy and fluid and thereby open and in pieces.

Turning away can emphasize rather than displace the visceral aspects of TTD viewing and the varied ways women incorporate and are close to images. Turning away also evokes sideways movements rather than developmental trajectories because viewers refuse the directives and interests of culture that are conveyed by images. Yet the women who oppose and dismiss TTD sessions are important to the coding of this form. Cooper and Eric are reliant on women's refusals of TTD practices as a means of asserting their knowledge and creative growth. Women also underscore the visual and affective potency of sessions by responding. Their evocations of shivering and embodied pain are testaments to the power of TTD images. They mark the women who do TTD sessions as cultural resisters and courageous explorers, moving through unfamiliar spaces and dealing with confining garb. Thus, women's beliefs about the value of their dresses and surprised responses are necessary for TTD to persist as unexpected, divergent from wedding rituals, and as a kind of cultural critique.

Promising Dirt

The term "trash the dress" undermines the demure aspects of wedding dresses and associated images. These women are brought up through garbage and infantilized by their link to excrement. TTD problematizes wedding culture since dirt "signals a site of possible danger to social and individual systems," according to Grosz, "a site of vulnerability."[121] Anthropologist Mary Douglas underscores how dirt is "matter out of place" that disturbs cultural categories.[122] Photographers use blogs and other methods to supervise cultural conceptions of TTD, particularly the forms of dirt and resistance that get coupled to this practice, and even establish less threatening names for sessions. Stone Ridge Photographers assures women that it "isn't interested in destroying anyone's dress."[123] There "may only be a tiny bit of dirt (similar to after the reception) on the hem which a dry cleaner can get out," writes photographer Stacy Able, and if "a bride is sentimental about archiving the gown, steps can be taken" to "minimize wear/dirt on the gown."[124] She points to the careful regulation of degrees of resistance. She also associates TTD with the rituals and features of weddings, including the likelihood of staining dresses, rather than the more usual distinctions between these practices.

Feminist considerations of abjection and fluid bodies offer critical models for considering how the TTD processes of getting wedding dresses wet and dirty disorder normative forms of femininity. Contemporary Western societies, as Grosz argues, negatively construct the female body "as a leaking, uncontrollable, seeping liquid; as formless flow; as viscosity, entrapping, secreting; as lacking not so much or simply the phallus but self-containment."[125] The gaze can be abject or render others as abject, according to Karen Jacobs, because its violent construction often conceptually rents the individuals viewed, it facilitates an ambivalent regard, it situates individuals too close to forbidden and polluted objects, and things that were previously unrepresentable and unseeable, but are now delivered by new technologies, generate fascination and horror.[126] This may include the persistent changeability of technologies. Abjection is an aspect of the gaze and incorporated into the body as sensations. Such forms of abjection as food loathing and other boundary disruptions trigger gagging and bodily spasms.

114 It's about "Creation, Not Destruction"

Some unappealing and spoiled foods make Kristeva's heartbeat increase and cause her to refuse to assimilate them.[127] Through these forms of subjectification, she simultaneously abjects and establishes herself. A group of individuals also shudder, look away, try to reject it, and end up abjecting and establishing themselves when thinking about TTD.

Dirty wedding dresses disturb some viewers but brides cover themselves in mud and reference such abject substances as pus, vomit, and shit. These experiences challenge the boundaries of the body and its whole and proper position. As Grosz writes, body fluids trace "the paths of entry or exit, the routes of interchange or traffic with the world."[128] The light-skinned Julianne highlights this porous and filthy body when she appears in white but directs a lover's kiss towards the mud-slathered shoe she holds.[129] Dirt rather than a groom has become the subject of her attention. Her flesh is scarred and legs caked with mud.[130] Under her soiled dress, the shape and texture of the muck is excremental. In another muddy session, Rema's bare feet shape the dirt into dung-like piles.[131] Her skin is turned dark gray by the black and white photography and her toes are so mired that they seem to be half formed by this muck and deteriorating into the wet and broken mass. This is horror photography because women fear small amounts of dirt will taint their dresses and Julianne and Rema appear to have been buried and exhumed. These depictions of repellent fluids and dirty bodies may briefly attract viewers but they also make women difficult to gaze at. During these instances of repulsed viewing, in the varied ways this term signifies, women are linked to the monster and monstrous. Threatened by "the sight of the monstrous," as film studies scholar Barbara Creed argues, "the viewing subject is put into crisis."[132] This breakdown occurs when Rema's separate toes melt into and are consolidated by the mud. Through such representations, viewers understand the precariousness of their position as coherent bodies. Stomachs hurt and other pains erupt as horror texts and TTD sessions figure the inside rushing outside and clothing and bodies dissolving.

This shift from clean to open body is emphasized by Emily's images. At the beginning of the session, the very pale and pink Emily rests cleanly and prettily in her wedding dress on a group of rocks.[133] A creek burbles near her feet. However, her dress is just draped over her upper thigh and she appears about to fall back and reveal her crotch and buttocks. Emily also sits on a mud bank and enters a pond. When leaving the water and viewed from the back, patches of dirt emphasize Emily's buttocks and evoke anal sex and evacuation. She also holds a red and purple bouquet so that it is aligned with her backside, appears as a corollary to the dirt print, and works as a stand-in for menstruation. An image of raspberry's once-white legs reveals pinkish-red stains near her hips and groin, a trail of rusty red dripping down her ankle, and blackened toenails. Like menstruation, these TTD messes leak, remain visible after drying, and are connected to out-of-control states. Iris Marion Young, in her study of women's corporeality, indicates how menstrual bleeding is culturally coded as "dirty, disgusting, defiling, and thus must be hidden."[134] However, these women intentionally get their wedding dresses dirty and thereby propose a kind of marriage to filth.

In Emily's last image, the grimy dress hangs out of a trash barrel and the bouquet is perched on the cover. Jessica "shoved the most expensive and symbolic item" from her "wardrobe into a giant green trashbag to haul home" from a TTD session.[135] She "couldn't wipe the grin off" her face as she listened to "the water swish inside the bag." Such dresses may be adopted, cleaned up, or discarded but something sticky and pleasurable remains. After reading about such filth-focused sessions, forum readers often decide that it is so much "FUN" that they should do one themselves.[136] According to Creed, such moments are appealing and abjection "is always there, beckoning the self to take up the place" where boundaries and meanings collapse.[137] The "subject is constantly beset by abjection which fascinates desire but must be repelled for fear of self-annihilation." sweetmelissa experiences such ambivalence when changing into her "dress in a seedy restroom," associating this TTD session with getting "every last ounce of joy out" of her gown, and trying to "put it on without letting the bottom touch the icky concrete floor!!!"[138] Remnants of TTD sessions linger on participants' bodies, are recorded in forum postings, and function as additional and improper skins. Their abject affect combines with, and is literally read through, the fingerprints and grease marks on computer screens to constitute Internet settings as messy rather than rational and ordered. These handprints are records of producing women and triggers for abjection. Such corporeal accretions point to embodied technologies and instances where women's practices and hardware intermesh.

Ass-Kicking Techno-Brides

Women combine conceptions of the corporeal and technological when arranging TTD scenarios and fighting zombies. In these sessions, women destroy dresses and use guns and other gear to render active and ass-kicking roles.[139] For instance, Jennifer and her future husband (FH) had an idea for a "'zombie-apocalypse' trash the dress" that she vetted and then depicted in the WeddingWire forum.[140] Jennifer and her "FH," who she does not specifically name, love to play "zombie shooter games" and were thinking about having their "friends" and the bridal party "dress up as zombies" and "slowly destroy the dress" as they "fight back." The couple conceptualizes this session as a condensation of their varied interests and as a way of representing themselves. She asks readers, "Is this too crazy?" and the women who read the forum support her proposal and reply that the concept is wonderful and that they would like to do a similar kind of TTD.

iconicaphotography describes how zombies disrupt the mannered aspects of Jennifer and her partner's wedding session: The "poor unfortunate newlyweds" were "enjoying a romantic photo shoot just after saying 'I do,' and out of nowhere comes a pack of ugly, disgusting and completely rude zombies. Not only did they try to eat one" of the photographer's "favorite couples, they also completely trashed the bride's dress!"[141] iconicaphotography then admits, "this scenario was rigged," "the bride and groom did plan this elaborate trash the dress photo shoot," and "it was an absolute blast." iconicaphotography articulates different origin stories for this session and diverse relationships to wedding photography. Wedding photography is depicted as a ritualistic and constrained practice that should not be disrupted and as something that can be parodied and undone so that couples and photographers can enjoy themselves.

Many TTD photographers associate such creative aspects of TTD with their practices. However, Jennifer's session and the associated women's wedding forum posts point to the artistic project of the bride and couple. For instance, Jennifer conceptualizes, assesses, and produces this session with and for the women who read WeddingWire as well as her FH. In a related manner, makeup artists Alexandra and Bill McCoy's zombie session is facilitated by the couple who are, according to Spectacle Photo, "Not only responsible for the demise of the zombies, but for the creation of them. Not only a quick hand with a gun, but with a make-up brush."[142] They are acknowledged as producers and credited with creating and destroying zombies. These zombie sessions and accounts thereby challenge claims that TTD is an act of creation rather than destruction. Cultural conceptions of zombies parallel this differentiation and conflation of creation and destruction. Zombies are conceptualized as monstrous because they are not procreative but uncontrollably and excessively reproduce. Their unrelenting spread is an interesting stand-in for generative wedding images, which encourage more types of sessions and representations, are available in multiples and reproducible, and are quickly reposted on numerous websites and social media settings.

The representations of Jennifer and her husband's zombie session begin with some traditional wedding photographs of the pale bride looking down at a mirror, neatly putting on her makeup, and producing herself as an attractive bridal subject.[143] These images seem to constitute brides and women as objects of the male gaze, and in some of them the groom looks at Jennifer as she shyly looks away. Then a female zombie head appears between the couple and ruptures their dyadic pairing. The couple screams and cowers as the mass of zombies hail the couple with reaching arms and open mouths that pose the dissolution rather than constitution of the individuals and couple. Jennifer dramatically holds the back of her palm to her forehead and opens her mouth in a shriek. She parodies the behavior of female victims in horror movies. In quoting these gestures, she highlights how women are rendered as weak and positions herself as a knowing subject who breaks out of wedding and horror conventions. Jennifer then self-presents as the empowered woman. Sherrie Innes and Gillis address similar performances and argue that aggressiveness is expected of female action heroes, who fight back rather than waiting for men to save them.[144] Gillis tempers this form of agency when noting that the fury of these women is coupled with their position as erotic subjects. Jennifer further adjusts this by resisting some gendered wedding conventions while positioning herself as the object of the gaze. For instance, she begins the TTD session wearing high-heels. At an important juncture in her transformation into the ass-kicking fighter, she replaces this shoe with sturdier knee-high lace-up boots.

Jennifer's boots support her revolutionary makeover because similar combat boots have been associated with active women in post-apocalyptic films, lesbians, riot grrrls, and punks and thus with people's resistance to norms.[145] Julia Emberley identifies the "violence in the 'punk-boot' that kicks back the waste of the bourgeoisie" in a "violent gesture designed to scare the shit out of 'them.'"[146] In a related manner, TTD participants and photographers conceptually kick the dress and some of the more limiting aspects of wedding culture back towards those maintaining conventions. Emberley also argues that the tendency to repeat such styles as punk, sometimes with less political intention, raises questions about using fashion subversively. Yet Jennifer has costumed and produced herself as an image of resistance and as a powerful woman who does not need help from and does not fear men or zombies.

At one point in the TTD session, the front ruffles of Jennifer's dress are ripped off to the upper thigh so that she can run and further show off her legs. Her husband gestures with outstretched guns but she out-mans him with her rifle. She lifts up her boot-clad leg on a metal drum, twists her mouth in a scream, and raises her gun but the pose also allows her to show off her boots, fishnet-clad upper-thigh, and blood-splattered skirt. By strapping on the boots, Jennifer forms her legs into dark phallic columns and articulates a more powerful role. She bases her claim to power on the recrafting of wedding garb and the ways that she wears these items. In another image, a female zombie lurches towards Jennifer while holding her muddy shoes and veil. When Jennifer raises the gun, she aims at the accouterments associated with her previous self and produces another image of commanding women. However, she also uses such actions as lunging at the violent other, kicking-ass, and kicking up the leg as moments of display.

Gillis rightly argues that depictions of ass-kicking techno-babes support male interests and fantasies. However, the versions of ass-kicking fighters that are produced by brides and photographers, and subsequently posted by women in wedding forums, are more likely to speak to women. The most extended dialogue about Jennifer's session was initiated by her and appears on WeddingWire.[147] In this setting, Jennifer has posted a variety of images, including a photograph of her wearing the dress and boots in the kitchen and the photograph of her kicking her leg up on the drum. With the kitchen image, Jennifer brings her interests back to a feminine sphere. This feminization of TTD and its audience is emphasized since the picture seems to have been taken so that she can share it with readers. These brides thus pose a TTD experience that women collaboratively produce and that they design so that the other women can see them.

Conclusion: Divorce TTD and Killing the Groom

TTD sessions and the destruction of dresses are marketed as expressions of brides' commitments to husbands and relationships. As GinaBee argues, "TTD symbolizes that you will never wear that dress again" and provides a way to "break into marriage in a fun artsy way."[148] While it used to be rare for women to wear their big white wedding dresses again, TTD has created a culture in which women can frequently don their gowns. TTD also connects a variety of occasions to wedding dresses. Photographer Jamie Salup indicates that people can do TTD to "relive the day, celebrate a marriage that will never break, or even symbolize a divorce and a new beginning."[149] In a similar manner, a group of event planners argue that TTD is an "intriguing concept for both weddings and divorces."[150] Eric's early TTD image of a muddy bride, which was used to represent the practice and marriage commitments, has more recently illustrated an article on how to throw a divorce party.[151] Pinterest "divorce" boards include images from Jennifer's and other couples' sessions.[152]

Some photographers express concerns about incorporating divorce sessions into their practices. Kevin's blog and his position as a wedding photographer are "usually filled with alot of love and laughter" so when a former client emailed about doing a TTD divorce session he "was just a little torn."[153] He wanted to work with her again but "wondered if the story belonged" on "the blog. After all," writes Kevin, "you don't see the word 'divorce' on a photographers website alot." Kevin points to the potential ideological and economic damage that divorce TTD sessions can cause to his business and to wedding culture. Of course, Kevin's comments also indicate the ways TTD is immediately correlated with blogging and the marketing of photographers and circulation of images of women. Kevin justifies the session by arguing that there is "still an awful lot of love" in his client's life because she "has four of the most amazing kids." In noting this, he connects TTD divorce sessions to ongoing reproductive and familial relationships, which are also emphasized in wedding photography. Kevin expresses concern but wedding photographers are incorporating the term "divorce" into their sites and marketing divorce sessions. For instance, Helene Cornell Photography asserts, "Forget Trash the Dress, Divorce shoots are the hottest new trend in wedding photography."[154] Helene Cornell Photography thereby makes the final outcome of the union and its representations into a process of separation, acrimony, and singleness.

Joelle Caputa's websites and unpublished book, which is titled *Trash the Dress: Stories of Celebrating Divorce in Your 20s*, also rework the rituals and meanings of TTD so that they are associated with divorce.[155] Caputa's websites have even supplanted the original concept because Eric removed many of the Trash the Dress! sites and she tactically uses "trashthedress" as part of her URLs. She designed her projects to show "women that divorce in your 20s is just the beginning of the life you were meant to live." Caputa writes, "Trash the dress, burry your wedding album in the back of your closet, and celebrate your divorce!"[156] She thereby associates trashing the dress with breaking up and getting rid of wedding symbols. Heterosexual marriages are also replaced with a culture that allows young divorced women to engage over life changes.

Caputa proposes communities of divorced women who are informed by TTD. Hanssie Trainor emphasizes communities of photographers and how they develop skills in TTD. In her image from a TTD training event, a blonde bride holds a blood-smeared knife to the cross hanging around her neck and severs her relationship with filial decency.[157] The bride's body is formed into an almost vertical columnar mass by the dress but the groom is more open because he is lying on the ground, his chest is smeared with blood, and his head is cropped out of the frame. Nick Yutaka's images from the session include the same blood-splattered bride with a circular saw as an accessory.[158] Yutaka describes his version of the bride and eviscerated groom. He writes, "torso: check. ripped out heart: check. severed foot: check. 'trash the dress' or stephen king's carrie?" Yutaka encourages readers to "peep the carnage" and foregrounds the ways TTD is associated with horror and horrified looking. Through this experience, Yutaka is also trained to include women who kill as part of TTD sessions. Varied women take up such violent images, represent the death of their spouses, and rescript their marital roles and relationships.

Sara conveys the death of her ex-husband in TTD pictures from the day the "divorce was finalized."[159] The extremely pale bride appears in a wrecked home with bloody handprints all over her gown. She clutches a (beef) heart; screams; and seems to be destroying the union, its consumerist structures, and her ex-husband. Sara's images of bridal rage exceed the visual functions of TTD because some viewers find them "almost too nightmarish" to "look at." Through these representations, Sara resists her feminine position as an appealing object and contributes to feminist methods of refusing the empowered gaze. Images like Sara's are disruptive because, as Tiina Mäntymäki notes in her study of novels about murderous women, "violence is culturally encoded as male."[160] The "woman who turns violent diverges from the script of femininity." Thus, Sara is not a productive stand-in for TTD customers because her relationship did not work and she is deemed to be too unattractive and threatening when smeared with blood.[161] Sara's session and gown, which is ordinarily associated with normative femininity, remove her from feminine categorizations.

Murderous women are also depicted in other kinds of wedding photography. For example, Lianne contacted Miller + Miller wedding photographers with an idea for an engagement session that adopts many of the murderous themes from TTD. The blogged session features the brown Lianne wearing a blood splattered white dress and holding a large bowie knife [Figure 3.2].[162] After kissing her dark-skinned fiancé, Lianne looks cunningly at the knife and then hides it behind her back. She holds her finger up to her mouth as if to indicate that she shares a childlike secret with the viewer. Lianne engages with her partner as

120 It's about "Creation, Not Destruction"

FIGURE 3.2 Miller + Miller Photography, Reprinted with permission. Engagement sessions also work against conventions by portraying agentive and murderous women.

she waits to kill him. Her movement is individually directed and antithetical to the usual progressions of brides. At the end of the rampage, she rides away on the motorcycle that her fiancé drove at the beginning of the session. If there is a romantic or visual connection in these images, it is the link between Lianne's white dress and the shining almost-white blade of the knife. Women are often correlated with jewels and other glittering things but in TTD sessions beringed fingers and shiny tools extend the body and propel its motions. In the horror genre, knives, nails, and improvised weapons also extend the body and make killing into a form of queer intimacy, including non-normative forms of passion and penetration.[163] Women such as Lianne, who adopt such queer imaging strategies before their divorce and act out the excision of their husbands, declare, whether intentionally or not, that the continuation of heterosexuality is impossible. Their wedding images are imaginings of familial separation and the literal severing of the groom. They allow women to pleasurably remain in the otherwise temporary bridal position.

Posters on women's wedding forums also propose ways of remaining in the provisional bridal position. Participants indicate that they find wedding sites, weddings, and connections with other women deeply pleasurable even after getting married. Through their TTD sessions and engagements in forums, they remain involved with wedding culture and in the role of the bride. For instance, MercyK stayed dedicated to the forums for "over a year after being married."[164] foxybride1024, who is married but remains associated with brides through her forum name, finds the setting "too great to leave."[165] Many participants are tied into other women's wedding planning. For instance, midnyteblue110609 has so "many friends on this site who aren't yet married."[166] midnyteblue110609 declares that she "might as well stay until they tie the knot" in a few years. She remains engaged with the position of the bride and cycles through the experiences and features of weddings. Of course, this commitment to other brides and weddings, as midnyteblue110609 suggests, can be delightfully never-ending since most women initially select these sites to plan their weddings. With these arrangements, repetition replaces linear development and monogamous heterosexual love is displaced by a love of weddings and brides.

Weddings are ordinarily associated with heterosexual love but wedding forums are also linked to women's passions for these events and other brides. MountainBride is "so over" her own wedding and the associated markers of her heterosexual union but remains named as a bride. She "LOVE[S] other peoples weddings, and weddings in general."[167] par228 expresses her "love" for weddings and "helping all the other soon to be MRS."[168] This is a love of a feminine culture where women do most of the planning for weddings. Women and wedding sites are engaged with dream days that might at one time have ended for individuals after the ritual. However, they no longer have to conclude because of their friendly and queer commitments to other brides. The threads on wedding forums, in a manner that is related to the addresses of other Internet settings, are calls for comment and ties that bind women to these structures. They encourage an intensive focus on weddings that is a prelude to and training ground for intensive mothering and intensive social networking.

Photographers and brides highlight women who are recently married and market their TTD sessions as a form of resistance and participants as resisters. Yet divorced women also render TTD as a form of connection and empowerment through resistance. In these cases, resistance means opposition to women's marriages. It also points to the diverse cohorts who produce women and claim to produce TTD sessions. TTD, which was and still is marketed as a way of indicating that weddings and commitments are eternal, also foregrounds the limits and frailties of relationships. TTD critiques, the queering of TTD representations, and theorizations of resistance can foreground these frailties and prevent sessions from furthering the more confining aspects of wedding culture. Women's erotica collecting and queer responses to TTD are reminders of the diverse desires that circulate in Internet settings. As the significance of Internet settings increases, it becomes more difficult to contain such queer engagements and forms of production, including instances of other sorts of growth and movement, with stories about traditional weddings and monogamous heterosexuality. The bloody, hungry, and ferocious behaviors of zombie walk brides, as I suggest in the next chapter, undermine even more aspects of weddings. For instance, zombie brides' interest in consuming everyone challenges the monogamous heterosexual features of weddings.

Notes

1. Etsy, "Etsy – Email Sign Up," 24 May 2014, http://www.etsy.com/emails/weddings
2. Etsy, "Etsy – About," 24 May 2014, https://www.etsy.com/?ref=about
3. Rock n Roll Bride, "Killer Style, Crazy Love – Alternative Wedding Inspiration," 29 January 2014, http://www.rocknrollbride.com
4. Lynette Seelmeyer, "True Blood," Rock n Roll Bride, 4 December 2009, 22 June 2014, http://www.rocknrollbride.com/2009/12/true-blood/
5. Lynette Seelmeyer, Picture This Photography, LLC, 7 August 2014, http://www.thepicturechick.com/
6. Kat, "Happy Halloween – Bride of Frankenstein," Rock n Roll Bride, 31 October 2009, 13 June 2014, http://www.rocknrollbride.com/2009/10/happy-halloween-bride-of-frankenstein/
7. There has also been an unfortunate incident where a bride died while participating in a TTD session. Ellen Connolly, "Bride falls to her death posing for wedding photos on waterfall in Canada," *GlobalPost*, 24 August 2012, 12 December 2013, http://www.globalpost.com/dispatch/news/regions/americas/canada/120824/bride-falls-her-death-posing-wedding-photos-waterfall
8. I have only found a small number of examples of same-sex couples performing in TTD sessions. Blue Olive Photography, "Margo & Sherwin's Granville Island Wedding," 3 October 2008, 13 June 2014, www.blueolivephotography.com/blog/2008/10/03/granville-island-wedding/
9. Miller, "Not Just Weapons"; Munro, "Resisting 'Resistance.'"
10. Thomas and Davies, "What Have the Feminists Done?"
11. Clover, *Men, Women, and Chain Saws*; Fuss, "Fashion and the Homospectatorial"; Lewis and Rolley, "Ad(dressing) the Dyke."
12. Kristeva, *Powers of Horror*.
13. Mayo, *Human Problems*.
14. Hargreaves, "Resistance and Relative Autonomy"; Miller, "Not Just Weapons"; Munro, "Resisting 'Resistance'"; Thomas and Davies, "What Have the Feminists Done?"
15. Abowitz, "Pragmatist Revisioning of Resistance," 878.
16. Munro, "Resisting 'Resistance.'"
17. Ortner, "Resistance and the Problem," 174.
18. Fleming, "Metaphors of Resistance"; Jermier, Knights, and Nord, *Resistance and Power*; P. Prasad and A. Prasad, "Stretching the Iron Cage"; Scott, *Weapons of the Weak*.
19. hooks, *Ain't I a Woman*; Butler, *Gender Trouble*; Diamond and Quinby, eds. *Feminism and Foucault*.
20. Thomas and Davies, "What Have the Feminists Done?" 720.
21. Kristeva, *Powers of Horror*.
22. Grosz, *Volatile Bodies*, 192.
23. Lori Adalsteinsson, as quoted in Donna Tam, "Wedding attire subjected to unconventional treatment," *Spokesman-Review*, 16 August 2007, 22 June 2014, http://news.google.com/newspapers?nid=1314&dat=20070816&id=9aBXAAAAIBAJ&sjid=cfMDAAAAIBAJ&pg=6925,4588516
24. Benkler, *Wealth of Networks*; Jenkins, *Fans, Bloggers, and Gamers*; Kahn and Kellner, "New Media."
25. Gillett, "Internet Web Logs," 28.
26. Khondker, "Role of the New Media"; Lotan et al., "Revolutions Were Tweeted."
27. Daniels, "Race and Racism."
28. Gillis, "(Post)Feminist Politics of Cyberpunk," 7.
29. Gibson, *Neuromancer*.
30. Edwards, "Blonde with the Guns."

31. de Lauretis, *Technologies of Gender*.
32. Helford, "Postfeminism."
33. Brown, "Gender and the Action Heroine."
34. Jamie Miles, "Infographic: The National Average Cost of a Wedding is $28,427," The Knot, 16 December 2013, http://blog.theknot.com/2013/03/07/average-wedding-cost-2013/. Critics such as William Oremus point out that this number can be misleading because the average includes people who spend a great deal of money on their weddings. The median was still 18,086 in Manhattan, NY, which had the highest wedding spending. It was 8,440 in Alaska. William Oremus, "The Wedding Industry's Pricey Little Secret," Slate, 12 June 2013, http://www.slate.com/articles/life/weddings/2013/06/average_wedding_cost_published_numbers_on_the_price_of_a_wedding_are_totally.single.html
35. Telegraph, "The great bridal train robbery," 1 May 2013, 13 June 2014, http://www.dailytelegraph.com.au/the-great-bridal-train-robbery/story-e6freuy9-1226632632496; Bride to Be, "The average cost of a wedding in Australia," 16 December 2013, http://www.bridetobe.com.au/article/planning-latest-trends-the-average-cost-of-a-wedding-in-australia; Jessica Irvine, "Here comes the bride, all dressed in red," *Sydney Morning Herald*, 7 April 2012, 12 June 2014, http://www.smh.com.au/opinion/society-and-culture/here-comes-the-bride-all-dressed-in-red-20120406-1wgsl.html
36. Telegraph, "Average wedding now costs more than £18,000," 22 May 2013, http://www.telegraph.co.uk/finance/personalfinance/10072716/Average-wedding-now-costs-more-than-18000.html; Brides, "Average Cost of Wedding in UK: Wedding Budget Breakdown," 7 January 2013, 22 June 2014, http://www.bridesmagazine.co.uk/planning/general/planning-service/2013/01/average-cost-of-wedding
37. Telegraph, "Average wedding now costs more than £18,000," 22 May 2013, 16 December 2013, http://www.telegraph.co.uk/finance/personalfinance/10072716/Average-wedding-now-costs-more-than-18000.html
38. Kayla Epstein, "Counting the cost: you won't believe what these wedding guests spent…," *Guardian*, 9 July 2013, http://www.theguardian.com/commentisfree/2013/jul/09/weddings-cost-readers-respond
39. Carey Purcell, "Being a bridesmaid is driving me into bankruptcy," Salon, 23 June 2014, http://www.salon.com/2014/06/23/being_a_bridesmaid_is_driving_me_into_bankruptcy_partner/
40. Lisa Ellis, "What It Costs To Trash Your Wedding Dress," WhatItCosts, 12 March 2014, http://weddings.whatitcosts.com/trash-wedding-dress-pg3.htm
41. Bambacas, "Thinking about White Weddings," 193.
42. Heise, "I'm a Modern Bride."
43. Lewis, "Working the Ritual."
44. Oswald, "Member of the Wedding?" 108.
45. Alicia Robichaud Photography, "Friends," Flickr, 11 July 2010, 13 June 2014, http://www.flickr.com/photos/aliciarphoto/4791673893/in/set-72157624305896841/
46. Alicia Robichaud Photography, "Mud Fight," Flickr, 11 July 2010, 13 June 2014, http://www.flickr.com/photos/aliciarphoto/4792297480/in/set-72157624305896841/
47. Stockton, *Queer Child*.
48. Bubbly Bride, "Bubbly Bride: Pole Dancing Lessons For Your Bachelorette Party!" OneWed, 8 June 2009, 13 June 2014, http://www.onewed.com/blog/savvy-scoop/category/bridal-beauty-hair-makeup/2009/06/07/bubbly-bride-pole-dancing-lessons-your-bachelorette-party
49. White, "Concerns about Being Visible."
50. John Michael Cooper, "Show Off! (a.k.a. Trashing the Dress)," Internet Archive, 1 February 2006, 17 December 2013, http://web.archive.org/web/20060207051456/www.wedshooter.com/2006/02/01/show-off-aka-trashing-the-dress

51. jmc, "Being Featured on Inside Edition," AltF, 26 October 2011, 18 December 2013, http://www.earth13.com/weddings/being-featured-on-inside-edition/
52. John Michael Cooper, "Show Off! (a.k.a. Trashing the Dress)," Internet Archive, 1 February 2006, 17 December 2013, http://web.archive.org/web/20060207051456/www.wedshooter.com/2006/02/01/show-off-aka-trashing-the-dress
53. Filax, "Resisting Resistors," 262.
54. John Michael Cooper, "Show Off! (a.k.a. Trashing the Dress)," Internet Archive, 1 February 2006, 17 December 2013, http://web.archive.org/web/20060207051456/www.wedshooter.com/2006/02/01/show-off-aka-trashing-the-dress
55. markeric, "The Godfather of Trashing- John Michael Cooper (alt f)," Trash The Dress! 14 June 2007, http://trashthedress.wordpress.com/2007/06/14/the-godfather-of-trashing-john-michael-cooper-alt-f/
56. Nead, "Seductive Canvases."
57. markeric, "The Godfather of Trashing- John Michael Cooper (alt f)," Trash The Dress! 14 June 2007, 19 April 2009, http://trashthedress.wordpress.com/2007/06/14/the-godfather-of-trashing-john-michael-cooper-alt-f/
58. Filax, "Resisting Resistors," 262.
59. Bergstein, "Artist in His Studio."
60. Robin Summerfield, "Trashing the dress," *Calgary Herald*, 13 July 2007, 13 June 2014, http://www.canada.com/topics/lifestyle/story.html?id=92e34b79-d8d7-48de-86c2-2deffef1df1e&k=74118
61. Izzy Grinspan, "Wedding trashers," Salon, 30 June 2007, 13 June 2014, http://www.salon.com/mwt/feature/2007/06/30/wedding_dress/
62. Political movements have deployed garments as part of their ethos and message. This includes the Black Panthers' and Black Power movement's use of afros, black berets, dashikis, and items with the black power sign; Chinese Communist Party's Zhongshan or Mao suits; and the Rastafari movement's dreadlocks and rastacaps. Davis, "Afro Images"; Kelley, "Nap Time"; Chen, "Dressing for the Party."
63. Theo, "Trash the dress Susanna Photo Gallery by Theo at pbase.com," Pbase, 9 July 2007, 14 October 2010, http://www.pbase.com/theo/trashsu
64. The Swimming Fully Clothed Blog, 17 December 2013, http://blog.swimmingfullyclothed.com/
65. Joel Wiebner, "The Godfather of Trashing- John Michael Cooper (alt f)," Trash the Dress! 13 June 2007, 19 April 2009, http://trashthedress.wordpress.com/2007/06/14/the-godfather-of-trashing-john-michael-cooper-alt-f/
66. Matt Adcock, as quoted in Michael Roney, "TRASH THE DRESS (TTD)," Wedpix Magazine, 22 June 2014, http://www.wedpix.com/articles/trash-the-dress/ttd-trash-the-dress-photo-sessions.html
67. Mark Eric, "'Trash the Dress' – It's About Creation, not Destruction," MCP Actions, 2 June 2009, 28 November 2013, http://www.mcpactions.com/blog/2009/06/02/trash-the-dress/
68. Eileraas, "Reframing the Colonial Gaze."
69. Cheltee T., "So many Choices," Something About You and Me, 15 January 2013, 13 March 2014, http://somethingaboutyounme.blogspot.com/2013/01/so-many-choices.html
70. Jessica, as quoted in Chris Honour, "Trash the Dress 'It's about creation, not destruction,'" East Orlando Photography, 20 August 2007, 28 November 2013, http://eastorlandophotography.com/blog/2007/08/trash-the-dress-it%E2%80%99s-about-creation-not-destruction/
71. ksl, "The Godfather of Trashing- John Michael Cooper (alt f)," Trash The Dress! 14 June 2007, 18 May 2009, http://trashthedress.wordpress.com/2007/06/14/the-godfather-of-trashing-john-michael-cooper-alt-f/

72. Jessica, "The Godfather of Trashing- John Michael Cooper (alt f)," Trash The Dress! 14 June 2007, 18 May 2009, http://trashthedress.wordpress.com/2007/06/14/the-godfather-of-trashing-john-michael-cooper-alt-f/
73. johnmichaelcooper, "The Godfather of Trashing- John Michael Cooper (alt f)," Trash The Dress! 14 June 2007, 18 May 2009, http://trashthedress.wordpress.com/2007/06/14/the-godfather-of-trashing-john-michael-cooper-alt-f/
74. markeric, "The Godfather of Trashing- John Michael Cooper (alt f)," Trash The Dress! 14 June 2007, 19 April 2009, http://trashthedress.wordpress.com/2007/06/14/the-godfather-of-trashing-john-michael-cooper-alt-f/
75. Mumby, "Theorizing Resistance."
76. John Michael Cooper, "Retiring Joan and Ophelia," AltF, 12 December 2008, 18 December 2013, http://www.earth13.com/anti/retiring-joan-and-ophelia/
77. John Michael Cooper, "Show Off! (a.k.a. Trashing the Dress)," Internet Archive, 1 February 2006, 17 December 2013, http://web.archive.org/web/20060207051456/www.wedshooter.com/2006/02/01/show-off-aka-trashing-the-dress.
78. Trash The Dress Australia! and Trash The Dress – Europe are still available but no one has posted any new blog posts since 2010. Trash The Dress Australia! 8 March 2010, 22 June 2014, http://trashthedressaustralia.wordpress.com/; Trash The Dress – Europe, 22 February 2010, 22 June 2014, http://trashthedresseurope.wordpress.com/
79. Mark Eric, "Published Work Free to Flaunt," Mark Eric Photo Journal, 29 May 2014, http://www.markeric.com/category/free-to-flaunt/
80. You & Your Wedding, 24 December 2013, http://www.youandyourwedding.co.uk
81. WeddingWire, "Weddings, Wedding Venues," 24 December 2013, http://www.weddingwire.com/
82. WeddingWire, "About WeddingWire, About Us," 24 December 2013, http://www.weddingwire.com/corp/about-us
83. Mulvey, "Visual Pleasure."
84. Mulvey, "Unmasking the Gaze."
85. Straayer, *Deviant Eyes, Deviant Bodies*; Kaplan, "Is the Gaze Male?"
86. Fuss, "Fashion and the Homospectatorial."
87. Ibid., 713.
88. Vänskä, "Why Are There No Lesbian?" 70.
89. Lewis and Rolley, "Ad(dressing) the Dyke," 179.
90. Fuss, "Fashion and the Homospectatorial," 714.
91. Lewis and Rolley, "Ad(dressing) the Dyke," 181.
92. halfbaked, "Re: 'Trash the dress.'" NYCityWeddings, 7 October 2009, 28 January 2014, http://www.nycityweddings.com/chat/topic.aspx?ID=642069&Highlight=trash
93. Boricua_Bride, "AWWW: Ghana_bride TTD pic teasers on blog…," Project Wedding, 2 March 2010, 18 December 2013, http://www.projectwedding.com/forums/awww-ghana_bride-ttd-pic-teasers-on-blog?page=1
94. cld606, "Trash the Dress Pictures," Project Wedding, 28 August 2009, 13 June 2014, http://www.projectwedding.com/post/list/trash-the-dress-pictures
95. Sarahinwonderland, "Trash the dress inspiration Post em ladies!" Project Wedding, 19 February 2009, 22 June 2014, http://www.projectwedding.com/forums/trash-the-dress-inspiration-post-em-ladies?page=2
96. WeddingWire, "Wedding Dress Photos, Wedding Dresses Pictures," 4 July 2014, http://www.weddingwire.com/wedding-photos/dresses
97. Pinterest, "Pinterest / Home," 22 August 2012, http://pinterest.com/; Slater, "Trading Sexpics on IRC."
98. misshammy, "{Trash the Dress}," Project Wedding, 18 June 2009, 27 March 2010, http://www.projectwedding.com/biography/list/MrsRaz/trash-the-dress; midnyteblue110609, "{Trash the Dress}," Project Wedding, 18 June 2009, 27 March 2010, www.projectwedding.com/biography/list/MrsRaz/trash-the-dress; misshammy, "TRASH THE DRESS TEASER PICTURES!" Project Wedding,

12 October 2009, 27 March 2010, http://www.projectwedding.com/post/list/trass-the-dress-teaser-pictures?page=3
99. MommyLynda, "Trash the dress inspiration Post em ladies!" Project Wedding, 19 February 2009, 22 June 2014, http://www.projectwedding.com/forums/trash-the-dress-inspiration-post-em-ladies
100. Lallysgirl, "AWWW: Ghana_bride TTD pic teasers on blog...," Project Wedding, 2 March 2010, 18 December 2013, http://www.projectwedding.com/forums/awww-ghana_bride-ttd-pic-teasers-on-blog?page=3
101. White, "Concerns about Being Visible."
102. Stockton, *Queer Child*.
103. Nicolette Photography, "Trash The Dress – Kari & Jay Reynosa," 3 December 2009, 13 March 2014, http://nicolettaphotography.com/blog/?p=48
104. Tanya Lea McConnell, "Trash the dress; fresh until death do us part," Bridal Vine, 1 April 2012, 13 March 2014, http://www.bridalvine.com/wedding-trends/trash-the-dress-fresh-until-death-do-us-part
105. Laura, "More on Trashing Wedding Gowns," The Thinking Housewife, September 2011, 13 March 2014, http://www.thinkinghousewife.com/wp/2011/09/more-on-trashing-wedding-gowns/
106. Lewis, "Looking Good," 94.
107. Elizabeth Freeman's research also identifies the queer possibilities in wedding rituals. Freeman, *Wedding Complex*.
108. Kat, "True Blood," Rock n Roll Bride, 4 December 2009, 23 May 2014, http://www.rocknrollbride.com/2009/12/true-blood/; Reilly, "True Blood," Rock n Roll Bride, 4 December 2009, 23 May 2014, http://www.rocknrollbride.com/2009/12/true-blood/
109. JoJo Bananas, "This Trash the dress was so exteme but i soooo loved it ...," Wedding Bee, 8 July 2014, http://boards.weddingbee.com/topic/this-trash-the-dress-was-so-exteme-but-i-soooo-loved-it/page/2#axzz36ulHKt4B
110. Miss Sushi, "Trash the Dress Part 2," Wedding Bee, 16 December 2013, http://www.weddingbee.com/2008/11/10/trash-the-dress-vancouver/#ixzz2nevWGIL1
111. redbullfanatic, "Trash The Dress – Anyone Done It?" Wedding Bee, 22 June 2014, http://boards.weddingbee.com/topic/trash-the-dress-anyone-done-it#ixzz2nesnz0Ks
112. Clover, *Men, Women, and Chain Saws*, 192.
113. AnneNM82, "Trash the dress...does this one go too far?" Wedding Bee, 16 December 2013, http://boards.weddingbee.com/topic/trash-the-dressdoes-this-one-go-too-far/page/4?replies=89#ixzz2netRbNGB
114. D.Marie, "Trash the dress...does this one go too far?" Wedding Bee, 16 December 2013, http://boards.weddingbee.com/topic/trash-the-dressdoes-this-one-go-too-far/page/3#ixzz2neu2zY2F
115. Pinedo, *Recreational Terror*.
116. Williams, "When the Woman Looks," 23.
117. AnneNM82, "Trash the dress...does this one go too far?" Wedding Bee, 16 December 2013, http://boards.weddingbee.com/topic/trash-the-dressdoes-this-one-go-too-far/page/4?replies=89#ixzz2netRbNGB
118. ginantonic, "Will you trash your dress?" WeddingBee, 13 June 2014 http://boards.weddingbee.com/topic/will-you-trash-your-dress
119. ant n tilde, "Re: 'Trash the dress' Photos," NYCity Weddings, 11 April 2007, 13 June 2014, http://www.nycityweddings.com/chat/topic-393980-1.html
120. Nicola Lambert Hyde, "Nicola Lambert Hyde – UK," Trash the Dress – Europe, 21 September 2008, 18 May 2010, http://trashthedress.eu/page/2/
121. Grosz, *Volatile Bodies*, 192.
122. Douglas, *Implicit Meanings*, 109.
123. Stone Ridge Photographers, "Stone Ridge Photographers Trash the Dress," 19 May 2010, http://www.stoneridgephotographers.com/TTD_SRP.htm

124. Stacy Able, "Trash the Dress you Say?" Stacy Able Photography, 15 May 2009, 18 May 2010, http://stacyable.com/blog/2009/05/15/trash-the-dress-you-say-what/
125. Grosz, *Volatile Bodies*, 203.
126. Jacobs, "Optic/Haptic/Abject."
127. Kristeva, *Powers of Horror.*
128. Grosz, *Volatile Bodies*, 195.
129. Alyssa Andrew Photography, "Lehigh Valley & Philadelphia Region Wedding Photographer | Alyssa Andrew Photography," 19 May 2010, www.alyssaandrew.com/main.php#imagegalleries/-%20galleries%20-/Trash%20the%20dress/8
130. Alyssa Andrew Photography, "Lehigh Valley & Philadelphia Region Wedding Photographer | Alyssa Andrew Photography," 19 May 2010, www.alyssaandrew.com/main.php#imagegalleries/-%20galleries%20-/Trash%20the%20dress/10
131. Partington Photography, "More from 'Rema trashes her dress'...," 16 November 2009, 14 December 2013, http://www.partingtonphotography.ca/2009/11/more-from-rema-trashes-her-dress/
132. Creed, *Monstrous-Feminine*, 29.
133. Troy, "Trashed !!! Emily TTD Session || May 31st," Bellagala, 3 June 2009, 19 May 2010, http://bellagala.com/photography/blogs/troy/index.php?m=06&y=09&entry=entry090603-071313
134. Young, *On Female Body Experience*, 107.
135. Jessica, as quoted in Chris Honour, "Trash the Dress 'It's about creation, not destruction,'" East Orlando Photography, 20 August 2007, 28 November 2013, http://eastorlandophotography.com/blog/2007/08/trash-the-dress-it%E2%80%99s-about-creation-not-destruction/
136. Chazitha, "Re: My TTD (no photos yet)," Easy Weddings, 1 March 2009, http://www.easyweddings.com.au/forum/viewtopic.php?f=9&t=16391&st=0&sk=t&sd=a&sid=e51bbdc4614d1565841bf21c9e120c24&start=10
137. Creed, *Monstrous-Feminine*, 10.
138. sweetmelissa, "You did WHAT with you wedding dress?" Brides.com, 22 August 2007, 18 May 2010, http://www.brides.com/forums/fashion-focus/thread.jspa?messageID=297570
139. iconicaphotography, "Zombie Trash the Dress Photo Shoot," Iconica Photography, 7 July 2012, 22 November 2013, http://www.iconicaphotography.com/recent-photos/zombie-trash-dress-photo-shoot/; Jervy Santiago, "Ingle + Aimee Cinematic E-Pictorial (trash-the-dress)," Jervy Santiago for Visionary Photography Hub, 22 November 2013, http://jervysantiago.com/blog3/?p=375; Spectacle Photo, "Till Death Do Us Part 1," 22 November 2013, http://www.spectaclephoto.com/till-death-do-us-part-1/
140. Jennifer, "Is this too crazy? Trash the dress idea...," WeddingWire, 8 April 2011, 22 November 2013, http://www.weddingwire.com/wedding-forums/is-this-too-crazy-trash-the-dress-idea/e043e8558956f1d0.html?page=1
141. iconicaphotography, "Zombie Trash the Dress Photo Shoot," Iconica Photography, 7 July 2012, 22 November 2013, http://www.iconicaphotography.com/recent-photos/zombie-trash-dress-photo-shoot/
142. Spectacle Photo, "Till Death Do Us Part 1," 31 August 2012, 29 December 2013, http://www.spectaclephoto.com/till-death-do-us-part-1/
143. iconicaphotography, "Zombie Trash the Dress Photo Shoot," Iconica Photography, 7 July 2012, 22 November 2013, http://www.iconicaphotography.com/recent-photos/zombie-trash-dress-photo-shoot/
144. Inness, "Boxing Gloves and Bustiers"; Gillis, "(Post)Feminist Politics of Cyberpunk."
145. Lewis, "Looking Good."
146. Emberley, "Fashion Apparatus," 49.
147. Jennifer, "Chinese Knockoff - My actual DH Gate Trash the Dress Dress vs. what's advertised," WeddingWire, 26 April 2012, 1 January 2014, http://www.

weddingwire.com/wedding-forums/chinese-knockoff-my-actual-dh-gate-trash-the-dress-dress-vs-whats-advertised/aab5d78d01140467.html?page=2; Jennifer, "Chinese Knockoff - My actual DH Gate Trash the Dress Dress vs. what's advertised," WeddingWire, 19 March 2013, 1 January 2014, http://www.weddingwire.com/wedding-forums/chinese-knockoff-my-actual-dh-gate-trash-the-dress-dress-vs-whats-advertised/aab5d78d01140467.html?page=2

148. GinaBee, "Trash the Dress Pictures, Project Wedding, 15 September 2009, 4 June 2014, http://www.projectwedding.com/forums/trash-the-dress-pictures
149. Jamie Salup, "Trash the Dress Photos," Jamie Salup Photography, 18 November 2013, http://www.jamiesalupphotography.com/capturing/trash-the-dress-photos/
150. Madeline Zamost, Dana Brown, and Kassie Budzinski, "Trash the Dress- an intriguing concept for both weddings and divorces," Philadelphia Event Planners, 17 June 2013, http://philadelphiaeventplanners.com/2013/06/trash-dress-intriguing-concept-weddings-divorces/
151. Snappening.com, "How to Throw a Divorce Party," 21 May 2013, http://www.snappening.com/blog/how-to-throw-a-divorce-party
152. yeager90, "divorce," Pinterest, 4 January 2013, http://www.pinterest.com/yeager90/divorce/
153. Kevin, "Carissa l Saskatoon Trash The Dress Photography," Organic Photography, 15 February 2011, 16 November 2013, http://www.organicphotography.ca/2011/02/15/carissa-l-saskatoon-trash-the-dress-photography-2/
154. Helene Cornell Photography, "The Newest Trend In Photography," 1 April 2011, 16 November 2013, http://photographybyhelene.com/2011/04/the-newest-trend-in-photography/
155. Joelle Caputa, "Trash The Dress Book: Stories of Celebrating Divorce in Your 20s," 29 November 2013, http://www.trashthedressbook.com/
156. Joelle Caputa, "Meet Joelle Author," Trash The Dress Book: Stories of Celebrating Divorce in Your 20s, 30 November 2013, http://www.trashthedressbook.com/?page_id=38
157. Hanssie Trainor, "for photographers: trash the dress ~ socal photog shootout," 20 October 2009, 5 January 2014, http://hanssietrainorphotography.com/2009/10/for-photographers-trash-the-dress-socal-photog-shootout/
158. Nick Yutaka, "socal photog shootout: trash the dress," nick yutaka photographer, 7 December 2009, 5 January 2014, http://www.nickyutakaphotographer.com/home/2009/12/7/socal-photog-shootout-trash-the-dress.html
159. Wedinator, "Trash the Dress to Celebrate the Divorce," 22 August 2010, 5 January 2014, http://wedinator.icanhascheezburger.com/2010/08/22/funny-wedding-photos-celebrate-the-divorce/#comments
160. Mäntymäki, "Women Who Kill Men," 442.
161. John, "Some chick took these photos the day her divorce was finalized (4 Photos)," theChive, 30 August 2010, 5 January 2014, http://thechive.com/2010/08/30/some-chick-took-these-photos-the-day-her-divorce-was-finalized-4-photos/
162. Miller + Miller Photography, "Jeremi + Lianne's Halloween Themed Engagement Photography," 27 October 2011, 4 January 2014, http://www.chicagoillinoisweddingphotography.com/2011/10/27/halloween-themed-engagement-photography/; Miller + Miller Photography, 7 August 2014, www.millermillerphotography.com
163. Clover, *Men, Women, and Chain Saws.*
164. MercyK, "Do you just come here for the boards?" Wedding Bee, 14 March 2014, http://boards.weddingbee.com/topic/do-you-just-come-here-for-the-boards/page/4#axzz2vzP6qRFk
165. foxybride1024, "How many think you will stop visiting the forum after the wedding?" Project Wedding, 7 December 2009, 22 June 2014, http://www.

projectwedding.com/forums/how-many-think-you-will-stop-visiting-the-forum-after-the-wedding
166. midnyteblue110609, "How many think you will stop visiting the forum after the wedding?" Project Wedding, 8 December 2009, 22 June 2014, http://www.projectwedding.com/forums/how-many-think-you-will-stop-visiting-the-forum-after-the-wedding
167. MountainBride, "How many think you will stop visiting the forum after the wedding?" Project Wedding, 7 December 2009, 22 June 2014, http://www.projectwedding.com/forums/how-many-think-you-will-stop-visiting-the-forum-after-the-wedding
168. par228, "How many think you will stop visiting the forum after the wedding?" Project Wedding, 8 December 2009, 22 June 2014, http://www.projectwedding.com/forums/how-many-think-you-will-stop-visiting-the-forum-after-the-wedding?page=2

4

DEAD WHITE WEDDINGS

Zombie Walk Brides, Marriages, and How-to Guides

Annette photographically depicts five "Zombie brides" in a park during a zombie walk.[1] Her image of people collaboratively enacting undead roles is posted on the Flickr photo-sharing site where such labels as "zombie" and "zombie bride" are commonly deployed. The depicted brides function as a series of copies, doubles, and mirrored couples rather than establishing the uniqueness of their garb or wedding. The two zombie brides on the left are portrayed from behind and function as white forms, with their bodies swathed from head-to-toe in tulle and lace. There are other gendered subjects in the image but the brides' spread skirts establish a homosocial and queer space. Another two zombie brides face each other with one bride reaching up to hail and touch the other. Her gestural call to her companion is a mirroring action. The other bride raises her arm and the two are similarly dressed in white wedding dresses. Such images pose women as linked and coupled because they are physically engaged and dressed to be married. Behind this bridal couple, an almost effaced bride, who also appears to be hailed by one of the brides on the left, suggests that this mirroring, same-sex coupling, and viral replication will continue. Annette foregrounds the importance and likelihood of such identifications by indicating that "Zombie brides" are "Very popular" and everyone is interested in them.

The gestures of other zombie brides further complicate the meanings of these women's raised hands. In a Flickr photograph of a pair of zombie brides, the women reach hungrily out at viewers.[2] Their doubled aspects and blood-red and smeared mouths, with dribbles of red coursing from their lips and across their bodices, are visceral articulations of monstrous and insatiable femininity that have and will continue to virally reproduce according to zombie mythologies. Certainly, Annette's argument about the popularity of zombie brides suggests that these femininities are repeated and embraced, and thus their raised hands are tools of making and unmaking that generate love and revulsion. The repetitions of zombie brides and the mirroring aspects of their poses also underscore the duplicative technologies through which they are generated, including photography and Internet remediation. These images and technologies reproduce and remake things in whole and in part and therefore underscore the ways people, cultural practices, and representations are like us and uncanny in their slight distinctions. New media and related technologies are often imagined to be alive and lively but the functions of these technologies are like zombies, especially when they are not processing information, and are a form of suspended animation.[3] The Internet and computer are neither alive nor dead. There are uneasy connections between the Internet and zombies, humans and zombies, and brides and zombie brides.

Zombie brides engage with and torque conceptions of femininity, heterosexuality, and whiteness while being envisioned as mostly blank and unspeaking subjects. Human individuals and parts are also envisioned as blank canvases that are available for zombie and other transformations. These zombie brides' verbal silences are related to and distort traditional wedding photography and its constitution of demure and downward glancing brides. Yet many images propose that the mouths of zombie brides hail individuals and underline the vulnerability and frailty of the human subjects that they address. For instance, another two zombie brides depicted on Flickr nestle together, with the shorter bride's breasts intimately filling the space below the other's chest, but the smaller bride's wide-open mouth and bloodstained chin are directed at other subjects. The photographer >>SuperMary<< argues that these zombies are "not… quite.. blushing" and that they undermine the virtue and cleanliness associated with brides.[4] jamie nyc's Flickr photograph also depicts women who refuse cultural expectations that they will remain proper and clean.[5] In this image, the bride's whitened skin, white dress, and splashes of blood-red across her face and chest emphasize her shift from bridal whiteness to grotesque almost deadness. She addresses one of her bridesmaids as if she is going to whisper in her ear but instead stretches her mouth across the woman's head and points to some odd ways that mouth and skull fit together. These zombie presentations propose how licking, mouthing, biting, and intermeshing constitute people as lovers and consumable in different ways than the spoken "hey you" of Louis Althusser's hail.[6]

Representations of brides at zombie walks, including groups of brides and brides coupled with other women, are more common than images of zombie grooms. This complicates the linking of female brides to males and heterosexuality. For instance, Georgette argues that the zombie bride in another Flickr image "got left at the altar … maybe she ate the groom" and challenges the monogamous heterosexuality associated with brides.[7] Zombie bride Helen would present a more languorous figure except she has a torn, bloodied, and bruised face.[8] The groom is missing from this Flickr photograph but bridesmaid Emma stands against Helen and hangs her arm in a similar pose. The photographer entitles the image "Undead Wedding" and helps to make these women into a couple. In a similar manner to women's participation in trash the dress (TTD) sessions, where they appear to be killing their husbands, these zombie brides embody murderous women who excise men from the picture and from their lives.

Most traditional weddings and photographs perpetuate feminine beauty and whiteness but zombie brides associate monstrosity, aggressiveness, dead whiteness, and queer sexualities with brides and wedding dresses. These zombie brides, including the women represented on Flickr and in how-to instructional guides on eHow, Instructables, and wikiHow, produce whiteness by combining numerous colors and looking unhealthy or dead. They thereby pose feminine whiteness as multihued, changeable, deathly, and unappealing instead of the more usual construction of it as stable, enlivening, and beautiful. In how-to demonstrations, light-skinned hands are associated with and deliver death. Whiteness is constructed by hand rather than natural. Carol Armstrong's and Craig Owens's studies of photographic repetition enable me to consider how these zombies are part of the culture of duplication. Zombies and copies are not the same as the things that they derived from; hence they construct, rather than convey, whiteness and other identities. The literature on whiteness and race, including Richard Dyer's writing on the undead, helps me to theorize the critical implications of associating whiteness with death.[9] Zombie brides' whiteness, with its monstrous and deathly features, unsettles the cultural association of feminine whiteness with beauty and health and provides some problems for the associated articulations of whiteness and Caucasian people as ideals.

Zombie Walks and Archives

The physical features of zombie walks help zombie brides to disorder white dresses and the monogamous commitments of weddings. The anthropologist Bryce Peake analyzes a zombie walk where dirt from the park mixes with "blood from the bodies of the undead."[10] As participants experience this wetness and mass of bodies, they are "fully transformed into zombies. Groaning, staggering, and reaching, the libidinous energy—sexualized by the moans, the touching, and the lack of clothing." These zombie walks, which are also called zombie mobs, lurches, shambles, shuffles, and crawls as ways of emphasizing the physical arrangements and movements of zombies, are organized public gatherings where people engage with zombie embodiment and behaviors. Zombie walks are held in urban settings where tight spaces encourage participants to experience their combined and hybrid bodies. These events tend to happen around Halloween when the rituals of dressing up are more likely to facilitate transgressive behaviors. Zombie walks also support ethical and fan components because organizers collect funds for charities and incorporate horror film screenings. Zombie walks have happened on most continents and are widely represented in Internet settings. The earliest zombie walk was called "The Zombie Parade" and held in 2001 in Sacramento, California as part of a promotional event for a midnight film festival.[11] Estimates indicate that there were 30,000 zombie walk participants in Minneapolis-Saint Paul and 25,000 in Buenos Aires in 2012.[12] The number of attendees at these events continues to increase and support the erotically affective mass that Peake chronicles. This is because zombies are a key cultural narrative and way of identifying.

The experiential features of zombies and zombie walks are documented, saved, commented upon, and reimagined in Internet settings. The characteristics of these digital forms of storage and transmission echo the cultural characteristics of zombies. In Matthew Kirschenbaum's consideration of computer inscription, he describes what formally and conceptually happens to hard drives when there are no commands or programmed requests for information. These instances of hard drive and information stasis are a "coma or walking death, oddly inert yet physically present."[13] There are instances when data is not in use. Hard drives and information stasis are thereby associated with the "uncanny, the unconscious, and the dead." Solid-state drives without moving parts and the storage of photographs of people intensify these renderings of walking death. Photographic images point to moments in time that are no longer happening and eventually represent people who were alive and are now dead. Roland Barthes considers the affective and death-like qualities of photographs in his search for an image that will emotionally express his dead mother. He presents a photograph of Lewis Payne, who is about to be executed, and argues, "He is dead and he is going to die."[14] Due to viewers' shifting experiences with such depicted subjects, photographs represent people as neither fully living nor completely dead. Digital sharing sites combine the suspended animation of image storage with the not-quite-dead features of people in photographs. Like data, photographs are often stilled and archived. This is magnified when photo-sharing sites archive zombie brides and other figures from zombie walks. There are problems with correlating digital storage and photography with the living and lively. These technologies construct gender and other aspects of identities and subjects.

Flickr and its-photo sharing functions are further related to walking death and zombie walks because the site was developed in 2004, which is about the same time as the term "zombie walk" was introduced.[15] Flickr offers zombie images that are associated with early zombie walks, although the dates attached to Flickr photographs are somewhat unreliable and some images have discrepant years of production.[16] These images produce a composite and mutable archive of zombie walk representations and near-death. The characteristics of zombies are designed to revise human categorizations and Flickr promises "new ways of organizing photos and video" and distinguishes itself from older media and the accompanying organizational and photographic histories where white children are transformed into heterosexual couples, get married, and have families of their own.[17]

Flickr claims to have reconceptualized imaging and relationships but its site icon is a paired blue and pink dot, which suggests that men should be romantically matched with women. Some of its site texts are also in blue and pink and further assert that binary gender and heterosexuality are part of the setting. Flickr and other sites use such icons and colors, in a similar manner to sites' informational "About" pages, and articulate settings and members. In Flickr's case, these site-wide features function as technologies of gender that bracket the diverse archive with binary gender distinctions. The functions of such features also make close textual analysis of the varied parts of sites important. Participants can extend, critically read, or work to undo these structural elements. For instance, members' images of zombie brides and their once white dresses point to possibilities for revision. They present deader versions of such blue and pink pairings and critical reminders of the ways people are rupturing cultural models of femininity, heterosexuality, and whiteness.

Flickr and the other Internet sites that are associated with zombie walks frequently offer instructions on self-representing as the undead. Internet how-to sites also provide tutorials on zombie identification.[18] For instance, eHow's zombie guides include: "How to Look Like a Zombie," "How to Do Zombie Makeup for Girls," "How to Do Dead Bride Makeup for a Halloween Costume," and "Rules for Zombie Walkers."[19] In some of these guides, zombie walks are the intended venue and zombie brides are exemplary characters.[20] They provide zombie tutorials and other information for non-experts, propose simplified methods for accomplishing tasks, and are envisioned as communities of people who share information and develop skills. For instance, Instructables defines the site as a "documentation platform where passionate people share what they do and how they do it, and learn from and collaborate with others."[21] With eHow, "Professionals in every field" are supposed to "come together to offer expert advice, backed by the additional support of a can-do eHow community."[22] Flickr also encourages participants to designate the cameras that they use and supports a community of individuals who think about photographic skills and "sharing."

They're Us: Zombies as a Critical Practice

Women produce zombie brides with the assistance of Internet sites, including how-to guides, and engage with contemporary identity categories. Cultural understandings of zombies suggest that these women's production of zombie brides is a critical strategy. For instance, reporter Doug Gross argues that we "love zombies so much" because they help "reflect whatever our greatest fears happen to be at the time."[23] Psychiatrist Steven Schlozman "will always love" the "original *Dawn of the Dead*" because it has "great social commentary."[24] eBay and Etsy sellers write about love in order to facilitate impassioned connections among feminine and sometimes derided subjects. They use these relationships to elevate their identities and empower themselves. Zombie enthusiasts also express passionate attachments as part of their embrasure of the critical possibilities of zombie texts, including transforming their bodies and identities. Rather than the distancing process that is associated with high culture, zombie and other fans perform critiques while loving and having a closer relationship to particular texts.

Representations of zombies are part of the larger cultural fascination with such undead creatures as ghosts and vampires. There are numerous films and television programs about zombies, many of them influenced by George A. Romero's *Night of the Living Dead* (1968). There are also hybrid literary forms such as Seth Grahame-Smith's *Pride and Prejudice and Zombies*, graphic novels, and zombie survival manuals.[25] This fascination and cultural engagement with the undead, which in the case of zombies has increased in the last few decades, is supported and extended by considerations of zombies in Internet and computer-mediated settings. There are forums about zombies and image sites with people self-presenting as zombies. Zombie-oriented computer games allow people to further identify with and kill the undead. The academic literature engages with the critical aspects of this zombie media and considers 1930s films about zombification in Haiti that reference colonialism, recent conceptions of zombies, zombies and theories of consciousness, and Romero's use of zombie films as a means of social and consumerist critique.[26]

Zombies trigger terror as well as critical commentary according to Sarah Juliet Lauro and Karen Embry's research on these constructs.[27] They engage fears of being devoured, which are directed mainly at the physical body, and dread of having one's individual consciousness absorbed by the horde. Zombie hailing, including the ways zombies address people with their hands and mouths, are representations and prompts for these fears. Contemporary zombies also challenge conceptions of biology and science by seeming to function beyond expectations for human physiology. Zombie brides reference cultural expectations about women's life stages, including heterosexual marriages and reproduction. However, zombie brides are no longer following these trajectories. Their developmental and forward growth is stalled and they remain permanently associated with the liminal category of "bride." Some brides and other female zombies assert their relationship to monstrous procreation by suspending developmentally stilled zombie fetuses from their abdomens.[28] They evoke people's fears about and interests in the destruction of the individual.

Characters in zombie media and viewers imagine becoming zombies and identify with zombies' disordered bodies and states. In George A. Romero's *Dawn of the Dead* (1978), humans look out at encroaching zombies on the other side of glass walls, theorize that they are drawn to the mall for similar reasons, and one of the characters declares, "They're us." Contemporary viewers and critics continue these forms of recognition in Internet settings. They are hailed and constituted as subjects by the mirroring features of zombies and new media. For instance, people's images are reflected onto screens and depictions and they are collapsed with the hand pointer and other technological representations of bodies. Zombie films and television programs offer individuals opportunities to identify by looking at the screen, which is related to the glass dividers in Romero's mall, and the zombies who are visible through these architectural features. Writer Gavon Laessig indicates, "People identify with the zombie because the zombie is us."[29] Reporter Peter Keough further details these forms of attachment. He argues, "Not only do people want to watch the undead," they "want to be the undead."[30] Peake articulates a trance-like conversion through which zombie walk participants become zombies. Their transformation is based on group contact and the feel of fluids and flesh. However, all of these individuals identify with and are turned into zombies because of cultural conceptions and contact with bodies and technologies.

Nic Crowe considers a group of women's zombie self-presentations and expands upon these arguments. Crowe writes, "Zombies let you be whatever you want. You can experiment with make up, body movement, everything. They are like a blank canvas" that allows women to render their own characteristics and subjecthood.[31] In Crowe's analysis, zombies enable postfeminist choices and allow women to move from being nothing to being what they want. Some bloggers, as I suggest in the following chapter and afterword, also identify nails as blank canvases that let women produce any kind of art and version of the self that they desire. Simal Yilmaz combines these concepts and argues, "Nails have become the new canvases for our zombie appreciation."[32] The idea that women's hands convey and deliver zombies is furthered by the materiality of nails, which are nearly dead or undead material that is embedded in the living body. They're us due to our partial composition from dead things. Zombies' hands are terrifying because these creatures are no longer human but their hands still function as active appendages that can stop people's agency and vitality. People's fears of appendages that are moving but dead extend some cultural sentiments about hands. As art historian Rose Marie San Juan indicates, "When a hand moves, there is always something of the stranger in it."[33] The hand "rarely seems to be in sync with the rest of the body" and casts doubt on cultural investments in the coherent individual and the "unifying power of consciousness." Hands are identified as precision tools that make individuals human.[34] Yet individuals also engage with their hands as strangers and representations of the zombie embodiment within themselves.

People see zombies everywhere and equate contemporary cultural experiences to zombie embodiment. Individuals who walk into things while texting are identified as zombies. Susan M. Behuniak, in her consideration of the ways zombies and Alzheimer's patient have been equated, argues that zombies have the "status of being 'not quite'; they are neither fully dead nor do they appear to be fully alive."[35] This "not quite" leads to eerie reflections of they're us. Indeed, all living people are undead because they are not deceased. Technologies are also undead because they are not and have never been alive but are understood as living. Zombies are "us" and not quite us, offering a duplication that has internal distinctions and translation errors. They encourage critical comparisons between versions of the self, including people's pasts and reflections, and thereby offer the opportunities to think about sideways growth into other timelines and constructions.[36] This copying and imprinting from one time and self to the other is also an aspect of photography and digital imaging. Thus, the intensity of the recognition that they're us is magnified through photographic and other forms of imaging.

Photographs, as Owens argues, are "one link in a potentially endless chain of reduplication; themselves duplicates (of both their objects and, in a sense, their negatives), they are also subject to further duplication, either through the procedures of printing or as objects of still other photographs."[37] This replication is continued and foregrounded in images with mirrors, which reduplicate the scene, and in photographs with similar subjects. These repetitions underscore photography's function as a mechanism of copying and a producer of zombie-like massification. Yet such processes are also prone to error and foreground slight distinctions. Armstrong analyzes Diane Arbus's photograph of identical twins and argues that almost at the same time as viewers notice the young women's sameness and that their clothing and environment are doubled, "comes the awareness of slight differences, brought on by the perception of sameness and all the almosts that go with it."[38] Photographic copies and twins also model sideways growth in their emphasis on relationality and parallelism rather than forward development.

These considerations of sameness and similarities are extended by zombie brides' resemblances to people, brides, and other zombies and the ways they are photographically and virally reproduced. For instance, two zombie brides who are portrayed together have comparable facial physiognomies, arm positions, puff-sleeved wedding dresses, and red blood splatters.[39] Their visual parallels and position as arm-in-arm brides, as Armstrong's analysis suggests, encourage viewers to at once see them as stilled versions of the same individual and note their differences. While both brides smile, the mouth of the woman on the right is more open, her face is larger, and her skin is whiter. Each bride has a dark smeared handprint as if someone had grabbed her around the neck in order to infect her but the mark on the left bride covers her chest and the one on the right runs along her cheek and throat. These brides and their technological reproduction thus emphasize the replication of zombie culture and the specific ways whiteness, blood, and feminine garb produce women. While Flickr's paired blue and pink dots continue the cultural linking of binary gender and heterosexuality, the zombie brides emphasize the parallels and particularities of female couplings.

The similarities between the two zombie brides constitute a community of shared features and values as well as some distinctions. Communities can make otherwise dismissed interests visible but participants tend to reject people who do not match their identities and standards.[40] Margaret Robinson, the organizer of a zombie walk, tells a reporter at the event, "We are all zombies tonight, we are all undead" and continues the idea that "they're us."[41] Yet her temporal qualifier of "tonight" raises questions about how people identify and are accepted at other times. Zombie walk forums and associated Internet sites enable people to extend such zombie walk engagements and attachments. Thus, these Internet sites offer settings in which zombies can be further kept "alive" through texts and technologies. They offer opportunities for hybrid identification and critical frameworks for thinking about the possibilities and problems with zombies and other constructions. Early academic and popular literature often describes Internet settings as places where any identity can be produced and remade. However, forum participants suggest a more ambivalent position in foregrounding their traditional identities through "before" images, changing their racial position with makeup and blood, and thinking about becoming "after" and an undead something else. People's zombie self-presentations are imagined as eternal and often persist through Internet images but the corporeal manifestations of participants' presentations are temporary.

How-to guide authors go beyond the relational equations proposed by Romero and other producers of "they're us" and assume individuals want to enmesh with and change into the undead. They provide instructions on how people can further produce themselves as zombies and underscore the ways humans and zombies are like each other. Meghan White offers simple makeup and costuming tips and indicates, "If you want to be the undead, you just have to act like a zombie."[42] In her account, people are so behaviorally close to zombies that identification is always available to those who want to be undead and act the part. Rain Blanken suggests that these connections are in themselves endangering: "One reason they are so frightening is because they are us" and we can imagine our bodies in the place of zombies.[43] Blanken supports Lauro and Embry's argument that people fear being eaten and absorbed by the throng.[44] Thus, zombie identification continues the bodily sensations that individuals experience when identifying with horror characters.[45] Associating with zombies may also pose that such actions will be replaced by vacancy and that even the repetitive waves of embodied shivering and shuddering at monsters will stop. This suggests that the affective aspects of horror are methods of foregrounding viewers' liveness.

Zombies are conceptualized as blanks. Traditional photographs are also blanks, which have imprinted information that cannot be seen or read before they are developed. This makes zombie photographs illegible and readable. Photographers pick up these varied forms of recognition when they see themselves and their photographic and other absences in zombies. Aimeesque provides a picture of a zombie photographer angling his camera at the attending photographer on Flickr and identifies the experience as the "twilight zone when the photographer and zombie in him met."[46] Georgette distinguishes a "Zombie Photographer Grrl" and adds that it is "Nice to see more than a few of us out there."[47] It is unclear whether another producing woman, photographer, zombie, or some combination of these triggers her identification. Viewers also recognize their zombie photographs on Flickr, name themselves, and become further enmeshed with zombie positions. suezq1342 posts an image of "a zombie guy" who "asked his zombie girlfriend to be his zombie bride in front of at least 2000 people" and RedandJonny respond with a "Whoa ! Thats us!!!"[48] In a related manner, Internet viewers make out their social positions, sexual and familial relationships, corporeality, and futures mirrored and threatened by zombies. Sherry Turkle argues in her research on people's relationships with technologies that character-based new technologies provide individuals with methods for identifying and working through their roles and relationships.[49] Bratich's indication that technologies are extensions of digits, hands, and bodies also poses these technologies as instances of self-recognition and actualization.[50]

Zombie positions offer viewers opportunities to experience the combined terror and pleasure of becoming zombies and critical strategies for thinking about identity positions and bodies. As the cultural geographer Jeff May argues, "Since zombies do not die normally, their presence represents a breakdown in the understood fabric of reality and creates ruptures in the subject 'human.'"[51] Zombies' challenges to the "human" go beyond the influences of their limited consciousness and position as neither alive nor dead. They can be deployed to think through and rework varied identity categories. For instance, zombies' white physiognomy and situation as not fully human offer opportunities to consider what ordinarily gets attached to race, including the links between Caucasians and beauty, intelligence, and agency, and the relationship between light skin color and racial privilege. People's construction and celebration of zombie physiognomy encourages further assessments of what whiteness means and how it can be politically deployed to undermine rather than enforce racial hierarchies and categories.

Zombies and Whiteness

Contemporary zombies' conceptual debt to filmic depictions of Haitian zombies, tendency to derive from white people, extreme paleness, and undeadness make them troubled white subjects who have mixed-race histories. Zombie how-to guides and Internet representations of zombie walk participants, particularly images of zombie brides, quote and complicate these layers of whiteness. This is significant since, as sociologist Chrys Ingraham argues, white wedding dresses and media representation of couples getting married, which almost always represent them as white, make weddings "code for whiteness."[52] Scholars study these and other Western conceptions of whiteness as a means of interrogating racial categories, the people who are raced, and the production and extension of racial inequalities.[53]

Individuals are not literally white, as Dyer's study of Western forms of whiteness demonstrates, but the "colour term, white, is the primary means" of identification.[54] Whiteness functions through a series of binaries that associate it with positive cultural characteristics and darker skin and other races with negative attributes. Cultural theorist Kobena Mercer critiques the ways whiteness was and continues to be "the measure of true beauty."[55] White, soft, and smooth skin was read as an indicator of women's beauty and moral purity through the nineteenth century in the West because it seemed to indicate that women did not have any sexually transmitted diseases.[56] Skin that was free of powder and other forms of makeup was also associated with innocence because cosmetics were believed to be a form of female deception that was designed to trick and seduce people, particularly unmarried men.[57] Kimberly Poitevin identifies how early modern English women used cosmetics to "accentuate differences between themselves and their foreign, darker-skinned counterparts" and thereby increased their economic and social opportunities.[58] Yet women who used these products, which could easily be applied and removed, also "revealed color to be an unreliable marker of race, class, or moral truth" and exposed the constructed aspects of gender and race. The whiteness of zombies continues and skews the features of earlier constructions of cosmetic whiteness and can thereby help to reveal the produced characteristics of gender, race, and sexuality.

People's whiteness is linked to privilege and agency but it is also connected to illness and death, including the ways reborn artists use grayed and blued Caucasian skin to represent premature babies. Until the early twentieth century, white cosmetic paints and skin lighteners often sickened women because they contained toxic materials.[59] Women in some communities still use unhealthy skin lightening products despite the risks of experiencing skin irritations, changes in pigmentation, skin hardening, paralysis, and death.[60] These connections between whiteness and death are also emphasized in films about the undead. According to Dyer, filmic vampires consume white victims and represent white society feeding upon and obliterating itself. J. Hoberman and Jonathan Rosenbaum study "midnight" films and identify *Night of the Living Dead* as "the most literal possible depiction of America devouring itself."[61] Romero's zombie films, according to Dyer, assert "whiteness as death."[62] White humans are often corrupt and murderous in these texts so there are no differences "between whites, living or dead, all whites bring death and, by implication, all whites are dead (in terms of human feeling)." People's self-representations as light-skinned zombies, especially when reproduced, further trouble the liveness of white subjects. These individuals are rendered as having no substance, according to game studies researcher Ewan Kirkland, because of the "translucence of white photographic representation, the transparency of white faces on film," and the "illumination of white figures in pictorial discourse."[63] Thus, zombie whiteness is part of the undead's and white subjects' dwindling.

Zombie Brides and Race

Zombies' connections to humanness and whiteness and reordering of selfhood and embodiment are condensed in the figure of the zombie bride. Brides, as I have already suggested, ordinarily support heterosexuality, monogamous coupling, familial and reproductive futures, consumerism, and whiteness. The overwhelmingly white racial composition of people at zombie walks, which is conveyed in Internet depictions, and how-to guides is worrying and should not be dismissed. Yet zombie brides also rework their whiteness and physiognomy. In Internet representations, they wear filthy and torn dresses, have broken bodies and reddish-brown scabbed skin, are drenched in blood, brandish bits of other people, and reach out to eat people. Their bodies are a record of violence against women, which is all too resonant in contemporary society. However, contemporary zombie brides are also imagined as active and agentive, as opposed to the association of zombies with blankness, while killing or otherwise losing their living husbands. In presenting these positions, the women who self-present as zombies contribute to the forms of developmental resistance and heterosexual uncoupling that are produced as part of weddings and that I consider in the chapter on TTD. There are troubling aspects of these murderous positions and some productive critical applications, especially when women who are otherwise posed as conventional and passive fight back.

Zombie brides are identified as a key type and figure of fascination and delight. Scott Snider believes that "It just wouldn't be a Zombie walk without at least one Zombie Bride in her wedding dress."[64] dr_dustbunny advises that "Everyone needs the ever soo hawt 'Bride Zombie', saw around ten of those."[65] "There is always a bunch of Zombie brides" at any "Zombie gathering," writes Deanna Gray, "They must be especially vulnerable!"[66] These posters assert the importance of brides in zombie culture and that these figures are appealing because they are recognizable, continue some features of dyadic gender, reference feminine beauty and appeal even as they move beyond these strictures, and are susceptible and thus available for transformation. Most photographers of zombie walks continue this focus, and support the centrality of brides in contemporary culture, by including images of brides in their Flickr sets. Photographers' interest in and documentation of zombie brides forward alternative conceptions of brides and, as the comment about "hot" brides suggests, constitutes monstrous women as erotically appealing. Images of grotesque zombie brides offer an antidote to the mandates for brides, and women more generally, to be conventionally attractive. Yet they also continue the association of women with abjection, including the idea that women are too filthy and fluid.

Instructions on how to create such zombie brides are part of Cody McCloy, Henry Hanks, and Nicole Saidi's reporting on a popular culture convention where attendees received zombie makeup tips and performed at a zombie walk.[67] In the accompanying "Zombie 101" Internet how-to guide, the makeup artist applies "a layer of liquid latex" that is lighter than attendee Suzanne Johnson's pale skin. The makeup artist also uses black makeup to "simulate dead, rotten flesh" and adds a "layer of white powder" to "give the skin the proper zombie pallor." While Johnson is blonde, pale, and wearing a white wedding dress, which as Ingraham suggests ordinarily signifies whiteness, the bright white gown acts as a color and smoothness swatch that her mottled coloration does not achieve.[68]

The how-to steps of applying Johnson's makeup are, as the remarks of Poitevin suggest, a reminder of how easily whiteness can be applied and removed.[69] Of course, cultural conceptions indicate that zombie whiteness has a life and undead expectancy that human whiteness cannot match.

Some of the people who structure zombie whiteness acknowledge the role of skin color as an organizing principle in social and cultural relations. For example, the dialog between Christine Grabig and kenndubeau highlights zombie skin. kenndubeau notes that the couple is "proud to be" portrayed in Grabig's "Mr & Mrs Zombie" photograph.[70] In a similar manner to RedandJonny, they accept and are produced through the photographer's address.[71] kenndubeau thinks the image is "Great" because Grabig "really brought out the decay in" the couple's "skin." Grabig replies, "I brought out the decay? Wow.. I'm... honored, I think ;)."[72] Her ironic hesitation recalls the standards of wedding photography, including the practice of making brides appear beautiful and unblemished, and the ways zombie images deviate from these norms.[73] Yet the couple is excited about their skin breaking down, shifting away from white, and having an unstable position. They begin to peel back skin, and material versions of this process are suggested by the consequence of decay, and examine its physical and ideological layers.

Christine Grabig's and kenndubeau's "Mr & Mrs Zombie" replaces racial stability with decay but they still focus on heterosexual unions. vanBuuren's "kiss the bride" photograph, which represents the pale groom's mouth pressed against the side of the extremely light bride's face, could also establish the primacy of white heterosexual romance.[74] However, the photographer inquires whether the zombie groom is "Kissing? or sucking her brains through a headwound?" In doing this, he challenges the white heterosexual coupling that is centered by the action and forwards non-normative and barely alive whiteness. The depicted bride shifts from exceptionally pale to dissolving because of the tonal qualities of the image and her light skin, blonde hair, and white veil. For example, the overexposed veil "eats" into her hair and dress. At one time, this image further decomposed the white body because, in a gesture that is related to zombies, the bride was absorbed by the blank white surface around the depiction. This is part of the larger tendency for depictions of whiteness to dissipate, which Kirkland identifies.[75] However, Flickr has replaced white with black borders. This has somewhat stabilized the images of white dissolution that appear on Flickr. eBay also offers black as the background to some detail views. Fortunately, this decomposition of whiteness still occurs in other Internet settings because of the illuminated features of most screen technologies and the wide scale use of white borders and backdrops.

The Undead Whiteness of How-to Guides

Zombie how-to authors produce and foil a racial "us" by using white bodies as the standard and ground from which zombies are rendered. Brides are featured as part of this transformation and move away from the normative and the human.

As the Zombie Maker site notes, "Blood looks great on white dresses."[76] While people's whiteness, as Dyer and others indicate, does not really correlate to the color white, one might also be directed to think that blood looks great on light skin.[77] This may figure whiteness as the aesthetic ideal for zombies but it also suggests that whiteness is best at being virally contaminated, rotten, rent asunder, wounded, and consumed. These connections between whiteness and death are supported by Zombie Maker, who advises that the "foundation" to becoming undead, and thus the recipe to nearing death, is access to cosmetic whiteness—"white cream makeup, the sort clowns wear," pressed powder, or talcum powder. Tom Walsham's "Zombie Makeup and Costume Tips" also suggest that it is advantageous to be white.[78] Images of an individual's grayed white cheek, a white woman with lighter makeup on half her face, and a light-skinned hand stand in for human transformations into zombies. These versions of whiteness are grotesque and the underlying people appear to be diseased. They have dripping goiters of flesh and hands that have rotted away until ligaments and bones are revealed. Since hands convey emotional and physical touching, sharing, and producing, these images figure the white touch, rather than contact with the other, as contaminating.

Zombie identifications challenge Western beauty standards and racial hierarchies by associating whiteness with ugliness and the grotesque. Indymogul produces zombies by building up layers of liquid latex and toilet paper until "you have some gross looking white skin."[79] In a related manner, Leah D'Emilio links ugliness to whiteness. She tells readers, "You look awful. Your skin is a strange hue of greenish-white. Your eyes are sunken in their sockets" and you "look great" because your "makeup has been applied to perfection!"[80] Her narrative points to how people who render themselves as zombies garner pleasure from being abject. Part of their enjoyment is based in creating monstrous versions of whiteness. Through this engagement, participants also undermine the purported perfection of whiteness and white people's relationship to beauty and health. Their appreciation of flaws and impurities are especially significant when they are associated with white brides who are still expected to be faultless and morally and physically clean.

Zombie whiteness provides methods for interrogating perceptions that whiteness is stable and coherent. The skin of zombies and humans is not one color and it does not remain constant over time. Assessments of skin color, according to the research of George Lipsitz and Rosenthal, are relational and rely on comparisons.[81] Such things as heat, cold, sun exposure, illness, and death influence skin color. The "Zombie Bride Make-up" guide from FunCostumes proposes a composite coloration that is produced from "near-white foundation" and "grey or dark blue."[82] To "attain a simple zombie look," writes Murrye-bernard, apply "white face paint or powder"; blend "a combination of black, purple or blue eyeshadow around your eyes"; and "apply black lipstick, or cover lips with white face paint."[83] The details of these "simple" makeup instructions indicate the complexity of zombie skin color and race. Yet each of these stages and combinations of color is necessary. By "following these steps, you will look as though you have risen from the dead." This is whiteness as death. However, it is related to and a reminder of the production of everyday whiteness. These zombie how-to guides reference everyday makeup techniques and advise people to use the cosmetics and other products that they have in their homes.[84] Rather than developing more beautiful physiognomies, zombie brides emphasize the composite layers of cosmetic production and the ways made-up women present a series of versions and therefore move beside themselves.

How-to guide representations of zombies, and indeed most zombie portrayals, convey layers of whiteness that are interspersed with other colors. For instance, McCloy, Hanks, and Saidi use the term "layer" when describing the application of latex and other materials to Johnson's zombie bride portrayal.[85] coreymarie figures herself as a zombie bride and uses the terms "Base Coat" and "layer."[86] She opposes a more coherent version of whiteness, and this resistance is advocated by critical theorists of race, and is not a "fan of the little tubes of 'Cream White.' They're always just a little too opaque." The term "layer" and depictions of each stage of zombie makeup application further foreground the constructed aspects of zombie physiognomy and race. These practices encourage the further peeling back of skin and consideration of its colors, structures, and meanings.

coreymarie's layers include such diverse materials as white baby powder, Elmer's glue, "Tan colored recycled paper napkins," oats, and "Brown, purple, yellow and green" eye shadow. In the accompanying images, she illustrates how she uses these materials to make her family into zombies. Her photographs and formulas displace cultural investments in smooth and pure white skin with the encrusted and multi-colored skin that is produced by this hodgepodge. For instance, she shows photos of a hand being made over with white baby powder and layers of brown napkins [Figure 4.1]. This employment of brown paper to render the skin of white people is notable. According to numerous popular accounts, whites and people of color in the United States used the color of brown paper bags to distinguish between light-skinned people of mixed race and darker-skinned African Americans and to exclude darker people from some social spheres.[87] By literally gluing white skin and brown paper together, coreymarie suggests that Caucasians can as easily be equated to black people and brown hues. She thereby uses zombie identities to trouble current conceptions of skin color and race.

Women also recognize the aesthetic problems with zombie identification and follow cultural mandates about being pretty and appealing. XaSkYlItLoVeX wants to be a zombie "but all the makeup looks are really disgusting looking."[88] She emphasizes the ways women are structured as to-be-looked-at-ness and articulates her desire for "something cuter" than the usual zombie presentations. Face Paint Heaven describes this "dilemma girls of all ages can identify with. You want to be a zombie . . . and need to look scary and, well, dead.

Dead White Weddings **145**

FIGURE 4.1 coreymarie, The all-new adventures of coreymarie.com. Brown paper is used in making a zombie hand.

But you still want to look cute!"[89] Some how-to guide authors respond to this "dilemma" and propose more appealing zombie self-presentations. For example, WordCustard demonstrates "how to look dead without looking repulsive."[90] When "you've got a hot date (dead or alive?)," writes WordCustard, "a girl needs to go to a little more effort." Of course, zombie bride and female zombie self-presentations also require time and expertise. The time that individuals commit to zombie self-presentations, like reborn doll producers' extreme forms of labor, are foregrounded by their focus on and evidence of layers. Producing women's layered works are sedimentary archives of the ways they construct their labor and identities.

White Heterosexual Zombie Walk Wedding Culture

Zombie wedding culture, including the many white couples self-presenting as zombies and holding their legal wedding ceremonies at zombie walks, further ensconces the idea that they're us and that enactments of these figures have proliferated. "Whether we like it or not," notes Cynthia, "zombies are everywhere in pop culture these days – even weddings."[91] Some people, as Cynthia suggests, do not accept the ways zombie wedding ceremonies challenge the expected physiognomy and demeanor of brides and grooms. At the same time, zombie walk weddings are linked to heterosexuality because the news stories report on the union of men and women. Holding weddings at zombie walks encourages viewers to associate all zombie walk brides and grooms with functional unions. Weddings, as Ingraham indicates, "prepare heterosexuals for membership in marriage as an organizing practice for the institution of heterosexuality."[92] Weddings assert that engaged and recently married people are normal, honorable, hardworking, responsible, mature, family-oriented, and properly gendered. Yet zombie walks, and especially zombie walk weddings, also reference deviations from social codes.

Christopher Downs and Amber Nolin's zombie walk wedding viscerally influenced viewers. Chelsea describes it as the "eeriest and bloodiest wedding" she has "ever seen" and "not for those with weak constitutions."[93] She associates the horror genre with this wedding and proposes a more uncomfortable experience than the usual affective experiences of familial bonding and normative delights. Of course, filmic and other kinds of popular representations have also linked weddings to people's panics over committing, discomfort with families and their expectations, boredom when surrounded by unknown people, and anger over the traditional relationships that are celebrated. Downs and Nolin's zombie walk wedding proposes a different correlation of physically touching and emotionally feeling than the traditional wedding. It included Nolin reaching out for other bodies during the ceremony and Downs "devouring the bride on the altar."[94] Reverend Heather Lynn Meyer encouraged this aggressive possession of the bride by noting, "you may now take your corpse bride and devour her."[95] Meyer's version of "you may now kiss the bride" evokes everyday but still violent and controlling statements such as "I could eat you up" and "love you to death."

The reporting about Tracey and Andy Monaghan's marriage further challenges normative weddings. They first had a traditional wedding that "was a big disappointment."[96] Romance and the "perfect" day were unavailable to Tracey because she was "pregnant," had "a stinking cold," and all she "wanted to do was go to sleep." Tracey lists her pregnancy as one of the unpleasant aspects of her first wedding but images of their zombie wedding, which are reproduced on numerous websites, emphasize the couple's racial and reproductive positions with images of their light-skinned child. Portraits of white babies, according to Shawn Michelle Smith's research on race and family albums, are an important feature of early photography and continue to forward whiteness.[97] Since these images and the associated offspring establish the white middle-class family's future, white women are expected to reproduce and maternally support white children. However, Tracey's uneven facial mask of raw red skin and brown scabs trouble her bodily integrity and thereby her ability to generate the white family. Tracey's depictions, if deployed in a similar manner to other wedding photography, act as a measuring stick to judge her physiognomy throughout her life. However, this comparison is distinctly different than the ways the dress, photography, and other facets of the wedding ceremony usually shape brides into thin, white, and clean forms.

The zombie bride is also deployed as a method of commenting upon brides and female roles. There are numerous wedding images where light-skinned brides are characterized as zombies. These identifications function as some combination of playful, funny, disapproving, and regulating. Brides tend to be identified as zombies when they gesture with their arms, including lifting up their arms and hands. For instance, sarah pants posts photographs of a passive bride with her hands cut out of the frame that she describes as "beautiful" and "perfect."[98] The bride is then identified as a zombie when she removes her arms from underneath the veil and reaches towards her face.[99] Such zombie identifications suggest that there is something awkward and surprising about brides, and perhaps women more generally, escaping from the bridal veil and actively doing things. The bride looks at herself in the mirror as a means of accomplishing this work and hails and constitutes herself as bride and other. Her self-production through mirror images also results in her queerly becoming a matching couple.[100] Many wedding images focus on feminine maintenance and repetition by presenting similarly dressed bridesmaids attending to the bride. In contrast to this necessity of being produced by others, images of zombie brides articulate these women's hands as flexible implements. The "zombie bride" label, with its implication that women's photographs and poses fail to meet norms, suggests some of the ways wedding culture is strained and managed.

Photographs of wedding parties encountering zombie walks further collapse the distinctions between heterosexual unions and zombie brides. For instance, a "Real bride and groom getting their wedding photo taken" with a "zombie bride and groom" mixes up these events and positions.[101] In the image, it is not fully clear who belongs to which ritual, especially since the two women pose together in the center of the representation. A sculpture of two united white spheres underscores the brides' similarities and their potentially erotic connections. Another "real bride, not zombie bride," tries to "keep the blood off her wedding dress," but she is incorporated into the zombie walk because of her gown.[102] While wedding gowns are one of the most recognizable features of weddings and are designed to distinguish the bride, these items connote zombie walk brides when placed in other situations. This confusion between brides and zombie brides is magnified in instances where wedding parties happily enact zombie gestures during ceremonies and turn conventional weddings into zombie walks.[103] In doing this, they recode individual participants' erotic interests and the heterosexual emphasis of these events.

The comments and engagements of some zombie walk participants more overtly replace heterosexual coupling with homosocial and potentially same-sex erotics. Kristin Petherbridge serves as a zombie bride, stands with her bridesmaids, argues she may have eaten the groom, and establishes her participation in a homosocial feminine setting.[104] Jim Reynolds presents an image of two zombie brides whose coupling is echoed by the twinned doors in the background. He "didn't see any grooms" at the zombie walk, which leads him "to believe that zombies may be more socially progressive in some areas" and that the brides are lesbians.[105] Zombie brides Loran and Krystle, according to photographer Ian

Aberle, "were on their way to the Bridal Show when the Zombie Apocalypse happened."[106] "Now they just eat the brains of the men they will never wed." Aberle provides a history of frustrated white femininity, heterosexual unions, and reproduction but the images suggest a more queer future. In them, Loran and Krystle are united by red fluid and a kiss.[107] Their actions propose that zombie brides replace heterosexuality with lesbian sexual attachments.

Conclusion: Zombie Nails and the Cosmetic Aspects of Zombie Culture

Zombies hail other subjects and constitute them as human and potentially other. Zombies are mechanisms in the interpellation process and figures that interrupt this structure. They stop people from being individuals and humans. Zombies' typical group hail associates them with the mass rather than the singular person. Arms and hands play an important part in this hailing and interpellation process. Hands allow people to point to individuals and others and are understood as body parts that make people human. Yet nails are one of the most visible dying and dead things embedded in the body. Due to the cultural connotations of hands and nails, zombie hands convey such hybrid positions as living-dead and dichotomies as living or dead. They point to the deadness within all individuals and the monstrosity of reaching hands that can transform individuals from subjects into something else.

The constructed features of zombie hands and bodies are based in technological and cosmetic practices that forward monstrosity rather than traditional forms of beauty. Zombie walk participants emphasize blood and filth in their how-to guides, including instructions on how to create zombie nail art applications.[108] An associated series of women's nail art challenges provide instructions on creating zombie nails.[109] In these participatory challenges, bloggers respond to a series of topics and post about applications over a period of time. Nail art challenges also provide opportunities for individuals to collaboratively communicate about and develop nail polish culture, including conceptions of what bodies are supposed to look like and how femininity is constructed. While women use zombie nails to offer a different model of embodiment, nail bloggers ordinarily associate femininity with neat nails and focus on painting within the "lines" of the nail and cuticle. For instance, Nail Art 101, whose identity is coupled with how-to instructions, chastises readers that, "It doesn't matter how cool your mani is if everyone is looking at your gross cuticles."[110] Nail Art 101 thereby points to the abject and monstrous aspects of women's bodies and asserts what needs to be maintained.

Most nail bloggers remove polish from their hands and cuticles after applying nail polish but the individuals who are engaged with zombie culture positively associate the gross and messy body with zombie nails. Emma offers a "gross, sloppy pic" before she cleaned up her zombie-themed nails because she thought it was "more thematic."[111] Sarah Eubanks did zombie nails and thought, "hell, why clean up" and happily gave up on feminine maintenance.[112] Instead, she added more material to make her "hands and cuticles look extra gross." Even when Eubanks shows pictures of her manicure without its veneer of filth, she still emphasizes how her fingers "look like they were rotting, bloody and bruised under" the nail. Kimberly Purcell foregrounds the violent aspects of these self-portrayals and describes this manicure as a "Good job!" that looks like the blogger "slammed both hands" in the "car door!!!!"[113] The dark black-purple at Eubank's nail beds makes it appear as if blood is collecting under the surface and the nails are swelling. This celebration of women's "good" work and production of the visual and visible body emerges from what is culturally marked as a feminine practice. Yet it renders a version of femininity that is contradictory in its careful crafting, messiness, and violence to the usual ways of being seen.

These women rework traditional femininity by documenting the destruction of their nails. This is especially significant since undamaged nails are a key resource for nail polish bloggers. For instance, Helena Rodero cut and ripped her nails. Her nails are streaked with what looks like blood and dirt is rubbed into the chewed and broken tips. While Rodero waited until her nails needed to be trimmed, she jokingly warns viewers that it is a "scary manicure, not apt for people with weak hearts."[114] Emma replies that they "look so scary" in the "best possible way" but she probably could not do the same thing.[115] FRANCINE is "proud" of her similar "mani and completely grossed out by it."[116] Her expressions of nausea are understandable. FRANCINE's nails are tipped with a deep burgundy and crumble away to reveal what looks like rotten flesh. She assures readers that they "were done using false nails, so no nails were harmed in the making of this mani." Jen views Kitties26's comparable manicure and "almost had a heart attack."[117] She thinks they are "quite scary to someone so attached to her nails!" Such views of damaged nails, in a similar manner to soiled wedding dresses, emotionally touch readers. In these cases, women experience damaged bodies and imagine having zombies' nails and hands touch their skin.

Kitties26 continues these narratives about being physically and emotionally touched and grasps the arm of her "victim" [Figure 4.2]. Her photographic rendering is "not a scary zombie 'grab you' kind of feel, it's more of a creepy cold zombie hand touching you vibe!"[118] Her comments underscore the relationship between physically touching and emotionally feeling and the ways these experiences can be delivered through images. She changes the hail, in which the individual reaches to call to the person who is being constituted as a subject, into an instance where zombies reach in order to touch and incorporate. This zombie touch highlights the fragility and mutability of skin. Kitties26 points to a faint white scar on her victim and holds the skin so that it is molded into pleats and furrows. These corporeal interventions are shifted when Kitties26 states that this touch is between her and her mother. Her dirty nails and fingers, which sometimes make her look sallow and at other times brown, appear over her mother's

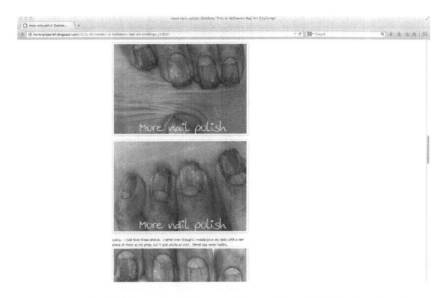

FIGURE 4.2 Kitties26, more nail polish. A zombie manicure is displayed against the skin of the blogger's mother.

clean and pale hand. The image thus complicates photography's role in producing the white family. The shifts in color and liveliness, which the texts suggest will occur as the daughter infects the mother, reverse the usual expectations about traits being transferred from parents to children. The child poses herself as the progenitor but she is the producer of death rather than life. The usual identifications of the mother and motherhood are also modified when Kitties26 holds raw meat instead of, but in the same manner as she held, her mother. This and other forms of holding are key functions of hands, which own and produce through these actions.

Zombie brides' hands, especially when they are reaching and damaged, also reshape femininity rather than constituting traditional female positions. Zombie brides reference one of the most traditional occasions in young women's "movement" towards womanhood while presenting non-normative forms of femininity and femaleness. Representations of zombie brides are becoming more common and are part of the growing influence of zombie texts. They suggest everyday identity categories are also being remade. Certainly, indications that whiteness is the foundation of zombie identification need to be more fully related to the cosmetics that are used for these procedures and the resultant physiognomies and self-conceptions. In trash the dress sessions, photographers and brides indicate that filth and fluidity, as well as "liberation" from norms, are flattering and a more apt representation of their identities than wedding photography. In zombie images and texts, the blood flowing through skin and life are coded as unflattering. Thus, people's zombie bride representations of whiteness point to different experiences with, cultural conceptions of, constructions of, and theories of whiteness. These feminine zombie representations can be used to develop a more extensive theory of the implications and uses of monstrous and deathly whiteness than Dyer proposes.[119] In my anticipated version of this account, whiteness is a "condition"—a restrictive expectation *and* a disease. From this position, dead whiteness can be critically deployed to curtail the empowered gestures and claims about beauty that are associated with white people.

Notes

1. Annette, "20-05-06_1406," Flickr, 4 July 2006, 30 June 2014, http://www.flickr.com/photos/hestia/182196498
2. Sean Doorly, "Zombie Bride," Flickr, 13 July 2012, 16 January 2014, http://www.flickr.com/photos/sdoorly/7587170402/
3. Kirschenbaum, *Mechanisms*.
4. >>SuperMary<<, "Zombie Brides," Flickr, 29 October 2005, 22 June 2014, http://www.flickr.com/photos/superscarymary/102258078
5. jamie nyc, "Zombie Bride & Bridemaids - NYC Zombie Crawl 2012," Flickr, 27 May 2012, 17 January 2014, http://www.flickr.com/photos/jimkiernan/7285363934/
6. Althusser, "Ideology and Ideological State Apparatuses," 105.
7. Georgette, "Undead and Undead Bride," Flickr, 22 June 2014, http://www.flickr.com/photos/saturation/5108741655/in/set-72157625102419331/
8. sjnewton, "Undead Wedding," Flickr, 27 October 2007, 22 June 2014, http://www.flickr.com/photos/77844986@N00/1779429957
9. Dyer, *White*; Frankenberg, introduction to *Displacing Whiteness*; Ingraham, *White Weddings*; Lipsitz, "Possessive Investment in Whiteness"; Mercer, "Black Hair/Style Politics."
10. Peake, "He is Dead," 54.
11. Chiara Bonello, "Zombies Take to the streets," *Malta Independent*, 4 November 2010, 25 January 2014, http://www.independent.com.mt/articles/2010-11-04/news/zombies-take-to-the-streets-282698/
12. Andy Mannix, "Zombie Pub Crawl breaks world record," City Pages, 14 November 2012, 18 January 2014, http://blogs.citypages.com/blotter/2012/11/zombie_pub_crawl_breaks_guinness_world_record.php; Leandro Avalos Blacha, "Buenos Aires, invadida por los muertos vivos," Revista de Cultura, 29 October 2012, 18 January 2014, http://www.revistaenie.clarin.com/escenarios/Buenos-Aires-invadida-por-los-muertos-vivos_0_800920101.html
13. Kirschenbaum, *Mechanisms*, 97.
14. Barthes, *Camera Lucida*, 95.
15. The first event that was labeled a "zombie walk" occurred in 2003 in Toronto, Ontario. Asbury Park Zombie walk, "The History of the Zombie Walk," *Asburied Park Press* 11, no. 1, 5 October 2013, http://www.njzombiewalk.com/zombiewalk/The_Zombie_Walk.html
16. Jason Schneider, "zombie tableau," Flickr, 12 February 2000, 1 February 2014, http://www.flickr.com/photos/layoutmonkey/57045687/; ~SwmpGrl~, "113," Flickr, 1 January 2002, 2 February 2014, http://www.flickr.com/photos/swmpgrl/6155718471/in/photostream/
17. Flickr, "About Flickr," 9 July 2014, http://www.flickr.com/about; Smith, "Baby's Picture."

18. The conventions of Internet how-to guides are related to the development of this form. European artisans and other specialized workers began to record their procedures starting around 1400. This expanded with the availability of the printing press. Karim-Cooper, "This Alters Not thy Beauty"; Eisenstein, *Printing Press*. While manuals and frequently asked questions files (FAQs) are more common formats for dispensing information in Internet settings, the Linux community and sites like The Linux Documentation Project produce operating system "HOW TOs." The Linux Documentation Project, "Single list of HOWTOs," 31 October 2011, 22 June 2014, http://www.tldp.org/HOWTO/HOWTO-INDEX/howtos.html
19. eHow Contributor, "How to Look Like a Zombie," eHow, 22 June 2014, http://www.ehow.com/how_2034320_look-like-zombie.html; Jessica Clouse, "How to Do Zombie Makeup for Girls," eHow, 22 June 2014, http://www.ehow.com/how_8258168_do-zombie-makeup-girls.html#ixzz1cOjUsg9l; Christina Sloane, "How to Do Dead Bride Makeup for a Halloween Costume," eHow, 22 June 2014, http://www.ehow.com/how_8174238_do-bride-makeup-halloween-costume.html; Jen Kim, "Rules for Zombie Walkers, 1 July 2014, http://www.ehow.com/info_10017292_rules-zombie-walkers.html
20. Julie Johnston, "How to Make a Cool Girl's Zombie Costume," eHow, 22 June 2014, http://www.ehow.com/how_8629469_make-cool-girls-zombie-costume.html#ixzz1y6uZvFQT; Louise Harding, "Female Zombie Costume Ideas," eHow, 22 June 2014, http://www.ehow.com/info_8257215_female-zombie-costume-ideas.html
21. Instructables, "About Instructables," 19 December 2011, http://www.instructables.com/about/
22. eHow, "About eHow," 22 June 2014, http://www.ehow.com/about-us.html
23. Doug Gross, "Why we love those rotting, hungry, putrid zombies," CNN, 2 October 2009, 22 June 2014, http://articles.cnn.com/2009-10-02/entertainment/zombie.love_1_zombie-movie-encyclopedia-white-zombie-peter-dendle?_s=PM:SHOWBIZ
24. Steven Schlozman, as quoted in Carol Memmott, "Novelist lets us in on 'Secret' about zombies," CNN, 25 March 2011, 22 June 2014, http://www.usatoday.com/life/books/news/2011-03-25-zombie_ST_N.htm
25. Grahame-Smith, *Pride and Prejudice*.
26. Aizenberg, "I Walked with a Zombie"; Dendle, "Zombie as a Barometer"; Fay, "Dead Subjectivity"; Harper, "Night of the Living Dead"; Horne, "I Shopped with a Zombie"; Lightning, "Interracial Tensions"; Loudermilk, "Eating 'Dawn'"; Lowenstein, "Living Dead"; Moody, "Conversations with Zombies."
27. Lauro and Embry, "Zombie Manifesto."
28. Justin Meyers, "Pregnant Fetus Sucking Zombies," WonderHowTo, 6 March 2014, http://halloween-ideas.wonderhowto.com/inspiration/pregnant-fetus-sucking-zombies-0131035/
29. Gavon Laessig, "Undead Like Me," Lawrence.com, 27 October 2008, 22 June 2014, http://www.lawrence.com/news/2008/oct/27/undead_like_me/
30. Peter Keough, "Voodoo economics: What vampire and zombie movies can tell us about the future of capitalism," *Boston Phoenix*, 21 May 2010, 22 June 2014, http://thephoenix.com/boston/movies/102380-voodoo-economics/
31. Kat, as quoted in Nic Crowe, "On feminist zombies," Libertine, 21 January 2014, http://www.interestedwomen.com/index.php/on-feminist-zombies
32. Simal Yilmaz, "19 Ominously Undead Manicures," Trend Hunter, 7 February 2013, 21 January 2014, http://www.trendhunter.com/slideshow/manicure-designs
33. San Juan, "Horror of Touch," 433.
34. Rowe, *Dead Hands*.
35. Behuniak, "Living Dead?" 80.
36. Stockton, *Queer Child*.

37. Owens, "Photography 'en Abyme,'" 85.
38. Armstrong, "Biology, Destiny, Photography," 38.
39. Andrew Smith, "Zombie brides," Flickr, 12 October 2013, 21 January 2014, http://www.flickr.com/photos/91682649@N02/10235515474/
40. Jowett, "Origins, Occupation"; Secomb, "Fractured Community."
41. Margaret Robinson, as quoted in Urmee Khan, "Zombie world record broken in Nottingham," *Telegraph*, 31 October 2008, 22 June 2014, http://www.telegraph.co.uk/news/newstopics/howaboutthat/3333085/Zombie-world-record-broken-in-Nottingham.html
42. Meghan White, "Handmeg does Halloween," *The Temple News*, 24 October 2011, 22 June 2014, http://temple-news.com/2011/10/24/handmeg-does-halloween/
43. Rain Blanken, "How-To Zombie Makeup," About.com, 22 June 2014, http://diyfashion.about.com/od/facepainting/ss/zombie_makeup.htm
44. Lauro and Embry, "Zombie Manifesto."
45. Clover, *Men, Women, and Chain Saws*; Pinedo, *Recreational Terror*.
46. Aimeesque, "the twilight zone when the photographer and zombie in him met…," Flickr, 11 June 2011, 22 June 2014, http://www.flickr.com/photos/aimeesque/5831214815/in/photostream
47. Georgette, "Zombie Photographer Grrl," Flickr, 24 October 2009, 18 January 2014, http://www.flickr.com/photos/georgie_grrl/4052791120/
48. suezq1342, "Toronto Zombie Walk 2009," Flickr, 25 October 2009, 18 January 2014, http://www.flickr.com/photos/suezq1342/4042990701/in/set-72157622535809385; RedandJonny, "Toronto Zombie Walk 2009," Flickr, 18 January 2014, http://www.flickr.com/photos/suezq1342/4042990701/in/set-72157622535809385
49. Turkle, *Life on the Screen*.
50. Bratich, "Digital Touch," 303.
51. May, "Zombie Geographies," 289.
52. Ingraham, *White Weddings*, 139.
53. Hartigan, Jr. "Establishing the Fact."
54. Dyer, *White*, 42.
55. Mercer, "Black Hair/Style Politics," 35.
56. Craig, "Race, Beauty"; Palmer, "Brazen Cheek."
57. Gwilliam, "Cosmetic Poetics."
58. Poitevin, "Inventing Whiteness," 63.
59. Palmer, "Brazen Cheek"; Peiss, *Hope in a Jar*.
60. Pierre, "I Like Your Colour!" Saraswati, "Cosmopolitan Whiteness."
61. Hoberman and Rosenbaum, *Midnight*, 125.
62. Dyer, *White*, 211.
63. Kirkland, "Caucasian Persuasion of Buffy."
64. Scott Snider, "Toronto Zombie Walk 2008-6222," Flickr, 19 October 2008, 22 June 2014, http://www.flickr.com/photos/sniderscion/3003562957/
65. dr_dustbunny, "the_infecte d: ZOMBIE WALK 2005," LiveJournal, 28 August 2005, 10 April 2011, http://community.livejournal.com/the__infected/14334.html
66. Deanna Gray, "Zombie Bride!" Flickr, 18 October 2008, 22 June 2014, http://www.flickr.com/photos/22490363@N02/2957373462/
67. Cody McCloy, Henry Hanks, Nicole Saidi, "So you wanna be a zombie," CNN, 4 September 2011, 22 June 2014, http://geekout.blogs.cnn.com/2011/09/04/so-you-wanna-be-a-zombie/?hpt=hp_c2
68. Ingraham, *White Weddings*.
69. Poitevin, "Inventing Whiteness."
70. kenndubeau, "Mr. & Mrs Zombie," Flickr, 22 June 2014, http://www.flickr.com/photos/wolfie/2770597212/in/set-72157606779725127/
71. RedandJonny, "Toronto Zombie Walk 2009," Flickr, 18 January 2014, http://www.flickr.com/photos/suezq1342/4042990701/in/set-72157622535809385

72. Christine Grabig, "Mr. & Mrs Zombie," Flickr, 16 August 2008, 22 June 2014, http://www.flickr.com/photos/wolfie/2770597212/in/set-72157606779725127/
73. Sobal, Bove, and Rauschenbach, "Weight and Weddings."
74. vanBuuren, "kiss the bride," Flickr, 26 October 2008, 22 June 2014, http://www.flickr.com/photos/bunnytek/2978549155/
75. Kirkland, "Caucasian Persuasion of Buffy."
76. Zombie Maker, "Zombie Maker – character – What was your zombie in their previous life?" 24 June 2014, http://www.zombiemaker.com/character/profession/
77. Dyer, *White*.
78. Tom Walsham, "Zombie Makeup and Costume Tips," 20 October 2011, http://zombies.tomwalsham.com/costume.html
79. Indymogul, "How to make zombie make-up," Curbly, 6 June 2007, 22 June 2014, http://www.curbly.com/indymogul/posts/1744-how-to-make-zombie-make-up
80. Leah D'Emilio, "How to Apply Scary Halloween Makeup," Maholo, 22 June 2014, http://www.mahalo.com/how-to-apply-scary-halloween-makeup/
81. Lipsitz, "Possessive Investment in Whiteness"; Rosenthal, "Visceral Culture."
82. FunCostumes, "Zombie Bride Costume," squidoo, 18 June 2012, http://www.squidoo.com/zombiebridecostume
83. Murrye-bernard, "Zombie Makeup Ideas," LoveToKnow, 10 September 2011, http://makeup.lovetoknow.com/Zombie_Makeup_Ideas
84. Christi Aldridge, "How to Do Zombie Makeup and Hair Easily," eHow, 23 June 2014, http://www.ehow.com/how_8330451_do-zombie-makeup-hair-easily.html#ixzz1cPZ1sxxS
85. Cody McCloy, Henry Hanks, Nicole Saidi, "So you wanna be a zombie," CNN, 4 September 2011, 22 June 2014, http://geekout.blogs.cnn.com/2011/09/04/so-you-wanna-be-a-zombie/?hpt=hp_c2
86. coreymarie, "Zombie walk photos & DIY zombie make-up," The all-new adventures of coreymarie.com, 23 October 2009, 24 January 2014, http://coreymarie.com/2009/10/zombie-walk-photos-diy-zombie-make-up/
87. Kerr, "Paper Bag Principle."
88. XaSkYlltLoVeX, "How to do cuteish Zombie Makeup?" Yahoo! Answers, 10 September 2011, http://answers.yahoo.com/question/index?qid=20110823134057AA7RVj3
89. Face Paint Heaven, "How to be a Cute Dead Zombie Girl," 15 September 2010, 15 September 2011, http://www.myfacepaint.com/379/cute-dead-zombie-girl/
90. WordCustard, "The Cute Zombie Girl Style Guide," Squidoo, 23 June 2014, http://www.squidoo.com/cute-zombie-girl
91. Cynthia, "A Sweet and Bloody Zombie Love Story Styled Wedding Shoot," Poptastic Bride, 31 October 2013, 8 January 2014, http://poptasticbride.com/2013/10/zombie-wedding/#.Us2ubPZszeB
92. Ingraham, *White Weddings*, 4.
93. Chelsea, "Wedding of the Zombies!" Practically Ever After, 3 December 2009, 5 June 2014, http://practicallyeverafter.com/links/wedding-of-the-zombies.html
94. Gavon Laessig, "Undead Like Me," Lawrence.com, 27 October 2008, 23 June 2014, http://www.lawrence.com/news/2008/oct/27/undead_like_me/
95. Heather Lynn Meyer, as quoted in FullMoonKC, "Zombie Wedding at Macabre Cinema," YouTube, 29 September 2010, 4 January 2014, http://www.youtube.com/watch?v=WtNKN0AE0nQ&list=PL8jL4ivTG2AnF2TPhTmZtLdge1UFo0GXm&index=10
96. Tracey Monaghan, as quoted in Daily Mail Reporter, "'Till death do us part': Horror film fans splash thousands on their fairytale 'zombie wedding,'" *Daily Mail*, 25 October 2010, 23 June 2014, http://www.dailymail.co.uk/news/article-1323555/How-undead-wed-Couple-dress-zombies-tie-knot-bloody-wedding.html
97. Smith, "Baby's Picture."

98. sarah pants, "beautiful," Flickr, 3 June 2006, 9 January 2014, http://www.flickr.com/photos/sarahpants/162618026/in/photostream/; sarah pants, "perfect," Flickr, 3 June 2006, 9 January 2014, http://www.flickr.com/photos/sarahpants/162618026/in/photostream/
99. sarah pants, "zombie bride," Flickr, 3 June 2006, 9 January 2014, http://www.flickr.com/photos/sarahpants/162618032/in/photostream/
100. sarah pants, "checking for tear damage," Flickr, 3 June 2006, 25 January 2014, http://www.flickr.com/photos/sarahpants/162622319/in/photostream/
101. ted_martens, "We crashed a wedding photo shoot," Flickr, 2 October 2010, 18 January 2014, http://www.flickr.com/photos/tedmartens/5045262087/
102. travel science, "A real bride, not zombie bride, tries to keep the blood off her wedding dress," Flickr, 11 June 2011, 18 January 2014, http://www.flickr.com/photos/travelscience/5823311520/
103. Lizzy Biggs, "Zombie Nation," Flickr, 18 September 2010, 24 January 2014, http://www.flickr.com/photos/1_lizzy/5370973703/; Melissa Squires, "zombies," Flickr, 28 August 2009, 24 January 2014, http://www.flickr.com/photos/mayize/4057589444/
104. Kristin Petherbridge, as quoted in Eric Collins, "Zombies unite in annual downtown death march," Katu.com, 26 October 2008, 25 January 2014, http://www.katu.com/news/33340734.html
105. Jim Reynolds, "Zombie Brides," Flickr, 30 October 2007, 25 January 2014, http://www.flickr.com/photos/revjim5000/1804831243/
106. Ian Aberle, "Zombie Brides and Cool Rides (Dark)," Zombie Ambience, 12 August 2010, 24 January 2014, http://zombieambience.com/2010/08/zombie-brides-and-cool-rides-dark/
107. Ian Aberle, "Kissing Zombie Brides," Flickr, 1 May 2010, 25 January 2014, http://www.flickr.com/photos/ianaberle/4577128483/in/set-72157623865916387/
108. Caralyn, "Zombie Accessories," Blink and You'll Miss It, 20 October 2011, 11 January 2014, http://blink-and-youll-miss-it.blogspot.com/2011/10/zombie-accessories.html; PShiiit, "(Tuto Vidéo nail art) DIY Zombie Nails // On se prépare pour la Zombie Walk!" 30 September 2012, 11 January 2014, http://pshiiit.com/2012/09/30/tuto-video-diy-zombie-nails-on-se-prepare-pour-la-zombie-walk/
109. Emily Esqueleta, "The Halloween Challenge: 'Trick or Treat' nail art," Macabre Manicures, 1 October 2012, 14 January 2014, http://macabremanicures.blogspot.com/2012/10/the-halloween-challenge-trick-or-treat.html; Elizabeth Lefevre, "Crumpet's Nail Tarts Halloween Challenge- Black Cats & Bats!" Not Too Polished, October 2013, 14 January 2014, http://nottoopolished.blogspot.com/2013/10/crumpets-nail-tarts-halloween-challenge.html;
110. Nail Art 101, "nail care," 19 October 2013, http://www.nail-art-101.com/nail_care.html
111. Emma, "Digit-al Dozen: Zombielicious," Manicurity, October 2012, 11 September 2013, http://www.manicurity.com/2012/10/digit-al-dozen-zombielicious.html
112. Sarah Eubanks, "Halloween Nail Art Challenge - Z is for Zombies 10/9," Samarium's Swatches, 9 October 2012, 11 September 2013, http://www.samariums-swatches.com/2012/10/halloween-nail-art-challenge-z-is-for.html
113. Kimberly Purcell, "Halloween Nail Art Challenge - Z is for Zombies 10/9," Samarium's Swatches, 9 October 2012, 11 September 2013, http://www.samariums-swatches.com/2012/10/halloween-nail-art-challenge-z-is-for.html
114. Helena Rodero, "Halloween Challenge #3: Zombies," Nail Wish, 9 October 2012, 10 January 2014, http://nailwish.blogspot.com.es/2012/10/hi-everyone-i-warn-you-this-is-scary.html
115. Emma, "Halloween Challenge #3: Zombies," Nail Wish, 9 October 2012, 10 January 2014, http://nailwish.blogspot.com.es/2012/10/hi-everyone-i-warn-you-this-is-scary.html

116. FRANCINE, "Naaaaiils⋯," The Polished Mommy, 15 October 2012, 11 September 2013, http://www.thepolishedmommy.com/2012/10/naaaaiils.html
117. Jen, "Zombies 'This is Halloween Nail Art Challenge,'" More Nail Polish, 15 October 2012, 23 June 2014, http://www.morenailpolish.com/2012/10/zombies-this-is-halloween-nail-art.html
118. Kitties26, "Zombies 'This is Halloween Nail Art Challenge,'" Flickr, 15 October 2012, 23 June 2014, http://morenailspolish.blogspot.com/2012/10/zombies-is-halloween-nail-art-challenge_15.html
119. Dyer, *White*.

5
NEVER CLEANING UP
Cosmetic Femininity and the Remains of Glitter

Glitter nail polish is "fun, feminine and manages to capture a generous amount of attention" according to the blogger alexandra.[1] She argues that glitter polishes and other "lovely feminine nail art" designs "attract only positive attention towards the hands and enhance their beauty." On a beauty site, hirra notes that glitter eye makeup extends women's "femininity" and makes women more "attractive for others."[2] alexandra and hirra associate glitter with femininity and the ways women are directed to function as visual objects and make themselves more appealing to other people. Their identification of glitter as an amplification of femininity is related to visual culture researchers John A. Walker and Sarah Chaplin's assertion that gleams and glitter "extend the self beyond bodily limits."[3] These comments about glitter also evoke Teresa de Lauretis's examination of the ways gender is produced through social technologies and Jack Bratich's classification of Internet technologies and settings as "extensions" of bodily digits, people, and ideas.[4] Glitter functions as a technology because it produces women and femininity; emphasizes women's visual features by illuminating them; and is rendered from small fragments of plastic, metal, and other materials that reflect light.[5]

Many women indicate that glitter fulfills their desires and encourages them to pleasurably look at their bodies. They thereby deploy some features of postfeminism and focus on the personal pleasures of feminine experiences. For instance, alexandra and Daneen find glitter to be enjoyable. Daneen's glitter nail polish "is sparkly," "fun," and "just so nice to look at while" typing.[6] She is engaged with her own in-motion visual features and technological practices rather than thinking about how others see her as a passive object. Glitter enhances her experience typing and thus her position as a producing woman. flinty also engages with her own interests and body when spending most of the time that she wore glitter nail polish looking at her nails: "Staring at them indoors," "staring at them during the day," "staring at them during the night," and "taking photos of most of that process" [Figure 5.1].[7] In doing this, flinty focuses on seeing and producing a version of herself rather than engaging in the purportedly more typical feminine process of seeing herself the ways others see her. She proposes something quite distinct from the male gaze, which I discuss in earlier chapters, by relating feminized forms of seeing women's bodies to producing and changing things.[8] These and related comments suggest that glitter is a multivalent shifter. It alters the visual appearance of objects and individuals' engagements with their bodies and the world. For instance, flinty's polish does not resemble a stable color. Her polish is "So changeable, so lovely" that she had to take "many photos in different types of lighting situations." This means that women cosmetically produce and then document different versions of their bodies in Internet settings, including examinations of the peripheral and dead parts of their fingernails, rather than seeing themselves as ideal and passive models of beauty. Yet these women are not completely detached from normative beauty culture.

Glitter cosmetics are part of the body-centric forms of femininity that are encouraged and regulated by contemporary society. According to feminist philosopher Sandra L. Bartky, normative femininity is focused on women's bodies, including their "appearance."[9] Individuals and cultural institutions produce conceptions of femininity and feminine norms by encouraging women to manage their appearance, including their application of makeup.[10] For women to be identified as fully, or even acceptably, feminine they must learn and perform a

FIGURE 5.1 flinty, Polish or Perish. Blog posts often show the different qualities of glitter polishes.

variety of complicated and time intensive beauty practices. They need to adopt accommodating poses and demeanor, remove facial and body hair, stay clean, manage bodily scents, maintain a toned and youthful appearance, and apply cosmetics. Women who do not follow the rules and disciplinary procedures of normative beauty culture are at risk of cultural dismissal, which may include negative commentary, social and sexual ostracization, limited job prospects, and institutionalization.[11] Yet the women who are invested in glitter makeup applications and Internet commentary are too often denigrated for their interest in what is deemed to be trivial and are denied power and respect. Women have varied investments in beauty practices and their produced bodies but no one can completely disinvest and remain culturally legible and accepted.

Feminist literature on the ways beauty culture objectifies and disciplines women and research on how women find enjoyment and agency in related practices are useful for my project. The combination of these approaches is suggested by Paula Black's study of the pleasurable aspects of the beauty industry and interrogation of the ways these structures still control women and their bodies.[12] Alexandra, Daneen, flinty, and other posters write about the delightful aspects of glitter materials and applications. There are also women who indicate how they feel constrained by cultural expectations. For instance, SaucyandSparkly wishes glitter was "socially acceptable" but she is inhibited by "rules" about cosmetics that she "cannot break."[13] Thus glitter is understood as an aspect of femininity and something that damages individuals' womanliness, especially when they deploy heavier applications of glitter. Women take an active part in Internet cosmetic cultures and propose and create products but the term "choice," when imagined to be only about personal decisions rather than also addressing cultural directives to make certain selections, is a too utopian way of describing beauty culture. As I have previously noted, postfeminism tends to perpetuate beliefs that women are empowered to freely choose between different options. Postfeminist theorization, especially when postfeminism is understood as contemporary practices that are aligned with feminism, poststructuralism, postcolonialism, and postmodernism, offers useful ways of interrogating these narratives. My analytical approach is to consider the ways beauty culture, and specifically Internet narratives about glitter cosmetics and practices, are connected to desires and displeasures and produce and trouble traditional femininity.

People's references to and applications of glitter are important to the production of femininity because glitter is a significant component of contemporary cosmetics through which women craft their appearance and position. Women also choose glitter for its disruptive features or find themselves at the boundaries of normativity because of glitter's mutability and range of negative references. Glitter functions as what N. Katherine Hayles describes as a flickering signifier and associates with computer and Internet processes because glitter makes the meanings of femininity and other things less stable.[14] Glitter drifts everywhere, contaminates things, refracts light, blurs the body, and dissolves the ability to see solid forms. In this chapter I consider how glitter is a feature of and produces femininity, threatens femininity, is managed, is produced by women, and is a technology for cultural opposition. These seemingly contrary and yet irrevocably intermeshed functions of glitter, and numerous other features of femininity function because women reference and try to manage similar discordances, suggest some interesting discrepancies within femininity that have political and theoretical potential. All of this makes the cultural coding and functions of glitter important to feminist studies and women's empowerment. However, glitter has been undertheorized. My interrogation of cosmetic glitter and the ways it is conceptualized on beauty sites and blogs offers methods for thinking about the construction of normative femininity and the critical possibilities of this evanescent material.

The Properties of Glitter

Glitter's capacity to visually alter the body and reorder cultural assumptions and stable categories is related to the ongoing instabilities of new technologies. For instance, morphing is identified as an aspect of new media and Internet settings because people change texts and switch between different identifiers and avatar representations.[15] The instability and changeability of morphing is part of the ontology of new technologies. Instability and changeability also occur with the appearance of new products, phasing out of older technologies, confusion about the uses of technologies and interfaces, the crashing of operating systems and software, and the disappearance of Internet sites.[16] Thus, Internet technologies can render flickering signifiers that allow texts and other things to be easily changed and do not support reliable meanings.[17] One version of this formal and ideological flickering is the use of HTML to simulate glittering texts and pointers that shift in and out of focus.[18] By using such glitter effects, women eBay sellers and other producers associate sites and products with femininity. For instance, "Girly Glitter Graphic Code" is further marked as female by including images of women covered in glitter, generating these sparkling experiences, and changing shape.[19] Such "glittered logos" and "sparkling" texts are part of Internet participants' engagements in femininity, according to Amy Shields Dobson's social networking research.[20] Nail polish bloggers also configure more normative forms of femininity, as I indicate later in this chapter, when they diffuse the color and sparkle of glitter by embedding it in layers of translucent polish.

Beauty bloggers emphasize their shared engagement in glitter through a variety of visual and textual strategies. Blogs are titled such things as Glitta Gloves, Glitter Geek, and Glitz & Glitter.[21] Glitter is also depicted in banners that are featured at the top of each blog. For instance, A Polish Addict's banner emphasizes her interests with photographs of glitter nail polish bottles and densely glittered fingernails.[22] Bloggers commonly employ photographs of nails and hands as a means of conveying the aspects of glitter. In doing this, they provide different renderings of the glittered body than the media's focus on the faces and torsos of stars. Bloggers' images of hands are related to broader Internet and computer conventions, including the continued deployment of hand-pointers. Images of hands also appear in beauty and craft tutorials as a way of demonstrating posters' skills and asserting individual forms of production.

Numerous forms of glitter are featured on beauty blogs and forums and sold in salons, stores, and websites. These nail swatches and reviews are accompanied by provisos about who should use these products and how they should be employed. Articles are titled "9 Ways to Wear Glitter Without Looking Like You Fell Off the Christmas Tree (PHOTOS)" and "How to Wear Glitter Eye Makeup and Not Look Like a Middle Schooler" as a means of suggesting that women inappropriately wear glitter makeup and need instruction.[23] The qualifications accompanying these how-to guidelines are notable since most major cosmetics manufacturers and many smaller brands market glitter versions of all kinds of makeup. Recommendations are ordinarily based in cultural expectations and warn women to control glitter's association with immaturity, personal indulgences, and gay and drag cultures or risk condemnation. Glitter, which becomes dirt when misplaced, must also be washed off at the end of the event or day. Of course, this cleaning process is extremely difficult since glitter tends to drift everywhere and attach itself to clothing and skin. Glitter is a feature of femininity and culturally disturbing, in a manner that echoes Mary Douglas's analysis of dirt, because it disrupts order and stable categorizations.[24]

Applications of glitter modify the sorts of cultural values and identity positions that are associated with women and femininity. Glitter, as popular culture scholar Hannah Priest argues, is a shifter and is at "once childlike and adult, innocent and sexualized."[25] Glitter generates fluctuating meanings, including understandings of it as dirt and matter out of place, which threaten normative femininity. Thus, glitter's association with particular age groups, sexualities, and identities makes these positions unstable. Glitter's incorporation into clothing, cosmetics, craft projects, ornaments, and toys also has an influence on the ways these things are understood. A common link between these varied artifacts is that they are frequently identified as frivolous and culturally devalued. Therefore, some narratives about glitter continue the historical association of cosmetics with a series of negative characteristics, including improper passions, overt sexuality, unruliness, and superficiality.[26]

Glitter can still be a cultural requirement. Philosopher Thomas Leddy argues that sparkle and shine are some of the core metaphorical concepts of beauty and positively pervade people's aesthetic lives.[27] Glitter is a synonym for sparkle and shine and promises to facilitate many of the same attributes.[28] These terms figure women as animated, bright, energetic, glowing, light (both in terms of color and mass), and vibrant. Thus, women are reliant on glitter's more figurative features to maintain their beauty, appeal, and very claim to being female. Beauty products promise to enhance the wearer's inner sparkle while producing physical shine. Women do not have to apply glitter makeup or glossy hair products but they are expected to achieve some of the features associated with these products. They can also extend these attributes in Internet settings and feminize their profile by deploying glitter codes and graphics. Glitter's tendency to render sparks of light makes it a technology of lightness that is not always positively coded.

Society also associates sparkle and shine with "such negative aesthetic qualities as 'glitzy' and 'gaudy' and the superficiality of 'glitter.'"[29] As this suggests, glitter has been linked to deception and lower-class values. Its purportedly excessive and ostentatious features are used to articulate and condemn class behaviors as well as the characteristics that are associated with other devalued identity positions. Poet William Drummond indicated in 1649 that "All is not Gold which glittereth" and writer Samuel Johnson similarly argued in 1784 that "All is not gold that glitters."[30] William Shakespeare referenced these sayings in *The Merchant of Venice*.[31] These beliefs about the fraudulence of glittering things are disturbing. Glitter is a means, at least through the related identification of such affects as warmth, luminosity, and sparkle, for women to be recognized. Ideas about glittering are connected to normative femininity because radiance and glow are associated with women who are in love, getting married, pregnant, and new mothers.

Many women find it difficult to manage glitter because of its ideological shifts. Glitter's material and affective qualities are linked to beauty, wealth, normative femininity, duplicity, lower-class values, sexual promiscuity, and gender nonconformity. Faced by these conflicting implications, women who are invested in traditional gender roles try to control glitter's negative influences. Women use Internet settings to indicate that there are acceptable times to wear glitter makeup, age groups who can sport this material, amounts of glitter that should be worn, and parts of the face and body where it can be applied. While being "glitzy" and wearing glitter on New Year's Eve is more culturally acceptable, being "gaudy" and wearing glitter at work is believed to mark women as being of a lower and tasteless class and being sexually promiscuous.[32] Even the women who decide to ignore these proscriptions often mention the rules associated with glitter makeup. Cultural conceptions of glitter cosmetics thus enforce particular kinds of female behaviors by indicating how specific cohorts should perform.

Feminist Responses to Beauty and Cosmetics

Feminists take varied political and theoretical stances in response to conceptions of beauty and the processes and rituals associated with beauty products. Some feminists argue that normative beauty culture maintains binary gender positions, limits women's agency, and supports the objectification of women.[33] Women's use of cosmetics, according to Bartky, is coded as an expressive and creative process. However, she identifies it as "a highly stylized activity that gives little rein to self-expression."³⁴ Thus, painting the face can "be described as painting the same picture over and over again with minor variations." Women are not permitted a wide range of choices in "what is considered appropriate makeup for the office and for most social occasions; indeed, the woman who uses cosmetics in a genuinely novel and imaginative way is liable to be seen not as an artist but as an eccentric." SaucyandSparkly supports this analysis by suggesting that creative makeup applications are culturally regulated.³⁵ Doing gender by employing cosmetics can thus threaten women's claims to normative femininity as well as bolster their position and status. Michelle M. Lazar argues in her research on postfeminist identity that in many cultures "'doing' beauty" is an expected part of traditional forms of doing gender and femininity.³⁶ There are rewards for meeting beauty ideals and penalties for not meeting expectations and following directives. As feminist philosopher Susan Bordo argues, "beauty remains a prerequisite for female success."³⁷ Like contemporary conceptions of motherhood, the "standards for" being beautiful and styling the self "have become more stringent, more rigorous, than ever." Women experience significant pressures to conform to exacting standards.

Beauty practices, according to Kathy Davis, do not solve women's appearance problems and cannot be separated from the "oppressive cultural constraints on women to be beautiful."³⁸ However, she indicates that some women use beauty procedures as methods of working within current cultural limitations. Davis's argument also applies to glitter cosmetic practices. Women wear glitter makeup as decorative and enhancing strategies but this material cannot be rendered in the same way and produce the same face because glitter tends to be unmanageable and drifts everywhere. For instance, Jessica's glitter makeup is "everywhere but" her "eyes" by the end of the day.³⁹ BLIX's addictive "crack" is glitter and she probably has it in her ass "crack since" she uses "it so much."⁴⁰ Some of these women embrace the uncontrollable aspects of glitter and apply it in order to interrogate norms. WonderHowTo demonstrates a "Bearded Bettie" makeup application that "catches you with her sparkly" eye shadow and "beard?!"⁴¹ daydream222 analyzes how "nail polish is intertwined with race, gender, and class" and presents an "unusual" color combination that distorts the association of pink glitter with femininity.⁴² Through these processes, women's glitter makeup applications do some of the same disruptive work as their zombie self-representations. They reference and disorder the limiting features of cosmetics and the associated mandates for women to keep themselves groomed and mannered.

Some recent scholarship on beauty culture, as I have begun to suggest, points to the pleasure that women experience when participating in beauty rituals and crafting their appearances.⁴³ Numerous beauty bloggers provide narratives about pleasurable glitter makeup undertakings and indicate the ways women produce their bodies and inventive applications through these approaches. Thus, these behaviors provide ways for women to develop and demonstrate skills and emphasize their roles as creators. Feminists have described the kinds of skills and identity positions that inform the work of women in salons.[44] However, research on beauty culture might expand to focus on the technical and creative skills that women employ when they work on and represent their own bodies for Internet viewers. Demonstrations and acknowledgments of such proficiencies have been an important aspect of beauty blogging and supported the kinds of polish production that I consider in the afterword. While feminists rightly associate beauty culture with producing and regulating women's and feminine roles, they might further consider how women produce material goods and affects through these systems.

Queering Glitter

Glitter is deployed in and associated with alternative cultures and lifestyles and can thus challenge the gender characteristics that produce and support normative womanhood. In contemporary society, gay and lesbian activists deploy "glitter bombing" as a way of queering homophobic political figures and interrogating their policies and values, including their opposition to same-sex marriages. Glam rock musicians, including Gary Glitter and Ziggy Stardust as performed by David Bowie, wore glitter in the 1970s as a way of representing their gender nonconformity and sexual lability, which are forms of flickering signifiers. The performer Sylvester James, according to sociologist Joshua Gamson, symbolizes the "1970s subcultures of glittery, druggy, self-celebrating fantasy worlds where gender was something you could try on and race was an exploding costume."[45] In Todd Haynes's film *Velvet Goldmine*, which is from the 1990s and depicts the 1970s, heaps, spills, and cosmetic applications of glitter activate an array of gender and sexual positions. Stephanie Meyer's Twilight novels and the related films from the early twenty-first century portray vampires, especially the male body of Edward Cullen, glittering and sparkling.[46] Due to such figures and texts, glitter's many references include male femininities.

Academics, in a similar manner to these cultural producers, suggest that some people use glitter because it can contest normative identity formations. For instance, women's studies scholar Loran Marsan identifies the performer Cher's use of glitter as an essential component of her drag.[47] Cher uses glitter to challenge the direct linking of female gender and sex formations. Normative forms of doing gender naturalize and stabilize binary sex categories by making male and female roles seem spontaneous, based in genital and other sex attributes, and part of the everyday world.[48] However, Cher offers a counter to this because, as Marsan writes, her "feminine identity is constructed as surface value primarily through excess and the use of *false* visual elements of femininity such as wigs and glitter that refute a connection between her representation of femininity and her female sex."[49] Cher's glitter applications draw attention to the construction of identity and, perhaps, to the inequitable hierarchies that are upheld by cultural beliefs about people's "essential" aspects and differences.

Cher renders overabundance and a queer body through her glittering self-presentations. Media studies scholar Adele Patrick theorizes this "predominantly female activity of constructing feminine excess" in relationship to Dusty Springfield—a mid-twentieth-century singer who used peroxide-produced blonde beehives, dark eye makeup, and shimmering gowns to produce feminine exaggeration.[50] Women's exploration of glitter is an engagement with such excessive female femininity, whether embraced or controlled, and a negotiation of the ways certain forms of femininity are associated with the queer. Indeed, Patrick studies Springfield because she provides an opportunity to associate feminine excesses with women's routines rather than their more usual association with men's performances as drag queens. Patrick's interest in the routine and gender dissonances is related to Judith Butler's interrogations of gender performativity and indication that repetitive enactments of gender can challenge the binary and the naturalizing features of these positions.[51]

Women's deployment of glitter provides opportunities to theorize positive engagements with and the management of overabundance. Becca posts Evelyn Murphy's photograph of a woman ecstatically experiencing a cascade of glitter. The model's breast is so encrusted in glitter that it looks like a disco ball. "Wearing glitter as clothing," blogs Becca, "Why not? You can never have too much."[52] Her comments reference and torque the mandate for women to buy commodity items. However, glitter is often believed to make people inappropriately look like a "disco ball" and be "too much."[53] Performance studies scholar Della Pollock argues that "too much" articulates the purportedly "intrinsic characteristics of unacceptable 'others' and their proper place on the moral/political gridwork of everyday social life: they are excessive, excluded, superfluous, at best marginal."[54] Objects and people are believed to be too much when they insistently emphasize their visual features and the ways they become present through artifice. When the individual's style is "too much," writes Jack Babuscio in his analysis of camp, "it results in incongruities: the emphasis shifts from what a thing or a person *is* to what it *looks* like; from *what* is being done to *how* it is being done."[55] Thus, too much points to conflicts in cultural conceptions of gender and other identity categories. It destabilizes and queers the structures by which we understand and navigate the world. Glitter, with its production of varied female and male femininities, extreme shine, and formlessness, helps reveal incongruities in the binary gender and sex system. Due to these features, glitter cannot fully support the mythos that there is a stable and natural female sex even though it is associated with, and produces, femininity.

Glitter's relationship to disproportionate femininity is supported by Priest's description of the "almost-excessive use" of glitter "by drag queens."[56] Glitter is one of the materials that drag performers deploy, whether female-to-female, male-to-female, or presenting other gender positions, to reform femininity beyond what Marsan refers to as "'normal' proportion."[57] This expansion or explosion of femininity and the body is also associated with horror and monstrosity. Carol

Clover and Barbara Creed indicate that cultural understandings of female bodies as too fluid, reproductive, and open are related to the dank caves in horror films, the reproduction of monsters, and the wounded bodies of horror victims and killers.[58] While we might worry, according to Priest, about how "glitter encourages girls to aspire to princess-like femininity," glitter (and the girl child in horror films) is also associated with the "sinister."[59] Glitter is combined with such icons of monstrosity and death as bearded ladies, coffins, skulls, weapons, and zombies and becomes matter that is out of synch with normative femininity.[60] There is a "subtle horror in glitter," according to Christopher Paul Andrews's consideration of the monstrous and camp.[61] People identify the dreadfulness of "youthful" glitter on "old" faces and the glitter traces of celebrations that cannot be cleaned up.

Glitter is contaminating because it deforms gender and sex roles and is physically unmanageable. It does not remain in the "right" place and inappropriately sticks. Comedian Demetri Martin identifies the polluting and contagious aspects of glitter. He argues that people should be "prepared to have it on" them "forever 'cause glitter is the herpes of craft supplies."[62] The musician Ke$ha supports these associations while more positively configuring glitter. Individuals near Ke$ha "get glitter" on them, which indicates their physical contact with her, and this "infuriates a lot of people."[63] Glitter acts as a record of past connections and can be seen as a kind of abject touching. Ke$ha shoots it "from glitter guns and out of every orifice" during performances and sometimes when she urinates "it is in the toilet."[64] Her goal is "to cover the planet in glitter" and thereby "take the fuck over."[65] Thus, Ke$ha links glitter to the fluid aspects of women's bodies and indicates that it helps subvert hierarchies and categories. This also means that glitter can queer things. Yet glitter complicates the more usual cultural renderings of the abject leakiness of the female body, which are explored by trash the dress brides and photographers.[66] Glitter is related to light and dryness rather than more typical references to dark, wet, and sticky vaginal fluids and blood and filth.

Producing Glitter Makeup and Its Meanings

Suze lists "10 things Ke$ha taught" her "about fashion" and asserts the personally empowering aspects of glitter and norms.[67] She blogs, "Enjoy glitter? Too much is never a bad thing. It can be your signature" and what "sets you apart from all those other girls on the dance floor. Just make sure to not wear too much to work. Unless you're a go-go dancer." Suze and other women's use of makeup is contrarily pleasurable and part of their application of norms to the body, in which the acceptability of wearing glitter on the dance floor at night is differentiated from wearing it to work and appearing to be "too" sexual. Such cosmetics convey, according to fashion theorist Jennifer Craik, "cultural preoccupations, representations of gender, codes of sexuality and qualities of personhood."[68] Doing beauty is thus a method of producing the self and world.

Women's cosmetic applications and other methods of restyling and controlling the body often make subjects into feminine, heterosexual, and consuming women. When used in excess, and there may not be any "appropriate" amount of glitter, or when cosmetics do not continue to fulfill their functions, makeup also torques the normative forms of these structures.

Women help to produce cultural conceptions of makeup and femininity in their beauty blogs and posts to cosmetics-oriented websites. Their procedures are related to zombie makeup narratives and applications, which sometimes deploy the same products. Yet their routines are not divorced from commercial and consumer cultures. The wide scale incorporation of bloggers into the fashion industry is mirrored by the ways beauty bloggers influence cosmetic companies and receive complimentary products, travel accommodations to events, and advertising requests from manufacturers.[69] Julie Fredrickson, who founded a network of beauty and fashion websites, estimated that there were thousands of beauty blogs in 2008.[70] The number of blogs has grown significantly since that time. There has also been a diversification of blogs, including specialized blogs about glitter makeup and nail polish. While beauty sites tend to convey a range of sentiments and cultural mandates about glitter cosmetics, blogs that focus on glitter makeup present more positive feelings.

Bloggers proscribe against certain uses of glitter makeup but many of them assert that women, who they often refer to as "girls," "like glitter."[71] For Lucy, "Having freshly painted, glittery nails is enough to make any girl happy."[72] According to her, glitter functions as a sort of stimulant and generates pleasure. In a related manner, JennySue loves "anything *shiny, sparkley, and glittery*" and believes that it is "the girly girl" in her "that finds glitter to be so much fun and glamorous."[73] Her girly side responds to or is even created by these products. Thus, glitter is believed to call to the feminine in its more "girly," or hyperfeminine and childish, forms. This is another version of Babuscio's too much.[74] Jane Smith evokes these feminine and excessive features when noting that glitter "brings back those memories of being a kid wearing sparkly nail polish" and makes her "feel like a Disney Princess."[75] Such moments of women celebrating girlhood, and thereby acknowledging the values of some girls, should not be dismissed.[76] Their enmeshed temporalities and experiences encourage women to grow sideways and thereby provisionally resist the proscriptions about adult female behavior.[77] Glitter is a form of growing sideways rather than being a controlled and "responsible" adult because it is associated with wishes for more pleasure, leisure, and luxury. Proscriptions against glitter also work to foreclose these possibilities.

Women's and girls' investments in such things as glitter are too often articulated in essentialist terms and related to insignificant choices. According to Priest, women's attraction to glitter is condemned by associating it with the "trivial and the teenage," "teen female sexuality," and the "hyperfeminine."[78] craig_serithor could be referencing these categorizations when he argues that girls are interested in glitter because they "like shiny, fluffy, cozy, warm and flashy things, its just in their nature."[79] Alice An, who is a makeup artist, also dismisses girlhood and femininity. "Glitter: all girls love it," writes An, "but very few know what to do with it."[80] In her narrative, women's adoring relationship with glitter does not equate to knowledge or skill. Women who sell on ecommerce sites also deploy narratives about deskilling but they use it as a means of marketing their position as stay-at-home mothers and as methods of avoiding some buyers' demands. In An's account, glitter threatens to disorder the areas where it is applied and the women who wear it. Glitter is associated with girls because it is not supposed to lead to authority or expertise. Yet readers, as I indicate later in this chapter, assert that the women who produce and document glitter polishes on blogs are knowledgeable and demonstrate creativity and technological skill.

Pam Pastor is also conscious of the cultural limits that are placed on glitter cosmetics. Her Internet news report about glitter begins by establishing a position that is mature and uninfluenced by the visual. Pastor is "NOT a glitter girl."[81] She used to believe that glitter nail polish was "messy, tacky and only for little girls." However, Pastor also provides a conversion account. She began wearing a bestselling glitter nail polish, "couldn't stop staring" at her nails, and realized that the polish "had turned" her "into a glitter girl." The visual aspects of glitter, especially when in contact with her body, lure Pastor and she becomes something else. Her narrative about changing interests and identifications is related to the other mutable features and cultural renderings of glitter as well as new media and its assertions about change. This glitter position offers some intriguing aspects. Pastor associates glitter with things that are chaotic, vulgar, and childish. Adopting glitter thus challenges social norms and the ways women are directed to do gender and other identities correctly. Yet by entitling her article "Grown-up glitter," Pastor tries to make glitter and its attributes more proper.

Some women indicate that conceptions of glitter, and the associated notions of age, class, gender, race, and sexuality, curtail their aesthetic and expressive options. katie would wear "face glitter to the post office, the library," and "dry cleaner" if such behaviors and materials were "socially acceptable."[82] katie imagines an everyday world where she can sparkle and indicates that such displays are not suitable for women. SaucyandSparkly feels forced to do gender in conventional ways because if she were to "walk into a college seminar with glitter covering" her "face, most people would probably think" she was "a cocaine addict."[83] More than seeing her as the eccentric, which Bartky indicates is how unconventional makeup applications are coded, SaucyandSparkly believes that people would associate her glitter surplus with even more culturally dismissed losses of control. In response, she proposes a world where glitter would be not only allowable but also curative: "Glitter could be that one entity where uptight women," instead of "turning to binge eating, drugs, or a mid-life crisis," could "throw some glitter on their faces and instantly feel like their lives are fun and have meaning." If "more people gave glitter a chance, maybe someone would discover that glitter cures cancer." She identifies glitter's compulsive pleasures as therapy. Unfortunately, this proposal also renders adult women as unhealthy and in need of remedies.

Directing Women

Beauty editors publish texts in women's and lifestyle magazines and have a role on beauty and cosmetics websites where they create a market for makeup and guidelines on how these products are supposed to be used. For instance, beauty editor Sarah Carrillo and her colleagues proclaim the importance of editorial instructions on a beauty site. According to them, beauty editors know about "new makeup products" and "write about *bad makeup*."[84] Yet they were embarrassed to find out from makeup artist Susmta Patel that glitter "shouldn't be worn by anyone over the age of 14."[85] Now that they "know" about these gender and age standards, they "can share these mistakes" so that readers "never walk out of the house with bad makeup (again)."[86] Through such Internet texts, beauty editors establish their knowledge and expertise. This renders the women who use makeup as initiates. Beauty editors also help construct the category of "bad makeup," which is linked to bad women, and indicate how readers can remain good adults. Similar narratives about values are deployed by other women's production cultures, including Etsy sellers and reborn doll producers.

Women are warned that they will seem older and even monstrous when they wear glitter. For example, blogger JennySue cautions, "if you've got lots of fine lines and wrinkles, or have skin that isn't aging well" then a glitter product is not "for you."[87] Stef and Tyna also advise, "There is nothing like glitters settling into wrinkles to draw attention to, even accentuate, them."[88] In these accounts, glitter is inappropriate for adult women, does not work with their characteristics, and is against their best interests. Given these proscriptions, it is not surprising that Stef feels "kinda dumb with too much glitter."[89] This is because glitter is "the equivalent of a big flashing arrow" that says, "hey, I'm old!" She identifies glitter's features—its sparkle and light refraction capacities—as a form of embarrassment and outing. Stef suggests that glitter makes women inappropriately visible. Glitter is contained to the sphere of girlhood and women's life stages are mapped and hierarchized by these ageist stereotypes.

The cultural correlation of glitter and age renders varied methods of controlling women. Adult women are warned against "too much," which suggests they need to manage their body and sexuality, as well as glitter applications. vfashiontrends links these forms of bodily management, specifically makeup applications and eating, when noting "Shimmer! Glitter! Sparkle! They're all so fun – but like eggnog, flashy makeup is best consumed in moderation."[90] According to Rachel Smith, "glitter eyeshadow is fine in moderation" but "there is a point at which there is tooooo much."[91] Anja Emerson writes that it is "important to know when to stop. Applying glitter with a heavy hand results in an over-the-top look that isn't pretty."[92] They suggest that excesses endanger women's visual appeal. Women are encouraged to disavow their own pleasures and instead manage all aspects of their bodies. Such threats are used to reorient women so that they more clearly support traditional femininity. These proscriptions are not surprising since Babuscio suggests that "too much" is a critical strategy that can undo traditional forms of gender and other identities.[93] Too much also highlights the constructed aspects of selves and renders dissonances.

Beauty "excesses" are associated with the purported immoderation of sex workers, who refuse traditional notions of female gender, emphasize the economic aspects of relationships, highlight women's active sexualities, and reject the correlation of sex with monogamous coupling. Earlier cultural associations of prostitution with cosmetics are still employed to dictate "appropriate" makeup applications and an array of other behaviors. For instance, Valerie warns women to "beware of applying too much" glitter eye shadow "because you might look like a hooker."[94] Jennifer Wright provides an article on "How To Wear Glitter Eyeshadow And Not Look Like A Prostitute."[95] She scorns women's pleasures and eccentricities when describing makeup use with so "much glitter" that the "girls looked like ladies of the evening" on New Year's Eve. Wright suggests that being chaste is more appropriate and asks readers, "Aren't you glad you stayed home like a hermit that night?" According to her, "it IS possible to apply glitter eyeshadow and make it look good. Tasteful, even." She references moral women and class expectations, in a manner that is related to beauty editor Carrillo's indications of how to avoid "bad" makeup.[96] These women support normative forms of womanhood and interlock culturally approved forms of taste, class, and sexuality.

Women also relate bad and excessive forms of glitter to drag queens. This allows them to articulate behaviors that go beyond the acceptable limits of femininity. In Daniel Harris's study of drag, he positively identifies such glittering materials as "sequins, rhinestones, satins, and lamés" as materials that men use in their drag.[97] Harris thus highlights the complicated gender coding of these items, and, by implication, the properties of glitter and glittering things. Stef and Tyna also suggest the varied genders and femininities that are associated with shine. However, they use it as part of a warning. They advise, "Wherever you choose to wear glitter, let that be the only place to have it proudly shine. Unless you're a drag queen."[98] In such accounts, moderation is identified as the key to remaining female. Other applications are associated with looking rather than being. Ellen Tarnapolsky instructs women "to be conservative" in their glitter usage "because there is a fine line you can cross and end up looking like a made up drag queen."[99] According to these women, glitter threatens traditional femininity and women's status. Women appear "made up" and highlight their production of gender and other identity characteristics rather than appearing natural. Babuscio proposes a similar argument about excessive practices, but in his reading this destabilization is welcome.[100] Butler also contends, "Drag exhibits the imitative structure of gender itself."[101] People often assert the naturalness of normative femininity but the links between traditional femininity, glitter, and drag compromise these claims. Dismissive references to old women and drag queens make it more difficult to exist within varied life stages and roles. However, warnings about the risks of glitter tie traditional feminine forms of identity to queer positions and performances.

Glitter Fallout

Glitter and other reflective materials "capture and intensify the light," according to Harris, and contribute to the "drag queen's glittering aura."[102] The intensification and spread of glitter can also provide women with drag auras and, as Babuscio and Butler argue, reveal that identity positions are produced. Thus, it is not surprising that one of the major concerns about glitter makeup is its tendency to drift to other areas of the face and body, become an intense effect, render a drag aura, and remain after the wearer has tried to remove it. This creep is seen as troubling because it can mar women's intended appearance and function as a kind of dirt or sexual trace of the past. Thus, glitter (and other makeup has some of these qualities) has a tendency to shift from what is deemed to be tasteful and feminine to what is monstrous and queer.

Fallout is one of the most referenced problems with glitter makeup. Frou describes "GLITTER EVERYWHERE!!"[103] This glitter is unmanageable and uncontainable. It does not remain in one place and becomes too much and matter out of place because its spatial positions and magnitude shift. In a related manner, Trish's application turns the delights of glitter into something less appealing. She loves "the look but the fallout makes it look like a fairy blew its nose" and she is covered in a form of disgusting bodily matter.[104] Karen encourages people to "go with the glitter and fallout. Resistance is futile" when using certain kinds of glitter makeup.[105] "It's kinda like the zombie apocalypse that way." Thus, glitter is viral and makes the user into something else. The term "fallout" references toxic contamination, especially nuclear fallout and an associated series of harmful transformations. Karen's reference to zombies, whose features are also sometimes linked to nuclear events, intensifies the connections between glitter, hazards, aversions, and embodied transformations.

Karen quotes *Star Trek* and its Borg manifesto with her "Resistance is futile" comment. The Borg, according to these texts, tries to absorb all societies and individuals into its hive-like collective. In a related manner, zombies are usually depicted consuming individuals and turning them into violent, unthinking, and voracious hordes. People are, as my study of zombies in the last chapter suggested, embracing these figures. They thereby challenge investments in the whole, coherent, and agentive self and normative forms of gender, race, and sexuality. Glitter can also overwhelm proper femininity. Nevertheless, the Borg and zombie metaphors suggest that glitter is another form of identity and embodiment that women consumers must accept, even though they find it more difficult to manage their identity positions when wearing it.

The bodies of the Borg and zombies are opened and linked through networking, the ingestion of flesh, and shared interests. While glitter is often deployed to articulate such specific parts of the body as eyes, cheeks, lips, and cleavage, it drifts everywhere. Such drifts and series of parts render the bodies of glitter wearers as open and uncategorizable. Glitter refracts the light, diffusing the "edge" of the body and opening up and extending the form. This extension of the body, as theorized by Walker and Chaplin, is magnified by the ways women with glitter nail polish move sparkling surfaces around their bodies with every gesture.[106] Feminist scholar Katherine Stern argues that such feminine self-presentations as "cascading layers, flounces, curlicues and tassels of hair and fabric" suggest a "pliancy of outline that merges figure and ground, blending the body with its surroundings."[107] This feminine artifice, including "accentuated eyes and lips" that "function like jewels," fragments and disintegrates the body. Glitter and its jewel-like properties also break down the body and cultural assumptions about bodily solidity. "Because of its overdone sparkling flashiness," writes Andrews, "glitter never seems integrated into the form it is on."[108] Instead, glitter creates "hollowness, a void within and underneath." Thus, glitter is also divorced from and empties out the body, physically and conceptually replacing essences with the excesses of visual features.

The openness of the glitter-produced body may result in pain as well as pleasure. Fallout is connected to physical discomfort, disordered identities, and aesthetic annoyances. For DarkSideChic87, "glitter fallout is unbearable."[109] An eye shadow's "huge chunks of glitter" got into her "eyes and made them sting and water." Karlie Tipton also had "large pieces" of glitter "falling" into her "eye and causing enormous amounts of pain."[110] These descriptions emphasize the cultural fears associated with fallout and the corporeal rather than conceptual experience of hollowing out the body. Glitter eye shadow is inadvisable, according to Kelly B., "unless you want to put out an eye."[111] The last time she used it her "eyelids were swollen and scratched for 3 days." Her phrase evokes the expression, "you could put an eye out with that," which is deployed to indicate that behaviors are stupid and juvenile. Glitter is also rendered as inane in varied ways. Health and makeup forum posters warn that cornea damage and other sorts of injuries can result from using glitter products that are not manufactured for cosmetic use but individuals also advise that sharp and unhygienic craft glitter can be used as eye makeup.[112]

Glitter and other forms of makeup do ideological violence to women's normative positions. Women's use of cosmetics as a means of establishing naturally white and smooth skin is undermined, as I have already noted in the last chapter, because these products and the underlying conceptions of skin and race can be easily applied and removed.[113] This demonstrates that white skin, Caucasian positions, and the associated conceptions of purity and beauty are unstable and exposes the constructed aspects of identities. While glitter makeup is less easily removed than other forms of cosmetics, its luminescent light remainders do not correlate with smooth and untouched skin. Glitter "outs" wearers because its last fragments glimmer in the daytime. It brings the night and celebratory behaviors into other times and places and disturbs the skin surface. As rmh notes, "you'll be left with some very obvious glitter specks all over."[114] These flecks visually pierce the skin with blank spaces and other colors and extend the body into space with beacons of light. Glitter thereby evokes the patchy, open, and diseased flesh that white makeup was designed to solidify and cover up.[115]

Glitter cosmetics and HTML effects disturb stable conceptions of skin color and surface because they seem to prick the skin and page with other colors. In a related manner, female nail polish bloggers describe how glitter and other forms of nail polish rupture stable conceptions of skin color and create unappealing forms of whiteness. Nail bloggers refer to "lobster hands" that they think are too pink because of the ways colored nail polishes change the appearance of their skin color.[116] They also describe "corpse" and "zombie hands," which are "too" white.[117] In some of these cases, "too much" is linked to monstrosity and causes bloggers to provide warnings and other provisos about their images to readers. Yet various bloggers also persist in exploring and embracing these visual effects. Their unflattering whiteness is related to the ways the authors of how-to guides construct disgusting and deathly zombie whiteness. All of these producers use cosmetics to unintentionally or tactically layer varied identities and shift between normative femininity and monstrous difference.

The Politics of Glitter Jelly Sandwiches

Nail polish bloggers, in a similar manner to reborn producers, use their practices as a means of establishing their identity and expertise. They develop and convey specific terminology, polishes, applications, imaging technologies, and values. They frequently refer to the polishes that they most covet and the people who pay a lot of money for polishes as "lemmings" because these animals, and by implication polish collectors, follow each other's undertakings.[118] This establishes the commitment of collectors and the collecting culture. Bloggers also describe the process of combining nail polishes and other materials as "frankening" and thereby part of monstrous Frankensteinian projects. Women layer translucent, or jelly, and glitter polishes and make "glitter jelly sandwiches."[119] They use these terms to create their own culture and to propose a series of innovative nail polish practices. Some of these producers develop a following and proficiency in frankening that allows them to become indie nail polish makers. Through their assertions that nail polish practices are meaningful and pleasurable, they challenge negative assessments of cosmetics and the associated dismissal of women and their interests.

Nail polish bloggers' assertions about the positive aspects of their pursuits and related commentary on contemporary culture are political. For instance, their production and writing about glitter jelly sandwich nail polish applications render different forms of feminine and domestic associations than men's directives for women to prepare them sandwich meals, which I considered in the introduction. Bloggers' revisions of this sexist conception have a force since glitter jelly sandwiches are extremely popular nail polish applications with thousands of dedicated posts and even more commentary. Their popularity has resulted in commercial cosmetic manufacturers offering polishes that produce similar effects. Anthea explores the creative aspects of nail polish applications and titles a post "Make Me A Sandwich!"[120] In doing this, she transforms beliefs that women should be focused on other people and that they should perform for men, which underlies the "make me a sandwich" directive. She chooses to produce a sandwich because it is something she has "been wanting to try for awhile" and shares it with her feminized readers, who she refers to as "lovelies."

Lizzy O. The DIY Lady, whose blog name emphasizes her ability to make things and that DIY is feminine, critiques men's sexist directive for women to make them sandwiches. If her "future husband" ever tells her "Make me a sammich Woman," a glitter jelly sandwich "mani or something like it, is what" she "SHALL RECREATE!!"[121] She thus articulates glitter jelly nail polish and the related beauty culture as a method of refusing rather than reinscribing women's more servile position within heteronormative culture. Lizzy O. The DIY Lady appends a "buhahahahahahahhahah" evil scientist laugh to her plan and thereby proposes that substituting glitter jelly sandwich applications for food is inventive and subversive. Nail polish bloggers also contend that women are experimental scientists and have technical skills when using terms such as "frankening" and narratives about doctor Frankenstein to describe their nail polish inventions. Their references, which I explore in the afterword, undermine the usual cultural associations of scientists and inventors with men.

Nail bloggers are motivated to make glitter jelly sandwiches because of the Internet and other women's creativity. G.'s "obsession with 'jelly sandwiches' began" when she "first saw the beautiful" blogged "creations" of her "pal Niki."[122] NICOLE is "always encouraging people to try" glitter jelly sandwiches.[123] Her post "even inspired Lesley to try one."[124] After reading it, drinkcitra is also "inspired" to try this application.[125] Their use of terms such as "inspired" establish the creative lineages of nail polish bloggers and the ways producers are in conversation. Rather than the more usual practice of identifying male lineages for women's work, which artist Mira Schor identifies as a politically troubling aspect of feminist art production and documentation, nail bloggers credit other women.[126] Bloggers collaboratively work with readers by asking for "ideas for jelly sandwiches."[127] The usual hierarchy between producers and users is not in place. For instance, Lisa Washington indicates to readers, "you can experiment with whatever colors you like, you might come up with an awesome combination that no one has tried yet!"[128] Her acknowledgment of a collaborative production community proposes a more intermeshed notion of production than reborn artists' recognition of sculptors and description of reborn sculpts as blanks that are brought to life through reborning. Washington articulates a culture that values sharing and innovations.

Bloggers' posts about glitter jelly sandwiches articulate different forms of femininity and women's positions than sexist directives to make men sandwiches. However, the women who produce and chronicle these applications still deploy gendered categories. In some cases, bloggers find glitter jelly sandwiches appealing because they diffuse the excessive and norm disrupting aspects of glitter. The Crafty Ninja likes the glitter jelly sandwich because it "dulls the glitter to create a more subtle, delicate, and girly look."[129] According to All The Pretty Polish, the glitter jelly sandwich "calms the glitter down a bit. You can still see it, but it isn't as harsh."[130] She suggests that glitter jelly sandwiches make women less abrasive and more properly feminine, although still engaged with the more production-oriented aspects of beauty culture. These posts are related to women's requests for pretty and feminine zombie makeup applications. Women try to negotiate conflicting demands because they recognize the centrality of zombies and glitter applications and pressures to follow contemporary identity strictures.

Glitter Visuality

Some women's narratives about glitter connect the gendered aspects of cosmetics to the larger cultural notion that women should be visually available. G. asks, "What is this" glitter mascara "going to look like on my lashes? Will it make them sparkle? Twinkle like little Christmas lights? Will everyone around me instantly become mesmerized and hypnotized when they look into my eyes?"[131] Walker and Chaplin present a similar, although less playfully excessive, understanding of glitter. They argue, "Gleams and glitter enable the wearer to be a centre of emanation" and "to attract the gaze of others."[132] Glitter, as they suggest, can extend the body and act like a shield and block people's ability to see. Glitter also sometimes makes women "too much" in ways that thwart other people's ability to gaze and interest in gazing. For instance, MEGHAN DEMARIA advises against wearing both glitter eyeliner and eye shadow because "you might blind people with your shimmer."[133] There are also instances where glitter-facilitated looking is antithetical to what people want to see and the ways they want to see it. For instance, extraH enjoyed referring to her glitter polish and saying, "'look at it! look AT IT!' over and over again to people" who are not interested in makeup and do not want to look.[134] Donna ironically suggests that extraH "should go wake your neighbors and show them" because they will "thank you for your generosity and consideration!"[135] These women direct people's gaze while using makeup to control what is viewed and how they are seen.

Some critical possibilities are suggested by women's creation of glitter products and applications and orchestration of people's view of their handiwork. Feminist visual culture studies scholar Griselda Pollock argues that it is politically important to consider the female spectator and the "possibility that texts made by women can produce different positions within" the "sexual politics of looking. Without that possibility, women are both denied a representation of their desire and pleasure and are constantly erased."[136] Many women who write about glitter polish express their pleasure in this material. They share their glitter makeup passions with posters and readers and use images and texts to constitute the ways glitter products are viewed. Their engagements with nail bloggers and readers are less erotic than women's wedding forum communications. However, they establish a visual and textual site where women's delighted views are detailed and skills are celebrated.

Women chronicle their pleasure in looking at glitter nail polish and themselves, even if it breaks cultural directives to be outwardly focused. Their narratives about staring at glitter nail polish may seem to be an intensification of vanity, which is one of the purported aspects of femininity and cosmetics that is culturally dismissed.[137] Yet these women assert and admire their handiwork and the aesthetic aspects of the material rather than their physiognomies, which glitter has multiplied, fragmented, and effaced. ~Leslie~ uses her blog to "show the world what" she can paint.[138] For Polish and Prose, nail blogging "unleashed a flood of inspiration. Color, Art, Glitter, and Writing all meshed into one creative space."[139] These women, as Polish and Prose suggests, are engaged in a series of inventive forms of production. They create elaborate layering combinations that change the texture as well as color of polishes, mix materials together to make unique varnishes, paint images, attach decorations, produce detailed texts, and use a variety of specialized photography techniques to provide images of their nails. However, their choice of mediums and identities, like the practices of stay-at-home mothers who are ecommerce sellers and artisans who make reborn babies, limit their respectability and the cultural acknowledgment of their artistic practices.

Women connect such creative forms as nail polish mixing and layering to the process of staring at their nails. Their positions are related to the ways artists shift between producing and looking at their work. They are thereby focused on production skills. For example, Nail Noir reviews a nail polish product, describes the process of admiring the color and staring at her nails, and wishes the readers who engage, "Happy painting!"[140] In a similar manner to glitter jelly sandwich producers, she acknowledges their shared production abilities and interests. After successfully layering different colors, Cristina F also "cannot stop staring at" her "nails."[141] Minty acknowledges Cristina F's artistry by noting, "You're layering skills are amazing."[142] In these cases, women's photographs of their nails are an instantiation of their staring, and bloggers usually include numerous images and focus viewers on what is significant. These images thereby indicate women's production cultures and forms of seeing and render the kinds of female spectatorship that Pollock mentions.

Nail bloggers direct the viewer's gaze at nails and glitter polishes, including shots of the bottle, rather than women's faces or whole bodies. In doing this, women propose feminine forms of looking that are engaged with alternative visual pleasures, including the refraction and dematerialization of the body and its parts. Jessica provides an image of the bottle and close-ups of her painted nails against the container.[143] These are common nail blog conventions. She "cannot stop staring at" her "nails" and invites the reader to "Look for yourself!" Viewers take Jessica up on this invitation, share her visual interests and spectatorial position, and "can't stop staring at" her "nails either."[144] However, her image conveys the features of glitter, and a slight dematerialization of the body, rather than an exacting image. Photographic hot spots and reflections from the glitter wash the purple nail polish out to a yellow-white. The glitter refracts the light so that long slashes seem to cut across the nails and pale fingers. Large white hot spots also appear in the center of Nail Noir's photographed nails [Figure 5.2].[145] These areas seem to be above the form and to hollow out the body. Such visual effects are features of glitter and glitter photography, which as Andrews indicates, create a negation.[146] Naily Daily supports this when promising to "kill your eyes with glitter."[147] She indicates the excessive aspects of glitter, including its light properties, and the ways glitter functions beyond vision. This move beyond the visible is continued in Internet settings where whiteness is challenged by the properties of the screen and dissipates.[148] In these instances, the representation and its promise of delivering a version of the body fail.

The women who use glitter products, especially nail polishes, suggest that the qualities of polishes, and thus the aspects of their extended corporeality, are difficult to detect through photographic processes and Internet settings. Thus,

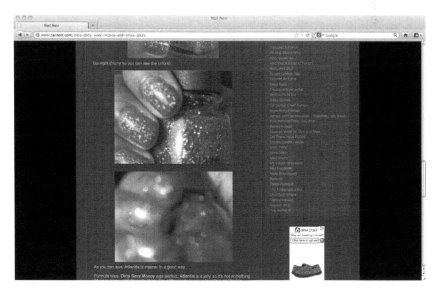

FIGURE 5.2 Nail Noir. Blur and hot spots demonstrate the aspects of glitter and break down the body.

glitter foils women's position as viewable and easily portrayed. Nail bloggers use phrases such as "photography doesn't do it justice" to indicate that glitter cannot be fully represented and cameras and other imaging processes are dysfunctional.[149] This is related to how eBay sellers use this phrase to specify that objects have a greater value than images imply and individuals can only fully experience things by buying, touching, wearing, and living with them.[150] "No matter how hard" A Polish Addict tried to represent glitter cosmetics, "the photos still could not do it justice."[151] Scrangie finds it "hard to show just how shiny and pretty glitter" looks "in photographs!"[152] These women undermine some of the intentions of their blogs, especially their interests in conveying the features of brands and innovative applications through photographs and Internet postings. Women labor at their depictions, and their narratives about work are an interesting corollary to the more usual identification of nail care as frivolous. However, the materials and technologies do not oblige and deliver a detailed view. For instance, glitter foils flinty's imaging processes. The "sparkle made" her "camera wiggy."[153] TGW's camera acts "all funny and out of focus" because of an eye shadow's "awesome glitterness."[154] These cameras and photographs are capricious vehicles rather than unbiased conveyors of material realities. Their limitations encourage further interrogations of the cultural association of photography with documentation and traces of the real.[155]

The stilled, and yet blurry as if they are in motion, glittered fingers depicted in nail blogs are the producing fingers of similar polishes, applications, and images. These women's hands thus actively function as subjects and objects. Bloggers' hands are central to their practices. They are tools that produce texts, nail polish applications, digital images, and sites. They are also marginal since their production techniques are culturally dismissed. Nail bloggers' images of their hands emphasize their role as producers and the handmade aspects of their crafts. In a related manner, reborn artists make assertions about artistry and emotional feelings with their images of human and doll hands. Technologies extend these hands and intermesh the different meanings of digital. However, technologies are flickering prosthetics, which insert further failures, changed meanings, and static into the body, and out-of-focus images of glitter look a lot like static.

Conclusion: The Body and Glitter's Touch

Women deploy glitter nail polish and blogging as methods of pleasurably dematerializing and reconfiguring the body and connecting with readers. Their positions refute indications that women narcissistically fall in love with themselves as passive models of beauty. This accusation is unfortunately directed at women even as they are told to focus on their appearance, seek validation from other people, and adopt the position of to-be-looked-at-ness that is interrogated by Laura Mulvey and other feminists.[156] This research has encouraged filmmakers and films theorists to interrogate the forms of visual pleasure that constitute women as objects. Pollock argues that female-focused production methods, forms of viewing, and visual constructions of the body are needed.[157] Nail bloggers engage with traditional conceptions of women and beauty practices. Yet they also offer photographic and other production techniques that focus on women's visual pleasures, including their shared delights in producing and looking at women's cosmetic applications, rather than offering views of the female body that allow viewers to distance themselves from the scene while enjoying its visual features. For instance, nail bloggers' out-of-focus techniques suggest that affective forms of visual seeing are superior to and more pleasurable than detailed and objectifying views. In indicating this, these women point to other visual and tactile methods of engaging. They help supplant the objectification of women's bodies with sensual and tactile experiences where women are situated in relationship and blurrily connected to viewers.

Glitter's conjunction with the blur, and thus the unknowable and obscured, renders a much less centered and comfortable viewing position than is ordinarily associated with photographs, films, and related camera technologies. Glitter encourages a critical rethinking of how photography and digital imaging are connected to visual seeing. After all, the continued identification of photography as indexical signs and traces of objects, even after shifts in technologies have changed the production mechanisms, implies that these images are the product of touching. Light from depicted objects "touched" the light sensitive surface of the negative or image. In a related manner, Roland Barthes argues that while the photographer and photographic practice are usually associated with the eye, he believes they should be related to the finger, including the photographer's control of the shutter.[158] This shift from looking to feeling is apt since Barthes provides an affective study of photography and how it influences individuals. Glitter photographs also provide felt images where webs of translucent tissue seem about to encase viewers. These blurs, especially when images are enlarged, cause viewers' eyes to try and refocus and result in mild dizziness. The chemicals in nail polish and people's emotional responses intensify these experiences. This happens when Cyśka is "dizzy with excitement" over glitter nail polish.[159] Nail bloggers foreground such dizzying and destabilizing fascinations. They refocus attention from men to cosmetics and thereby propose different methods of looking and subject/object relationships.

Women's blog posts about glitter jelly sandwiches and other nail polish applications emphasize notions of touch. This is related to Laura U. Marks and other film theorists' identification of the haptic aspects of cinema viewing, including grainy images and films, shifts in focus, camera positions that are close to the body, and depictions that evoke the senses.[160] The tactile aspects of glitter jelly sandwiches activate fingers, mouths, and tongues. For instance, nail bloggers experience these polishes as a combination of taste and texture and as being "yummy squishy goodness."[161] G. asks readers, "Want a bite of my Green Jello Jelly Sandwich?"[162] Christina offers "delicious pictures."[163] Their indications that nails and images of applications are sustenance are supported by women's positive responses to their creativity and skill, including "Yum yum!" and "nom nom!!!!" comments.[164] By calling this nail polish application a "sandwich" and providing narratives about its tastiness, they evoke the larger association of consumer items with food.[165] They also constitute glitter jelly sandwich images as versions of nail biting and cannibalistic self-engagement. Wedding-dress-clad zombies, including the women who are getting married to men at zombie walks, reach out hungrily at participants and express cannibalistic and polyamorous interests in all bodies. These couples thereby challenge aspects of the heteronormative wedding culture that they are enacting. In a comparable manner, glitter jelly nail polish bloggers propose a differently focused gaze and fascination with women's body parts. They assert that the hand rather than women's breasts and buttocks are of interest and edible. Nail bloggers' production of yummy squishy and other hand-made affects suggest that their Internet practices are instances of touching-feeling.[166]

Glitter nails are conceptualized through eating and incorporation but they are also physically and conceptually at the limit of liveness and the body. They are positioned as neither living nor cast off. After all, nails are dead tissue that is embedded in the body and glitter is a trace of the feminine and cosmetic that is not easily removed. These representations of boundary parts share some interesting links with conceptions of the undead, including zombies. Nails, glitter cosmetics, and zombies have ambivalent connections to liveness, trouble stable identity categories, and open up the body. Rather than painting the dead body and nails over and solidifying them, nail bloggers further dissolve the body through the dematerializing and out of focus aspects of glitter. For example, the gummy layers of glitter jelly sandwich applications further open up the nail with spatial strata and render it as squishy softness. All of this allows women to pleasurably stare at and blog about the intense diffraction of light and breakdown of form that was their body. This is not the hard, toned, and coherent body that all contemporary subjects are directed to achieve. Women use glitter to facilitate their femininity and to see their monstrous and fascinating parts.

Glitter jelly sandwich makers use the feminine aspects of beauty culture, such as emphasizing their nails and other physiognomic features, in order to playfully reference and critique other traditional feminine roles. By choosing these applications, they accept some of the conceptions of femininity that are part of nail polish culture, adopt beauty directions (and many glitter jelly sandwich posts include step-by-step directions), resist demands to prepare food, engage in a practice with other women, and invent and practice creative forms. The promises of wide-open choices and freedom that are consistently directed at women are rightly critiqued in postfeminist analysis. However, these studies do a disservice to some women's and feminist interests when they suggest that there are no productive choices within normative feminine cultures or that these choices are nothing more than purchasing decisions.[167] Choices can be limited but, like the decision to produce glitter jelly sandwiches and equate them to the make me a sandwich meme, they still have meaning. Traditional forms of femininity can be creatively deployed as ways of maneuvering within and reworking contemporary cultural positions.

Women's glitter makeup commentary and applications are part of an unexpectedly extensive and conflicted array of lived practices. They unsettle without permanently foiling the processes of normative femininity. Yet it is worth thinking about Ke$ha's and SaucyandSparkly's ideas of a world pleasurably covered and soiled by glitter that allows other politics to take over.[168] Such performances and writing can highlight the irreconcilable behaviors and beliefs that are incorporated into normative femininity. We might also consider how these women's projects would function if they tactically deployed rather than willingly coupled with familiar erotic positions and age hierarchies. Mainstream culture uses opposites as methods of articulating norms. Yet the ways incompatible positions, including conceptions of glitter, are corralled into norms and the behaviors that mainstream culture worries about are points of stress and thus possible places to rupture the system.

In the afterword, I continue these lines of inquiry by more fully considering how women elevate and compromise their creative production through links to monstrosity, which is referenced by normative culture but is not fully incorporable.[169] Women choose such identifiers as stay-at-home mother, mother-artist, and bride *and* embrace the monster and abjection. The women who "franken" and blog about nail polishes by making new formulas, colors, and combinations provide a site from which to elaborate on these behaviors. They use commercial polishes and other materials to create unique products, to allude to Frankenstein and his monster, and to refer to polish and nail art processes as monstrous. They also figure their hands as horrific and productive. These women's narratives and photographs of hands foreground their roles as producing women and active agents rather than constituting themselves solely as visual objects.

Notes

1. alexandra, "Lovely Feminine Nail Art Designs," jotzoom, 25 August 2013, http://jotzoom.com/lovely-feminine-nail-art-designs
2. hirra, "Glitter Eye Makeup," are 'n' style, 19 May 2013, 23 June 2014, http://www.carenstyle.com/glitter-eye-makeup.html
3. Walker and Chaplin, *Visual Culture*, 98.
4. de Lauretis, *Technologies of Gender*; Bratich, "Digital Touch."
5. The machinist Henry Ruschmann is credited with inventing glitter by developing a technique to grind up plastics and make large quantities of the material. His company, Meadowbrook Inventions, is a leading supplier of glitter. Aja Mangum, "Glitter: A Brief History," *New York Magazine*, 7 October 2007, 23 June 2014, http://nymag.com/shopping/features/38914/
6. Daneen, "Polished: How To Remove Glitter Nail Polish," spoiled pretty, 24 August 2011, 17 February 2013, spoiledpretty.blogspot.com/2011/08/polished-how-to-remove-glitter-nail.html

7. flinty, "Many, many pictures of OPI Rally Pretty Pink," Polish or Perish, 3 August 2011, 25 January 2013, http://polishorperish.blogspot.com/2011/08/many-many-pictures-of-opi-rally-pretty.html
8. Kaplan, "Is the Gaze Male?" Mulvey, "Visual Pleasure."
9. Bartky, "Foucault, Femininity," 81.
10. According to Kathy Davis's research on beauty practices, women's engagement with their appearance is "one of the central ways that femininity is constructed." Davis, "Remaking the She-Devil," 25.
11. Carey, Donaghue, and Broderick, "'What You Look Like'"; Hosoda, Stone-Romero, and Coats, "Effects of Physical Attractiveness."
12. Black, "Discipline and Pleasure."
13. SaucyandSparkly, "Things I wish were socially acceptable," 14 January 2012, 27 June 2013, http://saucyandsparkly.com/2012/01/14/things-i-wish-were-socially-acceptable/
14. Hayles, *How We Became Posthuman*.
15. Sobchack, ed. *Meta-Morphing*; Toffoletti, *Cyborgs and Barbie Dolls*.
16. A number of scholars argue that the newness of new media is "defined" by its lack of clear purposes and features. Through processes of cultural incorporation, people solidify the meanings and uses of new media. Chun, introduction to *New Media*; Gitelman and Pingree, "What's New?" Peters, "And Lead Us Not."
17. Hayles, *How We Became Posthuman*, 30.
18. This tendency used to be more common. 123cursors, "Glitter Cursors for Tumblr, Blogger and Websites," 4 March 2013, http://www.123cursors.com/cursor-category/76.html; FamilyLobby.com, "Create Glitter Text – Textured Text for your website," 3 March 2013, http://www.familylobby.com/create-glitter-text-graphics.asp; Html Best Codes, "Sparkles around mouse," 4 March 2013, http://htmlfreecodes.com/Sparkles_around_mouse.htm; snazzyspace, "Tumblr Codes: Mouse Sparkles – Tinkerbell Sparkle Trails on your mouse cursor," 4 March 2013, http://www.snazzyspace.com/tumblr-mouse-sparkles.php
19. WishAFriend.com, "Girly Glitter Graphics – Girly Glitter Graphics for Myspace," 4 March 2013, http://www.wishafriend.com/glitter/fun/girly/
20. Dobson, "Individuality Is Everything," 375–76.
21. Kirsten, "Glitta Gloves," 19 April 2014, http://www.glittagloves.com/; Arianne, "Glitter Geek," 19 April 2014, http://www.glittergeek.ca/; Shelby, "Glitz & Glitter," 19 April 2014, http://glitzandglitter.org/#sthash.aNG0atbG.dpbs
22. A Polish Addict, 19 April 2014, http://www.apolishaddict.com/
23. April Daniels Husar, "9 Ways to Wear Glitter Without Looking Like You Fell Off the Christmas Tree (PHOTOS)," The Stir, 28 December 2013, 20 April 2014, http://thestir.cafemom.com/beauty_style/166123/9_ways_to_wear_glitter; Nora Crotty, "How to Wear Glitter Eye Makeup and Not Look Like a Middle Schooler," Fashionista, 3 December 2013, 20 April 2014, http://fashionista.com/2013/12/how-to-wear-glitter-eye-makeup#awesm=~oC0hOUVLzqXdl3
24. Douglas, *Implicit Meanings*.
25. Priest, "What's Wrong With Sparkly Vampires?"
26. Craik, *Fashion*.
27. Leddy, "Sparkle and Shine."
28. Thesaurus.com, "Sparkle Synonyms, Sparkle Antonyms," 25 June 2013, http://thesaurus.com/browse/sparkle?s=t; Thesaurus.com, "Shine Synonyms, Shine Antonyms," 25 June 2013, http://thesaurus.com/browse/shine?page=3&qsrc=121
29. Leddy, "Sparkle and Shine," 260.
30. Drummond, *Works of William Drummond*, 222; Johnson, *Letters*, 413.
31. Shakespeare, *Merchant of Venice*. The play was registered in 1598. Wells and Dobson, eds. *Oxford Companion to Shakespeare*.

32. Courtney Leiva, "Glitzy Glitter Holiday Beauty (Without Going Overboard!)," Shecky's, 18 December 2012, 11 June 2014, http://www.sheckys.com/2012/12/18/glitzy-glitter-holiday-beauty-without-going-overboard/
33. Bordo, *Unbearable Weight*; Wolf, *Beauty Myth*.
34. Bartky, "Foucault, Femininity," 70.
35. SaucyandSparkly, "Things I wish were socially acceptable," 14 January 2012, 27 June 2013, http://saucyandsparkly.com/2012/01/14/things-i-wish-were-socially-acceptable/
36. Lazar, "Right to Be Beautiful," 37.
37. Bordo, "Beauty (Re)Discovers," 144.
38. Davis, "Remaking the She-Devil," 22.
39. Jessica, "It's All About the Glitter!" Makeup and Beauty Blog, 2 June 2009, 23 June 2014, http://www.makeupandbeautyblog.com/cosmetics/its-all-about-the-glitter/
40. BLIX, "Dark Red Wine Smokey Glitter Makeup look with Morgana Cryptoria," Glitter is my crack..., 2 November 2010, 19 April 2014, http://themoonmaiden-blix.blogspot.com/2010/11/dark-red-wine-smokey-glitter-makeup.html
41. WonderHowTo, "How to Create a freakshow 'Bearded Bettie' makeup look for Halloween," 19 April 2014, http://makeup.wonderhowto.com/how-to/create-freakshow-bearded-bettie-makeup-look-for-halloween-404164/
42. daydream222, "Thinking About Color...and a crazy NOTD," Polish or Perish, 13 April 2010, 23 June 2014, http://polishorperish.blogspot.com/2010/04/thinking-about-colorand-crazy-notd.html
43. Black, *Beauty Industry*; Brand, ed. *Beauty Matters*; Davis, *Reshaping the Female Body*.
44. Black, "'Ordinary People"; Harvey, "Becoming Entrepreneurs"; Kang, *Managed Hand*.
45. Gamson, "Sylvester," 140.
46. See for instance, Meyer, *Twilight*.
47. Marsan, "Cher-ing/Sharing Across Boundaries."
48. West and Zimmerman, "Doing Gender."
49. Marsan, "Cher-ing/Sharing Across Boundaries," 60.
50. Patrick, "Defiantly Dusty," 368.
51. Butler, *Bodies That Matter*.
52. Becca, "10 Ways to sneak fancy dress into everyday life," GypsyPixiePirate, 15 March 2013, 19 April 2014, http://gypsypixiepirate.com/2013/03/15/10-ways-to-sneak-fancy-dress-into-everyday-life/
53. Karen, "You'll Be Sparkling for Hours with the New Urban Decay Stardust Sparkling Lip Glosses," Makeup and Beauty Blog, 6 September 2011 http://www.makeupandbeautyblog.com/product-reviews/youll-be-sparkling-for-hours-with-the-new-urban-decay-stardust-sparkling-lip-glosses/; Marlena, "Top 10: Glitter and Shimmer Makeup," Makeup Geek, 23 June 2014, http://www.makeupgeek.com/articles-reviews/top-10-glimmer-and-shimmer-makeup-products/
54. Della Pollock, as quoted in Braziel and LeBesco, "Performing Excess," 9.
55. Babuscio, "Camp," 24.
56. Priest, "What's Wrong With Sparkly Vampires?"
57. Marsan, "Cher-ing/Sharing Across Boundaries," 53.
58. Clover, *Men, Women, and Chain Saws*; Creed, *Monstrous-Feminine*.
59. Priest, "What's Wrong With Sparkly Vampires?"
60. Glamour Doll Eyes offers "Bearded Lady - a medium to dark brown inspired by the luscious beards of the women of the sideshow. The silver shimmers throughout add a hint of femininity." Glamour Doll Eyes, "Bearded Lady - $1.25 : Glamour Doll, eye shadows to strut your stuff!" 23 June 2014, http://glamourdolleyes.com/index.php?main_page=product_info&cPath=92_95_100&products_id=870; Moi Minerals & Cosmetics, "Till Death do Us Part Zombie Shadow collection," 4 February 2012,

http://www.moiminerals.com/item_260/Till-Death-do-Us-Part-Zombie-Shadow-collection.htm
61. Andrews, *Blood and Glitter*.
62. Demetri Martin, "Demetri Martin: Glitter," Comedy Central Stand Up, 26 January 2012, http://www.jokes.com/funny/demetri+martin/demetri-martin--glitter; Demetri Martin, "Demetri Martin - Where Jokes Go," Comedy Central Stand Up, 13 January 2007, 23 June 2014, http://www.cc.com/video-clips/3v3ayf/stand-up-demetri-martin--where-jokes-go
63. Ke$ha, as quoted in Eric Spitznagel, "Ke$ha Spends More on Glitter Every Month Than Most People Spend on Rent," *Vanity Fair*, 10 February 2011, 23 June 2014, http://www.vanityfair.com/online/oscars/2011/02/keha-spends-more-on-glitter-every-month-than-most-people-spend-on-rent. Reporter Eric Spitznagel also codes Ke$ha as frivolous and childish and references the negative characteristics of glitter.
64. Ke$ha, "Ke$ha Loves Glitter, Glitter Loves Ke$ha," MTV Style, 2 September 2010, 23 June 2014, http://www.mtv.com/videos/interview/keha/554992/keha-loves-glitter-glitter-loves-keha.jhtml#id=1646375
65. Ke$ha, as quoted in Eric Spitznagel, "Ke$ha Spends More on Glitter Every Month Than Most People Spend on Rent," *Vanity Fair*, 10 February 2011, 23 June 2014 http://www.vanityfair.com/online/oscars/2011/02/keha-spends-more-on-glitter-every-month-than-most-people-spend-on-rent
66. Grosz, *Volatile Bodies*; Young, *On Female Body Experience*.
67. Suze, "10 things Ke$ha taught me about fashion," Suze Geeks Out, 25 July 2010, 20 April 2014, http://suzegeeksout.com/2010/07/25/10-things-keha-taught-me-about-fashion/
68. Craik, *Face of Fashion*, 175.
69. Pham, "Susie Bubble."
70. Julie Fredrickson, as quoted in Kayleen Schaefer, "Beauty Blogs Come of Age: Swag, Please!" *New York Times*, 31 January 2008, 23 June 2014, http://www.nytimes.com/2008/01/31/fashion/31SKIN.html?pagewanted=all
71. Channie Williams, "Girls Like Glitter," 31 January 2011, 24 April 2012, http://www.blogger.com/profile/03943163233090101164
72. Lucy, "CHILDS PLAY," mythology 20, 28 April 2011, 7 November 2011, http://www.mythology20.com/2011/04/childs-play.html
73. JennySue, "Glitter Makes Everything More Glamorous," JennySue Makeup, 3 October 2011, http://www.jennysuemakeup.com/2011/10/glitter-makes-everything-more-glamorous.html
74. Babuscio, "Camp."
75. Jane Smith, "Glitter Nail Polish!" LUUUX, 19 June 2014, http://www.luuux.com/viz/glitter-nail-polish-9
76. For further discussions of the importance of girl culture, see Kearney, *Mediated Girlhoods*; Kearney, "Pink Technology."
77. Stockton, *Queer Child*.
78. Priest, "What's Wrong With Sparkly Vampires?"
79. craig_serithor, "Why do girls like glitter?" Yahoo! Answers, 25 January 2013, http://answers.yahoo.com/question/index?qid=20111218072424AAIfAg2
80. Alice An, "Shimmer, sparkle and shine: Tips that will keep you glittering into the New Year," Examiner.com, 30 December 2011, 19 August 2013, http://www.examiner.com/makeup-in-new-york/shimmer-sparkle-and-shine-tips-that-will-keep-you-glittering-into-the-new-year
81. Pam Pastor, "Grown-up Glitter," *Philippine Daily Inquirer*, 28 January 2011, 23 June 2104, http://lifestyle.inquirer.net/fashionandbeauty/fashionandbeauty/view/20110128-317027/Grown-up-glitter
82. katie, "Are you a glitter girl, too?" thecoveted, 30 November 2009, 19 January 2012, http://the-coveted.com/blog/2009/11/30/glitter-girl/

83. SaucyandSparkly, "Things I wish were socially acceptable," 14 January 2012, 27 June 2013, http://saucyandsparkly.com/2012/01/14/things-i-wish-were-socially-acceptable/
84. Sarah Carrillo, "11 Makeup Mistakes You Don't Realize You're Making," Total Beauty, 9 August 2011, 23 June 2014, http://www.totalbeauty.com/content/gallery/makeup-mistakes-youre-making
85. Susmta Patel, as quoted in Sarah Carrillo, "11 Makeup Mistakes You Don't Realize You're Making," Total Beauty, 9 August 2011, 23 June 2014, http://www.totalbeauty.com/content/gallery/makeup-mistakes-youre-making/p92112/page11
86. Sarah Carrillo, "11 Makeup Mistakes You Don't Realize You're Making," Total Beauty, 9 August 2011, 23 June 2014, http://www.totalbeauty.com/content/gallery/makeup-mistakes-youre-making
87. JennySue, "JennySue Makeup Product Review - MAC'S Glitter Brillants," JennySue Makeup, 18 January 2009, 23 June 2014, http://www.jennysuemakeup.com/2009/01/jennysue-makeup-product-review-macs.html
88. Stef and Tyna, "Guest Blogger: We Heart This Talks Glitter," Birchbox, 23 June 2014, http://blog.birchbox.com/post/4043142484/guest-blogger-we-heart-this-talks-glitter
89. Stef, "How Do You Feel About Glittery Makeup?" Makeup and Beauty Blog, 22 October 2009, 23 June 2014, http://www.makeupandbeautyblog.com/cosmetics/how-do-you-feel-about-glittery-makeup/
90. vfashiontrends, "How to make your skin glow," 11 February 2012, http://www.vfashiontrends.com/makeup-tips/how-to-make-your-skin-glow
91. Rachel Smith, "Rant & Rave: Glitter Eyeshadow," temptalia, 10 January 2011, 23 June 2014, http://www.temptalia.com/rant-rave-glitter-eyeshadow
92. Anja Emerson, "Tips for applying glitter makeup," Helium, 11 September 2011, 23 June 2014, http://www.helium.com/items/2226310-tips-for-applying-glitter-makeup
93. Babuscio, "Camp," 24.
94. Valerie, "Urban Decay: Best of Urban," Review Stream, 23 June 2014, http://www.reviewstream.com/reviews/?p=78022
95. Jennifer Wright, "How To Wear Glitter Eyeshadow And Not Look Like A Prostitute," the gloss, 26 March 2013, http://thegloss.com/beauty/how-to-wear-glitter-eyeshadow-and-not-look-like-a-prostitute/
96. Sarah Carrillo, "11 Makeup Mistakes You Don't Realize You're Making," Total Beauty, 9 August 2011, 23 June 2014, http://www.totalbeauty.com/content/gallery/makeup-mistakes-youre-making
97. Harris, "Aesthetic of Drag," 64.
98. Stef and Tyna, "Guest Blogger: We Heart This Talks Glitter," Birchbox, 23 June 2014, http://blog.birchbox.com/post/4043142484/guest-blogger-we-heart-this-talks-glitter
99. Ellen Tarnapolsky, "New Year's Eve Make-Up Tips," Ezine Articles, 13 December 2011, 23 June 2014, http://ezinearticles.com/?New-Years-Eve-Make-Up-Tips&id=6755954
100. Babuscio, "Camp."
101. Butler, "Lana's 'Imitation,'" 2.
102. Harris, "Aesthetic of Drag," 64.
103. Frou, "MAC Mineralize Eyeshadow Duo (Engaging) Review, Photos, Swatches," Cosmeticized, 5 January 2012, http://www.cosmeticized.com/mac-mineralize-eyeshadow-duo-engaging/
104. Trish, "Rant & Rave: Glitter Eyeshadow," temptalia, 10 January 2011, 23 June 2014, http://www.temptalia.com/rant-rave-glitter-eyeshadow
105. Karen, "The Urban Decay Cowboy Junkie Shadows and Gloss Set Glitters Like a Starry Night," Makeup and Beauty Blog, 9 November 2010, 23 June 2014, http://

www.makeupandbeautyblog.com/product-reviews/the-urban-decay-cowboy-junkie-shadows-and-gloss-set-glitters-like-a-starry-night/
106. Walker and Chaplin, *Visual Culture*.
107. Stern, "What Is Femme?" 186.
108. Andrews, *Blood and Glitter*, 3.
109. DarkSideChic87, "Urban Decay • Midnight Cowboy Rides Again • Eye Shadow," MakeupAlley, 30 December 2007, 17 January 2012, http://makeupalley.com/product/x_showreview.asp?page=6/pagesize=10/ItemID=36112/
110. Karlie Tipton, "Rant & Rave: Glitter Eyeshadow," temptalia, 10 January 2011, 23 June 2014, http://www.temptalia.com/rant-rave-glitter-eyeshadow
111. Kelly B., "Rant & Rave: Glitter Eyeshadow," temptalia, 27 February 2012, 23 June 2014, http://www.temptalia.com/rant-rave-glitter-eyeshadow-2
112. Help.com, "how do you apply Heavy Metal eye glitter gels safely?" 16 April 2012, http://help.com/post/98844-how-do-you-apply-heavy-metal-eye-gl
113. Poitevin, "Inventing Whiteness."
114. rmh, "pretty! but the glitter lingers," Amazon, 22 November 2011, 4 March 2013, http://www.amazon.com/review/R1DJ95A6O3ME2J/ref=cm_cr_dp_title?ie=UTF8&ASIN=B003MZE8EY&channel=detail-glance&nodeID=3760911&store=beauty
115. Peiss, *Hope in a Jar*.
116. Beauty School Dropouts, "Champagne Bubbles New Year's Eve Manicure," 27 December 2011, 23 June 2014, http://thebeautyschooldropouts.blogspot.com/2011/12/champagne-bubbles-new-years-eve.html
117. Olive, "A pink Wednesday franken :)," Glittah Gloves, 28 September 2011, 23 June 2014, http://glittagloves.blogspot.com/2011/09/pink-wednesday-franken.html; Stefanie, "Back by Popular Demand: Work Appropriate Polishes – Rescue Beauty Lounge Edition," The Polish Addict, 29 August 2008, 27 March 2013, http://polishaddict.com/2008/08/29/work-appropriate-rescue-beauty-lounge-edition/
118. Francesca, "Nail Polish Lemmings – An Exposé," Polishment, 16 February 2012, 22 June 2013, http://definepolishment.com/2012/02/16/nail-polish-lemmings-an-expose/; The Polish Addict, "Lacquer Lexicon," 22 June 2013, http://polishaddict.com/lacquer-lexicon/
119. Allison Wheeler, "'Jelly Sandwich' Nails!" Lovelyish, 14 February 2013, http://www.lovelyish.com/2013/02/14/jelly-sandwich-nails/
120. Anthea, "Make Me a Sandwich," Nail Obsession, 15 July 2012, 18 June 2013, http://www.nailedobsession.com/2012/07/make-me-sandwich.html
121. Lizzy O. The DIY Lady, "Make Me A Sammich Woman!!!" The Do It Yourself Lady, 10 September 2012, 18 June 2013, http://www.thediylady.com/2012/09/make-me-sammich-woman.html
122. G., "A blueberry holo glitter jelly sandwich," Nouveau Cheap, 30 November 2011, 11 June 2013, http://nouveaucheap.blogspot.com/2011/11/blueberry-holo-glitter-jelly-sandwich.html
123. NICOLE, "White and Multi Glitter Jelly Sandwich," Polish Me, Please! 2 July 2012, 21 June 2013, http://polishmeplease.wordpress.com/2012/07/02/white-and-multi-glitter-jelly-sandwich/
124. Lesley, "Peanut butter jelly time! using Nicole's @PolishMePlease tutorial. t.co/lSiTfgCl," Twitter, 27 June 2012, 21 June 2013, https://twitter.com/misfitlesley/status/218211008978755585; NICOLE, "Mmmmm More Jelly Sandwiches," Polish Me, Please! 14 June 2012, 21 June 2013, http://polishmeplease.wordpress.com/2012/06/14/mmmmm-more-jelly-sandwiches/
125. drinkcitra, "White and Multi Glitter Jelly Sandwich," Polish Me, Please! 2 July 2012, 21 June 2013, http://polishmeplease.wordpress.com/2012/07/02/white-and-multi-glitter-jelly-sandwich/
126. Schor, "Patrilineage."

127. Goose, "Black and White Jelly Sandwich," Goose's Glitter, 8 February 2012, 12 June 2013, http://www.goosesglitter.com/2012/02/black-and-white-jelly-sandwich.html
128. Lisa Washington, "7 Tips on Doing a Jelly Sandwich Manicure ...," all women stalk, 11 June 2013, http://nails.allwomenstalk.com/tips-on-doing-a-jelly-sandwich-manicure/2/
129. The Crafty Ninja, "Glitter Jelly Sandwich Nails," 18 June 2012, 11 June 2013, http://www.thecraftyninja.com/jelly-sandwich-nails/
130. All The Pretty Polish, "Jelly Sandwich ft my newly nubbinized nails!" 22 August 2011, 13 June 2013, http://alltheprettypolish.blogspot.com/2011/08/jelly-sandwich-ft-my-newly-nubbinized.html
131. G., "Review: Maybelline Limited Edition Colossal Volum' Express Diamonds Mascara," Nouveau Cheap, 9 April 2010, 19 August 2013, http://nouveaucheap.blogspot.com/2010/04/review-maybelline-limited-edition.html
132. Walker and Chaplin, *Visual Culture*, 98.
133. MEGHAN DEMARIA, "How To: Wear glittery makeup on New Year's Eve (without going overboard)," GirlsLife, 28 December 2011, 23 June 2014, http://www.girlslife.com/print/2011/12/22/How-To-Wear-glittery-makeup-on-New-Years-Eve-without-going-overboard.aspx
134. extraH, "OPI Let Me Entertain You," Polish or Perish, 26 October 2010, 23 June 2014, http://polishorperish.blogspot.com/2010/10/opi-let-me-entertain-you.html
135. Donna, "OPI Let Me Entertain You," Polish or Perish, 29 October 2010, 23 June 2014, http://polishorperish.blogspot.com/2010/10/opi-let-me-entertain-you.html
136. Pollock, *Vision and Difference*, 85.
137. Festa, "Personal Effects"; Phillippy, *Painting Women*.
138. ~Leslie~, "Cracked Glitter Bomb," Nail Polish Art Addiction, 4 September 2011, http://polishartaddiction.blogspot.com/2011/09/cracked-glitter-bomb.html
139. Polish and Prose, "About | Polish and Prose," 29 April 2012, 23 June 2014, http://polishandprose.com/?page_id=2
140. Nail Noir, "Finger Paints Winter Wishes," 27 April 2012, http://www.nailnoir.com/finger-paints-winter-wishes
141. Cristina F, "Muffin Monday!! Jordana Bronze Fest," Let them have Polish! 5 March 2012, 23 June 2014, http://www.letthemhavepolish.com/2012/03/muffin-monday-jordana-bronze-fest.html
142. Minty, "Muffin Monday!! Jordana Bronze Fest," Let them have Polish! 5 March 2012, 23 June 2014, http://www.letthemhavepolish.com/2012/03/muffin-monday-jordana-bronze-fest.html
143. Jessica, "REVIEW ~ Spoiled - Are Mermaids Real?" Love Lacquer, 28 January 2012, 23 June 2014, http://www.loveforlacquer.com/2012/01/review-spoiled-are-mermaids-real.html
144. Lady Luck, "REVIEW ~ Spoiled - Are Mermaids Real?" Love Lacquer, 28 January 2012, 23 June 2014, http://www.loveforlacquer.com/2012/01/review-spoiled-are-mermaids-real.html
145. Nail Noir, "Misa Dirty Sexy Money and China Glaze Atlantis," 4 May 2012, http://www.nailnoir.com/misa-dirty-sexy-money-and-china-glaze
146. Andrews, *Blood and Glitter*.
147. Naily Daily, "Happy New Years! (time to kill your eyes with glitter)," 31 December 2010, 24 June 2014, http://nailydaily.wordpress.com/2010/12/31/happy-new-years-time-to-kill-your-eyes-with-glitter/
148. Kirkland, "Caucasian Persuasion of Buffy."
149. LauraSummer, "Weather inspired NOTD!" Laura-Summer Beauty, 13 July 2011, 26 March 2013, http://laurasummerbeauty.blogspot.com/2011/07/weather-inspired-notd.html
150. White, *Buy It Now*.

151. A Polish Addict, "Ciate Jewel Swatches (Super Sparkly!!)," 16 February 2012, 24 June 2014, http://www.apolishaddict.com/2012/02/ciate-jewel-swatches-super-sparkly.html
152. Scrangie, "OPI Burlesque Collection for Winter/Holiday 2010," 4 October 2010, 24 June 2014, http://www.scrangie.com/2010/10/opi-burlesque-collection-for.html
153. flinty, "Dare2Wear Prism swatches: Silhouette, Pirouette and Kiss the Rain," Polish or Perish, 30 May 2010, 24 June 2014, http://polishorperish.blogspot.com/2010/05/dare2wear-prism-swatches-silhouette.html
154. TGW, "Shiro Cosmetics: For Science collection," That Gurl Who, 17 June 2011, 30 April 2012, http://thatgurlwho.co.uk/2011/06/shiro-cosmetics-for-science-collection/
155. For commentary on the association of photography with traces of the real, see Barthes, *Camera Lucida*; Sontag, *On Photography*.
156. Mulvey, "Visual Pleasure."
157. Pollock, *Vision and Difference*.
158. Barthes, *Camera Lucida*, 15.
159. Cyśka, "Hello, Heffalumps!" DizzyNails, 26 January 2012, 6 February 2013, http://www.dizzynails.com/2012/01/hello-heffalumps.html
160. Cranny-Francis, "Touching Film"; Marks, *Touch*; Paterson, *Senses of Touch*; Verrips, "Haptic Screens."
161. The more general rendering of yummy squishy as a feminized and highly constructed pleasure is demonstrated by the use of this term to describe artificial looking pastel cakes, fake food, skeins of colorful yarn, babies, and other cute or "kawaii" things.
162. G., "Want a bite of my Green Jello Jelly Sandwich?" Nouveau Cheap, 21 August 2011, 11 June 2013, http://nouveaucheap.blogspot.com/2011/08/want-bite-of-my-green-jello-jelly.html
163. Christina, "Polish Days Jelly Sandwich," Right Hand Nails, 4 July 2012, 11 June 2013, http://righthandnails.blogspot.co.uk/2012/07/polish-days-jelly-sandwich.html
164. Archana, "mmm.. Jelly Sammich!!! Yum!" Sassy Shelly: Nails and Attitude, 9 August 2012, 13 June 2013, http://www.sassyshelly.com/2012/08/mmm-jelly-sammich-yum.html; Jossie, "Orange Jelly Glitter Sandwich!" Samarium's Swatches, 12 August 2011, 13 June 2013, http://www.samariums-swatches.com/2011/08/orange-jelly-glitter-sandwich.html
165. iMacs were offered in such "flavors" as "strawberry," "blueberry," "lime," "grape," and "tangerine." Wedding dresses are equated to cotton candy and cup cakes. Nail products are also identified as food when the colors evoke foodstuffs, the texture is similar to comestibles, and they are marketed as nourishing the body. Apple Matters, 22 June 2013, http://www.applematters.com/collections/imac-5-flavors/; grannyclosetjunk, "Cotton Candy White Bridal Wedding Dress Union Label size 6-8," Etsy, 22 June 2013, http://www.etsy.com/uk/listing/81262542/cotton-candy-white-bridal-wedding-dress; Taylor, "Jessica Biel's Wedding Dress Revealed! Justin Timberlake Jumps for Joy in First Photo From Their Big Day," E! Online, 24 October 2012, 22 June 2013, http://www.eonline.com/news/355909/jessica-biel-s-wedding-dress-revealed-justin-timberlake-jumps-for-joy-in-first-photo-from-their-big-day
166. Sedgwick, *Touching Feeling*.
167. Dana Schowalter describes "postfeminist citizenship where women are encouraged to use their purchasing power to buy unnecessary products instead of coming together to fight for a more just society that recognizes and corrects existing inequalities." Schowalter, "Silencing The Shriver Report," 220.
168. Ke$ha, as quoted in Eric Spitznagel, "Ke$ha Spends More on Glitter Every Month Than Most People Spend on Rent," *Vanity Fair*, 10 February 2011, 23 June 2014, http://www.vanityfair.com/online/oscars/2011/02/keha-spends-more-on-glitter-

every-month-than-most-people-spend-on-rent; SaucyandSparkly, "Things I wish were socially acceptable," 14 January 2012, 27 June 2013, http://saucyandsparkly.com/2012/01/14/things-i-wish-were-socially-acceptable/

169. Monstrosity has been used to code the other as female, feminine, of color, and queer. For instance, Elizabeth Young shows how Mary Shelley's *Frankenstein* and subsequent quotations of this text code the monster as female and black. Young, *Black Frankenstein*.

AFTERWORD

A Show of Hands: Franken Polishes, Mannequin Hands, and #ManicureMonday

Hypertext artist Shelley Jackson's girlhood "nails were chewed ragged and rimmed with dirt."[1] She would color them "black with pencil" or make "fake fingernails" out of "fruit leather" and stick them on "with spit." Her friends were disgusted but she "thought they looked glamorous." Through this and related personal and conceptual narratives, Jackson highlights the ways the body is produced and social norms are conveyed. She shows how the female body functions as part of a regulatory system that mandates work from women and enables women to understand themselves in varied ways. Jackson produces these divergent readings of the body and fingernails as part of the "my body" – a Wunderkammer hypertext. She emphasizes the self as a technology, which is mediated by varied Internet and social conventions, and a cabinet of curiosities—a precursor to the museum where fascinating things are more important than authenticity and categorical relationships. While Jackson renders her hands, fingernails, toenails, and many other sectioned parts of her body and the interface in detail, she leaves her face as a simple line drawing.[2] In the introductory image, she only depicts part of the head, which is presumably a bust of her, and uses the top of the screen to crop out her eyes.[3] This is different than the selfie and other Internet representations that tend to center the face and emphasize the eyes.

Shelley and Pamela Jackson's The Doll Games also references hands.[4] In this text, hands function as features of young female producers and queer chronicling subjects. The Jackson sisters use The Doll Games as a secret childhood and hypertextual "laboratory" where they can retell and queer their history of doll play and handcrafting and reflect on girlhood, bodies, and identities.[5] They present such things as a "Catalog of Objects Pertaining to The Doll Games" and its collection of the Jacksons' modified dolls and crafted artifacts. Their "Padded bra" entry from this catalog underscores the production of female bodies and the ways women produce themselves and creative objects.[6] The "breast-laden bra" is a technology and disrupter of gender that sits unevenly over the doll's flat chest and renders the female body as a series of created and prosthetic parts. The Jacksons emphasize this disturbance of the coherent body and the associated gender and sex positions in their accompanying story about "prosthetic clay breasts and penises" that can be "donned or discarded" in doll play. Through this text, the Jacksons reference contemporary theories about how bodies, gender, and sex are being culturally, medically, and technologically remade. They produce a critical object that is something like reborn artists' anatomically correct belly plates, which are designed to produce babies' sex but also underscore the dolls' artistic and prosthetic states. The Jacksons' image, which depicts the doll's head turned away from the viewer and breasts/bra illuminated, also highlights how women are visually objectified and, because of the clearly homemade aspects of the chest and breasts, the internal problems and incoherence in such viewing positions.

The Jacksons' "voyeurism" photo essay from The Doll Games engages with feminist psychoanalytic considerations of the ways women are rendered as passive and objectified [Figure A.1].[7] The practices of the Jacksons and other producing women suggest how women and their hands work along with, at counterpurposes to, and confuse these gendered conventions. Their photographs figure a penetrating gaze where individuals look at and into naked doll bodies. In the last image from this essay, the female doll is laid out for inspection but its grubby plastic skin, hacked hair, and uneven breast-laden bra are reminders that it is crafted and manipulated. Two hands in the foreground, which are presumably associated with the Jacksons and thereby long-term stakeholders in this doll's construction, hold a smart phone over the doll's body and get ready to photograph it. In doing this, they highlight empowered viewing subjects, who are ordinarily structured as male, and their ability to look at and imagine controlling the naked doll's body and the female bodies it references. Yet these positions are compromised because the spectator and hands are objects in the photograph as well as producing subjects. This correlation between the doll and viewers is foregrounded because the dolls' hands have a similar gap between fingers and thumb as the corporeal but depicted hands. These corporeal hands are physically proximate to the doll body and have and will continue to intervene in her position. In some areas they are the same color as the doll's pink plastic and in other places a better match for the brown background. These digits emphasize Internet digital production by centering the smart phone and camera and the networked bodies of the doll and producers.

The information age that facilitates such texts, as author Stephen Fenichell suggests, can equally be understood as the plastic age because of the centrality of plastics in digital media and technology production.[8] This has resonant implications for the ways the Jacksons and other women frame their bodies through plastics and other mutable materials. In Kim Toffoletti's research on dolls and cyborgs, she argues that the critical possibilities of Barbie and other dolls include

FIGURE A.1 Shelley and Pamela Jackson, The Doll Games. The "voyeurism" photo essay interrogates the ways objects and bodies are viewed.

their plasticity. Barbie's "synthetic sheen" evokes a sense of "mutability or a state of flux."[9] Her transformative plasticity challenges cultural understandings of dolls, and the women they reference, as passive and static. Other aspects of such dolls, including their jointless elbows and knees that prevent full movement, offer more disturbing renderings of the feminine and female. There are expectations that women "should stay still," according to art historian Joanna Frueh, as if they are always posing "for a picture."[10] Frueh also proposes that "monster/beauty," with its affective and mobile features that are related to the transformative aspects of plastics and alternative aesthetics, is a model that can break these norms. Monsters are key features of producing women and women employ monsters in their aesthetic and creative work.

Many women who participate in Internet production cultures deploy traditional femininity, including conceptions of passive and seemly women, but they also focus on monstrosity, plastic elasticity, and bodily fragmentation. For instance, Shelley Jackson refuses identification as the "author of a hypertext about an imaginary monster," which was her first text, and instead identifies as the "monster herself."[11] Female nail polish producers and bloggers, as I continue to suggest in this afterword, also reference norms and associate their creations and bodies with monstrosity. Rather than proposing a unified body, they render bodies in pieces and distinguish their nails and hands from the whole. This is notable because within society, as Jenny Slatman and Guy Widdershoven argue in their study of hand transplants, "being a unique individual, presupposes a wholeness or unity," including links between the hand and body.[12] Many nail bloggers emphasize hands instead of the more usual focus on faces, and reference beauty culture even as they produce and celebrate monstrous bodies. Their posting strategies estrange hands from the rest of the body. They reconfigure Rose Marie San Juan's argument that individuals disassociate moving hands from their self-conceptions because of the uncanniness of these features.[13]

The interface has been related to and even conceptualized as a face and hand. Apple's FaceTime offers individuals the opportunity to "Be in two places at once," and thereby seems to deliver unmediated people and experiences and a form of liveness.[14] It emphasizes the faciality of its interface through the name of the application, references to a temporal present, and its demo images of people's faces centered on the screen. FaceTime evokes the conception of "face-to-face," which as Warwick Mules indicates, "has become a signifier of pure communication—either an ideal to which all communication should aspire, or more critically, a false promise that obscures the entangled context of mediation as the real condition of any communicative event."[15] Apple deploys such deceptive promises in asserting that its technologies bring faces and people together in the same place. The interface and its faciality, according to Mules, promote face-to-face interaction and a "seemingly transcendent space of common experience." Yet hands and particularly hand-pointers, as I have previously suggested, are also markers of people's physical position and ability to control systems.[16] The term "face-to-face" suggests bodies are physically touching. However, the term is meant to convey liveness and realness. Rather than being in contact, faces ordinarily retain some distance in their closeness and are associated with evaluative forms of looking because the eyes are positioned in the face. Hands and hand-pointers more overtly reference touching and being touched. This focus on tactility and material connections has been extended with touch screens.

Pointing and showing hands are features of ecommerce listings, craft and beauty tutorials, and nail blogs. Polish bloggers tend to feature cropped images of their hands. Women use their hands to apply polishes and as stilled photographic subjects that demonstrate their work. Since individuals cannot simultaneously use the same hand to apply polish and have their hand polished, subject and object positions are always an aspect of nail polish applications. Nail bloggers' emphasis on body parts is related to Roland Barthes's indication that individuals can never see the whole self without mediation.[17] There is no unmediated face-to-face that allows individuals to see themselves. This body, which is supposed to be intimately known, can only be seen in pieces. Yet images of hands also connect different subjects by situating viewers as writers, photographers, and producers and showing what they can see and do. Michele advises bloggers and crafters to leave "your hands in some shots" as a way of connecting the actions of producers and readers. These images say, "I made this and so can you."[18] The associated hands establish all individuals as producers rather than solely functioning as visual objects that are viewed.

Images of hands evoke touching-feeling and physical and emotional connections but women's focus on their hands has often been identified as engagements with the aesthetic self. Women's interest in nail polish and other forms of beauty culture has thus been dismissed for being frivolous and self-involved. However, journalist Tracie Egan Morrissey argues that nail art provides women with creative outlets that have not been delimited by cultural norms.[19] For reporter Sarah Hampson, nail art is a "silent, powerful voice of unapologetic femininity."[20] Morrissey and Hampson refute the sole articulation of nails as bodily properties and associate women and their nails with thinking and creativity. This is a reconceptualization of the usual binary that correlates women with the body and emotions and men with the mind and rationality. Yet Morrissey and Hampson still associate nail polish culture with certain aspects of traditional femininity. Some polish bloggers propose more monstrous relationships between women and their polished nails.

Frankening the Monster

Women franken, or mix different polishes and other materials together, as a way of advancing their relationship with nail polish culture and rendering the polishes that they want. The term "franken" is an abbreviation of Frankenstein and references things that are monstrous, not fully alive, composite, and creative. The *Oxford English Dictionary* does not address nail polish frankening when indicating that it primarily conveys "depreciative" opinions of things that are genetically modified.[21] Some contemporary uses of the term continue Mary Wollstonecraft Shelley's expressed concerns in *Frankenstein: Or, the Modern Prometheus* about the uncontrollable and alienating aspects of technology, but nail polish bloggers propose more positive readings of these monstrous mixes.[22] Many nail polish frankeners emphasize that this practice is linked to the monster and unnatural animation. AliceRoared states, "the term is taken from the concept of Frankenstein, who is a monster made from several parts of dead humans."[23] According to RaynesOnyx, frankens are associated with "Frankenstein's creature (except with polish not dead people)."[24] RaynesOnyx situates frankeners in the position of scientific creators. While she suggests that frankeners start with polishes rather than dead people as their base, bloggers' comments associate death and reanimation with frankening.

Frankeners identify with the scientific work as well as the more irrational practices of Dr. Frankenstein and the monster. My Lucid Bubble references sound thinking through her blog name but describes feeling "like a mad scientist!"[25] STEPH associates frankening with putting on her "white lab coat" and "mixing nail polish colors like a mad chemist!"[26] Dami starts her post on frankening by noting, "It's alive!"[27] Dami suggests that she and other female nail bloggers imbue life into dead things. This animation includes the further activation of female nails and hands. Frankening is associated with bodily contact because these mixes are personally made and applied and, as Dami explains, frankening creates things you cannot otherwise "get your hands on." Frankens thus enable women to have closer relationships with polishes. While women's search for beauty is ordinarily an attempt at aliveness and liveliness, frankening figures a beauty culture where individuals are interested in touching death, as fingers touch and propagate nails, and being conjoined to dead things that may be provisionally animated.

Film and media versions of the Frankenstein scenario situate declarations about producing life and the monster in a lab setting that is usually defined as male, but nail polish frankeners associate their creative processes with the home lab and such feminine spaces as the kitchen. Reborn artists also reference home nurseries and studios as methods of coding their artistic practices and identities. Lynderella, who is an important figure in frankening and indie nail polish production, speaks about her creative space as a lab and kitchen and indicates that she sometimes finds glitter in her food.[28] Her practice and body are thus situated between things and open to consuming and being contaminated by glitter. While nail polish is usually manufactured in large commercial spaces, producers indicate that frankens are "created 'at home'" and are "home-made."[29] Their perspectives enhance the idea of the handmade by relating polishes to intimate bodily and spatial relationships. These producers may also convey the handmade aspects of all polishes because they are made for and on the hand.

Amanda Frankenpolish incorporates polish mixes into her blogging identity and offers "recipes" from her "very own franken lab!"[30] She depicts polish culture as something that arcs between home cooking and inventive creation and underscores the many forms of women's creative and informed work. Frankenpolish asserts, "Frankening is all about experimenting!"[31] Monstrous failures are accepted as part of the learning process, or even something that is desired. She has created her "fair share of hideous, blindingly ugly polishes that would make anyone shudder in disgust." Her "Scrambled Eggs" franken "is weird" maybe "even hideous looking!"[32] She works through her varied sentiments about and relationships to the product when noting she has "never seen a polish like this," "at least it's an original," and she "kinda" likes it but she likes "weird things."

Kajsa identifies it as "so ugly looking! Fuck it," she has to "have one just like it!"[33] These bloggers pose a nail polish counter-aesthetic that is not based in making hands look traditionally pretty. Creativity and desirability are linked to the unpleasant and monstrous. In some cases, this is articulated as monstrous beauty. For instance, an article on Dr. Frankenpolish is titled "Unleashing a Beauty Monster."[34] The affective aspects of these nails, hands, and frankens are evoked by Frueh's identification of "monster/beauty" as the "flawed and touchable, touching and smellable, vocal and mobile body that, by exceeding the merely visual, manifests" a "sensual presence."[35] Frueh's proposal and the comments of bloggers suggest that franken polishes have an importance and function that exceed the visual. Some proponents of glitter suggest a similar cosmetic position that is beyond seeing.

Bloggers' engagements with such non-normative positions and counter-aesthetics include their ambivalent associations of frankens with femininity and the visual position of women. arya duwipangga evokes media utterances about Frankenstein when announcing that she "Franken-Polished It!"[36] She could not find a "really light pink nail polish" with a specific texture so she decides to make it herself since she is a "DIY person" who has "mixed some really weird (and intriguing) colors." The resultant shade may be "beautiful" and "feminine" but she curtails these identifications by relating frankening to the weird. duwipangga further limits her relationship to femininity by declaring that she "can't wear ye ole regular pinks at all!" Evil Angel also restricts her connection with traditional femininity by indicating that she "frankened a very nice sparkly peachy pink" for when she has to "go 'normal.'"[37] Fairly Charming contextualizes her blog and nail polish practice with the phrase, "Dare to be bold."[38] She is excited about a new glittering blue polish but prefaces it with a "normy." Her choir encourages women to wear nail polish as a means of looking "more feminine" and disallows anything "bright/outlandish." Fairly Charming questions these practices and uses texts, including photographs of these varied polishes and positions, to distinguish between her interests and cultural norms.

Polish bloggers use icons and illustrations to forward frankens and other monstrous forms of beauty. For instance, Michelle Mismas accompanies an article on frankenpolish with an image of Frankenstein's monster grafted onto a nail polish bottle.[39] Mismas thereby correlates the monster with cosmetics and aesthetics. The Polish Monster uses the name and design of her blog to link monstrosity to beauty. The blog icon, which was designed by her friend Justin, is a pink nail polish bottle that has a Cyclopean eye and an open mouth with sharp teeth.[40] This illustration animates polish in a similar manner to narratives about frankens and associates them with inhuman physiognomies. The Polish Monster further feminizes this monstrous identification by employing shades of pink on her blog and identifying pink as her "signature color." She posts a nail polish manicure where she uses pink flock to make her nails fuzzy and attaches a plastic googly Cyclopean eye to the center of each nail [Figure A.2]. Her nails thus

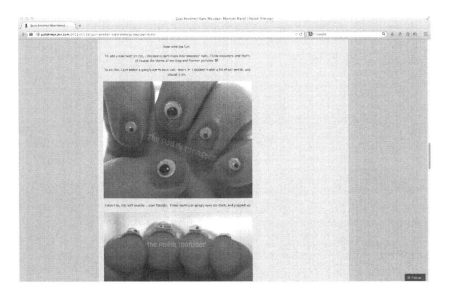

FIGURE A.2 The Polish Monster. Pink flock and plastic eyes are used to make monster nails.

become a digital version of the blog and its icon. She made them into "'monster' nails" because she loves "monsters, and that's of course the theme" of her "blog and franken polishes."[41] By producing this application and series of associations, The Polish Monster codes nails as fascinating and horrible on account of their feminine, plastic, technological, and undead features. She resituates and conflates seeing and feeling, which may also be how people experience images of hands, through these textured and plastic features. While fluidity and monstrosity have been negatively associated with femininity, The Polish Monster and other frankeners encourage women to self-identify with these positions and structure their bodies through these terms.

Women's pleasure in making and wearing franken polishes has led to a growing number of women becoming indie polish producers.[42] This culture has grown from and credits frankens and monsters for its successes. Lynderella is often recognized as the first indie brand to go public in 2011.[43] While there are women who produce indie polishes as their full-time jobs, most still identify this work as a hobby. Even larger indie companies only sell around 5,000 bottles a month.[44] Yet this has shifted the interests and identities of some nail polish bloggers and changed the overall polish industry. For instance, Christine thinks that the kind of glitter polishes that major brands produce "is a result of the rise of indie polish shops."[45] Kate's role as an indie polish producer has changed her bodily engagement and the position of her hands. She has "long, strong nails – the perfect canvas – but instead of spending hours painting" her nails, she spends time "playing with glitters and pigments trying to make sparkly happiness in a bottle."[46] Women and their hands are thus producers of applications and polishes. These indie polishes, according to Cassie Goodwin, are "by and large HAND MADE."[47] Their production is a labor intensive practice where one "person [is] bent over a tiny glass bottle mixing up beautiful potions to make your nails look amazing." Goodwin's use of the term "hand" suggests the individual nature of crafting and producers' personal experiences and products. Indie producers and bloggers understand hands as essential components in their work, body parts that labor, and features that do aesthetic work on other hands.

From Fleshy to Plastic

Women's descriptions of their monstrous hands remove them from the position of normative to-be-looked-at-ness. For instance, lifestyle blogger Ree Drummond accompanies her cooking instructions with comments about her "freaky pink alien hand."[48] With this account, Drummond self-presents as something other than normatively white and human. Her alien hand also refuses identification as the good mother. When Drummond's daughter tries to put her childish hand in the images and taste the food, Drummond's "Claw scratches and squeezes until the twelve-year-old punk whimpers and runs away." In Slatman and Widdershoven's study of hands, they suggest that a "malfunctioning organ," and Drummond's hand moves against normative codes, may result in "self-alienation."[49] Drummond's hand performs unusual acts and she sees, or at least describes, it as alien, and thus as a distant other. At the same time, she encourages viewers to see "Matching mother-daughter alien hands" and offers some resolution to warring body parts and familial and embodied dissolution. She explains that her "hand is always pink and freaky and bright white" so that she can properly expose the darker contents of the pot. Of course, Drummond could choose a different kind of photographic arrangement or light her images differently. By rendering and writing about her pink alien hand, Drummond emphasizes her strange role as producer, and women who are extremely successful producers are still unfortunately unusual, and the difficulties she has mediating between her envisioned creative and mothering positions.

Hands play a part in understandings of the self and are direct physical mediators between individuals and other people and things. Nail bloggers conceptualize polishes and colors as something that constitutes the self and view these elements and the accompanying hands as properties that can lead to disassociation. For instance, Sandi identifies a set of colors as "way outside" her "comfort zone" because they are not her style and not her personality.[50] When wearing them, "it's like seeing someone else's hands attached" to her "body." Mismas found that a "shimmery pinkish nude makes" her "nails look dead."[51] She thought that she "was looking at a corpse's hand" rather than at herself. Women also describe nails as canvases and thereby conceptualize nails as distinct from their bodies. Nails are artistically rendered elements that foreground women's creative self-production. Hands are thus technologies of the self, allowing people to do and change things. They structure the ways self and individual are understood.

Drummond's rendering of her pink alien hand is related to nail bloggers' classifications of their hands. Bloggers identify "zombie," "corpse," or "dead hands" when a polish causes hands to "look greenish, yellowish, or ashen."[52] These women use the term "lobster hands" to describe instances in which fingers look pinker. These experiences with hands are the sometimes-unintentional consequences of putting skin next to certain shades. They are moments when posters see themselves and do not recognize themselves. However, bloggers intentionally render methods of self-identification and distancing through "mannequin hands" and apply a color that matches their skin tone. This matching is not easily accomplished and there are not enough shades to meet the needs of participants. The analogous store mannequins usually come in a narrow range of skin colors and are often based on Caucasian skin tones. The women who blog about mannequin hands tend to focus on lighter shades. Some of them also hierarchize skin color by arranging bottles in a line from left to right and emphasize the lightest shades on the left.

There are nail polish bloggers who resist the ways mannequin hands privilege whiteness. Jackie S. replies to a thread on women showing their mannequin hands with an "UUGGGH!"[53] As an "African American, it is very hard" for her to "find 'nude' colors." Piff more overtly highlights the racist problems with the term "nude" and the production of a limited range of "nude" products. She "had a hard time finding a great creme nude, because 'nude' is usually nude for white people."[54] The nude is conceptualized as a kind of body. Yet this focus on "nude" also highlights how individuals with light skin do not fit within the norm. For instance, Nora does not "have the right coloring for 'nude' polishes." She is "too pale."[55] Such commentary critically puts nude in scare quotes and indicates the problems with uninterrogated and overarching uses of this term. Nevertheless, the underacknowledgment of the relationship between conceptions of nude, privilege, self, and beauty is more likely to disturb people of color who have already been disenfranchised in other ways.

Women produce mannequin hands by choosing colors that match their fingers and cuticles and thereby blend nails and hands so that they look like plastic models. According to Elizabeth, "most store mannequins are made either without distinct fingernails or with nails the same colour as the rest of the mannequin," so the practice of getting the polish to blend into the skin "is referred to as mannequin hands."[56] Mismas associates mannequin hands with the "use of a flesh toned nail polish to elongate the hands and give that plastic-y, doll-like effect."[57] Nancy Girl describes the "perfect nude/plastic Barbie/mannequin shade."[58] Some women add a matte topcoat to this application in order to get it as "plasticky as possible" and blend everything together.[59] They render a consistency of features that is distanced from animate flesh. In this case, and zombie whiteness operates somewhat differently, women's foregrounding and featuring of inhuman mannequin paleness allows them to propose alternative identity positions without addressing the relationship between skin color and Caucasian privilege.

Through these tactics, some women align with the plastic, mannequin, and doll, which have been used as aspersions. Yet women employ mannequin hand applications in order to self-identify with things that are produced and technological rather than natural. Women's shifts in corporeal identifications are supported by their illustration of posts with mannequin or plastic hands rather than the more usual practice of depicting their own hands. For instance, Mismas illustrates a post with a mannequin hand that has deeply carved nails that are the same color as the figure's painted skin.[60] Jenn Rice offers instructions on "How To Look Like A Hand Model, Via the 'Mannequin Hands Manicure'" but the accompanying picture is of a mismatched set of modeled mannequin hands rather than an ideal embodied model.[61] Women use these images and discourses to assert their alliances with other subjects and to extend ideas about what women and their bodies look and feel like.

Women sometimes indicate that their relationship with polish is more important than their appearance. For example, I Drink Nail Polish declares that she is not "breaking up with pastels" even though they do not enhance her skin tone.[62] Her blog name proposes that bloggers are more passionate than sensible about polish, nail polish is a form of sustenance, and these individuals consume a form of poison and are therefore something other than human. In playfully framing women's relationship to nail polish as resistant to break ups, I Drink Nail Polish articulates an intimate and loving relationship that exceeds corporeal bonds and conventions. Other women adopt a kind of erotic abjection. For instance, Kirsten loves how a polish looks on her "ghostly hands" even though the "contrast is almost alarming!"[63] Liz Krusenstjerna "would move to Vermont and marry" a nail polish shade because of how much she loves it.[64] In mentioning Vermont, where same-sex marriages were legalized before many other places in the United States, she suggests that polishes shift women's interests from heterosexual to lesbian and queer attachments. This extends Olivia S. and Morrissey's indications that women do not employ nail art applications in order to make themselves "more attractive to men" and "more appealing to men."[65] Instead, nail art producers actively and playfully render female and feminine engagements and queer relationships with objects. Through their queer ties, including associations with ghostly hands and girls, they refuse the usual beauty conventions and adult positions.

Nail bloggers engage with beauty culture and deathly references as part of their everyday practices. For instance, Nail Nerd created "Corpse Nails" for her visit to the "doctor's office."[66] Her nails provide the illusion that "blood and dirt" are "creeping out from the nail bed." She manufactures the ill and deathly for the medical establishment, which is familiar with such embodied states but ordinarily engages in evaluating and maintaining health. Nail Nerd further recodes the experiences of applying polish, especially the forms of femininity that are associated with these materials, by describing the completed application as "dead-and-done!" Nail Nerd thereby renders death rather than liveliness and aliveness as the conclusion of nail art applications. She provides a model for everyday zombie practices in which the bodies of women destabilize rather than assure and attract viewers. She foregrounds people's embodied reactions to such practices by indicating that "one of the nurses" told her, "those are CREEPY." By referencing a medical practitioner, who would not be easily influenced by visceral or depicted bloodshed, Nail Nerd intensifies the horror of her nails.

Nail Nerd's and other bloggers' narratives about horrific hands, which I also think about in relationship to TTD sessions, zombie brides, and zombie nails, should be intensified in descriptions of crafting accidents. However, these bloggers tend to identify crafting injuries as significant milestones in their position as crafters and as experiences that connect them to other practitioners. Wormie "posted about" her "first knit project," "first weaving project," and "first crafting injury" where she "slammed" the rotary cutter into her "index finger."[67] Ann is "sure you all can relate" to the glue gun burn on her finger.[68] She renders her blister as a form of "I made this" through images and descriptions. Readers connect to Ann and the other people who describe accidents through the affective touching-feeling that is generated by representations of accidents, the mirroring stories that they share, and their continued investments in craft production despite accidents and pain. Ann promises to "be back later to show you what" she is "working on."[69] She is "not gonna let a little glue gun burn end" her "plans." These injuries are thus testaments to crafters' loyalty and fortitude. For instance, Jolynn argues that she "gave" herself a blister because she cares that "damn much."[70] nltolonen connects crafting to feminine work and forms of suffering when indicating the "pain we women endure for crafting and beauty."[71] These bloggers' representations of crafting accidents establish a somewhat different relationship to horror than women who create monstrous nails. However, they echo the work of nail bloggers by undoing distinctions between passive looking and active doing and rendering past activities and methods of looking as feeling.

Conclusion: The Hand's Looks and Limits

Nail bloggers respond to images of nail polish applications and frankens as forms of active and creative production. However, a group of scientists worry that these practices encourage women to be passive and function as objects of the male gaze. For instance, scientist Hope Jahren expressed concern in November 2013 about young women's engagements in polish culture, including their posts on a Twitter feed that is also used by *Seventeen Magazine*. Jahren proposed a form of hashtag hijacking where individuals who are not in control of or associated with a meta data tag, which is used to group content, post different information than what is expected. She envisioned scientists "taking over" what she saw as *Seventeen Magazine's* ManicureMonday hashtag with "real pics of real hands doing real #Science."[72] Her intent was to "contrast real #Science hands against what @seventeenmag says our hands should look like." Through her proposal, Jahren distinguishes between young girls' interests in nails and hands, which she associates with looking rather than doing, and scientists' more recognized work and forms of production. In making these and related statements, Jahren and the participating scientific community acknowledge young women's investments but misidentify the many people who are interested in creating aesthetic and artful applications and producing polishes, including women, queers, and men. Jahren accepts that *"Seventeen Magazine* is not going away" and thereby identifies it as a problem but "then again, neither is Twitter, and so you'll find" her "over at #ManicureMonday for the long haul." In suggesting this, Jahren articulates participating scientists as more activist and informed than nail posters without considering their own association with sites like Twitter. She also misses the ways frankeners and polish bloggers conceptualize their work as science and experiment with materials.

Images from the #ManicureMonday intervention include "Scientist's hands coding, w Revlon" and a scientist's hand and purple nail polish application acting as a "size reference for coyote scat."[73] Scientists continue to post to the #ManicureMonday feed but most of them do not share nail art or notable manicures. For instance, Minibeast Mayhem displays an image of a leaf insect from the family Phylliidae perching on her nails and indicates that she is "going for leafy green extensions this week."[74] Her image received positive responses from the scientific community but it operates by making nail extensions into a joke. Like some of the discourses about glitter, scientists who participate in #ManicureMonday tend to relate nail polish to young girls, code it as frivolous, and indicate that the people who engage are in need of education. While Jahren and her peers are worried about the ways #ManicureMonday focuses on women's visual features, the hashtag tweet from Minibeast Mayhem is an example of how this scientific cohort emphasizes the visual features of hands, objects, and creatures.

Jahren's project includes an important feminist inquiry into the ways women are represented and their work is understood. However, she does not fully conceptualize girls', feminine, and women's cultures. In her reflection on the "#ManicureMonday #Science 'take-over,'" she describes her initial understanding of "everything associated with *Seventeen Magazine* as one big monolithic male gaze."[75] She modifies this statement to acknowledge the "teenagers" who "tweet their homemade nail art" and "pictures of what they feel makes their hands look great." Yet Jahren still associates these practices with the ways women are structured as to-be-looked-at-ness and understood as passive. She describes scrolling "past hundreds of painted disembodied hands" and wondering "who is attached to all those hands and what do those hands do when they aren't posing for a camera?" Of course, most photographs convey posed, or at least "stilled," things because they are representations of moments and activities. Women are doing something, including constructing conceptions of self and body, when they pose for their own images. In addition, these women are actively producing images and the associated nail polish applications. Jahren identifies nail polish enthusiasts' "disembodied hands" as a problem. However, I believe that these images propose different methods of viewing bodies and focus on the creative and aesthetic work of women and their hands.

Jahren is invested in a feminist view of science and female empowerment that she tries to convey through #ManicureMonday. Jason Bittel's report about the event is less focused on acknowledging women. What interested Bittel was "when everybody's favorite shark-guy, David Shiffman, started using the tag."[76] In other words, Bittel was intrigued by #ManicureMonday when the work of a male scientist appeared. He downplays people's concerns that the project would make women feel badly about their interests, conflates manicures with stupidity, and is a kind of "femme-shaming."[77] Such discrediting is implicit in his indication that the most interesting #ManicureMonday posts are by a man. Journalist Richard Horgan further dismisses women's voices and positions when reporting on the article and writing, "Femme-shaming!? That's ridiculous."[78] Thankfully, some posters provide more thoughtful perspectives and consider politically productive ways of engaging with women and other nail polish culture participants.

Momma PhD expresses a commitment to supporting young people through her ID.[79] She imagines that the project will allow young women to see that "you aren't alone in liking science and painting your fingernails." Reporter Laura Vanderkam associates the project with the "ongoing conversation about women in science," including women's struggles in being accepted as scientists and the ways they are held to and negatively judged for exhibiting traditionally feminine behaviors.[80] She thinks the photos show that you "can do serious work and enjoy girlie things." Scientist Joanne Manaster finds that #ManicureMonday's effectiveness as an outreach mechanism has been uneven.[81] She and these other women express their interest in the scientific, cultural, and aesthetic aspects of nail polish and thereby provide engaged addresses. For instance, Manaster's blog offers information on how to "make the world of beauty a bit more intellectually fascinating!"[82] This poses beauty culture as interesting and more disappointingly suggests that it is not thoughtful. In a video related to this project, Manaster chronicles her frustration in not being able to wear polish because of the constant hand washing in the lab, and provides a fascinating study of the use of such flammable materials as nitrocellulose in nail polish.[83]

A number of the women who participate in the Polish or Perish group blog describe the pleasures and difficulties in balancing science and nail polish culture.[84] They relate polish to academia and intellectual pursuits by re-envisioning the academic mandate to "publish or perish" and depicting a series of bottles imprinted with advanced degrees. Their tagline, which is "WOMEN WHO

HAVE ALMOST AS MUCH NAIL POLISH AS THEY HAVE EDUCATION," suggests that owning polish is less intense than commitments to education. These bloggers' interests in polish culture work along with and disrupt their roles in academia. For instance, kittytokaren's male colleague uses a desirable brand of polish for "sealing microscope slides" in the lab.[85] Rather than using polish in the most perfunctory and functional manner, kittytokaren describes him as a polish enthusiast who seems to "care about both quality and prettiness." She covets one of his polishes and thereby renders a polish culture that loosens gender and professional boundaries. LabMuffin's "love" of polishes with holographic and "thermal colour change effects," which shift hue in response to heat and cold, "inspired" her to write a "sciencey article on how thermochromic colour change pigments work."[86] Like Manaster, she is intellectually stimulated by the properties and science of beauty products. Other women respond by expressing their desire for the color change polishes and interest in the science. For instance, LabMuffin's posts make Michelle "love science again."[87] LabMuffin encourages women to be interested in and identify with science. These are the engagements that Jahren envisions.

Jahren is not interested in creating the fascinating and skillful nail polish applications that circulate on Twitter and appear in blogs. However, Manaster mentions Jayne Lim's "Nucleotide Skittles" manicure and other "amazing science inspired nail art," which she identifies as "inspiring."[88] As Manaster suggests, these practices inform each other as science stimulates nail art, nail art applications encourage viewers to create things, and bloggers and viewers get excited about science. Lim finds it difficult but valuable to combine science, nail art, and varied kinds of skills and knowledge. Frankeners and indie polish producers make similar comparisons while trying to make appealing polishes and learn about the chemical properties and reactions of different materials. For instance, indie polish producer Andrea of Indigo Bananas identifies her "interest in the chemistry of nail polish" and her dream of having a "full chemistry lab" and "making nail polish base from scratch."[89] These nail bloggers consider the visual properties of nails and the politics and procedures of beauty and science. They and other female producers challenge the borders between nail art and science, amateurism and skill, passive and active, and looking and being looked at.

Lim engages with these issues in her nail art application for the Scientista Foundation [Figure A.3].[90] This organization provides services for pre-professional women in the science, technology, engineering, and mathematics fields. She pays "tribute to some of the most notable women in science" by dedicating a nail to the achievements of Marie Curie, Rosalind Franklin, Ada Lovelace, and Barbara McClintock.[91] Her "science-inspired nail art" is "hard work," including the technical requirements to paint such images, but she feels "happiest" when sharing science and nail art with readers. Viewers such as BlushBug enjoy "looking" and learning things and love when Lim mixes "science and nail art together!"[92] They appreciate these hybrid forms of images and written texts and

FIGURE A.3 Jayne Lim, Cosmetic Proof. This manicure references women scientists and was designed to inspire pre-professional women.

creative and research engagements. Of course, the distinctions between these categories are blurred because the pictorial and creative features of Lim's nails include scientific diagrams. In producing and representing such manicures, Lim combines science, the work of women, a feminist project, Internet technologies, images of her hands, and art on her nails. She intensifies these connections in her Scientista nail painting of a laptop with a mouse directed towards viewers, who are also employing computers. Through this arrangement, Lim prompts bloggers and viewers to actively look and make things.

The nail bloggers and other producing women I study in this book widen current cultural conceptions of women, femininity, and creative practices. They offer a series of pleasures to women producers and readers, including interests that connect participants in queer engagements. Their production strategies amplify the lesbian looks that are figured in fashion magazines because of the ways women are encouraged to admire other women's bodies.[93] These producing women offer individuals different ways of seeing, making, and desiring. They generate terms and methods that make women's production cultures socially and economically viable. Some of them offer hybrid forms of viewing where distanced positions are made into instances of touching-feeling and looking-producing. For instance, nail bloggers' formal and conceptual shifts from the face to the hand underscore their interests in feeling and creating. This poses changed ways of understanding women's bodies.

Feminist studies of representations provide important considerations of the ways women are objectified, disempowered, and dismissed. This feminist research also calls for considerations of how women could look and be portrayed differently. This includes Griselda Pollock's call to rethink the female spectator and whether texts made by women can produce different viewing positions.[94] For Pollock, such positions and production practices are necessary features of acknowledging women and providing representations of their pleasure, rather than portrayals of what men and other subjects would like women to enjoy. Lim and many other nail bloggers link the visual delights of women's nails and hands to their practices of creating applications and products. The Jacksons create similar continuities between being looked at and making things. Their work indicates how important it is to simultaneously engage with all of the facets of producing women. Such combined analysis points to the problems and critical possibilities in representations of women, women's self-production, and women's cultures and work. These practices also demonstrate ways of producing and being varied sorts of women and other subjects.

Notes

1. Shelley Jackson, "Fingernails," "my body" – a Wunderkammer, 1997, 15 April 2014, http://collection.eliterature.org/1/works/jackson__my_body_a_wunderkammer/fingernails.html
2. Shelley Jackson, "The Body by Shelley Jackson," "my body" – a Wunderkammer, 1997, 27 May 2014, http://collection.eliterature.org/1/works/jackson__my_body_a_wunderkammer/body.html
3. Shelley Jackson, "'my body' – a Wunderkammer & (Shelley Jackson)," "my body" – a Wunderkammer, 1997, 21 April 2014, http://collection.eliterature.org/1/works/jackson__my_body_a_wunderkammer/
4. Shelley and Pamela Jackson, "the doll games," The Doll Games, 2001, 7 July 2014, http://www.ineradicablestain.com/dollgames/
5. Shelley and Pamela Jackson, "doll games: on little girls," The Doll Games, 2001, 7 July 2014, http://www.ineradicablestain.com/dollgames/littlegirls.html
6. Shelley and Pamela Jackson, "artifacts," The Doll Games, 2001, 15 April 2014, http://www.ineradicablestain.com/dollgames/artifacts.html
7. Shelley and Pamela Jackson, "voyeurism [8]," The Doll Games, 2001, 7 July 2014, http://www.ineradicablestain.com/dollgames/bod8.html; Mulvey, "Visual Pleasure."
8. Fenichell, *Plastic*.
9. Toffoletti, *Cyborgs and Barbie Dolls*, 70.
10. Frueh, *Monster/Beauty*, 1–2.
11. Shelley Jackson, "Stitch Bitch: The Patchwork Girl," 4 November 1997, 23 June 2014, http://web.mit.edu/m-i-t/articles/index_jackson.html
12. Slatman and Widdershoven, "Hand Transplants," 74.
13. San Juan, "Horror of Touch."
14. Apple, "Apple – iOS 7 – FaceTime, 23 April 2014, http://www.apple.com/ios/facetime/
15. Mules, "This Face."
16. White, *Body and the Screen*.
17. Barthes, *Roland Barthes*.
18. Michele, "How to Take Better Tutorial Photos with Framing and Cropping," CraftyPod, 6 November 2012, 10 April 2014, http://www.craftypod.com/2012/11/06/how-to-

take-better-tutorial-photos-with-framing-and-cropping/#sthash.sGOXPXyd.dpuf
19. Tracie Egan Morrissey, "Nail Art, the Last Bastion of Female-Centric Beauty," Jezebel, 7 August 2012, 12 January 2014, http://jezebel.com/5930229/nail-art-the-last-bastion-of-female+centric-beauty
20. Sarah Hampson, "How nail art is the new unapologetic emblem of femininity," Globe and Mail, 2 March 2013, http://www.theglobeandmail.com/life/fashion-and-beauty/beauty/how-nail-art-is-the-new-unapologetic-emblem-of-femininity/article9076963/
21. Oxford English Dictionary, "Franken-," 23 June 2014, http://www.oed.com.libproxy.tulane.edu:2048/view/Entry/252716?redirectedFrom=franken#eid
22. Shelley, *Frankenstein*.
23. AliceRoared, "Frankening polish," Beauty Haven, 30 July 2012, 25 April 2014, http://www.beautyheaven.com.au/forums/hands-and-feet/frankening-polish#
24. RaynesOnyx, "Franken Polish Creations," Onyx Polish, 28 May 2012, 23 June 2014, http://onyxnails.blogspot.com/2012/05/franken-polish-creations.html
25. My Lucid Bubble, "A Black Linear Holo Franken and How To Make Your Own," 26 April 2011, 23 June 2014, http://mylucidbubble.blogspot.com/2011/04/black-linear-holo-franken-and-how-to.html
26. STEPH, "My First Holographic Franken: Peacock Hour," STEPH'S CLOSET, 23 July 2009, 23 June 2014, http://www.stephscloset.com/blog/beauty/2009/07/614/my-first-holographic-franken-peacock-hour/
27. Dami, "Perfectly Polished Tips 34 - Franken Polish," Perfectly Polished Tips, 9 September 2008, 27 March 2014, http://perfectlypolishedtips.blogspot.com/2008/09/perfectly-polished-tips-34-franken.html
28. Mary, "Interview with Lynnderella," Body and Soul, 6 February 2011, 23 June 2014, http://www.body-soulbeauty.com/2011/02/interview-with-lynnderella.html
29. AmyGrace, "Ravishing Ruby - My 1st franken!" The Polished Perfectionist, 3 May 2011, http://the-polished-perfectionist.blogspot.com/2011/05/ravishing-ruby-my-1st-franken.html; Shilpa Gandotra, "How To Create Your Own Nail Polish - Steps To Create Indie Polish," Our External World, 27 November 2013, 24 June 2014, http://www.ourexternalworld.com/2013/11/how-to-create-your-own-nail-polish.html
30. Amanda Frankenpolish, "Welcome," Dr. Frankenpolish, 31 January 2009, 24 June 2014, http://drfrankenpolish.wordpress.com/2009/01/31/welcome/
31. Amanda Frankenpolish, "Frankenpolish 101: A Crash Course In The Art Of 'Frankening,'" Dr. Frankenpolish, 1 February 2009, 24 June 2014, https://drfrankenpolish.wordpress.com/2009/02/01/frankenpolish-101-a-crash-course-in-the-art-of-frankening/
32. Amanda Frankenpolish, "Scrambled Eggs," Dr. Frankenpolish, 26 May 2010, 24 June 2014, http://drfrankenpolish.wordpress.com/2010/05/26/scrambled-eggs/
33. Kajsa, "Scrambled Eggs," Dr. Frankenpolish, 26 May 2010, 24 June 2014, http://drfrankenpolish.wordpress.com/2010/05/26/scrambled-eggs/
34. Nails Magazine, "Unleashing a Beauty Monster," 1 December 2009, 6 October 2012, http://www.nailsmag.com/article/840/unleashing-a-beauty-monster
35. Frueh, *Monster/Beauty*, 2.
36. arya duwipangga, "I Franken-Polished It!" Eyelash Care and Eye Health, 9 July 2012, 11 June 2014, http://emiliorobin.blogspot.com/2012/07/i-franken-polished-it.html
37. Evil Angel, "Girly Franken and Claire's Flakies swatches," Black nail polish and lip gloss, July 2010, 25 April 2014, http://blacknailpolishandlipgloss.blogspot.com/2010/07/girly-franken-and-claires-flakies.html
38. Fairly Charming, 23 April 2014, http://fairlycharming.blogspot.com/

39. Michelle Mismas, "Customization: Frankenpolish & The Art Of Layering," All Lacquered Up, 25 September 2007, 9 May 2014, http://www.alllacqueredup.com/2007/09/customization-frankenpolish-art-of.html
40. The Polish Monster, "FAQ," 28 March 2014, http://polishmonster.com/faq/
41. The Polish Monster, "(Just Another) Mani Monday- Monster Nails!" 16 July 2012, 25 April 2014, http://polishmonster.com/2012/07/16/just-another-mani-monday-monster-nails/
42. Jim Walker, "Everything I know about the indie nail polish business, I learned from Waltham's Polish Pixelle," Brand New Watch, 13 November 2012, 10 August 2013, http://blogs.wickedlocal.com/brandnewwatch/2012/11/13/everything-i-know-about-the-indie-nail-polish-business-i-learned-from-walthams-polish-pixelle/#ixzz2bcZp1usP
43. Cassie Goodwin, "A Beginners Guide to Indie Nail Polish Part 1," Reluctant Femme, 6 August 2013, http://www.reluctantfemme.com/2013/08/a-beginners-guide-to-indie-nail-polish.html
44. Kerri Anne Renzulli, "Nail polish fans start making and selling their own lacquers," NewsObserver.com, 20 March 2013, http://www.newsobserver.com/2013/03/20/2766378/nail-polish-fans-start-making.html
45. Christine, "Say Hello to Indie Nail Polish," Temptalia, 11 December 2012, 11 August 2013, http://www.temptalia.com/say-hello-to-indie-nail-polish
46. Kate, "Indie Interviews: Mckfresh Nail Attire," Lacquerheads of OZ, April 2013, http://www.lacquerheadsofoz.com/2013/04/indie-interviews-mckfresh-nail-attire.html
47. Cassie Goodwin, "A Beginners Guide to Indie Nail Polish Part 1," Reluctant Femme, 6 August 2013, http://www.reluctantfemme.com/2013/08/a-beginners-guide-to-indie-nail-polish.html
48. Ree, "Homemade Chicken and Noodles," The Pioneer Woman, 25 January 2010, 25 March 2014, http://thepioneerwoman.com/cooking/2010/01/homemade-chicken-and-noodles/
49. Slatman and Widdershoven, "Hand Transplants," 76.
50. Sandi, "essie Bridal Collection 2008," Scrangie, 19 March 2009, 21 March 2014, http://www.scrangie.com/2009/03/essie-bridal-collection-2008.html
51. Michelle Mismas, "SpaRitual Mind.Body.Spirit Matte Nail Polish Swatches & Review," All Lacquered Up, 29 September 2009, 24 June 2014, http://www.alllacqueredup.com/2009/09/sparitual-mindbodyspirit-matte-nail.html#.T42RSI6fuHk
52. The Silver Nail, "Lobsters, zombies, and mannequins," 28 February 2012, 15 March 2014, http://thesilvernail.wordpress.com/2012/02/28/lobsters-zombies-and-mannequins/
53. Jackie S., "Show Me Your Mannequin Hands!" All Lacquered Up, 17 December 2009, 15 March 2014, http://www.alllacqueredup.com/2009/12/show-mannequin-hands.html
54. Piff, "THEME WEEK - My Favorite Nude," Polish or Perish, 16 May 2012, 28 March 2014, http://polishorperish.blogspot.com/2012/05/theme-week-my-favorite-nude.html
55. Nora, "Show Me Your Mannequin Hands!" All Lacquered Up, 22 December 2009, 15 March 2014, http://www.alllacqueredup.com/2009/12/show-mannequin-hands.html
56. Elizabeth, "Glossary," Did My Nails, 16 March 2014, http://www.didmynails.com/p/glossary.html
57. Michelle Mismas, "Show Me Your Mannequin Hands!" All Lacquered Up, 15 December 2009, 15 March 2014, http://www.alllacqueredup.com/2009/12/show-mannequin-hands.html
58. Nancy Girl, "MAKEUP MONDAY ♥ MANNEQUIN HANDS," 5 September 2011, 22 March 2014, http://nancyfashionfancy.blogspot.com/2011/09/makeup-monday-mannequin-hands.html

59. Smapte, "Mannequin Hands," That Thing I Like, 1 March 2012, 18 March 2014, http://thatthingilike.wordpress.com/2012/03/01/mannequin-hands/
60. Michelle Mismas, "Show Me Your Mannequin Hands!" All Lacquered Up, 15 December 2009, 15 March 2014, http://www.alllacqueredup.com/2009/12/show-mannequin-hands.html
61. Jenn Rice, "How To Look Like A Hand Model, Via the 'Mannequin Hands Manicure,'" SHEfinds, 20 June 2012, 29 March 2014, http://www.shefinds.com/2012/weve-got-a-serious-case-of-mannequin-hands-syndrome-do-you/
62. I Drink Nail Polish, "Revlon Facets of Fuchsia & Revlon Starry Pink," 30 September 2011, 24 June 2014, http://idrinknailpolish.blogspot.com/2011/09/revlon-facets-of-fuchsia-revlon-starry.html
63. Kirsten, "OPI Red Dazzle," Glittah Gloves, 26 September 2011, 24 June 2014, http://glittagloves.blogspot.com/2011/09/opi-red-dazzle.html
64. Liz Krusenstjerna, "Mannequin Hands: Zoya Farah and Barielle Buddaful," Lacquer Slacker Liz, 12 August 2013, 20 March 2014, http://lacquerslackerliz.blogspot.com/2013/08/mannequin-hands-zoya-farah-and-barielle.html
65. Olivia S., "Etude House Nail Polish Is Saving The Feminist Movement, Probably," xoVain, 2 August 2013, http://www.xovain.com/nails/etude-house-nail-polish; Tracie Egan Morrissey, "Nail Art, the Last Bastion of Female-Centric Beauty," Jezebel, 7 August 2012, 22 June 2014, http://jezebel.com/5930229/nail-art-the-last-bastion-of-female+centric-beauty
66. Nail Nerd, "How To Do Corpse Nails," 24 January 2012, 3 April 2013, http://www.nailnerd.com/how-to-do-corpse-nails/
67. Wormie, "My first crafting injury," Hooked on Crochet, 20 September 2009, 17 April 2014, http://hooked-on-crochet.blogspot.com/2009/09/my-first-crafting-injury.html
68. Ann, "Crafting Injury," November Rose, 19 November 2011, 17 April 2014, http://annsnovemberrose.blogspot.com/2011/11/crafting-injury.html
69. Ann, "Crafting Injury," November Rose, 19 November 2011, 17 April 2014, http://annsnovemberrose.blogspot.com/2011/11/crafting-injury.html
70. Jolynn, "I care so much it hurts......," Etsy, 20 April 2013, 19 April 2014, http://www.etsy.com/teams/7722/discussions/discuss/12175420/
71. nltolonen, "Crafting Injury story...," Splitcoaststampers, 26 March 2009, 19 April 2014, http://www.splitcoaststampers.com/forums/general-stamping-talk-f17/crafting-injury-story-t428240.html#ixzz2zRlAXffV
72. Hope Jahren, as quoted in Mindy Weisberger, "Scientists and #ManicureMonday: Nailed It," Storify, 30 April 2014, https://storify.com/LaMinda/scientists-and-manicuremonday-nailed-it
73. Lindy Elkins-Tanton, "ltelkins: Scientist's hands coding," Twitter, 18 November 2013, 29 April 2014, https://twitter.com/ltelkins/status/402442629205327872/photo/1; Rebecca Deatsman, "rdeatsman: #ManicureMonday pic," Twitter, 18 November 2013, 29 April 2014, https://twitter.com/rdeatsman/status/402496231483518976/photo/1
74. Minibeast Mayhem, "Minibeast Mayhem (minibeastmayhem) on Twitter," Twitter, 28 April 2014, https://twitter.com/minibeastmayhem
75. hjahren1, "What I learned from #ManicureMonday," #HOPEJAHRENSURECANWRITE, 20 November 2013, 29 April 2014, http://hopejahrensurecanwrite.com/2013/11/20/what-i-learned-from-manicuremonday/
76. Jason Bittel, "Scientist Hijacks Seventeen Magazine's #ManicureMonday," Slate, 20 November 2013, 28 April 2014, http://www.slate.com/blogs/future_tense/2013/11/20/manicuremonday_seventeen_magazine
77. sev, "sev (cheryltz on Twitter)," Twitter, 18 November 2013, 29 April 2014, https://twitter.com/HopeJahren/status/402519841765982209
78. Richard Horgan, "Hawaii Scientist Hijacks Seventeen Magazine Hashtag," FishbowlNY, 20 November 2013, 29 April 2014, http://www.mediabistro.com/fishbowlny/seventeen-magazine-manicuremonday-hope-jahren_b102410

79. Momma PhD, "Handy scientists nail #ManicureMonday," Geek Feminism Blog, 20 November 2013, 28 April 2014, http://geekfeminism.org/2013/11/18/handy-scientists-nail-manicuremonday-hashtag/
80. Laura Vanderkam, "What manicures, science have in common: Column," *USA Today*, 9 February 2014, http://www.usatoday.com/story/opinion/2014/02/09/manicure monday-science-women-scientists-column/5342551/
81. Joanne Manaster, "#ManicureMonday–A Lesson in Targeted Science Communication," PsiVid, Scientific American Blog Network, 25 November 2013, 29 April 2014, http://blogs.scientificamerican.com/psi-vid/2013/11/25/manicuremonday-a-lesson-in-targeted-science-communication/
82. Joanne Manaster, "The Science of Beauty," Joanne Loves Science, 6 May 2014, http://www.joannelovesscience.com/science_beauty.html
83. Joanne Manaster, "Flammability of Nailpolish," YouTube, 31 January 2010, 1 May 2014, http://www.youtube.com/watch?v=g9rHmFbFmrg
84. Polish or Perish, 7 July 2014, http://polishorperish.blogspot.com/
85. kittytokaren, "Grooming My (French) Poodle," Polish or Perish, 23 February 2010, 1 May 2014, http://polishorperish.blogspot.com/2010/02/grooming-my-french-poodle.html
86. LabMuffin, "Lab Muffin's Top 13 Polishes of 2013 Part 2: Indies," Polish or Perish, 6 January 2014, http://polishorperish.blogspot.com/2014/01/lab-muffins-top-13-polishes-of-2013_6.html; LabMuffin, "How do thermal polishes work?" Lab Muffin, 14 December 2013, 6 May 2014, http://www.labmuffin.com/2013/12/how-do-thermal-polishes-work.html
87. Michelle, "How do thermal polishes work?" Lab Muffin, 14 December 2013, 6 May 2014, http://www.labmuffin.com/2013/12/how-do-thermal-polishes-work.html
88. Joanne Manaster, "#ManicureMonday–A Lesson in Targeted Science Communication," PsiVid, Scientific American Blog Network, 25 November 2013, 29 April 2014, http://blogs.scientificamerican.com/psi-vid/2013/11/25/manicuremonday-a-lesson-in-targeted-science-communication/; Jayne Lim, "Molecular Nails–Nucleotide Skittles," Cosmetic Proof, 5 June 2012, 6 May 2014, http://www.cosmeticproof.com/2012/06/molecular-nailsnucleotide-skittles.html
89. Andrea, "Bakom Indigo Bananas: Andrea," Sminkan & Emma, 28 July 2013, 14 May 2014, http://www.sminkan.com/2013/07/bakom-indigo-bananas-andrea/
90. Scientista, "About – Scientista | Women in STEM," 9 June 2014, http://www.scientistafoundation.com/about.html
91. Jayne Lim, "Scientista Foundation | Nail Art Inspired by Women in Science," Cosmetic Proof, 8 July 2013, 28 May 2014, http://www.cosmeticproof.com/2013/07/scientista-foundation-nail-art-inspired.html
92. BlushBug, "Scientista Foundation | Nail Art Inspired by Women in Science," Cosmetic Proof, 28 May 2014, http://www.cosmeticproof.com/2013/07/scientista-foundation-nail-art-inspired.html
93. Fuss, "Fashion and the Homospectatorial"; Lewis and Rolley, "Ad(dressing) the Dyke"; Vänskä, "Why Are There No Lesbian?"
94. Pollock, *Vision and Difference*.

SELECTED BIBLIOGRAPHY

Books and academic journals are listed in this bibliography and in shortened citations in the endnotes. Detailed information about website references is included in the endnotes.

Abowitz, Kathleen Knight. "A Pragmatist Revisioning of Resistance Theory." *American Educational Research Journal* 37, no. 4 (Winter 2000): 877–907.
Aizenberg, Edna. "'I Walked with a Zombie': The Pleasures and Perils of Postcolonial Hybridity." *World Literature Today* 73, no. 3 (1999): 461–66.
Allison, Anne. "Portable Monsters and Commodity Cuteness: Pokémon as Japan's New Global Power." *Postcolonial Studies* 6, no. 3 (2003): 381–95.
Althusser, Louis. "Ideology and Ideological State Apparatuses." In *The Anthropology of the State: A Reader,* edited by Aradhana Sharma and Akhil Gupta, 86–111. Blackwell Publishing, 2006.
Andrews, Christopher Paul. *Blood and Glitter: Monster Subjectivity in a Concentration of Camp.* MFA Thesis, University of Notre Dame, 2010. 19 August 2013, http://etd.nd.edu/ETD-db/theses/available/etd-04152010-155142/
Arendell, Terry. "Conceiving and Investigating Motherhood: The Decade's Scholarship." *Journal of Marriage and the Family* 62, no. 4 (November 2000): 1192–207.
Armstrong, Carol. "Biology, Destiny, Photography: Difference According to Diane Arbus." *October* 66 (Fall 1993): 29–54.
Aronson, Pamela. "Feminists Or 'Postfeminists'?: Young Women's Attitudes toward Feminism and Gender Relations." *Gender and Society* 17, no. 6 (December 2003): 903–22.
Babuscio, Jack. "Camp and the Gay Sensibility." In *Camp Grounds: Style and Homosexuality,* edited by David Bergman, 19–38. Amherst, MA: The University of Massachusetts Press, 1993.
Bain, Alison L. "Constructing an Artistic Identity." *Work, Employment and Society* 19, no. 1 (2005): 25–46.
Balsamo, Anne Marie. *Technologies of the Gendered Body: Reading Cyborg Women.* Durham: Duke University Press, 1999.

Bambacas, Christyana. "Thinking about White Weddings." *Journal of Australian Studies* 26, no. 72 (2002): 191–200.

Barthes, Roland. *Camera Lucida: Reflections on Photography*, translated by Richard Howard. New York: Farrar, Strauss, and Giroux, 1981.

———. *Roland Barthes by Roland Barthes*, translated by Richard Howard. Berkeley: University of California Press, 1977.

Bartky, Sandra L. "Foucault, Femininity, and the Modernization of Patriarchal Power." In *Feminism and Foucault*, edited by Irene Diamond and Lee Quinby, 61–86. Boston: Northeastern University Press, 1988.

Baumgardner, Jennifer, and Amy Richards. *Manifesta: Young Women, Feminism, and the Future*. New York: Farrar, Straus and Giroux, 2000.

Behuniak, Susan M. "The Living Dead? The Construction of People with Alzheimer's Disease as Zombies." *Ageing and Society* 31 (2011): 70–92.

Benkler, Yochai. *The Wealth of Networks: How Social Production Transforms Markets and Freedom*. New Haven: Yale University Press, 2006.

Bergstein, Mary. "'The Artist in His Studio': Photography, Art, and the Masculine Mystique." *Oxford Art Journal* 18, no. 2 (1995): 45–58.

Betterton, Rosemary. "Prima Gravida: Reconfiguring the Maternal Body in Visual Representation." *Feminist Theory* 3, no. 3 (2002): 255–70.

Black, Paula. *The Beauty Industry: Gender, Culture, Pleasure*. New York: Routledge, 2004.

———. "Discipline and Pleasure: The Uncanny Relationship Between Feminism and the Beauty Industry." In *Feminism in Popular Culture*, edited by Joanne Hollows and Rachel Moseley, 143–59. Oxford: Berg, 2006.

———. "'Ordinary People Come Through Here': Locating the Beauty Salon in Women's Lives." *Feminist Review* 71 (2002): 2–17.

Bordo, Susan. "Beauty (Re)Discovers the Male Body." In *Beauty Matters*, edited by Peg Zeglin Brand, 112–54. Bloomington: Indiana University Press, 2000.

———. *Unbearable Weight: Feminism, Western Culture, and the Body*. Berkeley: University of California Press, 1993.

Bordo, Susan R. "The Body and the Reproduction of Femininity: A Feminist Appropriation of Foucault." In *Gender/Body/Knowledge: Feminist Reconstructions of Being and Knowing*, edited by Alison M. Jaggar and Susan R. Bordo, 13–33. New Brunswick, NJ: Rutgers University Press, 1989.

Bourne, Kristina A., and Pamela J. Forman. "Living in a Culture of Overwork: An Ethnographic Study of Flexibility." *Journal of Management Inquiry* 23, no. 1 (2014): 68–79.

Brand, Peg Zeglin, ed. *Beauty Matters*. Bloomington: Indiana University Press, 2000.

Bratich, Jack. "The Digital Touch: Craft-Work as Immaterial Labour and Ontological Accumulation." *Ephemera: Theory and Politics in Organization* 10, nos. 3–4 (2010): 303–18.

Bratich, Jack Z., and Heidi M. Brush. "Fabricating Activism: Craft-Work, Popular Culture, Gender." *Utopian Studies* 22, no. 2 (2011): 233–60.

Braun, Virginia. "'The Women Are Doing It for Themselves': The Rhetoric of Choice and Agency around Female Genital 'Cosmetic Surgery.'" *Australian Feminist Studies* 24, no. 60 (June 2009): 233–49.

Braziel, Jana Evans, and Kathleen LeBesco. "Performing Excess," *Women and Performance: A Journal of Feminist Theory* 15, no. 2 (2005): 9–13.

———, eds. *Bodies Out of Bounds: Fatness and Transgression*. Berkeley: University of California Press, 2001.

Breen, T. H. *The Marketplace of Revolution: How Consumer Politics Shaped American Independence*. New York: Oxford University Press, 2004.
Brooks, Ann. *Postfeminisms: Feminism, Cultural Theory, and Cultural Forms*. New York: Routledge, 1997.
Brown, Jeffrey A. "Gender and the Action Heroine: Hardbodies and the 'Point of No Return.'" *Cinema Journal* 35, no. 3 (Spring 1996): 52–71.
Brownmiller, Susan. *Femininity*. New York: Simon and Schuster, 1984.
Brundson, Charlotte. "Feminism, Postfeminism, Martha, Martha, and Nigella." *Cinema Journal* 44, no. 2 (Winter 2005): 110–16.
Bruni, Attila, Silvia Gherardi, and Barbara Poggio. "Doing Gender, Doing Entrepreneurship: An Ethnographic Account of Intertwined Practices." *Gender, Work and Organization* 11, no. 4 (July 2004): 406–29.
Buchanan, Elizabeth A., ed. *Readings in Virtual Research Ethics: Issues and Controversies*. Hershey, PA: Idea Group, 2004.
Bunting, Madeleine. *Willing Slaves: How the Overwork Culture is Ruling Our Lives*. New York: Harper Perennial, 2005.
Buszek, Maria Elena. Introduction to *Extra/Ordinary: Craft and Contemporary Art*, edited by Maria Elena Buszek, 1–21. Durham: Duke University Press, 2011.
Butler, Jess. "For White Girls Only?: Postfeminism and the Politics of Inclusion." *Feminist Formations* 25, no. 1 (Spring 2013): 35–58.
Butler, Judith. *Bodies That Matter: On the Discursive Limits of "Sex."* New York: Routledge, 1993.
———. *Gender Trouble: Feminism and the Subversion of Identity*. New York: Routledge, 1990.
———. "Lana's 'Imitation': Melodramatic Repetition and the Gender Performative." *Genders* 9 (Fall 1990): 1–18.
———. *The Psychic Life of Power: Theories in Subjection*. Stanford: Stanford University Press, 1997.
Carey, Renee N., Ngaire Donaghue, and Pia Broderick. "'What You Look Like Is Such a Big Factor': Girls' Own Reflections about the Appearance Culture in an All-Girls' School." *Feminism and Psychology* 21, no. 3 (2010): 299–316.
Casey, Catherine. "'Come, Join Our Family': Discipline and Integration in Corporate Organizational Culture." *Human Relations* 52, no. 2 (1999): 155–78.
Cataldi, Sue L. *Emotion, Depth, and Flesh: A Study of Sensitive Space*. Albany: State University of New York Press, 1993.
Chapman, Gwen E. "Making Weight: Lightweight Rowing, Technologies of Power, and Technologies of the Self." *Sociology of Sport Journal* 14 (1997): 205–23.
Chase, Cheryl. "Hermaphrodites with Attitude: Mapping the Emergence of Intersex Political Activism." *GLQ: A Journal of Lesbian and Gay Studies* 4, no. 2 (1998): 189–211.
Chen, Eva. "Neoliberalism and Popular Women's Culture: Rethinking Choice, Freedom and Agency." *European Journal of Cultural Studies* 16 no. 4 (August 2013): 440–52.
Chen, Gina Masullo. "Don't Call Me That: A Techno-feminist Critique of the Term Mommy Blogger." *Mass Communication and Society* 16, no. 4 (2013): 510–32.
Chen, Tina Mai. "Dressing for the Party: Clothing, Citizenship, and Gender-Formation in Mao's China." *Fashion Theory: The Journal of Dress, Body and Culture* 5, no. 2 (May 2001): 143–71.
Chun, Wendy Hui Kyong. Introduction to *New Media, Old Media: A History and Theory Reader*, edited by Wendy Hui Kyong Chun, 1–10. New York: Routledge, 2006.

Clover, Carol. *Men, Women, and Chain Saws: Gender in the Modern Horror Film.* Princeton: Princeton University Press, 1992.
Cole, Elizabeth R., and Alyssa N. Zucker. "Black and White Women's Perspectives on Femininity." *Cultural Diversity and Ethnic Minority Psychology* 13, no. 1 (2007): 1–9.
Collins, Patricia Hill. *Black Sexual Politics: African Americans, Gender, and the New Racism.* New York: Routledge, 2004.
Coltrane, Scott. "Household Labor and the Routine Production of Gender." *Social Problems* 36, no. 5 (December 1989): 473–90.
Corinne, Tee. *Cunt Coloring Book.* San Francisco, Last Gasp Publication, 1975.
Cornford, Matthew, and David Cross. "Inside Outside." *Third Text* 18, no. 6 (2004): 657–65.
Cott, Nancy F. *The Bonds of Womanhood: "Woman's Sphere" in New England, 1780–1835.* New Haven: Yale University Press, 1977.
Craig, Maxine Leeds. "Race, Beauty, and the Tangled Knot of a Guilty Pleasure." *Feminist Theory* 7, no. 2 (2006): 159–77.
Craik, Jennifer. *The Face of Fashion: Cultural Studies in Fashion.* New York: Routledge, 1994.
———. *Fashion: The Key Concepts.* Oxford: Berg, 2009.
Cranny-Francis, Anne. "Touching Film: The Embodied Practice and Politics of Film Viewing and Filmmaking." *The Senses and Society* 4, no. 2 (July 2009): 163–78.
Creed, Barbara. *The Monstrous-Feminine: Film, Feminism, Psychoanalysis.* London and New York: Routledge, 1993.
Culler, Jonathan. "The Closeness of Reading." *ADE Bulletin* 149 (2010): 20–25.
Cumberland, Sharon. "Private Uses of Cyberspace: Women, Desire, and Fan Culture." In *Rethinking Media Change: The Aesthetics of Transition*, edited by David Thorburn, Henry Jenkins, and Brad Seawell, 261–79. Cambridge, MA: MIT Press, 2004.
Daniels, Jessie. "Race and Racism in Internet Studies: A Review and Critique." *New Media and Society* 15, no. 5 (August 2013): 695–719.
Davis, Angela Y. "Afro Images: Politics, Fashion, and Nostalgia." *Critical Inquiry* 21, no. 1 (Autumn 1994): 37–45.
Davis, Kathy. "Remaking the She-Devil: A Critical Look at Feminist Approaches to Beauty." *Hypatia* 6, no. 2 (Summer 1991): 21–43.
———. *Reshaping the Female Body: The Dilemma of Cosmetic Surgery.* New York: Routledge, 1995.
Dawkins, Nicole. "Do-It-Yourself: The Precarious Work and Postfeminist Politics of Handmaking (in) Detroit." *Utopian Studies* 22, no. 2 (2011): 261–84.
de Chernatony, Leslie. "Brand Management through Narrowing the Gap Between Brand Identity and Brand Reputation." *Journal of Marketing Management* (1999): 157–79.
de Lauretis, Teresa. *Technologies of Gender: Essays on Theory, Film, and Fiction.* Bloomington: Indiana University Press, 1987.
Dean, Carolyn. "Boys and Girls and 'Boys': Popular Depictions of Childlike Adults in the United States, 1850–1930." *Journal of American Culture* 23, no. 3 (Fall 2000): 17–35.
Dendle, Peter. "The Zombie as a Barometer of Cultural Anxiety." In *Monsters and the Monstrous: Myths and Metaphors of Enduring Evil*, edited by Niall Scott, 45–57. Amsterdam, The Netherlands: Editions Rodopi B.V., 1994.
Dhaenens, Frederik. "Slashing the Fiction of Queer Theory: Slash Fiction, Queer Reading, and Transgressing the Boundaries of Screen Studies, Representations, and Audiences." *Journal of Communication Inquiry* 32, no. 4 (October 2008): 335–47.

Diamond, Irene, and Lee Quinby, eds. *Feminism and Foucault: Reflections on Resistance*. Boston: Northeastern University Press, 1988.

Dillaway, Heather, and Elizabeth Paré. "Locating Mothers: How Cultural Debates About Stay-at-Home Versus Working Mothers Define Women and Home." *Journal of Family Issues* 29, no. 4 (April 2008): 437–64.

Dimen, Muriel. "Sexuality and Suffering, Or the Eew! Factor." *Studies in Gender and Sexuality* 6, no. 1 (2005): 1–18.

Dobson, Amy Shields. "'Individuality Is Everything': 'Autonomous' Femininity in MySpace Mottos and Self-Descriptions." *Continuum: Journal of Media and Cultural Studies* 26, no. 3 (June 2012): 371–83.

Douglas, Mary. *Implicit Meanings: Selected Essays in Anthropology*. London: Routledge, 1999.

Douglas, Susan J., and Meredith W. Michaels. *The Mommy Myth: The Idealization of Motherhood and How It Has Undermined All Women*. New York: Free Press, 2004.

———. "The New Momism." In *Maternal Theory: Essential Readings*, edited by Andrea O'Reilly, 617–39. Toronto: Demeter Press, 2007.

Drummond, William. *The Works of William Drummond, of Hawthornden. Consisting of Those which Were Formerly Printed, and Those which Were Design'd for the Press*. Edinburgh: James Watson, 1711.

Duberley, Joanne, and Marylyn Carrigan. "The Career Identities of 'Mumpreneurs': Women's Experiences of Combining Enterprise and Mothering." *International Small Business Journal* 31, no. 6 (September 2013): 629–51.

Duncan, Carol. "The MoMA's Hot Mamas." In *The Expanding Discourse: Feminism and Art History*, edited by Norma Broude and Mary D. Garrard, 347–58. New York: Harper Collins, 1992.

Dyer, Richard. *White*. London: Routledge, 1997.

Edwards, Marlo. "The Blonde with the Guns: *Barb Wire* and the 'Implausible' Female Action Hero." *Journal of Popular Film and Television* 32, no. 1 (Spring 2004): 39–47.

Eileraas, Katrina. "Reframing the Colonial Gaze: Photography, Ownership, and Feminist Resistance." *MLN* 118 (2003): 807–40.

Eisenstein, Elizabeth L. *The Printing Press as an Agent of Change: Communications and Transformations in Early-Modern Europe*, vol. 1. London: Cambridge University Press, 1979.

Ekinsmyth, Carol. "Challenging the Boundaries of Entrepreneurship: The Spatialities and Practices of UK 'Mumpreneurs.'" *Geoforum* 42 (2011): 104–14.

Emberley, Julia. "The Fashion Apparatus and the Deconstruction of Postmodern Subjectivity." *Canadian Journal of Political and Social Theory* 11, nos. 1–2 (1987): 39–50.

Faludi, Susan. *Backlash: The Undeclared War Against American Women*. New York: Random House, 1991.

Fausto-Sterling, Anne. *Sexing the Body: Gender Politics and the Construction of Sexuality*. New York: Basic Books, 2000.

Fay, Jennifer. "Dead Subjectivity: White Zombie, Black Baghdad." *CR: The New Centennial Review* 8, no. 1 (2008): 81–101.

Fenichell, Stephen. *Plastic: The Making of a Synthetic Century*. New York: Harper Business, 1996.

Festa, Lynn. "Personal Effects: Wigs and Possessive Individualism in the Long Eighteenth Century." *Eighteenth-Century Life* 29, no. 2 (Spring 2005): 47–90.

Filax, Gloria. "Resisting Resistors: Resistance in Critical Pedagogy Classrooms." *Journal of Educational Thought* 31, no. 3 (1997): 259–69.

Fitzgerald, Louise. "'Let's Play Mummy': Simulacrum Babies and Reborn Mothers." *European Journal of Cultural Studies* 14, no. 1 (2011): 25–39.
Fleming, Peter. "Metaphors of Resistance." *Management Communication Quarterly* 19, no. 1 (August 2005): 45–66.
Foucault, Michel. "Technologies of the Self." In *Technologies of the Self: A Seminar with Michel Foucault*, edited by Luther H. Martin, Huck Gutman, and Patrick H. Hutton, 16–49. Amherst: University of Massachusetts Press, 1988.
Frankenberg, Ruth. Introduction to *Displacing Whiteness: Essays in Social and Cultural Criticism*, edited by Ruth Frankenberg, 1–33. Durham: Duke University Press, 1997.
Freeman, Elizabeth. *The Wedding Complex: Forms of Belonging in Modern American Culture*. Durham: Duke University Press, 2002.
Friedan, Betty. *The Feminine Mystique*. New York: W. W. Norton and Company, 1963.
Frueh, Joanna. *Monster/Beauty: Building the Body of Love*. Berkeley: University of California Press, 2001.
Fuss, Diana. "Fashion and the Homospectatorial Look." *Critical Inquiry* 18, no. 4 (Summer 1992): 713–37.
Gajjala, Radhika, and Annapurna Mamidipuni. "Gendering Processes within Technological Environments: A Cyberfeminist Issue." *Rhizomes* 04 (Spring 2002), 6 February 2013, http://www.rhizomes.net/issue4/gajjala.html
Gamson, Joshua. "Sylvester." *Camera Obscura* 65, 22, no. 2 (2007): 140–43.
Gauntlett, David. *Making Is Connecting: The Social Meaning of Creativity, from DIY and Knitting to YouTube and Web 2.0*. Cambridge: Polity Press, 2011.
Gerhard, Jane. "Sex and the City." *Feminist Media Studies* 5, no. 1 (2005): 37–49.
Gibson, William. *Neuromancer*. New York: Ace Books, 1984.
Gill, Rosalind. "Empowerment/Sexism: Figuring Female Sexual Agency in Contemporary Advertising." *Feminism and Psychology* 18, no. 1 (2008): 35–60.
———. "Postfeminist Media Culture: Elements of Sensibility." *European Journal of Cultural Studies* 10, no. 2 (2007): 147–66.
Gillett, James. "Internet Web Logs as Cultural Resistance: A Study of the SARS Arts Project." *Journal of Communication Inquiry* 31, no. 1 (January 2007): 28–43.
Gillingham, Lauren, Jennifer Henderson, Julie Murray, and Janice Schroeder. "Of Bombs, Baking, and Blahniks." *English Studies in Canada* 31, nos. 2–3 (June/September 2005): 22–30.
Gillis, Stacy. "The (Post)Feminist Politics of Cyberpunk." *Gothic Studies* 9, no. 2 (November 2007): 7–19.
Gitelman, Lisa, and Geoffrey B. Pingree. "What's New About New Media?" In *New Media, 1740–1915*, edited by Lisa Gitelman and Geoffrey B. Pingree, xix–xii. Cambridge, MA: MIT Press, 2003.
Goings, Kenneth W. *Mammy and Uncle Mose: Black Collectibles and American Stereotyping*. Bloomington: Indiana University Press, 1994.
Greenhill, Anita, and Melanie Wilson. "Haven or Hell? Telework, Flexibility and Family in the e-society: A Marxist Analysis." *European Journal of Information Systems* 15, no. 4 (August 2006): 379–88.
Greer, Betsy. "Craftivist History." In *Extra/Ordinary: Craft and Contemporary Art*, edited by Maria Elena Buszek, 175–83. Durham: Duke University Press, 2011.
Gregg, Melissa. "Learning to (Love) Labour: Production Cultures and the Affective Turn." *Communication and Critical/Cultural Studies* 6, no. 2 (June 2009): 209–14.
Groeneveld, Elizabeth. "'Be a Feminist or Just Dress Like One': BUST, Fashion and Feminism as Lifestyle." *Journal of Gender Studies* 18, no. 2 (June 2009): 179–90.

Grosz, Elizabeth. *Volatile Bodies: Toward a Corporeal Feminism*. Bloomington: Indiana University Press, 1994.

Guy, Donna J. "True Womanhood in Latin America." *Journal of Women's History* 14, no. 1 (Spring 2002): 170–73.

Gwilliam, Tassie. "Cosmetic Poetics: Coloring Faces in the Eighteenth Century." In *Body and Text in the Eighteenth Century*, edited by Veronica Kelly and Dorothea E. von Mücke, 144–59. Stanford: Stanford University Press, 1994.

Hall, Elaine J., and Marnie Salupo Rodriguez. "The Myth of Postfeminism." *Gender and Society* 17, no. 6 (December 2003): 878–902.

Hallstein, D. Lynn O'Brien. "Conceiving Intensive Mothering." *Journal for the Association of Research on Mothering* 8, nos. 1–2 (2006): 96–108.

Hardt, Michael, and Antonio Negri. *Multitude: War and Democracy in the Age of Empire*. New York: Penguin, 2004.

Hargreaves, Andy. "Resistance and Relative Autonomy Theories: Problems of Distortion and Incoherence in Recent Marxist Analyses of Education." *British Journal of Sociology of Education* 3, no. 2 (1982): 107–26.

Harper, Stephen. "Night of the Living Dead: Reappraising an Undead Classic." *Bright Lights Film Journal*, 50 (2005), 30 July 2012, http://www.brightlightsfilm.com/50/night.html.

Harris, Daniel. "The Aesthetic of Drag." *Salmagundi* 108 (Fall 1995): 62–74.

Hartigan, John, Jr. "Establishing the Fact of Whiteness." *American Anthropologist* 99, no. 3 (September 1997): 495–505.

Harvey, Adia M. "Becoming Entrepreneurs: Intersections of Race, Class, and Gender at the Black Beauty Salon." *Gender and Society* 19, no. 6 (December 2005): 789–808.

Hayles, N. Katherine. *How We Became Posthuman: Virtual Bodies in Cybernetics, Literature, and Informatics*. Chicago: University of Chicago Press, 1999.

———. *How We Think: Digital Media and Contemporary Technogenesis*. Chicago: University of Chicago Press, 2012.

Hays, Sharon. *The Cultural Contradictions of Motherhood*. New Haven: Yale University Press, 1996.

Heise, Franka. "'I'm a Modern Bride': On the Relationship between Marital Hegemony, Bridal Fictions, and Postfeminism." *M/C Journal* 15, no. 6 (2012), 17 June 2014, http://www.journal.media-culture.org.au/index.php/mcjournal/article/viewArticle/573

Helford, Elyce Rae. "Postfeminism and the Female Action-Adventure Hero: Positioning *Tank Girl*." In *Future Females, The Next Generation: New Voices and Velocities in Feminist Science Fiction Criticism*, edited by Marleen Barr, 291–308. New York: Rowman and Littlefield Publishers 1999.

Hellekson, Karen, and Kristina Busse, eds. *Fan Fiction and Fan Communities in the Age of the Internet: New Essays*. Jefferson, NC: McFarland and Company, 2006.

Hemmings, Clare. "Invoking Affect: Cultural Theory and the Ontological Turn." *Cultural Studies* 19, no. 5 (September 2005): 548–67.

Hewitt, Nancy A. "Taking the True Woman Hostage." *Journal of Women's History* 14, no. 1 (Spring 2002): 156–62.

Hilbrecht, Margo, Susan M. Shaw, Laura C. Johnson, and Jean Andrey. "'I'm Home for the Kids': Contradictory Implications for Work-Life Balance of Teleworking Mothers." *Gender, Work and Organization* 15, no. 5 (September 2008): 454–78.

Hill, E. Jeffrey, Joseph G. Grzywacz, Sarah Allen, Victoria L. Blanchard, Christina Matz-Costa, Sandee Shulkin, and Marcie Pitt-Catsouphes. "Defining and Conceptualizing Workplace Flexibility." *Community, Work and Family* 11, no. 2 (May 2008): 149–63.

Hoberman, J., and Jonathan Rosenbaum. *Midnight Movies*. New York: Harper and Row, 1983.

Hochschild, Arlie Russell. *The Time Bind: When Work Becomes Home and Home Becomes Work*. New York: Henry Holt and Company, 1997.

Hongladarom, Soraj, and Charles Ess, eds. *Information Technology Ethics: Cultural Perspectives*. Hershey, PA: Idea Group Reference, 2007.

hooks, bell. *Ain't I a Woman: Black Women and Feminism*. Boston: South End Press, 1981.

Horne, Philip. "I Shopped with a Zombie." *Critical Quarterly* 34, no. 4 (1992): 97–110.

Hosoda, Megumi, Eugene F. Stone-Romero, and Gwen Coats. "The Effects of Physical Attractiveness on Job-Related Outcomes: A Meta-analysis of Experimental Studies." *Personnel Psychology* 56 (2003): 431–62.

Humphreys, Ashlee, and Kent Grayson. "The Intersecting Roles of Consumer and Producer: A Critical Perspective on Co-production, Co-creation and Prosumption." *Sociology Compass* 2, no. 3 (2008): 963–80.

Ingraham, Chrys. *White Weddings: Romancing Heterosexuality in Popular Culture*. London: Routledge, 1999.

Jackson, Stevi. "Gender, Sexuality and Heterosexuality: The Complexity (and Limits) of Heteronormativity." *Feminist Theory* 7, no. 1 (2006): 105–21.

Jacobs, Karen. "Optic/Haptic/Abject: Revisioning Indigenous Media in Victor Masayesva, Jr and Leslie Marmon Silko." *Journal of Visual Culture* 3, no. 3 (2004): 291–316.

Jenkins, Henry. *Fans, Bloggers, and Gamers: Exploring Participatory Culture*. New York: New York University Press, 2002.

Jermier, John M., David Knights, and Walter R. Nord, eds. *Resistance and Power in Organizations*. New York: Routledge, 1994.

Johnson, Barbara. "Teaching Deconstructively." In *Writing and Reading Differently*, edited by G. Douglas Atkins and M. L. Johnson, 140–48. Lawrence: University of Kansas Press, 1986.

Johnson, Samuel. *Letters*, edited by George Birkbeck Hill. Oxford: The Clarendon Press, 1892.

Johnston, Deirdre D., and Debra H. Swanson. "Constructing the 'Good Mother': The Experience of Mothering Ideologies by Work Status." *Sex Roles* 54 (2006): 509–19.

Jowett, Donna. "Origins, Occupation, and the Proximity of the Neighbour." In *Who Is This "We,"* edited by Eleanor M. Godway and Geraldine Finn, 11–30. Montreal: Black Rose Books, 1994.

Juris, Jeffrey S. "Reflections on #Occupy Everywhere: Social Media, Public Space, and Emerging Logics of Aggregation." *American Ethnologist* 39, no. 2 (May 2012): 259–79.

Kahn, Richard, and Douglas Kellner. "New Media and Internet Activism: From the 'Battle of Seattle' to Blogging." *New Media and Society* 6, no. 1 (2004): 87–95.

Kang, Miliann. *The Managed Hand: Race, Gender, and the Body in Beauty Service Work*. Berkeley: University of California Press, 2010.

Kaplan, E. Ann. "Is the Gaze Male?" In *Powers of Desire: The Politics of Sexuality*, edited by Ann Snitow, C. Stansell, and S. Thompson, 309–27. New York: Monthly Review Press, 1983.

Karim-Cooper, Farah. "'This Alters Not thy Beauty': Face-Paint, Gender and Race in Richard Brome's *The English Moor*." *Issues in Review* 10, no. 2 (2007): 140–49.

Kearney, Mary Celeste. *Mediated Girlhoods: New Explorations of Girls' Media Culture*. New York: Routledge, 2006.

———. "Pink Technology: Mediamaking Gear for Girls." *Camera Obscura* 74, 25, no. 2 (2010): 1–39.

Kelley, Robin D. G. "Nap Time: Historicizing the Afro." *Fashion Theory: The Journal of Dress, Body and Culture* 1, no. 4 (November 1997): 339–51.

Kerber, Linda K. "Separate Spheres, Female Worlds, Woman's Place: The Rhetoric of Women's History." *The Journal of American History* 75, no. 1 (June 1988): 9–39.

Kerr, Audrey Elisa. "The Paper Bag Principle: Of the Myth and the Motion of Colorism." *Journal of American Folklore* 118 (2005): 271–89.

Khondker, Habibul Haque. "Role of the New Media in the Arab Spring." *Globalizations* 8, no. 5 (2011): 675–79.

Kim, L. S. "'Sex and the Single Girl' in Postfeminism: The F Word on Television." *Television and New Media* 2, no. 4 (November 2001): 319–34.

Kirkland, Ewan. "The Caucasian Persuasion of Buffy the Vampire Slayer." *Slayage: The Online International Journal of Buffy Studies* 5, no. 1, 17 (June 2005), 17 June 2014, http://slayageonline.com/essays/slayage17/Kirkland.htm

Krauss, Rosalind. *The Originality of the Avant-Garde and Other Modernist Myths.* Cambridge, MA: MIT Press, 1994.

Kristeva, Julia. *The Powers of Horror: An Essay on Abjection.* New York: Columbia University Press, 1982.

Kukla, Rebecca. "Talking Back: Monstrosity, Mundanity, and Cynicism in Television Talk Shows." *Rethinking Marxism* 14, no. 1 (2002): 67–96.

Lauro, Sarah Juliet, and Karen Embry. "A Zombie Manifesto: The Nonhuman Condition in the Era of Advanced Capitalism." *boundary 2* 35, no. 1 (2008): 85–108.

Lazar, Michelle M. "The Right to Be Beautiful: Postfeminist Identity and Consumer Beauty Advertising." In *New Femininities: Postfeminism, Neoliberalism and Subjectivity*, edited by Rosalind Gill and Christina Scharff, 37–51. London: Palgrave Macmillan, 2011.

Le Fanu, James. "The Hand: A Philosophical Inquiry into Human Being." *Journal of the Royal Society of Medicine* 97, no. 4 (April 2004): 201–2.

LeBesco, Kathleen. *Revolting Bodies?: The Struggle to Redefine Fat Identity.* Amherst, MA: University of Massachusetts Press, 2004.

Leddy, Thomas. "Sparkle and Shine." *British Journal of Aesthetics* 37, no. 3 (July 1997): 259–73.

Lerner, Gerda. "The Lady and the Mill Girl: Changes in the Status of Women in the Age of Jackson." *American Studies* 10, no. 1 (Spring 1969): 5–15.

Lewis, Charles. "Working the Ritual: Professional Wedding Photography and the American Middle Class." *Journal of Communication Inquiry* 22, no. 1 (January 1998): 72–92.

Lewis, Reina. "Looking Good: The Lesbian Gaze and Fashion Imagery." *Feminist Review* 55 (Spring 1997): 92–109.

Lewis, Reina, and Katrina Rolley. "Ad(dressing) the Dyke: Lesbian Looks and Lesbian Looking." In *Outlooks: Lesbian and Gay Sexualities and Visual Cultures*, edited by Peter Horne and Reina Lewis, 178–90. New York: Routledge, 1996.

Lightning, Robert K. "Interracial Tensions in *Night of the Living Dead.*" *Cineaction* 53 (2000): 22–29.

Lippard, Lucy R. *From the Center: Feminist Essays on Women's Art.* New York: Dutton, 1976.

Lipsitz, George. "The Possessive Investment in Whiteness: Racialized Social Democracy and the 'White' Problem in American Studies." *American Quarterly* 47, no. 3 (September 1995): 369–87.

Lopez, Lori Kedo. "The Radical Act of 'Mommy Blogging': Redefining Motherhood through the Blogosphere." *New Media and Society* 11, no. 5 (2009): 729–47.

Lotan, Gilad, Erhardt Graeff, Mike Ananny, Devin Gaffney, Ian Pearce, and danah boyd. "The Revolutions Were Tweeted: Information Flows during the 2011 Tunisian and Egyptian Revolutions." *International Journal of Communication* 5 (2011): 1375–405.

Lotz, Amanda D. "Postfeminist Television Criticism: Rehabilitating Critical Terms and Identifying Postfeminist Attributes." *Feminist Media Studies* 1, no. 1 (2001): 105–21.

Loudermilk, A. "Eating 'Dawn' in the Dark: Zombie Desire and Commodified Identity in George A. Romero's 'Dawn of the Dead.'" *Journal of Consumer Culture* 3, no. 1 (2003): 83–108.

Lowenstein, Adam. "Living Dead: Fearful Attractions of Film." *Representations* 110, no. 1 (Spring 2010): 196–200.

Mäntymäki, Tiina. "Women Who Kill Men: Gender, Agency and Subversion in Swedish Crime Novels." *European Journal of Women's Studies* 20, no. 4 (2013): 441–54.

Markham, Annette, and Elizabeth Buchanan with contributions from the AOIR Ethics Working Committee. "Ethical Decision-Making and Internet Research 2.0: Recommendations from the AOIR Ethics Working Committee." 2012, 27 July 2013, http://www.aoir.org/reports/ethics2.pdf

Marks, Laura U. *Touch: Sensuous Theory and Multisensory Media*. Minneapolis: University of Minnesota Press, 2002.

Marsan, Loran. "Cher-ing/Sharing Across Boundaries." *Visual Culture and Gender* 5 (2010): 47–63.

Martin, Joanne. "Deconstructing Organizational Taboos: The Suppression of Gender Conflicts in Organizations." *Organization Science* 1, no. 4 (November 1990): 339–59.

Matchar, Emily. *Homeward Bound: The New Cult of Domesticity*. New York: Simon and Schuster, 2013.

Mayo, Elton. *The Human Problems of an Industrial Civilization*. New York: Viking Press, 1933.

McRobbie, Angela. *The Aftermath of Feminism: Gender, Culture and Social Change*. Los Angeles: Sage, 2009.

Medved, Caryn E., and Erika L. Kirby. "Family CEOs: A Feminist Analysis of Corporate Mothering Discourses." *Management Communication Quarterly* 18, no. 4 (May 2005): 435–78.

Menon, Elizabeth K. "Virtual Realities, Technoaesthetics and Metafictions of Digital Culture." In *The State of the Real: Aesthetics in the Digital Age*, edited by Damian Sutton, Susan Brind, and Ray McKenzie, 151–61. London: I. B. Tauris, 2007.

Mercer, Kobena. "Black Hair/Style Politics." *New Formations* 3 (1987): 33–54.

Meyer, Laura, and Faith Wilding. "Collaboration and Conflict in the Fresno Feminist Art Program: An Experiment in Feminist Pedagogy." *n.paradoxa* 26 (July 2010): 40–51.

Meyer, Stephanie. *Twilight*. New York: Little, Brown and Company, 2005.

Milkie, Melissa A. "Contested Images of Femininity: An Analysis of Cultural Gatekeepers' Struggles with the 'Real Girl' Critique." *Gender and Society* 16, no. 6 (December 2002): 839–59.

Miller, Laura L. "Not Just Weapons for the Weak: Gender Harassment as a Form of Protest for Army Men." *Social Psychology Quarterly* 60, no. 1 (1997): 32–51.

Minahan, Stella, and Julie Wolfram Cox. "Stitch 'n Bitch: Cyberfeminism, a Third Place and the New Materiality." *Journal of Material Culture* 12, no. 1 (2007): 5–21.

Modleski, Tania. *Feminism without Women: Culture and Criticism in a "Postfeminist" Age*. London: Routledge, 1991.

Moody, Todd C. "Conversations with Zombies." *Journal of Consciousness Studies* 1, no. 2 (1994): 312–75.

Morreall, John. "Cuteness." *British Journal of Aesthetics* 33, no. 3 (1991): 39–47.
Morrison, Aimée. "'Suffused by Feeling and Affect': The Intimate Public of Personal Mommy Blogging." *Biography* 34, no. 1 (Winter 2011): 37–55.
Mules, Warwick. "This Face: a Critique of Faciality as Mediated Self-Presence." *Transformations* 18 (2010), 15 June 2014, http://www.transformationsjournal.org/journal/issue_18/article_01.shtml
Mulvey, Laura. "Visual Pleasure and Narrative Cinema." In *Visual and Other Pleasures*, 14–28. Bloomington: Indiana University Press, 1989.
———. "Unmasking the Gaze: Feminist Film Theory, History, and Film Studies." In *Reclaiming the Archive: Feminism and Film History*, edited by Vicki Callahan, 17–31. Detroit: Wayne State University Press, 2010.
Mumby, Dennis K. "Theorizing Resistance in Organization Studies: A Dialectical Approach." *Management Communication Quarterly* 19, no. 1 (2005): 19–44.
Munro, Petra. "Resisting 'Resistance,' Stories Women Teachers Tell." *JCT: An Interdisciplinary Journal of Curriculum Studies* 12, no. 1 (Spring 1996): 16–28.
Myzelev, Alla. "Whip Your Hobby into Shape: Knitting, Feminism and Construction of Gender." *Textile* 7, no. 2 (2009): 148–63.
Nakamura, Lisa. *Digitizing Race: Visual Cultures on the Internet*. Minneapolis: University of Minnesota Press: 2008.
Nathanson, Elizabeth. *Television and Postfeminist Housekeeping: No Time for Mother*. New York: Routledge, 2013.
Nead, Lynda. "Seductive Canvases: Visual Mythologies of the Artist and Artistic Creativity." *Oxford Art Journal* 18, no. 2 (1995): 59–69.
Negra, Diane. "'Quality Postfeminism?': Sex and the Single Girl on HBO." *Genders OnLine Journal* 39 (2004), 15 August 2013, http://www.genders.org/g39/g39_negra.html
———. *What A Girl Wants? Fantasizing the Reclamation of Self in Postfeminism*. New York: Routledge, 2009.
Nochlin, Linda. *Women, Art, and Power and Other Essays*. New York: Harper and Row, 1984.
Nurka, Camille. "Postfeminist Autopsies." *Australian Feminist Studies* 17, no. 38 (2002): 177–89.
Oberhauser, Ann M. "The Home as 'Field': Households and Homework in Rural Appalachia." In *Thresholds in Feminist Geography: Difference, Methodology, Representation*, edited by John Paul Jones, Heidi J. Nast, and Susan M. Roberts, 165–82. Lanham, MD: Rowman and Littlefield, 1997.
Ortner, Sherry B. "Resistance and the Problem of Ethnographic Refusal." *Comparative Studies in Society and History* 37, no. 1 (January 1995): 173–93.
Osborne, Jessica. "Feminism." In *Key Concepts in Cultural Theory*, edited by Andrew Edgar and Peter Sedgwick, 143–45. London: Routledge, 1999.
Oswald, Ramona Faith. "A Member of the Wedding? Heterosexism and Family Ritual." In *Lesbian Rites: Symbolic Acts and the Power of Community*, edited by Ramona Faith Oswald, 107–31. New York: Harrington Park Press, 2003.
Owens, Craig. "Photography 'en Abyme.'" *October* 5 (Summer 1978): 73–88.
Paasonen, Susanna. *Figures of Fantasy: Internet, Women, and Cyberdiscourse*. New York: Peter Lang, 2005.
Palmer, Caroline. "Brazen Cheek: Face-Painters in Late Eighteenth-Century England." *Oxford Art Journal* 31, no. 2 (2008): 195–213.
Parker, Rozsika. "'The Creation of Femininity,' from *The Subversive Stitch: Embroidery and the Making of the Feminine*." In *The Craft Reader*, edited by Glenn Adamson, 491–500. Oxford: Berg, 2010.

———. *The Subversive Stitch: Embroidery and the Making of the Feminine.* London: Women's Press, 1984.
Patrick, Adele. "Defiantly Dusty: A (Re)Figuring of 'Feminine Excess.'" *Feminist Media Studies* 1, no. 3 (2001): 361–78.
———. "Queening It: Women's Taste for Jewelry Excesses in Post-war Britain." *Women and Performance: A Journal of Feminist Theory* 15, no. 2 (2005): 119–46.
Patterson, Eleanor. "Fracturing Tina Fey: A Critical Analysis of Postfeminist Television Comedy Stardom." *The Communication Review* 15 (2012): 232–51.
Payne, Adrian, Kaj Storbacka, Pennie Frow, and Simon Knox. "Co-creating Brands: Diagnosing and Designing the Relationship Experience." *Journal of Business Research* 62, no. 3 (2009): 379–89.
Peake, Bryce. "He is Dead, and He is Continuing to Die: A Feminist Psycho-semiotic Reflection on Men's Embodiment of Metaphor in a Toronto Zombie Walk." *Journal of Contemporary Anthropology* 1, no. 1 (2010): 49–71.
Peiss, Kathy. *Hope in a Jar: The Making of America's Beauty Culture.* New York: Metropolitan Books, 1998.
Peters, Benjamin. "And Lead Us Not into Thinking the New Is New: A Bibliographic Case for New Media History." *New Media and Society* 11, nos. 1–2 (2009): 13–30.
Petersen, Anne Helen. "That Teenage Feeling: *Twilight*, Fantasy, and Feminist Readers." *Feminist Media Studies* 12, no. 1 (2012): 51–67.
Pham, Minh-Ha T. "Susie Bubble is a Sign of The Times." *Feminist Media Studies* 13, no. 2 (2013): 245–67.
Phillippy, Patricia. *Painting Women: Cosmetics, Canvases, and Early Modern Culture.* Baltimore: Johns Hopkins University Press, 2006.
Pierre, Jemima. "'I Like Your Colour!' Skin Bleaching and Geographies of Race in Urban Ghana." *Feminist Review* (2008): 9–29.
Pinedo, Isabel Cristina. *Recreational Terror: Women and the Pleasures of Horror Film Viewing.* Albany, NY: State University of New York Press, 1997.
Plant, Sadie. *Zeroes and Ones: Digital Women and the New Technoculture.* New York: Doubleday, 1997.
Poitevin, Kimberly. "Inventing Whiteness: Cosmetics, Race, and Women in Early Modern England." *The Journal for Early Modern Cultural Studies* 11, no. 1 (Spring–Summer 2011): 59–89.
Pollock, Griselda. *Vision and Difference: Femininity, Feminism and the Histories of Art.* London: Routledge, 1988.
Portwood-Stacer, Laura. "Do-It-Yourself Feminism: Feminine Individualism and the Girlie Backlash in the DIY/Craftivism Movement." October 2005, 27 November 2012, http://citation.allacademic.com//meta/p_mla_apa_research_citation/1/6/9/6/3/pages169635/p169635-1.php
Prahalad, C. K., and Venkat Ramaswamy. "Co-creation Experiences: The Next Practice in Value Creation." *Journal of Interactive Marketing* 18, no. 3 (Summer 2004): 5–14.
Prasad, Pushkala, and Anshuman Prasad. "Stretching the Iron Cage: The Constitution and Implications of Routine Workplace Resistance." *Organization Science* 11, no. 4 (July–August 2000): 387–403.
Press, Andrea L. *Women Watching Television: Gender, Class, and Generation in the American Television Experience.* Philadelphia: University of Pennsylvania Press, 1991.
Priest, Hannah. "What's Wrong With Sparkly Vampires?" The Gothic Imagination, 20 July 2011, 4 February 2012, http://www.gothic.stir.ac.uk/guestblog/whats-wrong-with-sparkly-vampires/

Railla, Jean. *Get Crafty: Hip Home Ec.* New York: Broadway Books, 2004.

Ray, Tapas. "The 'Story' of Digital Excess in Revolutions of the Arab Spring." *Journal of Media Practice* 12, no. 2 (2011): 189–96.

Rheingold, Howard. *The Virtual Community: Homesteading on the Electronic Frontier.* Cambridge, MA: MIT Press, 1993.

Rich, Adrienne. *Of Woman Born: Motherhood as Experience and Institution.* New York: Bantam Books, 1976.

Rind, Bruce, and Prashant Bordia. "Effect of Server's 'Thank You' and Personalization on Restaurant Tipping." *Journal of Applied Social Psychology* 25, no. 9 (May 1995): 745–51.

Ritzer, George, and Nathan Jurgenson. "Production, Consumption, Prosumption: The Nature of Capitalism in the Age of the Digital 'Prosumer.'" *Journal of Consumer Culture* 10, no. 1 (2010): 13–36.

Roberts, John, and Stephen Wright. "Art and Collaboration." *Third Text* 18, no. 6 (2004): 531–32.

Roberts, Mary Louise. "True Womanhood Revisited." *Journal of Women's History* 14, no. 1 (Spring 2002): 150–55.

Robertson, Kristy. "How to Knit an Academic Paper." *Craft Perception and Practice: A Canadian Discourse* 3 (2007): 85–92.

———. "Rebellious Doilies and Subversive Stitches: Writing a Craftivist History." In *Extra/Ordinary: Craft and Contemporary Art*, edited by Maria Elena Buszek, 184–203. Durham: Duke University Press, 2011.

Rosenthal, Angela. "Visceral Culture: Blushing and the Legibility of Whiteness in Eighteenth-Century British Portraiture." *Art History* 27, no. 4 (2004): 563–92.

Rousseau, Signe. *Food and Social Media: You Are What You Tweet.* Lanham, MD: AltaMira Press, 2012.

Rowe, Katherine. *Dead Hands: Fictions of Agency, Renaissance to Modern.* Stanford: Stanford University Press, 1999.

Ruddick, Sara. "Maternal Thinking." In *Maternal Theory: Essential Readings*, edited by Andrea O'Reilly, 96–113. Toronto: Demeter Press, 2007.

San Juan, Rose Marie. "The Horror of Touch: Anna Morandi's Wax Models of Hands." *Oxford Art Journal* 34, no. 3 (2011): 433–47.

Saraswati, L. Ayu. "Cosmopolitan Whiteness: The Effects and Affects of Skin-Whitening Advertisements in a Transnational Women's Magazine in Indonesia." *Meridians: Feminism, Race, Transnationalism* 10, no. 2 (2010): 15–41.

Sarikakis, Katharine, and Liza Tsaliki. "Post/feminism and the Politics of Mediated Sex." *International Journal of Media and Cultural Politics* 7, no. 2 (2011): 109–19.

Sayer, Liana C. "Gender, Time and Inequality: Trends in Women's and Men's Paid Work, Unpaid Work and Free Time." *Social Forces* 84, no. 1 (September 2005): 285–303.

Schaefer, Tali. "Disposable Mothers: Paid In-Home Caretaking and the Regulation of Parenthood." *Yale Journal of Law and Feminism* 19 (2008): 305–51.

Schor, Mira. "Patrilineage." *Art Journal* 50, no. 2 (Summer 1991): 58–63.

Schowalter, Dana. "Silencing The Shriver Report: Postfeminist Citizenship and News Discourse." *The Communication Review* 15, no. 3 (2012): 218–31.

Schudson, Michael. "Citizens, Consumers, and the Good Society." *The Annals of the American Academy of Political and Social Science* 611 (May 2007): 236–49.

Schultz, Susanne. "Dissolved Boundaries and 'Affective Labor': On the Disappearance of Reproductive Labor and Critique in Empire." *Capitalism Nature Socialism* 17, no. 1 (March 2006): 77–82.

Scott, D. Travers. "The Postfeminist User: Feminism and Media Theory in Two Interactive Media Properties." *Feminist Media Studies* 10, no. 4. (2010): 457–75.
Scott, James. *Weapons of the Weak: Everyday Forms of Peasant Resistance*. New Haven: Yale University Press, 1985.
Secomb, Linnell. "Fractured Community." *Hypatia* 15, no. 2 (2000): 133–50.
Sedgwick, Eve Kosofsky. *Touching Feeling: Affect, Pedagogy, Performativity*. Durham: Duke University Press, 2003.
Shakespeare, William. *The Merchant of Venice*. New Haven: Yale University Press, 2006.
Shelley, Mary Wollstonecraft. *Frankenstein: Or, the Modern Prometheus*. New York: Penguin Books, 1994.
Showden, Carisa R. "What's Political about the New Feminisms?" *Frontiers* 30, no. 2 (2009): 166–98.
Siles, Ignacio. "Web Technologies of the Self: The Arising of the 'Blogger' Identity." *Journal of Computer-Mediated Communication* 17 (2012): 408–21.
Slater, Don. "Trading Sexpics on IRC: Embodiment and Authenticity on the Internet." *Body and Society* 4, no. 4 (1998): 91–117.
Slatman, Jenny, and Guy Widdershoven. "Hand Transplants and Bodily Integrity." *Body and Society* 16, no. 3 (2010): 69–92.
Smith, Shawn Michelle. "'Baby's Picture Is Always Treasured': Eugenics and the Reproduction of Whiteness in the Family Photograph Album." *Yale Journal of Criticism* 11, no. 1 (1998): 197–220.
Snitow, Ann. "Feminism and Motherhood: An American Reading." *Feminist Review* 40 (Spring 1992): 32–51.
Sobal, Jeffery, Caron Bove, and Barbara Rauschenbach. "Weight and Weddings: The Social Construction of Beautiful Brides." In *Interpreting Weight: The Social Management of Fatness and Thinness*, edited by Jeffery Sobal and Donna Maurer, 113–35. New York: Aldine de Gruyter, 1999.
Sobchack, Vivian, ed. *Meta-morphing: Visual Transformation and the Culture of Quick Change*. Minneapolis: University of Minnesota Press, 2000.
Sontag, Susan. *On Photography*. New York: Penguin, 1977.
Stern, Katherine. "What Is Femme? The Phenomenology of the Powder Room." *Women: A Cultural Review* 8, no. 2 (1997): 183–96.
Stockton, Kathryn Bond. *The Queer Child, or Growing Sideways in the Twentieth Century*. Durham: Duke University Press, 2009.
Stolle, Dietlind, Marc Hooghe, and Michele Micheletti. "Politics in the Supermarket: Political Consumerism as a Form of Political Participation." *International Political Science Review* 26, no. 3 (2005): 245–69.
Stoller, Debbie. *The Happy Hooker: Stitch 'n Bitch Crochet*. New York: Workman Publishing Company, Inc., 2006.
———. *Son of Stitch 'n Bitch: 45 Projects to Knit and Crochet for Men*. New York: Workman Publishing Company, Inc., 2007.
———. *Stitch 'n Bitch: The Knitter's Handbook*. New York: Workman Publishing Company, Inc., 2003.
Straayer, Chris. *Deviant Eyes, Deviant Bodies*. New York: Columbia University Press, 1996.
Tasker, Yvonne, and Diane Negra. Introduction to "In Focus: Postfeminism and Contemporary Media Studies." *Cinema Journal* 44, no. 2 (Winter 2005): 107–10.
Taylor, Stephanie. "Negotiating Oppositions and Uncertainties: Gendered Conflicts in Creative Identity Work." *Feminism and Psychology* 21, no. 3 (2010): 354–71.

Thomas, Robyn, and Annette Davies. "What Have the Feminists Done for Us? Feminist Theory and Organizational Resistance." *Organization* 12, no. 5 (2005): 711–40.

Thomas-Hunt, Melissa C., and Katherine W. Phillips. "When What You Know Is Not Enough: Expertise and Gender Dynamics in Task Groups." *Personality and Social Psychology Bulletin* 30, no. 12 (December 2004): 1585–98.

Thurer, Shari L. *Myths of Motherhood: How Culture Reinvents the Good Mother.* New York: Houghton Mifflin, 1994.

Toffoletti, Kim. *Cyborgs and Barbie Dolls: Feminism, Popular Culture and the Posthuman Body.* London and New York: I. B. Tauris, 2007.

Turkle, Sherry. *Life on the Screen: Identity in the Age of the Internet.* New York: Simon and Schuster, 1995.

Vänskä, Annamari. "Why Are There No Lesbian Advertisements?" *Feminist Theory* 6, no. 1 (2005): 67–85.

Verrips, Jojada. "'Haptic Screens' and Our 'Corporeal Eye.'" *Etnofoor* 15, nos. 1–2 (2002): 21–46.

Vincent, Carol, and Stephen J. Ball. "'Making Up' the Middle Class Child: Families, Activities and Class Dispositions." *Sociology* 41, no. 6 (2007): 1061–77.

Wacjman, Judy. *TechnoFeminism.* Cambridge, UK: Polity, 2004.

Wakeford, Nina. "Developing Methodological Frameworks for Studying the World Wide Web." In *Web Studies*, 2nd. ed., edited by David Gauntlett and Ross Horsley, 34–50. London: Arnold, 2004.

Waldby, Catherine. "Biomedicine, Tissue Transfer and Intercorporeality." *Feminist Theory* 3, no. 3 (2002): 239–54.

Walker, John A., and Sarah Chaplin. *Visual Culture: An Introduction.* Manchester: Manchester University Press, 1997.

Walters, Suzanna Danuta, and Laura Harrison. "Not Ready to Make Nice: Aberrant Mothers in Contemporary Culture." *Feminist Media Studies* 14, no. 1 (2014): 38–55.

Weeks, Kathi. "Labor, Feminist Critique, and Post-Fordist Politics." *Ephemera: Theory and Politics in Organization* 7, no. 1 (2007): 233–49.

Wells, Stanley, and Michael Dobson, eds. *The Oxford Companion to Shakespeare.* Oxford: Oxford University Press, 2001.

Welter, Barbara. "The Cult of True Womanhood: 1820–1860." *American Quarterly* 18, no. 2, part 1 (Summer, 1966): 151–74.

West, Candace, and Don H. Zimmerman. "Doing Gender." *Gender and Society* 1, no. 2 (June 1987): 125–51.

Wharton, Carol S. "Finding Time for the 'Second Shift': The Impact of Flexible Work Schedules on Women's Double Days." *Gender and Society* 8, no. 2 (June 1994): 189–205.

White, Michele. "Babies Who Touch You: Reborn Dolls, Artists, and the Emotive Display of Bodies on eBay." In *Political Emotions*, edited by Janet Staiger, Ann Cvetkovich, and Ann Reynolds, 66–89. London: Routledge, 2010.

———. *The Body and the Screen: Theories of Internet Spectatorship.* Cambridge, MA: MIT Press, 2006.

———. *Buy It Now: Lessons from eBay.* Durham: Duke University Press, 2012.

———. "Concerns about Being Visible and Expressions of Pleasure: Women's Internet Wedding Forum Considerations of Boudoir Photography Sessions." *Interstitial: A Journal of Modern Culture and Events* (2013), 17 June 2014, http://interstitialjournal.com/

———. "The Dirt on 'Trash the Dress' Resistance: Photographers, Brides, and the Mess of Post-wedding Imaging Sessions." *Critical Studies in Media Communication* 29, no. 2 (2012): 113–31.

———. "Dirty Brides and Internet Settings: The Affective Pleasures and Troubles with Trash the Dress Photography Sessions." *South Atlantic Quarterly* 110, no. 3 (Summer 2011): 645–72.

———. "Killing Whiteness: The Critical Positioning of Zombie Walk Brides in Internet Settings." In *Monster Culture in the 21st Century: A Reader*, edited by Marina Levina and Diem-My T. Bui, 209–25. New York: Bloomsbury Academic, 2013.

———. "'Trash the Dress': Wedding Conventions and Resistance." *Communication Currents* 7, no. 5 (October 2012), 23 July 2014, http://www.natcom.org/CommCurrentsArticle.aspx?id=2811

Williams, Kristen A. "'Old Time Mem'ry': Contemporary Urban Craftivism and the Politics of Doing-It-Yourself in Postindustrial America." *Utopian Studies* 22, no. 2 (2011): 303–20.

Williams, Linda. "When the Woman Looks." In *The Dread of Difference: Gender and the Horror Film*, edited by Barry Keith Grant, 15–34. Austin: University of Texas Press, 1996.

Wilson, Frank R. *The Hand: How Its Use Shapes the Brain, Language, and Human Culture*. New York: Pantheon Books, 1998.

Wolf, Naomi. *The Beauty Myth: How Images of Beauty Are Used Against Women*. New York: William Morrow and Company, 1991.

Wollstonecraft, Mary. *A Vindication of the Rights of Woman: With Strictures on Political and Moral Subjects*. Boston: Thomas and Andrews, 1792.

Young, Elizabeth. *Black Frankenstein: The Making of an American Metaphor*. New York: New York University Press, 2008.

Young, Iris Marion. *On Female Body Experience: "Throwing Like a Girl" and Other Essays*. New York: Oxford University Press, 2005.

Zeiler, Kristin, and Anette Wickström. "Why Do 'We' Perform Surgery on Newborn Intersexed Children?: The Phenomenology of the Parental Experience of Having a Child with Intersex Anatomies." *Feminist Theory* 10, no. 3 (2009): 359–77.

Zelizer, Viviana A. "The Creation of Domestic Currencies." *The American Economic Review* 84, no. 2 (May 1994): 138–42.

INDEX

#ManicureMonday 202–203
404 error message 20–21

abject 100, 107, 113–115, 143, 166; death 1, 86; filth 99, 114, 115, 143; women 100, 113, 141, 148, 181, 200
about page 5, 10, 40, 51, 66, 108, 134
adult 68, 70, 74, 85, 102, 161, 167, 169
affect 42, 51, 67, 86, 110, 113, 115, 133, 162; Barthes on 133, 179; glitter's production of 162; hand's production of 22, 33, 69, 81, 88, 98, 196; horror as 86, 87, 111–113, 138, 192, 196; love 69, 98; maternal feeling 22, 51, 56, 69–70, 75; Sedgwick on 22, 51, 67; touching feeling 22, 69, 77–80, 179, 180, 196, 201; wedding's production of 97–98, 111, 146
affective labor 42, 76
ageism 19, 23, 85, 169
agency 4, 139, 140; crafting as 19; ecommerce as 35; postfeminist assertions of 8, 159; technology's association with 19, 139; white heterosexual men's 9, 139; women's 10, 53, 116–117, 162–163; zombies' association with 136
Althusser, Louis 67, 131
Apple: FaceTime, 193; iPad 19
Armstrong, Carol 132, 137
artifice 165, 172
artist 69, 176; collaboration 73–74, 80; elevation of 71, 74, 105–108, 178; gender and 65, 67, 70, 78, 105; guild 71–72; hierarchy and 14, 47, 50, 71, 73, 106; mother and 22, 45, 49–51, 54, 65, 67–68, 70, 74–75, 79, 85–87; painful work of 54–56, 76; passion of 51, 69, 72; professionalism of 22, 68, 71; self-discovery of 50, 69; skill of 56, 66, 69, 71, 72
authority 100; hailing as 78; opposition to 101; women's 20, 35, 105, 168
authorship 18, 73
avatar 4, 5, 25, 53, 150

Barthes, Roland 133, 179, 194
Bartky, Sandra L. 158, 162–163
beauty 23, 111, 140, 157, 158–160, 161–164, 166, 170, 172–173, 178–179, 180, 195, 204; monster 148, 192, 196; refusal of 143, 192, 196, 200; whiteness' relationship to 3, 23, 81, 132, 139–140, 143, 151, 172–173, 199; zombies' influence on 23, 132, 139, 141, 143, 148, 167
beauty blogging 160–161, 163–164, 167
belly plate 22, 83–84
blank 136, 138, 142, 173; bride as 131; nail as 73, 136; photograph as 138, 142; reborn as 65, 73, 175; wedding dress as 107; zombie as 136, 138, 141
blog 14–17, 68, 101, 118, 167. *See also* beauty blogging; mommy blogging; nail polish blogging
blood 98, 137; defiling 23, 117, 119, 130–132, 148, 149, 166, 200; disrupts

wedding 98, 143, 146; liveliness of 76, 150; race and 138, 143; residue of violence 97–98, 119, 121, 130–132, 141, 146; symbol of love 98; women's relationship to 114, 137, 141
blur 79, 205; glitter's production of 159–160, 177–179; women's role as 53, 55–56
bodily sensation 22, 67, 82, 86, 111–113, 138; abjection 86, 113–114, 115, 143; eew factor 86; pain 52, 76, 112–113, 114, 172, 201; shivering 86, 138, 111–113, 138
body 5, 6, 136, 148, 178–181; construction of 4–5, 23, 67, 73, 76, 163, 190–191; contact with 33, 51, 69, 78–80, 86, 132, 136, 138, 168, 193, 195; control of viii, 7, 100, 102, 159, 166–167, 169–170, 190; dematerialized 69, 177–178, 180, 198; extended 33, 55, 120, 139, 157, 165, 172, 175, 191; fat 15–16; fragmented 112, 172, 176, 193–194; gendered 5, 15–16, 82–84, 113, 164, 191, 194; interrogation of 24, 55, 87, 99, 100, 114, 139, 146, 158, 159, 172, 179–180, 191, 200; monstrous 1, 112, 130, 148, 193; open 114, 119, 132, 135, 141, 159–160, 166, 172, 173, 177, 180; raced 5, 20, 81, 142; reborn 73, 76–77; technological 2, 70, 135, 178; unruly 23, 106, 112; viewing of 85, 109, 149, 157–158, 179, 201, 203, 205
Bordo, Susan 5, 163
boudoir photography 103, 110
Bratich, Jack 19, 33, 139, 157
Bride of Frankenstein 1–2, 7, 24, 98, 112
Butler, Judith 39, 67, 165, 170–171

camera 16, 109, 178, 179, 191
camp 165, 166
cannibalism 115, 138, 141, 146, 147, 148, 180
Caputa, Joelle 118–119
Cher 164–165
childishness 1, 23, 70, 103, 106, 111, 167, 168
choice 159, 167; consumer 9, 163, 180; feminist critique of 13, 180–181; postfeminist promise of 8–9, 15, 37, 47; technological 9, 97; TTD as 107; wedding as 103; workplace and 41
class viii, 13, 19, 23, 106, 140, 162, 170
close reading. *See* textual analysis

Clover, Carol 112, 165–166
collaborate 16, 18, 23, 35, 71–73, 117, 130, 148, 174–175
collectible 65, 66, 74, 78
collecting 110, 121
collector 35, 65, 69, 74, 79, 83, 85, 110, 173
community 137; affective labor as 42; blogger 174–175; craft 34; ecommerce 21, 33–36, 38, 40–45, 52–54, 96
cooking 11, 14, 15, 174–175, 180–181, 195, 198
Cooper, John Michael 104–109, 111, 113
copy 2, 16, 18, 116, 130–132, 136–137, 140, 146
cosmetics 2–3, 23, 82, 116, 138, 140, 141–144, 148–150, 157–181
counter-aesthetic 104–106, 143–144, 162, 192, 196
crafter 12, 18–20, 49, 50, 53, 194, 201
crafting: community and 34; ecommerce and 37, 47–49, 53, 55–56, 96; family and 13, 42, 48–50, 52–53; feminism's relationship to 12–14; hand and 15, 34, 51–52, 161, 178, 193–194, 198, 201; new domesticity's relationship to 12, 18–21, 49; reborn and 65, 69, 76; resistance and 18–20, 149; as technology 24–25; women's relationship to 12–13, 15, 19–21, 24–25, 34, 53, 55–56, 190, 201
craftivism 19, 20
Craftster 19–20, 24
Culler, Jonathan 3, 4
cult of true womanhood 11–12

de Lauretis, Teresa 6, 101, 157
dirt 99, 112–115, 132, 161; challenges femininity 99, 104, 106, 112–115, 149, 161, 166, 171; childishness and 103; fingernails and 149, 190, 200; glitter as 161, 171; race and 149–150; wedding dress and 98, 100
divorce 22, 118–121
doing business 40
doing gender 39–40, 163, 164, 166
Doll Games, The 190–192
domesticity 2, 3, 7–8, 9–12, 14, 24, 37, 42, 50, 56, 174. *See also* new domesticity
domestic work 6, 13, 37
Douglas, Susan J., and Meredith W. Michaels 39, 74
drag 23, 161, 164–165, 170–171
Drummond, Ree 15–18, 45, 198–199
Dyer, Richard 132, 139, 140, 143, 151

Index

empowerment 3, 5, 8, 9, 17, 18, 101, 121; bride's 98, 103, 106, 116, 119; crafting as 18–21, 24; ecommerce as 20–21, 35, 37, 50, 54, 134; feminist critique of 6, 7, 16, 38, 108–109, 160, 191, 203, 205; glitter as 166; postfeminist descriptions of 8–9, 12, 15, 35, 159; race and 6, 10; technological 9, 10, 24, 100–101
engagement ring 15, 97, 102
engagement to be married 15, 97, 98, 102, 110, 119–120
Eric, Mark 105–108, 113, 118
erotica vii, 106–107, 110, 112
expertise: consumerism and 46; downplaying of 14–15, 16, 45–46, 168; women's association with 34, 50, 72, 145, 169, 173

face 1, 2, 147, 161, 163, 176, 190, 193–194, 205
Facebook 10, 42
FaceTime 193
failure 114, 139, 178, 195
fake fingernails 190, 202
family 13, 34, 45, 46, 56, 69, 70, 71; corporation's use of 33, 36, 38, 42; crafting's association with 12, 13, 48–53, 70; wedding's structuring of 2, 98, 101, 120, 146; whiteness and 2, 146, 149–150; women's association with 7–8, 9, 13, 18, 36–38, 40, 41, 48–53
fan 18, 51, 132, 135
feminism 2, 5, 7–9, 11–17, 25, 37, 70, 83, 99, 100, 113, 174, 202; beauty culture and 23, 25, 158–160, 162–164, 172; crafting and 12–14, 19, 25, 48–49; domesticity and 11–14, 15; film theory and 6, 16, 111; gaze and 23, 109–110, 119, 175–176, 191, 205–206; motherhood and 34–35, 38–42; postfeminism and 7–9; resistance to 11, 12–13; second-wave 12–14, 37, third-wave 13–14
feminist research 2, 4
film theory 6; haptic 179; horror 86, 112, 114, 166; psychoanalytic 16, 108–109, 114, 178–179; race and 140
fingernails. *See* nails
fingers 33, 51, 78, 97, 98, 120, 178, 179, 195
flexible work 41, 43, 48, 55
flickering signifier 159, 160, 164, 178

Flickr 130–132, 133–134, 137, 138, 141, 142
franken 24, 173, 174, 181, 194–201, 202, 204
Frankenstein 1, 24, 86, 173, 174, 181, 194–196
free labor 22, 42, 44, 46, 50, 51, 56
Fuss, Diana 109

gaze 79, 99, 108–109, 191; abject 113; difficult to 114, 175; heterosexual 101, 108–109; men as object of 17; women as object of 101, 116–117, 201–202; women's empowered 16, 17, 119, 158, 175–176; women's erotic 23–24, 108–109, 180. *See also* lesbian gaze; male gaze
genitals 1, 19, 22, 65, 83–85, 105, 164, 191
Gillis, Stacy 101, 116–117
glitter jelly sandwich 11, 173–175, 176, 197–181
good: bad behavior and being 198; eBay members as 40–41, 46; ecommerce's construction of 39, 41; mother as 12, 39, 41, 46, 74; women as 149, 169, 170
Greer, Betsy 19, 20
groom 111; death of 1, 98; killing of 22–23, 98, 112, 120, 131, 147; marriage and 23, 96, 116, 131, 145–146; murderous 98, 142
Grosz, Elizabeth 100, 113, 114
growing sideways 69–71, 85–87, 135, 136–137; reborn and 70–71, 75, 79, 84; resisting adulthood as 85–87, 98, 103, 104, 167; resisting heterosexuality as 111, 121
guild 71–72

hail 67–68, 78–80, 116, 130, 131, 135, 147, 148–149
hand: connection through 52, 77–80; corpse 173, 199; crafting and 15, 34, 67, 69, 115, 178, 181, 190; creativity and 15, 80; death and 22, 132, 136, 148, 198–199; disruption of 98, 180, 191, 198; domesticity and 2; emotion through 52, 67, 69, 77–80, 97–98, 143; extension of 33, 139, 178; femininity and 22, 98, 147–150, 157, 196; hailing 69, 78–80, 135, 148; human's relationship to 15, 80, 136, 198; lobster 24, 173, 199; mannequin 198–200; monstrous 24, 148, 181, 193,

198, 201; nail polish and 24, 193, 198; photographs of 160–161, 178, 191, 193–194, 202–203; pointer vii, 78, 80, 135, 148, 161; power represented through 10, 15, 33, 161, 191; race and 10, 15, 22, 81, 132, 143, 144, 199; technology and 52; touch and 22, 33, 51, 52, 67, 79–81, 193, 194; violence and 97–98, 149; work and 2, 52, 76, 198, 202–203; zombie 24, 173, 199; zombie's relationship to 130–136, 143, 147, 148–50

handcraft. *See* crafting; handmade

handmade: ecommerce and 20, 47; emotion through 53; family and 34, 42, 53, 70; feminist implications of 175; good of 12; hand and 15, 195; individuality and 12, 198; love represented through 51, 96–97; nail polish and 195; queering 190; touch through 51, 96; women's relationship to 12, 53, 56; work of 51

Hardt, Michael, and Antonio Negri 42, 56

Hayles, N. Katherine 4, 5, 159

heterosexuality 15, 24, 103; challenge to 1, 8, 17, 69, 70, 98, 101, 104, 106, 112, 120, 131, 141, 174, 180; ecommerce's construction of 20, 36, 96; gaze's relationship to 17, 23, 24, 109; gender and 10, 24, 108, 137, 200; Internet's construction of 8–9, 10, 24, 134; race and 145–148; TTD and 23, 99, 101, 102, 104, 109–10, 112, 119; wedding ring and 15, 98; wedding's relationship to 1, 2, 102–104, 111, 121, 146; women's forum and 98, 104, 108–111, 120–121; zombie's challenge to 121, 131, 135, 137, 141–142, 145–148, 180

home studio 50–51

horror 120; embodied 86, 111–112, 114, 138; glitter as 166; reborn as 86; theory of 111–112, 165–166; TTD as 23, 97–98, 111–112, 114, 116, 119; viewing as 111–113; wedding culture and 23, 98, 114, 146; women's bodies and 86, 112, 165–166, 201; zombie walks and 132

how-to 23, 132, 138, 139, 142, 145, 148, 161, 173

Index

Kramer, Leah 19, 24
Kristeva, Julia 86, 100, 114

layer 76, 139, 141–142, 143–145, 160, 173, 176, 180
lesbian 98, 103, 105, 147–148, 164, 200
lesbian gaze 109–110, 205
Lewis, Reina, and Katrina Rolley 109–110, 111
limited edition 65, 72–73
Lim, Jayne 204–205
liveness 79, 81, 86–87, 131, 136–138, 140, 180, 193
logo 10, 20, 160
love 51–52, 69; affect 51, 131; of crafting 34, 51–53, 104; ecommerce's construction of 44, 46, 48, 51, 96, 134; of glitter 167–168, 171; hand's association with 51; heterosexual 70, 96; maternal 36, 38, 51–52; monster 197, 200; of nail polish 197, 200, 204; queer 69, 98, 121, 178, 200; reborn and 65, 69, 75–77, 79; of technology 10, 110; of weddings 96–97, 110, 121; work as 76; zombie and 134, 146

make me a sandwich 11, 174–175, 180–181
male gaze 101, 109, 116, 158, 201, 202. *See also* gaze
Manaster, Joan 203–204
ManicureMonday 202–203
mannequin hand 199–200
Marlboro Woman, The 16–18
marriage 103, 146; challenge to 22, 98, 112, 121; crafting and 70; heterosexual 98, 103; TTD and 98, 103, 112, 118–119, 121; zombie's dissipation of 23, 146
Marsan, Loran 164–165
masculinity: artistry's relationship to 39, 70, 105; challenge to 65, 84; normative 6, 10, 84; race and 6, 10; technology and 5, 10, 24, 39; women's performances of 110
Matchar, Emily 12, 14
maternal reproduction 19, 42, 85; artistry's relationship to 3, 47, 49, 67, 85; challenge to 1–2, 98, 70, 135; crafting's relationship to 42, 76; monstrous 2, 85–86, 116, 130, 137, 166; production's relationship to 25; queer 70, 75, 85; race and 146; reborn and 70; script of 2, 98, 102, 118, 146; as work 36. *See also* technological reproduction

mess 114, 115, 148–149, 168
Miller + Miller Photography 119–120
mommy blogging 18, 43
monster 193; baby as 87; beauty 192; bride of Frankenstein 1; challenges norms 112; nail polish as 194–198; women as 112, 114, 166, 192
monstrous 1, 7, 114, 132, 148, 173, 193; body 165, 193; challenges norms 23, 132, 148, 198; franken as 194–198; glitter as 166, 169, 171; hand as 148, 198; nail polish as 24, 173, 181; nails as 201; wedding and 2; whiteness 23, 132, 143, 151; women as 86–87, 101, 114, 130, 135, 141, 148, 169, 180–181, 193, 194; zombie as 116
morphing 70, 160
mother-artist 54, 65, 181. *See also* mother-producer
motherhood 37; commodification of 18, 43, 75; community through 18; construction of women through 2; as controlling concept 38–39; creativity and 37, 47, 49–50, 53, 70; ecommerce's construction of 47; ecommerce seller and 36–38, 53–54; feminist consideration of 38–40, 74–75; normative 34, 43, 78, 163; postfeminism and 39, 47; reborn and 75, 85; revision of 18, 34, 75, 85, 150
mother-producer 42, 65, 68, 76, 87. *See also* mother-artist
mud 103, 104, 106, 114, 117, 118
Mulvey, Laura 16, 108–109, 181

nail art 148, 157, 181, 194, 200–202, 204
nail polish blogging 24, 73, 160–161, 167, 177; assertion of skill through 173, 174, 176, 178; body parts and 177, 178, 180, 193–194, 198; challenge to norms through 174–175, 178–180, 196; community through 174; creativity and 168, 174, 178, 201, 204; franken and 173, 181, 195–196; monstrosity and 173, 193, 194, 196–197, 201; nails' value for 149; norms through 148, 160, 169, 193; race and 173, 199; self-production through 136, 173, 198–199
nails 180, 194; as blank canvas 73, 136; dirty 15, 148–149, 190, 200; distinct from body 177, 180, 199–200, 203; embedded and dead 136, 148, 158, 180, 195, 198, 201; feminine 15, 148, 158, 201–203; glittered 160–161; horrific 97,

101; looking at 157–158, 168, 176–177; monster 196–198, 201; photographing 24, 160, 176, 178; as weapon 101, 120; zombie 148–150
new domesticity 3, 12–14, 18–19, 25, 47, 49

original 18, 52, 72, 73, 102, 107
Owens, Craig 132, 137

painting 68–69, 70, 71, 73, 76, 81, 109–110, 148, 163, 176
passion: commodification and 51; ecommerce selling as 36; for glitter 161, 176; horror as 120; reborn and 69, 72, 78, 86; shopping as 45; TTD and 98, 104; wedding as 121; between women 134; zombie and 134
personalization 9, 44, 97
photography 107, 179; affective 133, 179; death and 133; divorce 118–120; duplicative 131, 132, 137; failure of 178, 198; gender and 14, 102, 105; glitter 160, 177, 179; heterosexuality and 142; horror 114; looking and 109–110, 176, 191; queer engagement with 109–111; race and 140, 142, 146, 150; recognition through 137–138; resistance through 106; skill and 14, 134; tactile 79, 179; TTD 104–106; wedding 22, 96, 99, 102–104, 106, 107, 116, 118–119, 131, 146
pictures do not do it justice 178
Pie Near Woman 16–18
Pinterest viii, 110, 118
Pioneer Woman, The. *See* Drummond, Ree
Pioneer Woman Sux 16, 18
plastic 79, 84, 191–192, 197, 199–200
Pollock, Griselda 70, 175–176, 178–179, 206
porn. *See* erotica
postfeminism 7–9; choice and 8–9, 15, 47, 136, 159, 180; empowerment and 18, 35; feminism and 12, 13; individualization and 33, 35, 41, 50; motherhood and 37, 39
pregnant. *See* reborn pregnant
professional 7, 9, 22, 37, 41, 45, 50, 71
professionalism 7, 39, 45, 111
prosthetic 2, 178, 191

queer 165; brides as 23, 121, 130, 132, 147; femininity as 165; glitter as 165, 166, 171; Internet settings as 121; intimacy 120, 200, 205; nail polish production as 200; normative identity as 7, 23, 70, 121, 148, 171, 200; reborn producer as 69–70; theory 25, 39, wedding as 98, 104, 120; women's wedding forum as 98, 110, 121
queer child 69–70, 103, 110, 190, 200. *See also* growing sideways
queering 16, 17, 105, 121, 164

race 139, 144, 146; beauty and 139–140; challenge to 1–2, 139, 141, 142–143; construction of 2, 81–82, 140, 144, 172–173; hand distinguishing 15, 81, 198; Internet and 4, 9, 10, 20–21, 177; monster and 24; nail polish and 24, 163, 173, 199–200; reborn and 81–82; skin color 82, 144, 173; theory and 6, 139–140; wedding and 98, 139, 142, 145–148; whiteness 1–2, 81–82, 132, 140–144, 172–173, 198–200; zombie's reordering of 138–139, 140–142
Railla, Jean 12, 13
reborn pregnant 85
recognition 78, 135, 137–139
reddit 110–111
reproduction. *See* maternal reproduction
reproduction of objects 116, 131, 137, 146
resistance 2, 50, 171; crafting as 20, 50; to gender norms 16, 37, 65, 99–101, 106, 117, 119; to heterosexuality 69–70, 99, 112–113; Internet practice as 19, 101; to photographic convention 99, 104–108; to racial hierarchy 144, 199; theory of 50, 99–101; TTD as 23, 99, 104–106, 113, 121; to weddings 102, 106, 116–117, 141
Rock n Roll Bride 1, 97

scientist 174, 194–195, 201–205
sculpt 65, 72–73, 82, 174–175
Sedgwick, Eve Kosofsky 22, 51, 67, 78
Seelmeyer, Lynette 97, 111
self-actualization 68, 69, 139
Shanine, Bean 86–87
shine 161–162, 165, 170
skill: artistry as 66, 71, 104; beauty practice as 163–164, 168, 176; community and 16, 20, 134, 176, 179–180; crafting as 13, 50, 56; gender and 9, 11, 20, 39, 45, 50, 74–75; hand and 24, 67, 161; as inheritance 13, 20; inspiration and 16, 174; nail polish as 11, 174, 204; race and 9, 20; reborn

artist and 67, 71–72; stay-at-home mother and 45, 50, 56, 80, 104–105, 168; technology and 4, 9, 104, 168, 174; TTD and 104, 119; women's self-deprecation and 14, 20, 45–46, 104, 204
skin: beauty and 139–140, 169, 172; color 76, 79, 81–83, 96, 99, 114, 131–132, 137, 139–144, 172–173, 199–200; damaged 23, 140–142, 146, 149, 173; feel of 76, 79, 82, 86, 115, 149
Slashdot 5, 110–111
social networking 9, 40, 42, 96, 101, 102, 121. *See also* Facebook; Flickr; reddit; Slashdot; social news; Twitter
social news 5, 9, 10–11
sparkle 23, 160, 161–162, 167–169
spectatorship: challenge to 16, 17, 108–109, 114, 119, 158, 175–176, 180, 191, 206; feeling and 79; feminist theory of 99–100, 108–109, 113–114; glitter and 158, 175; horror 112–114; lesbian gaze 23, 109–110; male gaze 101, 109, 116, 201, 202; nail polish and 176–177; queer 23, 109–110; women and 16, 17, 158, 175–176, 206
stain 97–99, 113–114, 131
Stitch 'n Bitch 13, 18
Stockton, Kathryn Bond 69–70, 75, 103
Stoller, Debbie 13, 49

tactile 52; affect as 51, 67, 78; connecting through 51, 179; glitter as 179; hand and 33, 51, 193; reborn as 65, 67, 78–79
technologies of gender 6, 101, 134, 157, 191
technologies of the self 6, 8, 199
technology: as alive 131, 133, 136; changeability of 113, 160, 178, 194; crafting as 18, 24; duplicative 131, 137; empowerment and 8–9, 19, 33, 101, 168; free labor and 42–43; gender and 6, 7, 9–11, 24, 101, 104, 133, 134, 157, 168, 191; hand's connection to 33, 34, 51, 52, 115, 135, 139, 157, 178, 198–199; newness vii, 160; people produced by 5, 6, 24, 101, 157, 191; race and 10, 20–21, 142; resistance through 100–101, 160. *See also* Internet
telework 41, 43, 54
textual analysis 3–5, 7, 87, 134
thank you 43–44
they're us 135–139, 145
too much 165–167, 169–171, 173, 175
touch 52, 149; connection through 15, 69, 73, 77; emotion and 22, 51–53, 69, 73, 78–80, 82, 86, 149; enliven through 52, 67; glitter as 166; hand's relationship to 15, 33, 52, 67, 80, 193, 195; photography as 179; production through 69; queer 103; race and 81–82, 143, 173; reborn and 22, 67, 69, 73–74, 77, 78–82, 86
touching feeling 51, 67, 78–80, 143, 146, 149, 180, 194, 201, 205
trace 107, 114, 166, 171, 178, 179, 180
Twitter 101, 201–204

unique 2, 69, 73–74, 96–97, 107, 130, 181

viewing: challenge to 99, 104, 109, 113–14, 119, 175, 179, 191, 194, 198, 203–206; feeling and 22, 67, 73, 75, 77–80, 86, 112, 149, 179, 201; feminist theory of 99–100, 108–109, 113–114; glitter and 157–158, 175–179; horror 111–112, 135–136; Internet 5, 10; lesbian gaze 23, 99–100, 109–110, 205; male gaze 101, 109, 116, 158, 201; motherhood structured through 66–67, 69, 75, 78–80; nail polish and 24, 176–177, 180; queer 16–17, 111; women and vii, 16–17, 23, 66–67, 69, 108–109, 157–158, 175–177, 179, 202, 206
visual pleasure 176–177, 178–179

wedding 22–23, 102–104; challenge to 1, 98–100, 104, 106–107, 113, 131–132, 141; cost of 102; divorce and 118–119; duplication and 130, 137; ecommerce's use of 96–97; growing sideways and 98, 103, 111; heterosexuality in 99, 101, 145–148; horror and 98, 112–113, 116; monstrosity and 2; normative 2, 100; photography vii–viii, 1, 97–99, 102, 104–105, 106, 116, 118–120, 131–132, 142, 150; queerness of 98, 103–104, 110–111, 130, 180; whiteness and 99, 105, 139, 141; zombie 145–148
wedding dress 2, 22, 96, 108, 147; challenge to tradition 1, 99, 104, 106, 113, 114, 117, 130; cost of 102; heterosexuality and 2, 99; horror and 97, 112; queer eroticism and 109–111; soiled 9, 22, 97–100, 113–115, 119, 137, 149; TTD and 98–99, 104, 106, 107,

112–120; whiteness and 2, 23, 131–132, 139, 141, 143; zombie and 130, 132, 137, 141, 147, 180

wedding forum 23, 98–99, 104, 108–111, 115–117, 120–121, 176

Welter, Barbara 11–12

whiteness 23, 131–132, 137, 139–143, 151, 172; challenge to 8, 143, 177, 200; cosmetic production of 2, 23, 143, 172–173; deathly 87, 131–132, 143–144, 151; dissipation of 142, 177; ecommerce and 36; failure of 1; gender and 9–10, 20, 23; hand and 198; heterosexuality and 2, 96, 133, 142; monstrous 173; race and 1, 10, 81–82, 105, 132, 139–146, 172, 199; reborn and 81–82; technology and 9–10, 20, 24

women's movement 8, 12–14, 37, 38–39. *See also* feminism

yummy squishy 179–180

zombie marriage 23, 145–147, 180

zombie nails 24, 148–150, 173, 199, 201

zombie walk 87, 130, 132–134, 148; bride at 141; marriage at 145–147; queer 180; race and 23, 139–141; they're us, 137–138; transformation at 136